David Crockett

DAVID CROCKETT

Watercolor portrait by Anthony Lewis DeRose

David Crockett
The Man and the Legend

by James Atkins Shackford

Edited by John B. Shackford

Introduction by Michael A. Lofaro

University of Nebraska Press
Lincoln and London

© 1956, 1986 by the University of North Carolina Press
All rights reserved
Manufactured in the United States of America

The paper in this book meets the minimum requirements of American National
Standard for Information Sciences—Permanence of Paper for Printed Library
Materials, ANSI z39.48–1984

First Bison Book printing: 1994
Most recent printing indicated by the last digit below:
10   9   8   7   6   5   4   3   2   1

Library of Congress Cataloging-in-Publication Data
Shackford, James Atkins.
David Crockett: the man and the legend / by James Atkins Shackford; edited by
John B. Shackford; introduction by Michael A. Lofaro.
p.   cm.
Originally published: Chapel Hill: University of North Carolina Press, c1986.
Includes bibliographical references and index.
ISBN 0-8032-9230-9
1. Crockett, Davy, 1786–1836.   2. Pioneers—Tennessee—Biography.   3. Ten-
nessee—Biography.   4. Legislators—United States—Biography.   5. United
States. Congress. House—Biography.   I. Shackford, John B.   II. Title.
F436.C95S47   1994
976.8'04'092—dc20
[B]
94-21656   CIP

Reprinted by arrangement with the University of North Carolina Press, Inc.

To my wife,
ADA MORROW SHACKFORD,
this book is affectionately dedicated.

Contents

PART FIVE—*Out*

INTRODUCTION

By Michael A. Lofaro

In the following pages I have endeavoured to give the reader a plain, honest, homespun account of my state in life, and some few of the difficulties which have attended me along its journey, down to this time. . . . I know that obscure as I am, my name is making considerable deal of fuss in the world. I can't tell why it is, nor in what it is to end. Go where I will, everybody seems anxious to get a peep at me. . . . But just read for yourself, and my ears for a heel tap [the bit of liquor left in a glass after drinking], if before you get through you don't say, with many a good-natured smile and hearty laugh, "This is truly the very thing itself—the exact image of its Author,

DAVID CROCKETT."
from *A Narrative of the Life of David Crockett of the State of Tennessee*[1]

The famous frontiersman turned politician revealed a good deal about himself and his era in these brief excerpts from the preface to his autobiography. He presented himself to his readers as a truthful, "down-home" country boy who was modestly bemused at his fame and who simultaneously recognized the political appeal of portraying the events in his life with a thoroughly engaging and genial sense of humor. The publication of this best-seller in 1834 also marked Crockett's first major attempt to separate himself from his growing legend, a legend that would literally engulf "the exact image of its Author" within a few years.

Timing is often a crucial factor in the creation of a historical or legendary hero. David Crockett at least inherently sensed that the "considerable deal of fuss in the world" that he now made gave him a rare opportunity for true historical greatness. His *Narrative* was in part a corrective to what he called the "catchpenny errors," "outlandish" language, and "false notions" of the "autobiographical" work published under his name by Mathew St. Clair Clarke a year earlier in 1833 and was in part a campaign biography designed to pave the way for a presidential bid in the election of 1836 when Andrew Jackson was to step down from office.[2] His dilemma was that he had to deny the "outlandish" Crockett to succeed as a serious candidate, yet could not totally divorce himself from the same backwoods image that was the source of much of his political appeal.

Crockett arrived at this dramatic juncture in his career through his own efforts, but also because of the era in which he lived. Born in 1786, fifty-two years after the birth of Daniel Boone and only ten years after the Declaration of Independence, Crockett matured with the new nation. By the time that Boone's *Biographical Memoir* and Crockett's *Sketches and Eccentricities*, the first full-length biographies of both men, appeared in 1833, it was clear that the role of the frontier hero had been redefined and had exerted considerable influence upon American politics, as witnessed by Jackson's election and the age ushered in by his presidency.[3] The American ideal of the dedicated and noble pioneer of the eighteenth century had given way before the brash and cocky backwoodsman of the nineteenth century, just as the centers of political power had begun to move from the drawing room to the tavern, from the control of the upper class to within reach of the common man.

Ironically termed the "gentleman from the cane," Crockett was viewed as an unsophisticated and unrefined politician by some of his fellow members of the Tennessee legislature early in his career. They thought that he had stepped directly from the wild recesses of a West Tennessee canebrake onto the floor of the House. Crockett turned their mockery to his advantage by pinning to his shirt a fancy cambric ruffle of the same cut as that of his main antagonist, a Mr. James C. Mitchell. When David rose to speak after one of Mitchell's particularly informative addresses, his newly affected finery stood out on his backwoodsman's shirt in such a ridiculous fashion that the members of the House burst into a prolonged tide of laughter that forced an embarrassed Mitchell from the chamber.[4]

Crockett was no fool. He knew his image and continued to manipulate it to his political advantage, especially in his early campaigns.[5] His run against Dr. William E. Butler in the state elections of 1823 provided some of the best examples of this same type of humor and wit. Crockett played up his "gentleman from the cane" image and labeled Butler as an aristocrat. When visiting his opponent's house and noting the expensive furnishings, he refused to walk upon a particularly handsome rug and subsequently incorporated a telling comparison as a high point in his speeches: "Fellow citizens, my aristocratic competitor has a fine carpet, and every day he *walks* on truck finer than any gowns your wife or your daughters, in all their lives, ever *wore!*" He told Butler that he would have a buckskin hunting shirt made with two pockets large enough to hold a big twist of chewing tobacco and a bottle of liquor. After a prospective voter took a taste of "the *creature*," Crockett said that he would immediately hand him a replacement for the "chaw" he had to discard to take the drink and thus "he would not be worse off than when I found him; and I would be sure to leave him in a first-rate good humour." Crockett once even memorized Butler's standard campaign speech and delivered it word for word just before it was Butler's turn to speak.[6] The two men fortunately remained on good terms, and Butler often enjoyed Crockett's brand of entertainment as much as the rest of their audiences.

David Crockett's sense of humor was one of the reasons that he was perhaps more emblematic of the spirit of Jacksonian democracy than Jackson himself. Never achieving the heights of Jackson's great successes in the military and political arenas, he was never removed from a realm deemed approachable by the average citizen. His humor and, somewhat ironically, his lack of extraordinary success and achievement may well have kept Crockett a more attainable and attractive ideal in the popular mind during his public career. Again, timing was critical. Had he not opposed Jackson so vehemently, had he not taken time from his congressional duties to tour the northern and eastern states as a possible presidential candidate, he might not have lost his bid for reelection to the House in 1835 to Adam Huntsman, a peg-legged lawyer supported by Jackson and Governor Carroll of Tennessee, by 252 votes.[7] It was because of this defeat that he decided to explore Texas, or as Crockett himself put it: "Since you have chosen to elect a man with a timber toe to succeed me, you may all go to hell and I will go to Texas."[8] At this point, he had no intention of joining the fight for Texan independence. His last surviving letters, however, show that Texas changed his plans. Crockett literally rejoiced at the opportunities before him and spoke confidently of the fact that Texas would allow him to rejuvenate his political career and to acquire the wealth that had eluded him all his life by becoming the land agent for the new territory.[9] He clearly felt that he was in the right place at the right time.

While the death of the historical *David* Crockett at the Battle of the Alamo on March 6, 1836, assured that he would replace Daniel Boone as the then preeminent hero of the American frontier, it also loosed the floodgates for the unrestrained expansion of the image of the legendary *Davy* Crockett in the popular media of his day and ours.

David had, in fact, already become Davy to a certain extent. The *Sketches and Eccentricities*, his *Narrative, An Account of Colonel Crockett's Tour to the North and Down East* (the Whig account of his three-week campaign swing in 1835, probably written by William Clark),[10] and the posthumously published *Col. Crockett's Exploits and Adventures in Texas* contained a number of tales that had taken root in fertile soil. As part of the vanguard of what was later termed the "humor of the old Southwest," these stories were reprinted in a series of very popular Crockett Almanacs that were published from 1835 to 1856.[11] The early fictional Davy was not yet a full-blown "ring-tailed roarer" in the first Almanac, but, building upon the historical David's ability to give vent to a humorous boast, Davy became a screamer who could "run faster,—jump higher,—squat lower,—dive deeper,—stay under longer,—and come out drier, than any man in the whole country." The ante escalated rapidly in the hands of the Boston literary hacks who created tall tales for the next six Almanacs of the "Nashville" series. In the 1836 issue, for example, Davy had an epic underwater battle with the twelve-foot long "monstratious great Cat-Fish," and in the next volume saved the United States from destruction by wringing the tail off Halley's Comet. Davy, however, wanted nothing more to do with "see-less-tial bodies" after this experience for, as he explained,

I was appointed by the President to stand on the Alleghany Mountains and wring the Comet's tail off. I did so, but got my hands most shockingly burnt, and the hair singed off my head, so that I was as bald as a trencher. I div right down into the Waybosh river, and thus saved my best stone blue coat and grass green small clothes. With the help of Bear's grease, I have brought out a new crop, but the hair grows in bights and tufts, like hussuck grass in a meadow, and it keeps in such a snarl, that all the teeth will instantly snap out of an ivory comb when brought within ten feet of it.[12]

This adventure was but a mild warm-up for America's first comic superman. In later Almanacs, Crockett convinced his pet alligator to bite its tail and churn like a paddle wheel so he could ride up Niagara Falls; he also became a Promethean figure who saved the solar system by unfreezing the "airth" and sun that had "friz fast" to their axes with hot bear "ile" and then "walked home, introducin' the people to fresh daylight with a piece of sunrise in my pocket. . . ." But there was as well a darker side to Davy's "comedy" which proved a less flattering cultural mirror of America's past. His creators used him as an ardent warrior in the cause of territorial expansionism, with Mexico and Oregon as only the nearest of his targets. And perhaps most distasteful to modern sensibilities, Davy was the "humanitarian" who killed and boiled an Indian to make a tonic to help cure his pet bear's stomach disorder.[13] Blacks and other "sub-humans" fared no better.

The violent, jingoistic, and racist Davy of the Almanacs competed with and was eventually subsumed by a far longer standing tradition of Davy as the hero of romantic melodrama. From Nimrod Wildfire, James Kirke Paulding's Crockettesque character in his play *The Lion of the West* (1831), to Frank Mayo as the co-author and lead in the very long running *Davy Crockett; Or, Be Sure You're Right Then Go Ahead*, the heritage was passed on through a series of silent and modern films that culminated in the Davys played by Fess Parker and John Wayne, who were equally at home in the theater or in rerun after rerun on the television screen. Nineteenth-century drama and twentieth-century film always presented a heroic Crockett in the kindest light.[14] Courageous, dashing, and true blue, this nobleman of nature protected his country and all those who were helpless with equal fervor.

The Walt Disney–Fess Parker–inspired Crockett craze of the mid-1950s was without question the high-water mark of the impact of this legendary Crockett. A media-generated event, it occurred at the point when television had begun to reach a mass market and as Walt Disney entered that fledgling media with his innovative premise that children were a constantly changing and renewable audience. James Atkins Shackford's masterful biography of David Crockett was, simply by coincidence, published on June 2, 1956, near the height of the craze. The timing for this first thorough delineation of the historical Crockett could not have been worse. As the youth of America clamored for coonskin caps and fringed deerskin jackets and pants, as department stores set up special Crockett sections to sell the clothes and other Crockett paraphernalia (such as records, lunch boxes, towels, wallets, athletic equipment, baby shoes, and even women's panties), as the total Crockett industry realized sales of approximately $300 million, Shackford faced the monumental task of rescuing a nearly unknown David Crockett from the obscurity caused by the popularity of the earlier legendary Davys and deepened by Disney. His direct competition was no easier. Grosset and Dunlap's *The Story of Davy Crockett* sold at 10,000 copies per year before 1955; during the craze, sales increased to thirty times that figure.[15] By selling out all copies within a year of publication, Shackford's book was a hot item too, when judged by academic press standards. But the fact that the slightly larger than normal press run amounted to only 2,500 copies underscored the magnitude of the problem.

Since his manuscript was completed before the Crockett fad was well under way, one can only speculate as to how Shackford might have reacted to a legendary overlay that was so complete that most people today, and certainly nearly all those under the age of forty, visualize Fess Parker whenever they think of Crockett.[16] Clearly, however, both Shackford's purpose and the need for his work would only have intensified. His dedication to and scrupulous accuracy in unearthing the facts of Crockett's life produced a splendid biography, which in turn provided later scholars a firm foundation for the study of the man and the legend as well as their effect upon each other and upon the American people.

As one reads this book, Professor Shackford's somewhat disparaging views on the legendary Davy require explanation. He stated that he "ignored the mythological Crockett, save where he is deliberately introduced as such for a specific purpose. . . ." Those purposes usually arose in situations where the legend was presented and accepted as fact through common usage. Such correction was obviously necessary. However, in addition to "correcting the time-honored fictional versions of his life," Shackford also aimed "at counteracting the new emphases, and the unfortunate consequences thereof, which scholars have given those incorrect fictional versions within the last twenty years." He used the word "fictional" perjoratively in both instances and seemed to have the Almanacs in mind when he went on to say that "we would not now, if we could, eliminate 'Davy' from the delightful arena of the bedtime story. . . ." Beleaguered by the preponderance of scholarship on the legend that ignored historical data because it was not available in print, Shackford sought to sever the relationship between myth and man to bring the "Crockett God made" fully into focus, even though some of the evidence which he published for the first time revealed how David both used and helped to construct the image of Davy.[17]

Once this bias is understood, Shackford's *David Crockett: The Man and the Legend* is a delightful treasure trove of information. Amazingly, it stands in need of little correction after thirty years. The only significant area that requires additional comment concerns the much disputed facts surrounding Crockett's death at the Alamo. Based on the evidence available to him, Shackford built a case supporting the eyewitness oral accounts of Madam Candelaria, who testified that David was one of the first defenders killed and that he died unarmed. Shackford was not totally convinced on the matter and rightly asserted that "too much has been made over the details of *how* David died at the Alamo."[18]

New information has come to light that surprisingly indicates that the story as given in the "fictional" *Col. Crockett's Exploits and Adventures in Texas* is substantially correct. The two key works on which this view is based are *With Santa Anna in Texas: A Personal Narrative of the Revolution*, the eyewitness diary of Lieutenant José Enrique de la Peña, and a study of it and several corroborating accounts by Dan Kilgore in *How Did Davy Die?* Lieutenant de la Peña identified Crockett as one of the six or seven survivors who were captured when Mexican troops took the Alamo about six o'clock in the morning and were taken before Santa Anna under the protection of General Manuel Fernández Castrillón, who hoped to have them spared despite Santa Anna's orders to take no prisoners. Angered by Castrillón's insubordination, he ordered them executed immediately. Although according to de la Peña, the battle-proven "commanders and officers were outraged at this action and did not support the order, hoping that once the fury of the moment had blown over these men would be spared," several officers, who had not fought and were evidently hoping to flatter Santa Anna, carried out his wishes. It is likely that the entire episode from capture to execution took place within only a few minutes.[19]

With the addition of this material, Shackford's definitive biography of David Crockett is essentially up to date. He need not have feared that the sometimes cumbersome duty of recording all the facts necessary to depict the "Crockett God made" would allow his book to be eclipsed by Davy's ever-lengthening legendary shadow as "a less lively tale," for it is simply a different tale, one never before told in such intriguing detail or with such expertise. And if he extends himself beyond his evidence in his epilogue to claim that Crockett is a symbol of "the spiritual frontier of universal brotherhood where all men are their brother's keepers," he does no more than all who gaze into the life of a cultural hero and come away with the reflection of their own best hopes for mankind.[20] In the final analysis, James Atkins Shackford's ground-breaking achievement makes this biography the unequivocal starting point for everyone interested in the Crockett of history and legend. Here he gives us the Crockett who was the source of it all; the one who, in the estimate of historians and mythologists alike, is truly a "gen-u-ine original."

Notes

1. David Crockett, *A Narrative of the Life of David Crockett of the State of Tennessee*, ed. James A. Shackford and Stanley J. Folmsbee (1834; rpt., annotated facsimile edition, Knoxville: University of Tennessee Press, 1973), pp. 6, 7, 10–11.

2. Crockett, *Narrative*, pp. 3, 4, 5; [Mathew St. Clair Clarke], *The Life and Adventures of Colonel David Crockett of West Tennessee* (Cincinnati: published for the Proprietor, 1833). The latter work will subsequently be cited by its best-known title under which it was reissued that same year: *Sketches and Eccentricities of Col. David Crockett, of West Tennessee* (New York: J. & J. Harper, 1833). Although Crockett pleaded ignorance of the identity of the author, it was surely he who provided the bulk of the biographical information to his friend Clarke (see Crockett, *Narrative*, p. 3, n. 3).

3. Timothy Flint, *Biographical Memoir of Daniel Boone* (Cincinnati: N. & G. Guilford, 1833).

4. [Clarke], *Sketches and Eccentricities*, pp. 57–59; James A. Shackford, *David Crockett: The Man and the Legend*, ed. by John B. Shackford (1956; rpt. Chapel Hill: University of North Carolina Press, 1986), pp. 52–53.

5. Crockett did not seem to exercise the same control over his image in the national arena. When he first went to Congress in 1827, the Jacksonians applauded his backwoods virtues (in part as a means of exerting some sway over his vote) and the Whigs just as vigorously ridiculed him as a bumpkin and a fool. When Jackson was elected to a second term as president in 1832, the Whigs exploited Crockett's growing animosity toward Jackson, courted him as an anti-Jackson candidate for the presidential election of 1836, and reversed their portrayal of him. Quite naturally, the supporters of Jackson then took up the old Whig depictions. Crockett's increased prominence made him a valuable tool for others to manipulate and correspondingly decreased his own ability to shape his image.

6. Shackford, pp. 64–65; Crockett, *Narrative*, 168–70.

7. Shackford, pp. 203–5; Crockett, *Narrative*, p. 211, n. 18. The official returns were Huntsman 4,652 and Crockett 4,400.

8. [Richard Penn Smith], *Col. Crockett's Exploits and Adventures in Texas. . .Written by Himself* (Philadelphia: T. K. & P. G. Collins [Carey & Hart], 1836), p. 31; Shackford, p. 212.

9. Shackford, pp. 214–16.

10. (Philadelphia: Carey & Hart, 1835). The other of Crockett's Whig books is not included in this list because it consists mainly of artless invective rather than tales. See [Augustin Smith Clayton], *The Life of Martin Van Buren, Heir-Apparent to the "Government," and Appointed Successor of General Andrew Jackson* (Philadelphia: R. Wright [Carey & Hart], 1835.

11. For a brief summary of the history of the Crockett Almanacs, see Michael A. Lofaro, "The Hidden 'Hero' of the Nashville Crockett Almanacs," in Michael A. Lofaro, ed., *Davy Crockett: The Man, the Legend, the Legacy, 1786–1986* (Knoxville: University of Tennessee Press, 1985), pp. 46–49. John Seelye first proved the Boston origins of the "Nashville" Almanacs. See his "A Well-Wrought Crockett: Or, How the Fakelorists Passed through the Credibility Gap and Discovered Kentucky," in Lofaro, *Davy Crockett*, pp. 21–45.

12. Lofaro, "The Hidden 'Hero' of the Nashville Crockett Almanacs," pp. 51–57.

13. Richard M. Dorson, *Davy Crockett: American Comic Legend* (New York: Spiral Press for Rockland Editions, 1939), pp. 10–12, 16–17, 157–58, 138–39, 152.

14. For the best survey of the range of this material and its significance, see Richard Boyd Hauck, "Making It All Up: Davy Crockett in the Theater," in Lofaro, *Davy*

Crockett, pp. 102–23. In the same volume, see also pages pp. 125–[36] for an example of the legendary Davy in a 1916 silent film.

15. Margaret J. King, "The Recycled Hero: Walt Disney's Davy Crockett," in Lofaro, *Davy Crockett*, pp. 148, 143; for information on the music of the craze, see Charles K. Wolfe, "Davy Crockett Songs: Minstrels to Disney," in Lofaro, *Davy Crockett*, pp. 177–87. For all the information in regard to the publication of Shackford's book, I am indebted to David Perry of the University of North Carolina Press.

16. Fess Parker unintentionally further muddied the waters by his prime-time portrayal of Daniel Boone in 165 episodes of the television show of the same name that aired from September 24, 1964, to May 7, 1970.

17. Shackford, preface. Had Shackford known the Almanac tales thoroughly, rather than just the versions published by the "mythologists," he probably would not have termed them "bedtime stories." It is also interesting to note the absence in this book of any mention of the growing "myth-symbol" school of criticism. Shackford was surely aware of Henry Nash Smith's *Virgin Land: The American West as Symbol and Myth*, published in 1950, but chose not to include it in his discussions, perhaps because he saw that approach to the meaning of the frontier in American life as peripheral or antithetical to his own.

18. Shackford, pp. 229–35, 238.

19. José Enrique de la Peña, *With Santa Anna in Texas: A Personal Narrative of the Revolution*, trans. and ed. Carmen Perry (College Station: Texas A&M University Press, 1975), p. 53; Dan Kilgore, *How Did Davy Die?* (College Station: Texas A&M University Press, 1978); see also Richard Boyd Hauck, *Crockett: A Bio-Bibliography* (Westport, Conn.: Greenwood Press, 1982), pp. 50–54.

20. Shackford, preface and page 251.

Selected Bibliography

The following material is intended as a guide for the interested reader who wishes to pursue more information about Crockett. A good beginning point for those curious about the historical Crockett is of course Crockett's own *Narrative*. The work of Stanley J. Folmsbee, both as a sole and joint author, compliments, amplifies, and in a few instances corrects that of James Atkins Shackford. Richard Boyd Hauck's lively scholarship provides an excellent recent view of David and Davy. For the newest and most wide-ranging treatment of the legendary Crockett, see the essays in Michael A. Lofaro's *Davy Crockett*.

The present selected bibliography updates that of Shackford for both David and Davy through March 31, 1986. It focuses on materials that deal specifically with Crockett and excludes the following: the large amount of children's and juvenile literature from dime novels and comic books to biographies of the historical and legendary Crockett; and the fiction based on Crockett's life, such as Dee Brown's *Wave High the Banner* (1942). Because of its special concentration on Crockett, it similarly excludes group studies of famous frontiersmen, American heroes, and the like, thematic studies such as Richard Slotkin's *Regeneration Through Violence* (1973), and work centered on the Alamo.

For a quick expansion of the Shackford bibliography beyond that listed below, one could check the annotated bibliography contained in his 1948 dissertation on Crockett at Vanderbilt University (cross-check it with the most recent edition of *American Literary Manuscripts* for manuscript materials), the bibliography in Hauck's *Crockett*, together with his comments entitled "The Crockett Record" in that book (pp. 134–45), and the works cited in the "special features" and notes of Lofaro's *Davy Crockett*. Since 1986 marks both the bicentennial of Crockett's birth and the sesquicentennial of his death at the Alamo, a number of other studies may soon come into print. These include several books: a volume of new articles from the Crockett Bicentennial Celebration at Limestone, Tennessee, on August 15–17, 1986, to be published by the Tennessee Historical Commission (also, a collection of the often difficult to locate essays that were originally published in local and regional historical journals may be in the offing from the Commission); a reissuing of Hauck's *Crockett* in paperback; and a facsimile edition of the second series of "Nashville" Crockett Almanacs (1839–41) to be issued by the Tennessee Folklore Society as a complement to Franklin J. Meine's edition of the first series for the Caxton Club. Finally, a critical study and complete facsimile edition of all the Crockett Almanacs is presently under way by Michael A. Lofaro.

Works below that are devoted all or in substantial part to the historical Crockett are designated by an asterisk.

Albanese, Catherine L. "Citizen Crockett: Myth, History, and Nature Religion." *Soundings: An Interdisciplinary Journal* 61 (1978): 87–104.
———. "King Crockett: Nature and Civility on the American Frontier." *Proceedings of the American Antiquarian Society* 88 (1979): 225–49.
———. "Davy Crockett and the Wild Man; Or, The Metaphysics of the Longue Durée," in Lofaro, *Davy Crockett*, pp. 80–101.
———. "Savage, Sinner, and Saved: Davy Crockett, Camp Meetings, and the Wild Frontier." *American Quarterly* 33 (Winter 1981): 482–501.
*Arpad, Joseph John. "David Crockett, An Original Legendary Eccentricity and Early American Character." Ph.D. dissertation, Duke University, 1969.
———. "The Fight Story: Quotation and Originality in Native American Humor." *Journal of the Folklore Institute* 10 (1973): 141–72.
———. "John Wesley Jarvis, James Kirke Paulding, and Colonel Nimrod Wildfire." *New York Folklore Quarterly* 21 (1965): 92–106.
*———, ed. *A Narrative of the Life of David Crockett of the State of Tennessee*. New Haven, Conn.: College & University Press, 1972. For the best text of Crockett's autobiography, see Crockett, David.
Blair, Walter. *Davy Crockett—Frontier Hero: The Truth as He Told It—The Legend as His Friends Built It*. New York: Coward-McCann, 1955. Reissued in a revised edition as *Davy Crockett, Legendary Frontier Hero*. Springfield, Ill.: Lincoln-Herndon Press, 1986.
Boorstin, Daniel. "Heroes or Clowns? Comic Supermen from a Subliterature," in his *The Americans: The National Experience*. New York: Random House, 1965, pp. 327–37.
Bruce, Norman. "A Newly Discovered Silent Film: An Article on Davy Crockett (Oliver Morosco Photoplay Co.)," in Lofaro, *Davy Crockett*, pp. 125–[36].
Burke, James Wakefield. *David Crockett: The Man Behind the Myth*. Austin, Texas: Eakin Press, 1984. Blends history, oral history, and the historical novel in an attempt to make "the past live again."
*Cooper, Texas Jim. "A Study of Some David Crockett Firearms." *East Tennessee Historical Society's Publications* 38 (1966): 62–69.
*Crockett, David. *A Narrative of the Life of David Crockett of the State of Tennessee*. Philadelphia: Carey & Hart, 1834. Facsimile edition with annotations and introduction, edited by James A. Shackford and Stanley J. Folmsbee. Knoxville: University of Tennessee Press, 1973.
*Davis, Curtis Carroll. "A Legend at Full-Length: Mr. Chapman Paints Colonel Crockett—and Tells about It." *Proceedings of the American Antiquarian Society* 69 (1960): 155–74.
Dorson, Richard M. "The Sources of Davy Crockett, American Comic Legend." *Midwest Folklore* 8 (1958): 143–49.

*Downing, Marvin. "Davy Crockett in Gibson County, Tennessee: A Century of Memories." *West Tennessee Historical Society Papers* 37 (1983): 54–61.

*Folmsbee, Stanley J. "David Crockett and his Autobiography." *East Tennessee Historical Society's Publications* 43 (1971): 3–17.

*_____. "David Crockett and West Tennessee." *West Tennessee Historical Society Papers* 28 (1974): 5–24.

*Folmsbee, Stanley J., and Anna Grace Catron. "The Early Career of David Crockett." *East Tennessee Historical Society's Publications* 28 (1956): 58–85. This is the first of a series of three chronological articles on the life of Crockett.

*_____. "David Crockett: Congressman." *East Teneessee Historical Society's Publications* 29 (1957): 40–78.

*_____. "David Crockett in Texas." *East Tennessee Historical Society's Publications* 30 (1958): 48–74.

Harrison, Lowell H. "Davy Crockett: The Making of a Folk Hero." *Kentucky Folklore Record* 15 (1969): 87–90.

*Hauck, Richard Boyd. *Crockett: A Bio-Bibliography*. Westport, Conn.: Greenwood Press, 1982.

_____. "Making It All Up: Davy Crockett in the Theater," in Lofaro, *Davy Crockett*, pp. 102–24. Contains a filmography.

*_____. "The Man in the Buckskin Hunting Shirt: Fact and Fiction in the Crockett Story," in Lofaro, *Davy Crockett*, pp. 3–20.

*Heale, M. J. "The Role of the Frontier in Jacksonian Politics: David Crockett and the Myth of the Self-Made Man." *Western Historical Quarterly* 4 (1973): 405–23.

Hoffman, Daniel G. "The Deaths and Three Resurrections of Davy Crockett." *Antioch Review* 21 (Spring 1961): 5–13.

*Kilgore, Dan. *How Did Davy Die?* College Station: Texas A&M University Press, 1978.

King, Margaret Jane. "The Davy Crockett Craze: A Case Study in Popular Culture." Ph.D. dissertation, University of Hawaii, 1976.

_____. "The Recycled Hero: Walt Disney's Davy Crockett," in Lofaro, *Davy Crockett*, pp. 137–58. Contains a "Crockett craze" bibliography.

Leithead, Edward J. "Legendary Heroes and the Dime Novel." *American Book Collector* 18, no. 7 (1968): 22–27.

Lofaro, Michael A., ed. *Davy Crockett: The Man, the Legend, the Legacy, 1786–1986*. Knoxville: University of Tennessee Press, 1985.

_____. "From Boone to Crockett: The Beginnings of Frontier Humor." *Mississippi Folklore Register* 14 (1980): 57–74.

_____. "The Hidden 'Hero' of the Nashville Crockett Almanacs," in Lofaro, *Davy Crockett*, pp. 46–79.

*McBride, Robert M. "David Crockett and His Memorials in Tennessee." *Tennessee Historical Quarterly* 26 (1967): 219–39. Reprinted in *More Landmarks of Tennessee History*. Nashville: Tennessee Historical Society and Tennessee Historical Commission, 1969.

Meine, Franklin J., ed. *The Crockett Almanacks: Nashville Series, 1835–1838*. Chicago: The Caxton Club, 1955.

*Miles, Guy S. "David Crockett Evolves, 1821–1824." *American Quarterly* 8 (1956): 53–60.

*Peña, José Enrique de la. *With Santa Anna in Texas: A Personal Narrative of the Revolution*. Translated and edited by Carmen Perry. College Station: Texas A&M University Press, 1975.

Sann, Paul. "The King of Nothing: Davy Crockett," in his *Fads, Follies and Delusions of the American People*. New York: Crown Publishers, 1967, pp. 27–30.

Seelye, John. "A Well-Wrought Crockett: Or, How the Fakelorists Passed through the

Credibility Gap and Discovered Kentucky," in Lofaro, *Davy Crockett*, pp. 21–45.

Smith-Rosenberg, Carroll. "Davey [*sic*] Crockett as Trickster: Pornography, Liminality, and Symbolic Inversion in Victorian America." *Journal of Contemporary History* 17 (1982): 325–50.

Stiffler, Stuart A. "Davy Crockett: The Genesis of Heroic Myth." *Tennessee Historical Quarterly* 16 (1957): 134–40.

Taylor, Joshua C. *America as Art*. Washington, D.C.: Published for the National Collection of Fine Arts by the Smithsonian Institution Press, 1976, pp. 88–94. Contains an aesthetic discussion of the woodcuts that illustrate the Nashville Crockett Almanacs.

Wolfe, Charles K. "Davy Crockett Songs: Minstrels to Disney," in Lofaro, *Davy Crockett*, pp. 159–90. Contains checklists of traditional and of published Davy Crockett songs.

_____. "Davy Crockett's Dance and Old Hickory's Fandango." *Devil's Box* 16 (Sept. 1982): 34–41.

Preface

THE PURPOSE of this work is to present an authentic biography of David Crockett against the background of his times, a new and creative period of American history, so that the reader may see him as an individual, as a type, and as an exponent of a type—a true pioneer not only of advancing geographical frontiers but also of the frontiers of a new democratic spirit. Crockett's life and writings can shed a needed light upon the issues of our era. Incidentally, by presenting the real Crockett, this study aims at correcting the time-honored fictional versions of his life which seem first to have taken root in the legend and literature of backwoods America more than a hundred years ago. It also aims at counteracting the new emphases, and the unfortunate consequences thereof, which scholars have given those incorrect fictional versions within the last twenty years. So shrouded in fiction and myth and error has Crockett become that only the most careful and painstaking research into all available sources can hope to recapture the man himself. This will make necessary the introduction of much of the evidence into the body of this work; for only so can the true man now be reclaimed as authentic in the mind of the reader.

A popular notion initiated by recent students of American literature is that the historical David Crockett is unknowable, a notion which has resulted in an unsalutary neglect of the historical man and of his authentic *Autobiography*. Writing in an otherwise fine article which he called "Six Davy Crocketts," Professor Walter Blair too readily wrote off as unrecapturable "the Crockett God made," the historical Crockett of this biography, and turned his attention to the other five Crocketts, all various combinations of newspaper creations and folklore. If one had to depend merely on secondary sources and on all of the political, journalistic, and "literary" capital which has been made of David for a good deal more than a hundred years, as Mr.

Blair did, and had his assumption been sound that few authentic records of David existed inasmuch as few had been published, his conclusion would have been correct. The assumption was in error. Though none of the Crockett writers had ever gone to many of the original sources for their work, such sources did exist: holographs, court records of the counties where he lived, documents of the Creek Indian War in which he fought, archives of the state where he dwelt for most of his life, legislative and Congressional records, authentic reminiscences about him by those who had known him during the various periods of his life. Nevertheless, the erroneous assumption was made, and the historical Crockett was dismissed as being forever lost.

Professor Blair's obsequies over the historical Crockett, however, were but a late consummation to a movement which he, together with Mr. Franklin J. Meine, seems to have helped initiate back in 1933. In that year these men jointly published *Mike Fink* and Mr. Meine published *Tall Tales of the Southwest.* By ignoring Crockett, the historical man, and by dismissing his *Autobiography* from the anthology, Mr. Meine depicted Crockett as having only a mythical existence. (*See* his introduction to *Tall Tales*, where he neglects Crockett in his treatment of the rise of humor in the South and Southwest; or the selections in that anthology where, though including material from the realistic writings of A. B. Longstreet, he represents David Crockett only by a selection from the entirely spurious *Texas Exploits*—the only Crockett book with which David had *nothing* to do—and includes nothing from the *Autobiography*, his one work of real merit.) They thus paved the way a year later for Miss Constance Rourke's fictional *Davy Crockett*, which gave "Davy" the identical tall-tale treatment Mr. Meine had given him and which both Mr. Meine and Mr. Blair had given Mike Fink. The trend seems to have been established, and such names as those of V. L. O. Chittick, R. M. Dorson, Howard Mumford Jones, Walter Blair, E. J. Mayer, Carl Van Doren, and Irwin Shapiro, in books and in articles, swelled the chorus into a gala folklore festival which has covered a period of about the last twenty years. None of these men knew much about the historical Crockett, because nothing much was available in print. They wrote about the "Crockett men made," the legendary folk hero, a realm in which anything was acceptable, from Hebrew history to Paul Bunyan.

This cluster of scholarly names and reputations in support of the myth had several unfortunate consequences. One was the practical loss to American literature, because of elimination from anthologies, of the only valuable Crockett work, the *Autobiography*—as an examination of anthologies before 1933 and since that time will reveal. A second was, naturally, an almost complete substitution in anthologies of the mythological character for the historical man. A third unfortunate result has been a neglect of the historical man and of those documents which could form a basis for a fairer judgment of him. Where the historical figure has been remembered at all, it has been in terms of an unjustly cruel caricature, originally limned by his enemies, and continuing to persist because of a lack of all that evidence which might supply a basis for a more sympathetic interpretation.

The Crockett writers acted in good faith and were innocent of intending to destroy a classic from American literature or an interesting and important figure from American history. Unfortunately their contributions largely had that effect. Perhaps they will be willing to aid in restoring the proper balance which they have been instrumental, albeit unintentionally, in upsetting and will help to give back to American literature and history this book and this man who ought not to be thus neglected because of the "Davy of the typescript."

It is, of course, perfectly true that Crockett is important as a folklore hero, nor could one begrudge the study of him as such had it not been carried on to the complete exclusion of the real man and his work. We would not now, if we could, eliminate "Davy" from the delightful arena of the bedtime story. Rather we would claim for *David* a simultaneous and rightful place on the lifetime and deathtime playgrounds of the children of men. With so much granted in the myth's behalf, I must add this about the present study. I have here ignored the mythological Crockett, save where he is deliberately introduced as such for a specific purpose, and have made the effort to stick to the record so as to give an account of the "Crockett God made." If the result is a less lively tale, I am sorry for that. The choice was between doing as I have done or of not writing at all. I could find no justification for again abusing the public's continued interest in Crockett and for perpetrating again the sort of fabrications indulged in so many times before in these hundred-odd years since his death.

The present volume offers for the first time, I think, sufficient authentic material for a just estimate of the man. I believe a fairer judgment is due him than that which dismisses him as an insignificant, vain, stupid, egotistical, and corrupted, hack politician. No historian or scholar will want to accord him less than justice, and some correction of the popular interpretation may therefore be in order. Surely he deserves the tribute of a carefully constructed biography in which the essential man is revealed through the medium of authentic biographical facts. Up to the present writing, no such work exists. It is a tragic, and yet a grandly victorious story—the story of the destruction of our last frontiersman and of the birth of a new pioneer world citizen.

I wish to acknowledge here the efforts of all those who have aided me in this work—libraries and librarians, historical societies and their staffs, individuals I have unfortunately never met, universities, teachers, relatives, acquaintances, and friends. No work of this sort could possibly be completed without the undemanding generosity of many people. To them all I would express my deep appreciation.

Editor's Foreword

WHILE ENGAGED in the process of revising the present volume, my brother was stricken with a progressive muscular atrophy that deprived him of the use of his hands and threatened his life. In the spring of 1953 I agreed, with great trepidation, to undertake the work of revising the manuscript, in the hope that he might live to see a copy of the published work. All research for the biography had been completed with a meticulous thoroughness. My task was simply to reorganize the narrative so as to preserve the continuity without destroying the scholarly argument. Fortunately, I had been in close touch with my brother while the book was taking shape. At my suggestion the narrative had been organized as a tragic pattern involving five movements. But there remained the perplexing problem of attaining a balance between two interests which threatened the unity of the book: the narrative proper and the technical scholarship necessary to establish the authorship of the various books attributed to David Crockett. To the extent that I have succeeded in my task, I am indebted to the editorial assistance so generously given by the staff of The University of North Carolina Press.

JOHN B. SHACKFORD

PART ONE

The Long Haul

Chapter 1

THE BACKWOODS CONTEXT:
SWEET AND BITTERSWEET

Europe stretches to the Alleghanies; America lies beyond.
                                    —Ralph Waldo Emerson

THE frontiersman was history's agent for wresting land from the American Indian. How often—and how well—did he play his bitter role! Pursued by civilization which crowded him too closely behind, he arrived inevitably at the "final" boundary set by the latest Indian treaty. In front of him lay the rich wilderness and the trail of the retreating game upon which his very life depended. Pushed from behind, pulled from in front, he moved on inexorably into Indian territory.

Just as inexorably, the Indians resisted his encroachment. Angered by this betrayal of their established rights, they attempted to enforce the white man's treaties in the only way they knew, by attacking the invaders—by pillage, burning, and scalping. Then came a new "war," and a new treaty. Always the new treaty gave legal sanction to the latest accumulation of lands illegally acquired by these frontiersmen. No power on earth short of overwhelming physical force could have made them retrace their steps and abandon their "improvements" and the wild game on which they lived. Then the cycle would be renewed: new encroachments upon the new treaty, the inevitable massacres, the consequent accommodating treaty,—and new encroachments. So dwindled the hunting grounds of the redskin.

The story of the migration and death of David's grandfather is a case in point.[1] This earlier David, who took his family, including the later David's father, John, across the Appalachian Mountains in the year of Lexington, met death by violence at the hands of the aborigines and bequeathed to us his namesake as the abiding sign of the undertaking. Shortly after the middle of the eighteenth century the Crocketts arrived in Piedmont North Carolina. In the Lincolnton Court House, on the eastern side of the Appalachians, one may still find records of grandfather David and of two of his older sons, dated as early as March 6, 1771.[2] Shortly thereafter, history released the protected East into the great new life of the West, and about 1775 grandfather David slowly made his way up, across, and beyond the mighty mountain barrier.

William Byrd's diaries have acquainted Americans with his survey of the boundary line between North Carolina and Virginia in 1728-29. Less well known is the fact that the survey was not completed for another fifty years, and that as a result of this survey North Carolina recouped territory from the extreme western tip of Virginia, from which were formed two new counties, first Washington, then Sullivan. The settlement there, known as Watauga Settlement, governed itself at first. However, in the summer of 1776, Indian attacks caused it to petition the North Carolina legislature for annexation. Both grandfather David Crockett and his son William signed this petition.[3] In 1777 the Long Island Treaty was signed with the Indians; then legislation set up land-purchase offices in all North Carolina counties, and the movement across the mountains took on serious proportions. One year later (1778) North Carolina passed a law forbidding whites to enter or survey land within the Indian Boundary. Before the law was passed the land speculators had already made entries for more than a million acres within the Indian territory. The Long Island Treaty itself had lowered an older line of a former treaty and hence had deprived the Indians of lands formerly guaranteed them. By 1776 and 1777 the red men, dismayed and hostile, were engaging in depredations against the white "aliens" encamped within their nation.

It was in this situation that grandfather David lost his life. The *Autobiography* recounts the murder of the grandparents by Creeks and Cherokees in 1777 near what is now Rogersville, Hawkins County, Tennessee. They were probably among the unnamed twelve officially listed as murdered in the letter that Colonel Charles Robertson wrote to Richard Caswell, Governor of North Carolina, on April 27, 1777:

Sir:
The many hostilities committed by the Cherokee and Creek Indians on this frontier since the departure of the Gentm. Delegates from this county,

to the legislature of North Carolina, merits [*sic*] your Excellency's consideration.... There have been to the number of about twelve persons killed since the Delegates departed.[4]

The grandparents were massacred at this place, under these conditions, and at about this time. By August 19, 1778, their deaths had been made a matter of the slow-moving, frontier court, records.[5] The state of Tennessee finally, on July 12, 1927, unveiled a bronze tablet, in Rogers Cemetery on Crockett's Creek in Rogersville, commemorating the tragedy.[6] Stark danger was a fact in the context of a backwoodsman's life.

Several of the Crockett boys were away from home when the incensed red men descended upon the Crockett homestead. Happily for our story, David's father John was among them. However, Joseph and James were at home. Joseph, more fortunate than James, suffered only a broken arm from the impact of a rifle bullet. "Deaf and dumb" Jimmy was kidnapped by the Indians and held captive for twenty years before he was rescued by the other brothers. For years thereafter he tried unsuccessfully to relocate gold and silver mines he had visited blindfolded while a captive of the tribes. John Crockett was then serving as a ranger along the frontier outposts and so escaped injury, capture, or death.

Poverty, as well as danger, was the birthright of the pioneer; and John Crockett inherited his full share of it. The earliest record found for him is a court order for February 28, 1778, less than a year after the massacre of his parents, authorizing Isaac Shelby to take his deposition.[7] Around 1780 John married Rebecca Hawkins and settled in Washington County, North Carolina, within a large land plot sometimes known as Brown's Purchase, bought from the Indians by Colonel Jacob Brown of South Carolina for as much merchandise as a single pack-horse could carry. Three years later, when a new county, Greene, was created from a part of Washington County, John, whose home lay in the new county, was made constable in April, 1783, and again in 1785 and 1789.[8] David's *Autobiography*, speaking of his father's various hardships, mentions particularly a mill he built with "Thomas Galbreath," swept away by a "Noah's fresh." * Records re-

---

* The source of quotations throughout the text not otherwise documented is *A Narrative of the Life of David Crockett, of the State of Tennessee* by David Crockett and Thomas Chilton, referred to as the *Autobiography*.

veal a permit issued in 1794 to Thomas Galbraith to build a mill upon Cove Creek in Greene County.[9]

It should be a matter of later interest to note that Andrew Jackson, state's attorney in 1794, had received his first law license at the court where John Crockett presided as a magistrate. (Later James K. Polk received his first license in the court where David had served for several years as justice of the peace.) There are many cases in which John appeared as a juror. Once, in November, 1796, the state charged him with petit larceny. However, he pled not guilty, and was so found.[10]

One of the ways the backwoodsman had of attempting to escape debt was to speculate in land. There are several records showing that John tried his hand at it. On October 10, 1783, he bought for fifty shillings per hundred a two hundred acre homestead, which he sold for fifty pounds on June 4, 1787.[11] The bill of sale was signed by both John Crockett and his wife, Rebeckah Crockett. Another tract, which John bought on April 14, 1792, was evidently David's home place during his early years after 1794, and therefore has a peculiar interest for us: three hundred acres lying on Mossy Creek in Jefferson County.[12] The Crocketts did not move to it until after the disaster to the Cove Creek Mill in 1794. Its sale on November 4, 1795, under the sheriff's hammer, reveals John's failure to escape debt. The father either remained in possession of a remnant of these acres, or perhaps continued to live there in the employ of the purchaser. Certainly it was here that he built the tavern David describes in the *Autobiography*, so that David continued to live there for several more years. A few phrases of the sale record bear quoting:

> ... commanding the said Sheriff that of the goods and chattels, lands and tenements of John Crockett be caused to be made the sum of Four hundred dollars ... and also the sum of Forty three dollars ten cents, costs and charges in said suit, ... and whereas ... the said [William] Line ... was the highest bidder and bid the sum of forty Dollars ... therefore the said Robert McFarland Sheriff ... hath bargained and sold ... the said tract of land containing three hundred acres lying and being on the South side of the Main Holston road and within a few miles of Perkinses Iron Works on Mossy Creek the waters of Holston River ... together with all Hereditaments and appurtenances to the same appertaining being the land granted to John Crockett by grant no. 1050 and dated the fourteenth day of April 1792. To have and to hold the said tract of land ... to the said William Line his heirs and assigns forever. ...[13]

The location of this land and of John's tavern was in the extreme northern part of Jefferson County in the direction of Morristown.[14]

Many other records testify to John's humble circumstances. An inventory of the Gideon Morriss Estate lists a note against him for "13 bushels Indian Corn" for September 17, 1783. The court records that in 1801 the note was still "desperate" (disparate). An inventory of the Isaac Lambert Estate indicates that as late as October 23, 1810, he was a "debtor" to the amount of $2.25.[15] Other scattered records pursue him into Middle and West Tennessee, as he followed his son on the long trek, until we reach the final document making David administrator of his father's estate in Gibson County on September 15, 1834.

To achieve an accurate view of John Crockett's whole pioneer type, the twentieth-century reader must hold clearly in mind the realization that in an earlier day in the West a formal education did not constitute the measure of a man. The subduing of the wilderness allowed neither idle hands nor leisure for an education. To forget this fact is to risk the sort of misjudgments about these men from the cane that the "quality folk" of that day were guilty of. Our standardized spelling, for example, is but one aspect of the stereotypy of a machine age. Shakespeare found many different ways to spell his name; and Mark Twain roundly declared his lack of respect for any man so unoriginal as to be capable of spelling a word in only one way. In frontier life, action necessarily overbalanced reflection. An age such as our own, inclined to conformity and research, must avoid the temptation to identify ultimate truth with its own conventions if it is to make a proper evaluation of these pioneers.

John Crockett did have some rudiments of an education: he was a petty court official, and he signed the bill of sale in 1787 with his own name, not, like so many in those days, with "his mark." His hardships were deepened by misadventures that brought debts and creditors rather than fortune. Nevertheless, though he died as he had lived, a poor man, we find ourselves writing about him and his progeny more than a century later. It is in just such raw, uneducated pioneers of the late eighteenth century that we discover the vigorous roots of the new world. By the time of the death of Lincoln, even some among the "Boston Brahmin" were belatedly discovering this fact: "new birth of our new soil, the first American"—though Lincoln, Lowell's first discovery, was *not* the first-born American.

Civilization and *refinement* are relative terms. Judged by European standards, of that time, American life along the Atlantic coast, even in the most fashionable centers, was provincial and unpolished. Yet compared to the new life among the transmontane settlers, the American seaboard was a refined and civilized order. One gets a view of the great contrast between seaboard and inland America from descriptions of the hinterlands by the literary figures of the times. As "quality folks," they view with some contempt the rough, ugly new roots which the human plant was putting out into uncivilized ground. Madame Knight, William Byrd, Alexis de Tocqueville saw in this frontier class a seething, unfrugal, illiterate group of renegades and ne'er-do-wells—an irresponsible lot who loved an aboriginal life and sheer idleness much more than they did the respectable values of conventionalized religion, solid ownership of property, and all that round of activities which polite society invents for its titillation and points to as proof of its own superiority. And because the backwoodsman *was* unlettered, it was not until about the time of David Crockett that he began to give his impudent reply to quality folk—to express for the first time in American literature the essential spirit of the hardy new plant that was to seed a continent.

The annals of David Crockett's life prior to his twelfth year are practically confined to half the length of a poor man's tombstone: according to the *Autobiography*,[16] he was born on August 17, 1786, "at the mouth of Lime Stone, on the nola-chucky river," in Greene County. A stone slab now commemorates the spot at Strong Springs twelve miles east of Greeneville. The only additional information, likewise from the *Autobiography*, consists of a bit of genealogical data, some childhood reminiscences, and a brief description of the tavern that his father built in Jefferson County.

Our narrative must begin, then, with David's brief account, in a tone of apparent retrospective surprise, of how his father hired him out (probably in 1798) to Jacob Siler to help drive a herd of cattle to Rockbridge County, Virginia. One must remember the poverty of his father, his large family, and the fact that he had recently lost his homestead.

On this trip, David learned of the deceit of men, and responded to his lesson with a determination and physical vigor characteristic of the later man. Mr. Siler attempted to detain him by force beyond the completion of the service for which he had contracted. To escape, he stole away from the house in the dead of a snowy night, and walked seven miles in two hours through knee-deep snow. Finally, he encountered a party of travellers who agreed to furnish him a passage home; they were acquainted with David's father and his tavern back in Tennessee. One of the party, a Mr. Dunn, tried to persuade David to remain with him. Homesick and homeward bound, David took to the road, arriving home in the winter of 1798 or the early spring of 1799 after an absence of several months. There he remained until the following fall.

David, like Daniel Boone, found his independence threatened by the shadow of a birch rod. But whereas Daniel's difficulty had been with the teacher, David's arose out of an assault upon one of the canebrake scholars. Because he feared severe punishment either at the hands of the master, Mr. Benjamin Kitchen, or of his irate father, Crockett connived with his brothers to pretend at home, that he was attending school, and at school, that he was ill at home. In the meantime he enjoyed the pastimes natural to a young boy recently turned thirteen and possessed of an unexpected gift of borrowed time.

The inevitable discovery was at length made by virtue of a diplomatic communiqué to the father from Mr. Kitchen. David's choice simplified itself into whether to continue his educational career on the *de facto* side of a caning, or to draw back his forces precipitately, protect his flanks, and terminate the engagement altogether in a "strategic withdrawal." This decision was made for him by the uncontrolled wrath of his father and the size of the hickory which he brandished. David took to his heels upon another journey.

He hired himself to go immediately as a helper with a Mr. Jesse Cheek, who was driving a herd of cattle to Front Royal, Virginia. David says that one of his elder brothers went with him, but he does not tell us which one.[17] After driving through Abingdon, Wytheville, Lynchburg, Charlottesville, and Chester Gap, they finally disposed of the cattle to a Mr. Vanmetre at Front Royal late in the fall of 1799. Hoping that the enemy's forces might by now have been dispersed, David commenced the return trip with Jesse Cheek's brother, leaving his own brother behind to come along with the rest of the company. But the Cheek brother would ride and never "tie," there being but one horse between them, and David dropped astern after having been given four dollars to bear the expense of the four-hundred-mile journey home.

At this point he ran into Adam Myers, another waggoner from Greeneville, Tennessee, who persuaded him to go along and help him on a trip to Gerardstown, below Winchester, Virginia. Myers promised that as soon as the journey was completed, they would return immediately to Tennessee. David persisted in this agreement even after a meeting with his brother, who had overtaken him. Deaf to his brother's pleas to go home, he went on to Gerardstown. However, Myers, unable to get the return load for which he had hoped, ran local loads about Alexandria for the remainder of the winter. Meanwhile, David remained in Gerardstown, ploughing and doing day-labor for John Gray at twenty-five cents per day.

In the spring of 1800, Crockett and Myers set out for Baltimore. On the way the horses were scared by "some wheelbarrow men, who were working on the road." The wagon tongue and axletrees were broken, and David was rather shaken up. While the wagon was being repaired, David visited the wharf and dreamed of faraway places. Like Ben Franklin, he agreed, with the captain of one of the ships, to make a voyage to London, and returned to his lodgings for his clothes and money. But Myers, threatening him with his whip, adamantly refused to release him. Though David shortly thereafter escaped from Myers, he had to leave without his money, and he abandoned the projected London voyage. Setting out on the road again, he had not gone far before he encountered another waggoner and another Myers, this one named Henry. When Henry asked him about his troubles, David burst into tears and brought forth his story. Henry was enraged. He swore that he would return and force from Adam Myers the money David had left in his keeping. Henry's wrath was fruitless; Adam had spent the money and could not replace it. David set forth once more upon the road, with his newly-won protector. A few days later, when their ways parted, Henry took up a collection of three dollars for the boy and sent him on his homeward journey—afoot.

At Montgomery, Virginia, his money gave out and he set to work, first, for James Caldwell, and then for Elijah Griffith. After some eighteen months Griffith became involved in debt and departed the country, leaving David with an empty bag. David found employment at odd jobs for a few months longer, got together a little money and some clothes, and set out once more for home. In February or March of 1802, he made a dangerous crossing of the stormy New River in a borrowed canoe. Finally, he arrived at the home of his father's younger brother, Joseph Crockett, in Sullivan County. By strange coincidence, he here found his own brother, the one who had originally accompanied him on the trip into Virginia. After a visit of some weeks with their Uncle Joseph, the two boys set out homeward, arriving just at nightfall in the early spring of 1802.

David was now almost sixteen years old. He had been away from home for two and a half of a boy's "growingest" years. Having seen the first fringes of down come upon his face in an alien land and among foreigners, Crockett played the stranger and tested his age, experience, and acquired knowledge against the unsuspecting memory of his family. Staying inconspicuously out of the highlights and talking little, he went unnoticed until he was called in to supper. Then his eldest sister, plumbing his anonymity, "recollected" him, sprang up and seized him about the neck, and proclaimed his return.

As David tells the story, a touching reunion followed. He learned that the family had had no word of him since he had parted from his brother more than two years before. Nor was he disappointed in his belief that the school episode would be overlooked, and he could relax and enjoy his homecoming in the reflection that at sixteen he had not yet learned the first letter of the alphabet.[18] David's experience was doubtless repeated many times over in the backwoods, serving many men with reason or excuse for the proximate illiteracy that stood them in such good political stead in later life.

The *Autobiography* gives a brief account of the poverty of John Crockett and of his indebtedness to one Abraham Wilson to the amount of thirty-six dollars; and to another, a John Kennedy, a Quaker from North Carolina, for forty dollars. David worked out the first note in six months at his father's request. He also undertook to discharge the second in a similar time as a surprise to his father, who, by David's account, was visibly moved when the sacrifice was revealed to him. Perhaps for political reasons, he needed to soften the portrait of his father and of the filial relationship more harshly drawn in the anonymous work of 1833. This was in the spring or summer of 1803.

Being in dire need of clothes, he continued to work for the Quaker on his own.

That summer the Quaker's niece came to visit her uncle. To David she was all that was strange and fair. However, she was forespoken, and all his attentions could not weaken her loyalties. Envious and chagrined, he began to reflect on his own deficiencies. After taking an inventory of his rival, he concluded that a lack of learning was the seat of his misfortune; so he straightway set about putting a patch upon it. The Quaker had a married son living nearby who was "keeping school." David agreed with him to work for two days a week in exchange for board and four days' schooling. The arrangement continued for some six months until David had acquired an ability to read a little and to write less, and "to cypher some in the first three rules of figures." This, he says, was all the schooling he ever had in the way of "formal" education—four days a week for six months, and the hardly invaluable five days at his earlier indoctrination, or a total of about one hundred days.

All this schooling was only a means to the promised end: David was determined to capture a petticoat for himself. His mind made up, he went about his affairs in a most businesslike way. Shortly after completing his education, he "found a family of very pretty little girls," and set up to one of them, "whose name is nobody's business." He found she took it very well. She and David waited on the Quaker's niece when that young lady was married, and the fires were thereby fanned. His suit prospered and he pried out her consent to marry him. However, he reckoned without thought of woman's inconstancy—though it is yet said about the little town of Dandridge, Tennessee, where lived the Margaret Elder who had given David her troth, that he got pretty much what he deserved. For on the week-end of Saturday, October 19, 1805, when he should have been strengthening the bonds of his troth, David took his long rifle and went to a frolic. He tells us, in his own story, of his exploits with the rifle that week-end, and of how he won a whole beef with his marksmanship. He fails to mention the partying, the dancing, and the carousing in which he doubtless engaged, though we may be sure that the "men folks" whom he had outshot saw to it that Margaret got the word. It is probable that this side of the story is told with great accuracy by the anonymous

Life of 1833. Evidently this was one of the episodes which Crockett's *Autobiography* of 1834 aimed at abridging.

After the fun had drawn to an end on Sunday, David recalled the original object of his journey and went into Dandridge on the following Monday morning to pay a visit to the court house. One may still find there the official record of that visit:

> State of Tennessee—Jefferson County: To any licensed minister of the gospel or justice of the peace—Greeting: I do authorize and empower you to celebrate the rite of marriage between David Crockett and Margaret Elder and join them together as husband and wife. Given at my office in Dandridge, the 21st day of October, 1805. J. Hamilton, Clerk.[19]

David says that the marriage was to take place on a Thursday—probably the first Thursday following issuance of the license, or October, 24, 1805. Dilatory tactics were foreign to the frontier. To this nineteen-year-old the birds must have sung sweetly that Monday morning as he followed the forested wagon trail to Margaret Elder's —however sternly his conscience may have reminded him of a misspent week-end. But when he stopped within two miles of Margaret's for a friendly visit with her uncle, conscience had its revenge. There it was that Margaret's younger sister, in a burst of telltale tears, revealed that Margaret was going to marry another man on the following day. She loyally urged him to go on and attempt to change Margaret's mind, adding that the parents preferred David's suit to the other's. Crockett was too bitterly astounded by this revelation to read the meaning of the sister's too-sympathetic tears. He would not go on, but withdrew sorely bruised, concluding that he "was only born for hardships, misery, and disappointment."

With men of the backwoods, heartache was a luxury. The backwoodsman had to arrive at journey's end restored and prepared for the next stage. The whole of a twenty-year sorrow had to be crammed into a fistful of heart's-ease gathered along the way of a day's journeying through the forest. Crockett describes his sorrow in realistic terms, and he leaves us under the impression that he cherished it lone and long: "I continued in this down-spirited situation for a good long time." Yet, in less than ten months he had not only recovered, but had already found another, and had wooed, won, and wed. By following his account and the records, we understand him. The blood of a stricken heart may coagulate, and the heart-wound heal. But a young man may well-nigh die of a wounded pride.

One day while hunting, Crockett stopped at the house of a Dutch widow who had a daughter "as ugly as a stone fence." The daughter, observing his gloomy condition, tried to cheer him up with the promise that she would introduce him to a real beauty, if he would come to their reaping. Although he feared that the ugly girl might have herself in mind, he agreed to come. His fears were groundless. At the appointed time, the widow's daughter introduced him to the mother of the "beauty," the girl herself being at the moment absent. The Irish mother bantered David, saying she had a sweetheart for him, and later in the evening, in the young girl's presence, she laughingly called him her son-in-law. Although this somewhat nettled him, he went on the old saying of "salt the cow to catch the calf." Things went off well at the reaping, to say nothing of the frolic which lasted until daylight thereafter.

Back home at the Quaker's, he made arrangements to work for a cheap horse. Some weeks later he journeyed to see the girl and to find out what sort of people they were at home. He found her mother quite as talkative as ever, and her father a very affable old fellow. The girl herself was out at a meeting. When she returned, escorted, David tried unsuccessfully to outsit his rival. Finally, by pretending that he was about to leave, he discovered the truth of the matter: the girl preferred him and gave him her complete attention. However, salting the cow had only caught the calf, for David discovered, to his chagrin, that the mother was in his rival's barn. Nevertheless, he payed a stiff suit over the week-end before returning to work the following Monday morning.

The affair continued to be auspicious. Some three months after the date of their first meeting, in the meantime having earned enough with his gun thrown in to buy the horse, he was ready to tempt his fate once more. The question answered to his satisfaction, David went to his father's house to make arrangements for the infare. When he returned to ask consent of the girl's parents, he found a house divided against itself. The father was willing enough, but the Irish mother treated him "as savage as a meat axe" and practically ordered him out of the house. David reminded her of the coaxing she had earlier given him, and concluded the matter by making arrangements with the daughter to come away with him on the following Thursday. As he took his leave, the old lady was still shouting that he would not have her daughter. Undaunted, he made his engagement with the justice of the peace and got his license.

Once more, David has neglected to give us the names of the characters in this domestic comedy, but fortunately the records are more precise. The father and mother were William and Jean Finley; the daughter, Mary, nicknamed Polly. David obtained this second marriage license at the Dandridge Courthouse [20] on Tuesday, August 12, 1806, five days before his twentieth birthday. He had come a dozen miles from the north into the clerk's office in Dandridge, bringing with him as bondsman his friend Thomas Doggett.

On Thursday, August 14, 1806, David took two of his brothers, a sister-in-law, an unmarried sister, "and two other young men, and cut out . . . to get her." When the party drew near the Finley cabin, Crockett sent his attendants in advance with empty flagons, according to a custom of the times. Mr. Finley filled them, and they were brought back as tokens of welcome to the impatient bridegroom. The company drank freely of them and proceeded on their way.

Upon arrival at the bride's dwelling, David, without dismounting, asked Polly if she were ready to ride, and bid her mount. However Mr. Finley intervened. Stopping David at the gate, he apologized for his wife's tongue and requested that they stay and be married there. David consented on the condition that Mrs. Finley apologize. When she complied, the wedding party dismounted. "I sent off then for my parson," David says, though he had earlier spoken of having engaged a justice of the peace. Which of the two actually performed the ceremony is not recorded, but more to the point is the fact that it was satisfactorily performed. Afterwards, the party spent the night at the Finley's and next morning set out for David's father's, where a large company had been awaiting their arrival for twenty-four hours. "Having gotten my wife," says Crockett:

I thought I was completely made up, and needed nothing more in the whole world. But I soon found this was all a mistake—for now having a wife, I wanted every thing else; and, worse than all, I had nothing to give for it.

David's hard life was to grow no whit easier with marriage. We have seen that David was poor. The Finleys were equally poor. David says that as a marriage portion he and Polly were given two "likely" cows and calves, and that was about all they ever got—was, in fact, more than he had expected. His father-in-law's will, drawn up on April 3, 1818, and probated in the June session of the 1819 court, soon after Mr. Finley's death, testifies to the Finley poverty. To his sons and daughters, except Polly, he was able to leave only "the sum of two dollars each." As for Polly, the will includes this statement: "I do also give to my daughter Mary Crocket's three children, John, William, and Polly two dollars each...." Polly's inheritance was left to her three children, for, by that date, April 3, 1818, Polly was dead.[21]

The three Crockett children—John, William, and Polly—were born in that order; and though the daughter took her mother's nickname, she was christened Margaret instead of Mary, after one of David's sisters.[22]

Polly and David rented a small farm and cabin and went to work. The Quaker gave him an order for fifteen dollars on a store. With that and Polly's Irish skill at the spinning wheel, their cabin was "fixed up pretty grand." Yet the going without capital and on rented land was not easy. David describes it thus:

We worked on for some years, renting ground, and paying high rent, until I found it wan't the thing it was cracked up to be; and that I couldn't make a fortune of it just at all. So I concluded to quit it, and cut out for some new country. In this time we had two sons, and I found I was better at increasing my family than my fortune. It was therefore the more necessary that I should hunt some better place to get along; and as I knowed I would have to move at some time, I thought it was better to do it before my family got too large, that I might have less to carry.

The Duck and Elk river country was just beginning to settle, and I determined to try that. I had now one old horse, and a couple of two year old colts. They were both broke to the halter, and my father-in-law proposed, that, if I went, he would go with me, and take one horse to help me move. So we all fixed up, and I packed my two colts with as many of my things as they could bear; and away we went across the mountains. We got on well enough, and arrived safely in Lincoln county, on the head of Mulberry fork of Elk River. I found this a very rich country, and so new, that game, of different sorts, was very plenty. It was here that I began to distinguish myself as a hunter, and to lay the foundation for all my future greatness; but mighty little did I know of what sort it was going to be. Of deer and smaller game I killed abundance; but the bear had been hunted in those parts before, and were not so plenty as I could have wished. I lived here in the years of 1809 and '10, to the best of my recollection, and then I moved to Franklin county, and settled on Bean creek, where I remained till after the close of the last war [Creek Indian].

Though all of the facts in this quotation are accurate enough, the "best of his recollection" has played Crockett a trick. He did not leave the mountains of east Tennessee in 1809.[23] He left two years later, in the fall of 1811. The first two children, John Wesley and William, were born before the migration.

Crockett left east Tennessee some time after September 11, 1811, early enough in the fall to get himself established before winter. William Finley went with him and lent him an extra pack horse. He doubtless remained with them in middle Tennessee long enough to help them prepare for winter, since that was obviously one of his reasons for making such an extended journey.[24]

The frontier was moving on, from North Carolina to east Tennessee, and now to middle Tennessee. The last inundation was engulfing the last continent, and David was moving with it. His apprenticeship was done, and he was riding out upon an impulse of the race. But that, perhaps, he could not know. What he had learned and did know was that life contains its bitters; and that its sweets lie in the hope that looks to new horizons.

Chapter 2

WHITE MAN'S THUNDER

EARLY in 1813 Crockett left Lincoln County and arrived on Rattlesnake Spring Branch of Bean's Creek in Franklin County, ten miles south of Winchester and a few miles north of the present Alabama line.[1] He named his claim "Kentuck," perhaps reflecting his aspirations for a future move. A few months before his arrival, the latest Indian massacres had occurred there.[2] The whites had continued to push the Indians back and to violate the applicable treaty in that area. Now the Indians, encouraged by the British and exhorted by Tecumseh, were in a sultry and rebellious mood.

The conventional story of the outbreak of the Creek Indian War designates the Indian attack on Fort Mimms as its first engagement. However, the truth is that the whites, not the Indians, struck the first blow. The whites knew that the Indians were unquiet and thought they were getting arms and ammunition from the Spanish at Pensacola and from the British at other places. Accordingly, in the summer of 1813 some 180 white recruits intercepted a band of from sixty to ninety warriors returning from Pensacola and opened fire upon them without warning as they lay at rest during the noon meal at Burnt Corn Creek in south Alabama. The Indians were scattered by the ambush, but the whites failed to follow up the initial advantage. Stopping to scramble for Indian booty, they were effectually counterattacked and ignominiously defeated shortly afterward by the inferior force of Indians.

After this first unofficial act of war, the inhabitants along the Tensaw and Little Rivers in south Alabama, many of them of mixed and Creek blood, recognized the *de facto* state of war and gathered

18

around the residence of Samuel Mimms, an old Indian countryman, one mile from the Alabama River near its junction with the Tombigbee. There they built an almost square stockade, inclosing about an acre of ground and several buildings, and named it Fort Mimms.[3] All feared retaliation for the ambush, nor were they disappointed. Yet it seems, except for dereliction of duty on the part of the officer in charge, the attack on Fort Mimms might have been harmless, and rather a matter of prideful gesture than of open warfare. However, the United States Government had already decided on a war of approximate extermination of the Creeks in order to acquire the Indians' land and to secure the nation's position with respect to the threat of war with the British.

In the latter part of August, 1813, 553 persons had gathered in Fort Mimms. Of these, about 265 were soldiers under command of Major Daniel Beasley of the Mississippi Volunteers. The danger of attack was clear, and Major Beasley had been repeatedly instructed by his superiors to strengthen his position. On the very day of attack he notified General Claiborne that he had taken every precaution. In point of fact, it seems that he was not apprehensive, for he had neither materially strengthened his barricades nor even so much as closed his gates.

Meantime, the Indians were gatherings. Their leader in the attack was William Weatherford, an Indian known to be friendly to the whites. It is also well-established that the Creek Nation, as a whole, had not been cordial to Tecumseh or receptive to his plans to unite all the Indian nations in a concerted attack on their enemies. The evidence indicates that Weatherford earnestly entreated the Creeks not to avenge Burnt Corn, but could not prevail. Unable to stop them, he therefore led them in the attack, expecting, as he later said, to find the gates securely fastened, and trusting in the impregnability of the garrison to furnish him with argument for calling off the battle after a brief, symbolic skirmish. The fact that, when events turned out otherwise, he dissociated himself from the battle early in its course helps to establish the reliability of his story, as does his character and his later affiliation with Andrew Jackson. To his horror, Weatherford found the gates open and the posts completely undefended. He was powerless to prevent what followed.

At high noon of August 30, 1813, Beasley and other officers were engaged in a game of cards, and the soldiers and some young girls were dancing, the gate standing wide. The attack struck, and Beasley attempted to close the gate. Its path was clogged by sand, and he fumbled in his effort. He was thus struck down by the advancing one thousand warriors, the first to fall from the effects of his own fool-hardiness.

The Indians poured through the open gate. For two or three hours they butchered the inmates and then withdrew, to return a little while later. The survivors had by then closed the gates, but the enraged Indians set fire to the buildings with flaming arrows, and all those who remained alive crowded into "the bastion"—one immense solid mass of human beings herded together in a slaughter house. When the Indians finally left around five o'clock, all who had not escaped or been taken prisoner were dead and, for the most part, so thoroughly mutilated as to defy identification by their closest of kin. Only some fifty or sixty in all escaped, including the Negroes, who were probably taken captive rather than killed. The remainder, some five hundred, lost their lives, including a number of women and about one hundred children.

Thus opened the Creek War in which David participated. A runner dispatched immediately after the attack to Andrew Jackson passed close to David's country. Before Jackson had the news, the recruits were falling out and organizing along what is now the Alabama line. Jackson did not receive word of the massacre until about September 12, 1813. On September 9, and again on September 11, if Crockett's account is accurate, troops were mustering in Winchester. David was with them.[4]

On September 20, after gathering in Winchester, Franklin County, David's company marched to Beaty's Spring, a small place south of Huntsville, where the troops were to assemble. Crockett reports that while the company awaited muster, a Major Gibson arrived looking for volunteers to go with him to scout out the movements of the Creeks on the other side of the Tennessee River.[5] For this expedition Captain Jones recommended Crockett, who was accepted and then allowed to choose a companion. He chose George Russell, the young son of "Major" William Russell, early settler of Franklin County whom David undoubtedly knew prior to the war.[6] Major Gibson objected that the boy hadn't beard enough—that he wanted men, not boys, for such an undertaking. David persisted in his choice with some heat. He replied that if courage was measured by the beard, a goat would have preference over a man. George was allowed to go with him.

Major Gibson, David, George, and ten others set out that very afternoon, crossed the Tennessee River at Ditto's Landing, due south of Huntsville, and proceeded a few miles beyond by nightfall. The next morning they split into two groups to reconnoiter, Major Gibson to visit a friendly Cherokee, Dick Brown (who was to become a colonel in the liaison forces and to fight with Jackson's men), and Crockett to drop in on Dick's father—all to rendezvous at evening some miles beyond. The major failed to arrive at the point of rendezvous either that night or the next morning; and David, feeling his new responsibility and unwilling to return with no news and few rumors, insisted on going ahead.

Crockett's contingent arrived, during the afternoon of the second day, at the house of one Radcliffe, a white man living within the Creek Nation and married to a Creek woman. Radcliffe appeared quite apprehensive when Crockett's party descended on him. He stated that within the very hour ten painted warriors had left his house, and he was terrified lest they should return and destroy him and his family for harboring the enemy. Crockett himself was uneasy, for he blustered about the matter considerably. After a good meal he and his men saddled up and moved on. David was actually more afraid to return than go forward, for he did not relish the jibes back at camp. He insisted, therefore, upon going ahead, despite protests from some of his men: for, he says, he knew that some of the volunteers would go with him and that the rest would not have the courage to go back alone.

A man may, as the years roll on, forget dates and names. But as long as he lives there will remain clear in his memory and along the ridge of his spine the recollection of shadowy night scouting in hostile territory, where the condition of the light of the moon may determine whether he is, in the next instant, to live or to die. When, therefore, David tells us that "the moon was about the full, and the night was clear; we therefore had the benefit of her light from night to morning, and I knew if we were placed in such danger as to make a retreat necessary, we could travel by night as well as in the day time," we know that he speaks fact. For the story, as story, would have been more dramatic had the night been described as dark and ominous.

Along the way, through moonlight and shadow, they met two Negroes fleeing from their Indian captors. One of these they sent on to Ditto's Landing, and the other they drafted as a guide. Finally they reached the camp of some friendly Creeks, forty men, women, and children. The Indian boys were shooting arrows by the light of the fire, where David joined them while the Negro guide talked with the Indians. When the guide communicated to him the friendly Creeks' apprehension lest they be found entertaining Jackson's scouts, Crockett brought a laugh with his boast that he would scalp any unfriendly Indian who showed his face. Then, tying up their horses with the saddles on, his party retired, guns in arms.

David was startled out of a doze by what he describes as the sharpest scream that ever escaped a human throat. The Negro soon arrived at his side and reported that an Indian, whose war scream had so startled Crockett, had just come into camp with the news that the Creek war party had been crossing the Coosa River all day at the Ten Islands (near present Gadsden, Alabama), on their way to meet Jackson. "I felt bound," David remarks, "to make this intelligence known as soon as possible to the army we had left at the landing; . . ." David appears to have been delighted finally to get some sort of news that obligated him to return!

Travelling headlong through the night, by ten o'clock the next day they had covered the sixty-five miles and had arrived to report the news to Colonel Coffee—about ten hours after the scream. Colonel Coffee paid little attention to Crockett's story until Major Gibson returned on the following day with a similar tale of even worse proportions than David's, whereupon the colonel ordered that breastworks be hastily erected and sent a runner posthaste to Jackson at Fayetteville, calling for aid. David reflects:

This convinced me, clearly, of one of the hateful ways of the world. When I made my report, it wasn't believed, because I was no officer; I was no great man, but just a poor soldier. But when the same thing was reported by Major Gibson!! why, then, it was all as true as preaching, and the colonel believed every word.

This and similar incidents made David an inveterate hater of army "brass," and later enriched the arguments he was to level in Congress against the regular army as opposed to the volunteers, and against West Point and what he regarded as the aristocratic tendencies of that institution.

Colonel Coffee's Indian runner may have arrived at Jackson's headquarters the night of the same day of Major Gibson's return to Ditto's Landing. According to S. P. Waldo's *Memoirs of Jackson,* on October 8 Jackson received Coffee's "express" in Fayetteville, where he had arrived the previous day weakened by a bad wound received in a recent duel.[7]

Major Gibson had probably returned to Ditto's Landing on the 8th of October. Crockett's arrival back at camp had been on October 7, after travelling ten furious hours. The ride back was on the night of October 6 and the early hours of the following morning. The almanacs verify that the moon was full on October 10 of that year.[8] Hence Crockett's account of his midnight ride when "the moon was *about* the full," a matter to which he alludes a second time, turns out to be quite accurate. Also, his comment that they "therefore had the benefit of her light from night to morning" is astronomically correct, for when the moon is full its shining coincides with the duration of the darkness.

It is interesting to find David at the source of this historic march of the stern General Jackson, hoax though the entire alarm was. Upon arriving at Ditto's Landing, Jackson dispatched a force of some eight hundred men back along David's previous route, to explore the Black Warrior and Tombigbee (Etomb-ig-aby) Rivers and to "feel out" the enemy. When they arrived at Radcliffe's, they discovered the secret: it was Radcliffe who had sent the Indian runner into camp with his midnight scream in order to frighten the scouts and send them back with a false report. His sympathies evidently lay with the people of his adoption. "To make some atonement for this," David concludes, "we took the old scoundrells's two big sons with us, and made them serve in the war."

It comes not within the purpose of this biography to relate the whole story of the Creek War, certainly not to excuse or justify it. Though the roots of the plant contain its strength, crude strength is not of itself lovely. Our interest in the Creek War must be confined to David's participation in it.

Pushing on into Alabama, the Jackson forces struck towards the headwaters of the Black Warrior River, where they helped themselves to the provisions of the Black Warriors Town—the inhabitants all having fled before them—and burned it to the ground. From here they turned back northeast to the headwaters of the Alabama River, site of the present Gadsden, on the Coosa. On the lower course of this river, near Montgomery, where the Coosa and the Tallapoosa join, lay the Creeks' strongholds; and along this stretch of river Jackson intended to establish forts as he went south, to protect his rear and to keep open his lines of communication and supplies. On the way to the present Gadsden they established Camp Wells. The Jackson forces were now augmented by more Tennessee troops under Captain Cannon. Colonel Coffee was raised to the rank of general; and Captain Cannon, promoted to colonel, was, on October 29, placed in charge of David's regiment.

From Camp Wells the army marched to the Ten Islands (Gadsden) and established Fort Strother. A few days later, on information brought in by scouts, General Coffee sent out troops to destroy an occupied Creek town about eight miles away. Crockett tells the story quite accurately, but perhaps General Coffee's official report to Jackson should be quoted for contrast.

The battle of Tallussahatchee was fought on November 3, 1813, and the Coffee report was dated the next day after the troops had returned to the Ten Islands Camp:

... It was after sunrise when the action was brought on by Capt. Hammond's and Lieut. Patterson's [companies] ... their destruction was very soon completed; our men rushed up to the doors of the houses, and in a few minutes killed the last warrior of them; the enemy fought with savage fury, and met death with all its horrours, without shrinking or complaining: not one asked to be spared, but fought as long as they could stand or sit. In consequence of their flying to their houses and mixing with the families, our men, in killing the males, without intention, killed and wounded a few of the squaws and children ... not one of the warriors escaped to carry the news, a circumstance heretofore unknown.[9]

Beneath the camouflage of the official documents, one sees the clear picture: a massacre as cruel as that of Fort Mimms—which was at least a fort and was presumed to have had some defenses. Nine hundred men had surrounded and killed to the last man 186 warriors.

Nor is David's account so conscience-salving as to attribute the killing of women to accident or of the braves to their resistance. "We shot them like dogs," he relates. He describes the angry killing of one squaw who "had at least twenty balls blown through her"; and he states that "most" of the warriors wanted to be taken prisoner. Well might Jackson, in his report of the "battle" to Governor Blount, say: "We have retaliated for the destruction of Fort Mims." The official report is the romance, and David's account the facts, of the battle.

In his vivid, eye-witness account of this battle, David describes such incidents as setting fire to a house with forty-six warriors inside, and the next day eating potatoes from its cellar stewed in "the oil of the Indians we had burned up on the day before [which] had run down on them." So accurate is his relation where it can be tested by other evidence, that the *Autobiography* must be considered a source document on this, as on most of the other matters it treats. It is in some respects obviously more accurate than the official reports.[10]

Four days after Tallussahatchee, Jackson received word from runners that some Creek Indians friendly to the whites were besieged in Fort Talladega, thirty miles southeast, by hostile Creeks attempting to take the fort. In his official report to Blount, Jackson states that he received the news on November 7 and took up the march between 3:00 and 4:00 A.M., after learning that General White, in command of the East Tennessee troops and a political opponent of Jackson's, had refused to protect his rear. The report continues:

The infantry were in three lines—the militia on the left, and the volunteers on the right. The cavalry formed two extreme wings... advance in a curve, keeping... rear connected with... advance of... infantry lines, and inclose the enemy in a circle. The advance guard I sent forward to bring on the engagement... but owing to some misunderstanding, a few companies of militia commenced to retreat.... The victory was very decisive.

Again the official report covers up the facts—the retreat under fire of the front-line troops in this attempt to duplicate the manoeuvres employed at Tallussahatchee. With reference to the escape of the Creeks, David is more truthful:

... but at length they made their escape through a part of our line, which was made up of drafted militia, which broke ranks, and they passed.

In a corrected report of November 13, Jackson gives the Indian casualties as "killed and counted 299 plus some not found. If the line had not given way, would have repeated Tallussahatchee."

Having come thus far south into the strongholds of the Creeks and having let 700 of them escape through the lines, faced too with inadequate provisions, grumbling men, and lack of support from General White, Jackson, white with anger, was forced to retreat to Fort Strother. From there he wrote General Claiborne on December 18: "I was compelled by a double cause—the want of supplies and the want of cooperation from the East Tennessee troops, to return to this place." Also, the time of a number of the troops who had been with him on the Natchez expedition had, according to *official* records, expired, and there was serious grumbling.

It must have been at about this time that Crockett is supposed to have participated in the following amusing incident. A particular company, in which there was "a private, an awkward, boy-like soldier" (David, of course), had become restive and even insubordinate, and the officer made known to his men that he would not remain captain of a disobedient company. He informed them that he was going to put the matter before General Jackson and ask him what to do. When the captain set out for the general's quarters, Crockett called out that he was going along to "see what the old general says." So the captain and the private called on the general, and when the cause of the visit had been carefully explained, the general broke silence with: "Don't you make any orders on your men without maturing them, and then you execute them, no matter what it costs; and that is all I have to say"—a witty representation of Jackson's pith and brevity.

The two returned to the company, and when several of the uneasy ones asked David what the general had said, Crockett's briefer and pithier summary was: "The old General told the captain to be sure he was right, and then go ahead." Colyar says General Moore testified that the aphorism spread all over the army, then everywhere throughout the backwoods, and he adds: "I am sure, from the circumstantial detail with which it was given to me by General Moore, who was always much esteemed by General Jackson, that these are the facts of its origin." Colyar means that this was the origin of the motto which has become so inseparably attached to Crockett—the one, indeed, with which he inscribed his *Autobiography* in 1834: "Be always sure you're right—then go ahead!" [11]

Back at Fort Strother and closer to home the troops became unruly to the point of mutiny. David, in justifying his own supposed part in the mutiny, says, "for our sixty days had long been out, and that was the time we entered for." Now, for the first time, he puts in material manufactured from the whole cloth. He describes the determination of the troops to go home, Jackson's refusal to allow it, and his ordering of an armed guard to prevent their return. David recounts with glee how the mutineers called Jackson's bluff and marched past the guard, their own guns primed and cocked, and so to Huntsville and home; and the general's comment that they were "the damned'st volunteers he had ever seen in his life; that we would volunteer and go out and fight, and then at our pleasure would *volunteer* and go home again, in spite of the devil." [12]

The true story is, in the first place, that, though the troops did mutiny, Jackson singlehanded, with his rifle resting across the neck of his horse, one arm still practically useless from the duelling wound, held them at bay for some minutes, officers and men, with the assertion that he would shoot dead the first one who made a move to leave. Then some of the officers began to fall in behind Jackson and the mutiny was quelled. However, Governor Blount, for political considerations at home, ordered their release. It was not they who called Jackson's bluff, but he theirs; and from that day on many of them hated Jackson in their hearts—among them, perhaps, David; for hatred of Jackson was finally to be David's undoing. [13]

In the second place, David was not even among the first revolting troops, who were neither cavalry nor mounted volunteers, but infantry. David's mounted volunteers and the cavalry under General Coffee had, before the incident of the infantry's mutiny, already been released "to recruit their horses for a few days" and thereafter to rendezvous on December 8, 1813, at Huntsville.

In the third place, according to the payroll and muster records, Crockett did not leave until the expiration of his ninety days, on December 24, 1813. [14]

In writing the *Autobiography* in 1833, David had in mind his political future as well as his historical past. In order to build up his own "heroic" participation in a mutiny against Jackson, he found it necessary to represent that his term of service expired prior to the mutiny in order to justify his action. If David did actually participate in the mutiny, he had no legal grounds to support him, for his enlistment was not for sixty, but for ninety days; and he had not been on the Natchez expedition. Actually, he seems to have had no part in the mutiny. Because David confused and abused the record and subscribed to the story of his own desertion, a false rumor, which some have credited and tried to cover up, has persisted through the years that David once deserted during the Creek War. Though the records prove this false, a peculiar coincidence has given the rumor an appearance of truth. Incredibly there was another David Crockett in this same war at this same time who *did* desert—as verified by official records.[15]

Furthermore, the *Autobiography* exaggerates the extent of David's military service in 1814. In that narrative, Crockett writes that he returned to the army early in January, 1814, joined "Major" Russell's forces, and participated in the battles of Emuckfau Creek, January 22, and Enotachopco Creek, January 24, battles which drove Jackson back again to Fort Strother. David describes both battles well enough, relying probably upon either J. Reid and J. H. Eaton or Waldo. However, the official War Department records show that Crockett was not among these forces; and a study of the records and verification of them by The Adjutant General[16] proves that David did not return to the army again, after his release on December 24, 1813, until late in the following year, on September 28, 1814. His political ambitions of 1834 were applying the bellows to his military exploits of 1814. We ignore these engagements, then, as well as the remainder of the Creek War proper, as not belonging to the biography of Crockett. In fact, what he did for the next eight months, beyond the usual occupations of a backwoods farmer returned to his log cabin home after having been away to war for three months, must remain altogether a matter of speculation. The record for this period is completely silent.

About six months after Jackson had slaughtered the Creeks disastrously at the Battle of Horse-shoe Bend on March 28, 1814, and about six weeks after he had concluded his treaty with them on August 10, it became necessary to outfit an expedition to Pensacola. Some of the Creeks had fled to that area rather than submit to the terms proposed in the treaty, and the Spanish authorities at Pensacola had, on

August 25, allowed the British to land 300 soldiers, and given permission to the British officers to equip and train the Creek Indians. The British scheme was to employ these Creeks in a movement planned against Mobile and New Orleans. Crockett came in again in response to this fresh call for troops, joining "Major" Russell's "Separate Battalion of Tennessee Mounted Gunmen." The payroll and muster records of his company reveal that he entered as third sergeant in Captain John Cowan's company and served from September 28, 1814, to March 27, 1815.[17] David modestly refrains from telling us in his *Autobiography* that he served out his last six months as a noncommissioned officer.

David's company of 130 men left Fayetteville, crossed Muscle Shoals at a place called Melton's Bluff (present site of Florence), and started back over their previous route to the headwaters of the Black Warrior River. They then passed down this river due south until they reached the point of the junction of the Tombigbee and the Alabama Rivers, a few miles north of Mobile. Here, at the "cut off" on the east side, Fort Mimms had stood, scene of the earlier massacre. Two days before their arrival Jackson's forces had departed for Pensacola, on foot, for lack of forage for the horses. David's company set out on foot after them. Jackson was at this time Commander of the 7th Military District, having been promoted to Major General, U.S. Army. After prolonged dickering with Washington for permission to stem the Spanish breach of neutrality with force, and after much blustering with the Spanish commander, Jackson had "taken the responsibility," probably with "unofficial" official approval, and proceeded to Pensacola directly with his troops. He stormed and took Pensacola on November 7, 1814. David's company arrived around noon of November 8, too late even to see Fort Barrancas which had been blown up early in the morning by the Spanish themselves. David's part in this war was not exactly destined to end heroically. He was in time, however, to witness the departing British sails from the harbor, the single solace for the 80-mile jaunt from the "cut off."

With the departure of the British, the Indians whom they had been training fled into the swamps. It was, therefore, necessary to destroy them, or, if this were impossible, to keep up a rear-guard action against them. It was also necessary to keep an eye on Pensacola, while Jackson and the main army proceeded to Mobile, New Orleans, the British, and glory. So it was that David's military career terminated in mere bushbeating. "Major" Russell now finally became Major Russell. A regiment under the command of a regular army Major, Uriah Blue of Virginia, was formed by joining Major Russell's battalion and another battalion under Major Childs, of Knox County, Tennessee.

The information on this bushbeating command is extremely sparse, except for David's own account of aimless wandering by troops so short of rations that their main objective had much less to do with war or an enemy than with keeping alive by foraging.

After Jackson departed for Mobile and New Orleans, Major Blue's regiment returned to Fort Montgomery, a new fort erected that fall by Colonel Thomas H. Benton, about a mile and a half from old Fort Mimms, to resupply and rest. The regiment then set forth on its mission, striking for the territory north and east of Pensacola along the Escambia, Conecuh, and Yellow Water Rivers, toward the eventual destination of the Apalachicola River and the "seceded" Creeks, or Seminoles. David mentions only two encounters in the Pensacola area. In one, the two advance guards, Indians themselves, tricked two other Indians into friendly conversation and killed them when their backs were turned. David participated with the Indians in this ritual of mutilation. The other encounter was a skirmish along the east banks of Pensacola Bay, where a number of prisoners were taken. The Indian escort in whose keeping these prisoners were sent back to Fort Montgomery, as Crockett later heard, scalped them all as soon they were out of sight of the regiment.

About January 1, 1815, the troops set out for the Apalachicola River, despite the fact that they had already been out thirty-four days on only twenty days' rations. Blue's orders were to strike the Seminole towns only "if his supplies would justify." The enterprising and perhaps promotion-conscious "regular" Major pushed on despite what Crockett describes as the "extreme suffering for want of something to eat, and [exhaustion from] our exposure and the fatigues of our journey." Under these conditions, they accomplished nothing except near starvation. They entered and burned Holm's village, a deserted town on the Apalachicola, but found no provisions there. It was decided to split the forces. Major Childs and his men were to go on to join Jackson; Major Russell and his battalion were to make a beeline for Fort Decatur on the Tallapoosa, which would lie in their path of march northwestwardly to Fort Strother. They sent Indians ahead to blaze a trail and bring back provisions from Fort Decatur "to prevent us from absolutely starving to death." As the troops marched, they hunted squirrels, hawks, birds—anything they could find—throwing all into a pile at night and having a general division.

Just short of starvation, Crockett and a friend had the good fortune to get some turkeys and a buck. At the same time, the Indians who had been sent ahead returned with food, and Crockett sent them on to the troops in the rear. The Indians arrived just as Captain William Russell, son of Major Russell, "had had his horse led up to be shot for them to eat." They finally had a good feast, and were able to reach Fort Decatur. Even there they could get only one ration of meat and not a mouthful of bread. Back among the friendly Indians who had agreed to Jackson's peace treaty, David went bartering gunpowder and rifle bullets for corn. They went on next day to the Hickory Ground, former stronghold of the Creeks, some thirty miles beyond Fort Decatur. Here they got little to eat ("nothing," Crockett says) and so pushed on forty-nine miles to Fort Williams, going north toward Strother. David relates that the horses were giving out, and he recalls having seen thirteen good ones abandoned in one day, the saddles and bridles also being discarded. Passing by the former battleground at Fort Talladega, where Indian skulls still lay scattered about like gourds in a great gourd patch, they camped that night a few short miles from Fort Strother.

Next morning they met new recruits going to Mobile, Crockett's *youngest* brother among them. Crockett spent the night with the recruits, and in the morning, taking his leave, crossed the Coosa River to Fort Strother, from where, several days later, he struck out, by way of Ditto's Landing and Huntsville, for Bean's Creek in Franklin County—and family.

When shortly thereafter Crockett was called to go back down into the Black Warrior River country to hunt for more Indians (his time lacked about a month of being up), he hired a young man to go in his place for the remainder of his wages. Such a course was permitted at that time, though the official records make no comment of David's failure to complete his term of service, and indeed his discharge certificate was dated, not toward the end of February, when he says he came out for good, but towards the end of March at the expiration of his normal term.[18] Whether David (entered a 3rd sergeant, discharged a 4th sergeant) actually returned home toward the end of February or the end of March, we cannot be sure.

David concludes the account of his military adventures with another reference to the possibility that he may be "forced" to consent to take the Presidential chair. At the time of writing, in late 1833, such a proposal had been made to Crockett by the Mississippi Convention. David, in retelling his military exploits, was fully aware that fame was the doorway to large political office, and obviously his political ambitions had led him to add certain features to the account which the records will not support. It should be stressed, however, that of the entire *Autobiography*, only a few pages in this portion appear to be inaccurate as a result of deliberate intent.

Chapter 3

"I JUST NOW BEGAN TO TAKE
A RISE...."

TOWARD the beginning of 1815 Mary Crockett gave birth to a third child, a girl, who was named Margaret and nicknamed Polly. By the end of the following summer, Mary Crockett was dead. David does not say whether Mary's death was in any way related to Margaret's birth. When he had returned home from war in February or March, he had apparently found all the family in good health. His entire account of the events of the next several years is sketchy. He says only that he continued working his farm for two years after he came out of the war and "in this time.... Death, that cruel leveller of all distinctions ... entered my humble cottage, and tore from my children an affectionate good mother, and from me a tender and loving wife." We know neither exactly when she died, nor the cause of her death. About the whole event there is almost complete silence except for these brief words of David's and the implications of William Finley's will.

Mary Crockett died in Franklin County in the summer of 1815,[1] and was buried there, in a grave today without any other marker than the coarse field stones which have been placed beside it.[2] She left David, a rough, peripatetic backwoodsman, with three children, one an infant for whom he was hard put to provide properly. He first tried the solution of calling his youngest brother, who was married, to come and live with him. Finding, after a short trial, that this arrangement was unsatisfactory, he decided to marry a second time.

In the neighborhood there lived a young widow, Elizabeth Patton, who had lost her husband in the Creek War. She had two children, George and Margaret Ann, and also a tidy little farm. As Crockett viewed the situation, he thought she would make both a fine mother for his children and a fine partner for his future. Having made his decision, he seems to have lost little time in paying his suit.

Elizabeth Patton was born in Swannanoa, Buncombe County, North Carolina, May 22, 1788. Her father, Robert Patton, had settled in the territory later to become Buncombe. The first church structure in western North Carolina and the first graveyard there used by whites had both borne his name. The Pattons were a prominent family, and Elizabeth's father, for those times, was quite well-to-do. Elizabeth had removed to Tennessee with her first husband, James Patton. She was a large woman, a sensible woman, and she evidently had greater managerial ability and more regular habits than David. Apparently his marriage to her and into this family marked a distinct upward turn in his career. At any rate, within a year after the marriage his political fortunes "took a decided rise in the world."

David's awareness of the practical advantages of this marriage is reflected in an anecdote happily surviving in the unpublished reminiscences of Mr. James B. Gowen's grandfather. When Gowen, a personal friend of David's, saw Crockett shortly after his marriage to Elizabeth Patton, he began joshing Crockett about the rumor that she owned $800 in cold cash. David reportedly remarked upon the continuing applicability of the old saw, that the "sass" of the goose ought in all justice to be equally the "sass" of the gander, and that in their contemplated move west, this was just the sort of "sass" they would both need most.

How long David courted Elizabeth is conjectural. The marriage did take place in the spring or summer of 1816 in Franklin County, something more than a year before Crockett and Elizabeth moved west to what was to become Lawrence County. It was Lieutenant Crockett, not 4th Sergeant Crockett, who married the Widow Patton. Less than three months after his discharge from the army, the esteem of his friends had led to his election, on May 21, 1815, as a lieutenant in the 32nd "Regiment of the Militia of this state," a Franklin County Regiment.[3] David makes no mention of this fact in the *Autobiography*.

Another anecdote brings before our eyes the wedding party assembled for the solemn event.[4] It is probable that a justice of the peace had officiated at David's first marriage. His marriage to Elizabeth Patton was celebrated with greater solemnity. A minister had been provided. The guests had gathered from the backwoods, and were seated, self-consciously no doubt, around the "living room" of Mrs. Patton's home. All eyes were fixed expectantly on the doorway through which the bride might, at any moment, enter. Suddenly, to the consternation of the adults and the delight of the youngsters, the peculiar noise of a grunting pig issued through that doorway. Then, with a porcine nonchalance in contrast with the painful formality of the wedding party, in came—the pig itself. A titter of laughter swept through the company. David, rising to the occasion with serious mien, strode over to it and ushered it with ceremony out the door, remarking, with deep gravity, as he did so: "Old hook, from now on, I'll do the grunting around here."

Not long after his marriage, David made a trip into Alabama to explore the possibility of settling there. In the *History of Alabama and Dictionary of Alabama Biography*,[5] Thomas M. Owen calls attention to the fact that the Alabama territory between the Cahaba and the Black Warrior Rivers, present site of Birmingham, was first opened by the Creek War when Tennessee troops built a wagon road to Baird's Bluff, near the Blount County line. These pioneering soldiers had observed this territory closely for likely settlement sites. David had been with these very troops, and it is interesting to see that a few months after his marriage he set out for that country in search of "more elbow room," heading for the spot where once had stood the Black Warrior's Town he had helped to burn.

He does not say exactly when he started on this trip, only that it was "the next fall after" his second marriage. He does tell us that he went first to Jones's Valley, "where several other families had settled," and then on to Tuscaloosa. We can date the trip, and further verify his marriage date, from information supplied by Mr. Owen on Jones's Valley. This valley was first settled *in the fall of 1816*, and it was named for "Devil" John Jones, one of the first settlers. David tells us a little later that "the *next* fall" after this trip to Alabama he moved his family west; and records for November, 1817, pick him up again at the exact spot where he tells us he located after that move. The chronology seems, therefore, definitely established: he married in the spring or summer of 1816, set out in the fall of 1816 to look for new lands in Alabama, and in the fall of 1817 made his move west to Lawrence County.

In the fall of 1816, then, he started out, with three neighbors, for the "Creek country.... determined to explore new" land. Their route is not hard to mark out. They left Bean's Creek, crossed the Tennessee River at Ditto's Landing below Huntsville, struck the head of the Black Warrior River, followed it through Jones's Valley, and finally approached the site of the present Tuscaloosa. In either Blount or Cullman County one of the neighbors was bitten by a poisonous snake and had to be left behind. One night near the old Black Warrior's Town, the horses broke loose, and all the next day, carrying a heavy rifle and travelling fast, David tried to overtake them, covering, by his estimate, fifty miles afoot. At the end of the day he gave up the pursuit and stopped at a house by the wayside to spend the night.

Next morning David was attacked by nausea and "a dreadful headache." Crockett could not know it, but he was evidently suffering from malaria. Letters of the period, including Crockett's own, diagnosed this illness as anything from pleurisy to cholera, and applied the patent treatment, whatever the diagnosis, of bloodletting. At any rate, David made the effort to rejoin his companions, but was overcome before he reached them. Some friendly Indians, who were passing by, found him lying by the side of the trace. After interrogating him for awhile, they finally signed to him that he was going to die, "a thing," he says, "I was confoundedly afraid of myself." They helped him to the nearest house a mile and a half down the trail, and there he spent another night in high fever and delirium. When next day two of his Tennessee neighbors came along, travelling in his direction, they took him with them, first on one horse and then on the other, until, still in high fever, he arrived back where his companions awaited him. Since he was obviously in no condition to travel further, his friends took him to the nearby house of Jesse Jones, bought themselves new horses, and took their leave of him. David lay near the point of death for about two weeks, generously attended by these people. Then he began to mend, and before long he was able to travel a little. A passing waggoner, who lived within twenty miles of his place, agreed to take him along. When he finally arrived home, he "was so pale, and so much reduced," that "his face looked like it had been half soled with brown paper."

His reappearance astonished his homefolks, for his original companions had meantime long since returned. So surely had they been convinced he would die that in returning David's horse, which they had found with their own, they had exaggerated the story and reported not only that they had left him dying, but that they had later talked to men who had seen him draw his last breath and had helped to bury him.

Speaking of the report of his death, David says: "I know'd this was a whapper of a lie, as soon as I heard it." Here, perhaps, we catch the traditional folk humor of the early backwoods in the act of passing into the finished product of permanent literature. Mark Twain's "the reports of my death have been grossly exaggerated," like so much of the literary humor of the latter part of the nineteenth century, was no self-originating comet bursting suddenly into the literary firmament, but a luminous star of a larger constellation extending in unbroken pattern back to its origin in an earlier folk tradition. An interesting "coincidence" is that David's people and Twain's father lived for years together in the same frontier town.[6]

"Civilization" continued to crowd David. Early in the fall of 1817, he again set out exploring, going now into the western territory soon to become Lawrence County. On September 20, 1816, Andrew Jackson, D. Meriwether, and J. Franklin had negotiated a final treaty with the Chickasaw Indians for the territory in south Tennessee east of the final turnback of the Tennessee River. The fact of this newest treaty may have been David's reason for settling there instead of back in Alabama. After travelling eighty miles, he was again stricken, this time with what he calls "ague and fever," which he supposes was brought on by camping out—not a bad guess at that date for a contingent cause of malaria. He liked the country so well that he decided to move there. He tells us the precise spot he selected, "on the head of Shoal Creek," where the first records of his activities in that county place him.

Crockett reports that he and his family lived in their new location "some two or three years, without any law at all," except such "temporary government" of their own as the backwoodsmen found it necessary to set up. They met and appointed their magistrates, of whom he was one, and their constables. This was kept up

till our Legislature added us to the white settlements of Giles county; and appointed magistrates by law, to organize matters in the parts where I lived. They appointed nearly every man a magistrate who had belonged to our corporation. I was then, of course, made a squire according to law.

At this point Crockett has confused the record with one of his in-accurate recollections as to the passage of time. The records show that the county was actually organized on October 21, 1817, that the legislature made Crockett a legal magistrate there on November 25 following, and that the first court was held there early in the next year. Nor do the records reveal that the territory where David settled —near the center of Lawrence County—ever was *officially* "added ... to the white settlements of Giles county."

My reconstruction of what happened is this: David and his family made the move in late September, 1817. In a very short while the new settlers got together and selected their unofficial magistrates, whose names were then submitted to the legislature, according to custom. Pending action on them, this new settlement conducted its business in touch with, but not legally annexed to, the next settlement back east in Giles County, which had been set up in 1809. David was at this time completely ignorant of legal procedures and by his own confession barely able to write his own name, having to depend on his constable to issue the necessary warrants. He could hardly be expected in later years to have a clear recollection of that confusing new business of becoming a public official. When, therefore, he says they remained for two or three years without any law at all, he must be recollecting the two or three first years when, though *officially* there was law, *in fact* there was very little. David himself officially became a justice of the peace on November 25, 1817, about two months after his arrival in the county.[7] He had lost a couple of years in his chronology by attributing his stay in Lincoln County to 1809 and 1810, and here, at the wrong place, he recoups them.

From the point of view of one who had later served for years as a state legislator and a Congressman, these first days of organizing the county, with the first meetings of its court at the home of one of its members and the "farming out" of much of the new court's business to court referees, must have seemed, in recollection, comparatively lawless. David was soon appointed one of the court referees.[8] The entry of one of his decisions as court referee appears for May 4 and 5, 1818,[9] surrounded by entries about "wolf scalps over four months old" which had been brought in and the bounties paid.

That both court and citizens were agreeable to placing such decisions in David's hands is testimony of his fairness and popularity at this time. If the official records are to be believed, David greatly exaggerates the leeway given him in his decisions. Anyway, Crockett says that his judgments

were never appealed from, and if they had been they would have stuck like wax, as I gave my decisions on the principles of common justice and honesty between man and man, and relied on natural born sense, and not on law, learning to guide me; for I had never read a page in a law book in all my life.

The popular esteem in which Crockett was held is revealed by his election "about this time" to colonel of the local militia regiment. In those days each county was required by law to have at least one regiment of militia, with the following officers properly elected and recorded in the State Commission Book at the capitol: a colonel (in time of war at least two colonels, one a colonel commandant), a first and second major, lieutenants, ensigns, and so on.

The manner of Crockett's entry into the election campaign is characteristic. A Captain Matthews informed David that he was running for election as colonel of the Lawrence County Regiment and urged, against David's objections, that the latter run with him for first major, with the design, of course, of getting Crockett's support for his own election. Finally, Crockett agreed. Later, at a "frolic" Matthews gave for electioneering purposes, David discovered that Matthews was simultaneously running his own son for the very position of first major for which he had persuaded Crockett to run. Thereupon David took the father aside and won from him an admission of his son's candidacy. The father said the son hated to run against Crockett worse than against any other man in the county. Crockett replied that the son need give himself no concern about that matter, for he had decided not to run for first major after all. No, he would not run against the son, but instead he would run against the daddy, for the colonelcy.

Matthews evidently had both a sense of humor and a sense of sportsmanship; getting the attention of the gathering, he himself announced that David was to be his opponent. Crockett then made a speech, explaining the grounds for his action. He told the crowd "that as I had the whole family to run against any way, I was determined to levy on the head of the mess." When election time came, he concludes, "he and his daddy were both badly beaten." [10]

It is a mistaken notion that "Colonel" was a gratuitous title assumed by every Southern gentleman who knew how to mix a mint julep. A county had at least one colonel, sometimes as many as four, elected legally and entitled to retain the rank indefinitely upon good behavior. When a colonel moved to another county, he naturally would carry his title with him, though not of course his official rank. By law, a new colonel had to be elected immediately. In those times of continuous migrations, there were many duly elected colonels long before the backwoods had become plantations.

Crockett's election in 1820 to the legislature of Tennessee was an early manifestation of the political power of that "squatter democracy" which was to raise Jackson to the Presidency in 1828. There were wide differences between Crockett's brand of equalitarianism and the Jeffersonian brand. It was an article of faith among Jeffersonian democrats "that all men are created equal." However, the vulgarity and ignorance of the pioneers offended sensibilities refined and sharpened by education. Before 1825-30, "gentlemen" found the drab facts of backwoods life disgusting, and they were simply not amused by the "tall-tale" humor with which the backwoodsman lightened his burden. Backwoods electioneering—"treating" it was called —offended them deeply. As the Yankee Jonathan expressed it, "With us, you know that a man who would thus traverse the country in search of suffrages would meet with little else than general contempt...." In their opinion, the office should seek the man; "office seeker" and "candidate" were terms of opprobrium. Prior to the rise of Jacksonian democracy the homeliness of David's *Autobiography* would have been contemptuously dismissed as "low" writing.

With the general acceptance of Jacksonian democracy, some of the squeamishness was eliminated from the democratic idea; with the emergence of the early school of realistic writing (Crockett's work, Longstreet's *Georgia Scenes*, Seba Smith's *Jack Downing*, and others), the superficial distinction between "high" and "low" subjects began to disappear. In 1826 William Gibbs Hunt, scholarly New England editor, did not smile when a riverboat captain in Nashville, in explanation of his vessel's arriving rudderless from New Orleans, said: "Gentlemen, the naked truth is, that my boat ran so fast between this place and Baton Rouge, that the rudder could not keep up with her." Yet by 1830 the beliefs and practices of the backwoods had captured the public imagination, so that Crockett was to arrive in Washington at precisely the right moment to become the center of the frontier tradition. As Parrington remarks, the crude homespun of David's equalitarianism has, in retrospect, the dignity of an epic.

By 1818, Crockett had passed from private, to sergeant, to lieutenant, and finally to lieutenant colonel-commandant in the military sphere, and from neighbor to justice of the peace and court referee in the civil. His next "rise," to the position of town commissioner for Lawrenceburg, must have taken place sometime during the early months of 1818. Under date of April 1, 1818, there survive copies of five depositions taken before him and other town commissioners of Lawrenceburg. These are the depositions of Henry Rutherford, Thomas Gellaspie, Joseph Kilpatrick, Thomas (his mark) Wright, and James Hibbets, made for the purpose of identifying 4000 acres of land "on Indian Creek of Tennessee River" claimed by James Kerr and Isabella Falls. The commissioners and witnesses had all assembled in the woods on the plot to be identified. The witnesses testified that they had been with General Rutherford on March 7, 1784, "when he was acting as a commissioner to lay off the land for the officers & soldiers; and in running what is called the milatary [sic] line." These records give interesting insight into the psychological reasons behind such placenames as Indian Creek and Cathey's Creek, names which have long since become drab and unexciting with familiarity.[11]

Many records of David stud the court minutes for this period. On November 2 he was made custodian of funds to be collected from John Lockhard "for the support of a bastard child by him begotten on the body of ———," the mother's name being charitably omitted. On the same day he was placed on a "Jury of view" to select land "for the purpose of erecting Iron works." [12] Again, on February 1, 1819, David was among those selected [13] by the court from its own body "as a court of Quorum for the trial of all Jury causes by ballots."

Back in November, 1818, he had been appointed by the court to take lists of taxable property and polls, as well as lists of voters, "according to a late act of assembly making provision for taking the census," and on May 16, 1819, he turned in these lists, containing a total of seventy names.[14]

Toward the end of 1819, Crockett resigned as justice of the peace.[15] Perhaps he was already growing restive as the frontier settlement grew and the wild game retreated. He had been in one spot for almost two years, and there was no condition of war to keep him rooted longer. He may already have been contemplating the move he eventually made in 1822. A more conscious reason for the resignation was probably his decision to seek higher political office. At any rate, the resignation is down in the record for November 1, 1819, between the ubiquitous entries of bounties for wolf scalps. From this point on his name occurs less frequently among the records.

The history of the backwoods is inseparable from the story of the backwoods roads. The first roads were the rivers. Courts appointed "Juries of View" from along the route to mark off the line the road was to follow. The juries reported back to the court, and the court in turn appointed a foreman for the roadbuilding and upkeep, drafting all hands on either side to perform the job. As one reads these records and identifies the first faint beginnings of what is now a modern highway, history steps out of her shrouds and touches him with a new sense of the continuity of life and of the tangible reality of those ephemeral lives long since passed on.

One anecdote about David the trailblazer, belonging though it does to a later period, will help bring to life the reality lying behind the dry brevity of the actual records. In west Tennessee the lands were flat and swampy, the soil alluvial and diluvial. Once the "roads," wagon traces not to be confused with the "roads" of our lexicons, were built, it was necessary to cut down timbers, split them, and lay them crosswise athwart the way to form those corduroy roads called "rail roads," in the backwoods vernacular. One day while David was in Congress someone was advocating the laying of rails for the locomotive engine in the East at a cost of many thousands of dollars per mile, referring to them of course as railroads. Crockett arose and jokingly replied that in his country they constructed rail roads at little or no expense other than honest labor, and that there were some things the East might learn from the West. The Eastern newspapers, eager to oppose this backwoods Jacksonian, picked up his pun and made it appear that Crockett was an ignoramus who had never heard of a modern railroad.[16]

On January 1, 1821, David resigned his position of Commissioner of Lawrenceburg, having offered his name as legislator for Lawrence and Hickman Counties.[17] The *Autobiography* gives us an account of a curiously nonchalant campaign opening. He announced his candidacy in February. Then, "about the first of March," he "started ... with a drove of horses to the lower part of the state of North Carolina. This was in the year 1821, and I was gone upwards of three months." This would have brought him back about June first. The elections were scheduled for the following August, and for the next two months David went electioneering through Hickman and Lawrence counties. Thus David was launched into a political career that would ultimately lead him to his bitter end.

Crockett was new at campaigning and unfamiliar with the intricacies of state and national politics. However, he was not nearly so ignorant of procedure as he would lead us to believe, and he was relatively no worse off than many of his fellow legislators. Going first into Hickman County, he was soon in hot water with two rival parties over the question of moving the Hickman county seat from Vernon to a point nearer the county center or retaining it at Vernon. David pretends that he had not the slightest idea what they meant by "moving a town." He kept silent and sided with neither. From the success of his campaign, we suspect that he sided with both.

About this time a great squirrel hunt was projected, to be held on Duck River. Politicking in the canebrakes was an occasion for partying and fun. The hunt was to last two days, and the hunters divided into two parties to compete in the kill. At the end of the hunt, all were to meet and count squirrel scalps. The party having the fewest scalps was bound to foot the bill for the big public barbecue and country frolic to follow.

David joined one of the parties, and, according to his own account, his superior marksmanship enabled his group to outscalp their opponents. Then came the politicking as a prelude to the dancing. When David was called on for a political speech, he tried to beg off with the excuse that in the polished forensic arts he was no match for his opponent. Nevertheless, since he was forced to speak, he adopted the canny tactics he was to follow throughout his political career—tactics based upon a shrewd recognition that what these backwoods people really wanted to relieve their sense of isolation amid the hardships of frontier life and to satisfy their hunger for social companionship and fun, was not enlightenment, but entertainment. David had a peculiar gift for entertaining. He told them numerous jokes, including one hilariously appropriate to his own predicament. He compared his present situation to that of a man he had heard of not long before who, found beating on the head of an empty barrel and asked what he thought he was doing, replied that there *had* been cider in that barrel a few days before, and he was determined to get some of it out. There had been a little speech in himself a little while ago, David explained, but it seemed that something had happened, for he didn't believe he would have much success now in getting it out, beat about as he might.

When he saw that he had the crowd "in a first-rate way," he concluded with a remark that he was as dry as a powder horn and he thought it time for all parched throats "to wet a whistle." Whereupon he got down and led the way to the liquor stand, leaving few customers indeed for his opponent's wares. Throughout his opponent's speech he remained at the liquor stand telling good yarns to a delighted audience. This incident probably occurred at Centerville in Hickman County.[18]

On another electioneering occasion, a barbecue was held in Vernon, on a Saturday before court convened on the following Monday, a real occasion for a big week-end gathering. The candidates for Congress, for Governor, and for the legislature all attended, and in this company Crockett was understandably uneasy. But he analyzed the situation with good sense:

... as good luck would have it, these big candidates spoke nearly all day, and when they quit, the people were worn out with fatigue, which afforded me a good apology for not discussing the government. But I listened mighty close to them, and was learning pretty fast about political matters. When they were all done, I got up and told some laughable story, and quit. I found I was safe in those parts, and so I went home, and didn't go back again till after the election was over. But to cut this matter short, I was elected, doubling my competitor, and nine votes over.

In this manner Crockett won his first seat in the Tennessee State Legislature.

Thereafter he recounts a public meeting in Pulaski between himself and James K. Polk, who was to be Clerk of the State Senate during David's first term in the legislature, 1821-22, and who in 1823-24 was himself to become a representative in that legislature. (In 1825 Polk was elected to the first of seven consecutive terms to the national Congress, so that for the whole of Crockett's legislative and Congressional careers he served in the company of James K. Polk.) In the presence of a large gathering, Polk said to Crockett, "Well, colonel, I suppose we shall have a radical change of the judiciary at the next session of the Legislature." David replied, "Very likely sir," and, as he avers, "put out" from there as fast as he decently could, for he had no idea that there was such a thing as a "judiciary" in all of nature. Again we get that pose of pretended ignorance which so pleased his constituents then and so pleases his readers today. Even scholars, Parrington among them, have apparently been deceived by this pose into overemphasizing his ignorance. The reader can judge for himself whether or not a man who had been around the judiciary for four years as a justice of the peace, court referee, and town commissioner, being daily in the courts and signing official records, having been elected to several political positions of military rank and now to the state legislature, would be unfamiliar with the word "judiciary" in the summer of 1821, at thirty-five years of age.

PART TWO

The Stiff Climb

4

"I ... SERVED OUT MY TIME ... AND MOVED...."

D AVID'S first term as a state legislator was a quiet one, but not so quiet as the less-than-one-page that he devotes to it in his *Autobiography* might lead one to believe. In fact, events took place in this first term which give significant insight into his thinking at that time, and it will be worthwhile examining his record at some length.

The first session of the Fourteenth General Assembly convened on September 17, 1821, at Murfreesborough, Tennessee, and Crockett was present representing Hickman and Lawrence Counties. On the following day he was placed on the Standing Committee of Propositions and Grievances, the only one on which he served during the session. Our interest in this session is chiefly concerned with Crockett's activities relating to the west Tennessee lands.[1]

On September 25 he voted to release landowners in the Western District from paying double tax assessments for delinquent taxes during 1820. Again, on September 28, he submitted a preamble and resolution to prevent the Register of west Tennessee from issuing two or more grants of land on the same warrant. When this passed and was carried to the Senate, Crockett, on October 9, introduced a bill incorporating the provisions of this resolution; on October 22 he withdrew this bill for amendment. Later on in the same week he moved that the House proceed to consideration of the Senate resolution of October 22 requiring surveyors south and west of the Congressional line to present full and correct lists of all entries involving two or more grants made on one and the same warrant. Finally, on November 6, he introduced a bill for the benefit of the occupants south and west of the Congressional line.

As this matter of the west Tennessee Lands was to be Crockett's major concern for the rest of his political life—and finally to prove his undoing—an explanation of certain subjects relating to the disposition of these lands will be pertinent from time to time. First, the story of the Congressional line: when North Carolina in 1789 had offered to the Federal Government the territory later to become the state of Tennessee, for the purpose of creating that state, it had done so under the condition that all of the innumerable land warrants which North Carolina had previously issued or should issue, to her officers and soldiers for their service in the Revolutionary War or to redeem the Specie Certificates she had used to defray the expenses of that war, would be satisfied in and honored by the new state. The Government accepted the land with this stipulation. By Act of Congress of April 18, 1806, Tennessee was authorized to begin satisfying these warrants within a specified area, for which purpose a line was run across the state from north to south at a point some distance west of its center. This line was known as the Congressional Reservation Line. The North Carolina warrants were to be satisfied in the larger eastern portion, covering approximately three-fourths of the state. The smaller, western portion was to be reserved as public lands unpreempted.

However, this eastern portion was unfortunately insufficient to satisfy the warrants. Unethical practices may have been involved in the multiplication of these warrants, issuing warrants in the names of persons long dead to benefit present heirs or land speculators who could buy up claims from present heirs, post dating, and so on. In fact, the records had been so inaccurately kept and warrants so promiscuously issued that no one could know just how much land would be necessary to satisfy them all, or by what date they would be settled. To satisfy these warrants, it was at length necessary to throw open the land west of the Congressional line. Eventually, in self-defense, the State of Tennessee established a date, first east of the line, then west, after which no more North Carolina warrants would be satisfied. As the situation existed in 1821, a man who had received land on a warrant might, after having built his home on it and improved it, be moved off by anyone holding another warrant of earlier issue. This might happen to a man, not once, but many times. Of course the pioneer "squatter" on public lands, with no money to purchase a warrant of any sort, was being moved constantly further west as a result of action under this provision and of fear of such action.

As we have seen, Crockett had offered resolutions and bills about the practice of allowing a number of entries to be made upon the same warrant. One example of how this practice operated will suggest the sort of confusion and corruption that it invited. A man with a warrant for a thousand acres of land "fit for cultivation," as the warrants read, could, if he wished, split that up into ten parcels of one hundred each, or a hundred of ten each, or any combination he desired, in order to get only land "fit for cultivation." Thus he could run his lines so as to leave out barren land, hilltops, or any ground he pleased, and could take in the very best land of a number of good river bottoms. The result was a strange assortment of unclaimed land between surveys, a configuration of lines so intricate that it was next to impossible to determine the amount of unclaimed public lands remaining at any given time. There was a quick pre-emption of the very best lands in a territory generally poor in soil to begin with. Consequently only the worst of the poor soil remained for holders of other warrants.

Other complications will require elaboration later on. The important point to note here is that David, in the very first session of his first legislature, was actively interested in the public land policies west of the Congressional Reservation Line and in all things affecting the people already moving into that area. This was to be the dominant interest of his life from now on—from which all else that he did took its course. It is primarily in the light of this interest that one must come to an understanding and judgment of David Crockett.

It has previously been suggested that Crockett may already have been half-seriously contemplating a move further west. By September 29, such a move had become a necessity, and this fact perhaps accounts for his great interest in west Tennessee lands at the first session. On that date, twelve days after the session opened, Crockett was given a leave of absence. The occasion for this leave is best described by Crockett himself:

About this time I met with a very severe misfortune, which I may be pardoned for naming, as it made a great change in my circumstances, and kept me back very much in the world. I had built an extensive grist mill, and powder mill, all connected together, and also a large distillery. They had cost me upwards of three thousand dollars, more than I was worth in the world. The first news that I heard after I got to the Legislature, was, that my mills were—not blown up sky high, as you would guess, by my powder establishment,—but swept away all to smash by a large fresh, that came soon after I left home. I had, of course, to stop my distillery, as my grinding was broken up; and, indeed, I may say, that fortune just made a complete mash of me. I had some likely negroes, and a good stock of almost every thing about me, and, best of all, I had an honest wife. She didn't advise me, as is too fashionable, to smuggle up this, and that, and t'other, to go on at home; but she told me, says she, "Just pay up, as long as you have a bit's worth in the world; and then every body will be satisfied, and we will scuffle for more." This was just such talk as I wanted to hear, for a man's wife can hold him devlish uneasy, if she begins to scold, and fret, and perplex him, at a time when he has a full load for a rail-road car on his mind already.

And so, you see, I determined not to break full handed, but thought it better to keep a good conscience with an empty purse, than to get a bad opinion of myself, with a full one. I therefore gave up all I had, and took a bran-fire new start.

David remained long enough to cast his vote in behalf of General William Carroll for Governor of Tennessee, governors and senators being elected by the legislature in those days. Carroll was a known liberal and in most things a supporter of the Tennessee forces preparing to run Jackson for the Presidency. He had fought as a colonel under Jackson in the Creek War. Carroll won this significant election and took the oath of office on October 1.

Carroll's election was related to the call of a constitutional convention. On September 27 the two Houses had met in a Joint Session to determine whether to recommend to the people that they vote at the next general election on the question of calling a Constitutional Convention. David voted with the simple majority in favor of the recommendation—a two-thirds majority being required for approval. On October 11, presumably two days after he returned from his leave, the resolution was tried again and tabled. Crockett voted for tabling. When, on October 18, a majority voted to postpone the same resolution until a second session, *provided one should be called,* Crockett voted for postponement. On the surface it may appear that David voted for the motion at first, and then twice against it. However, once Carroll had been elected governor it was a foregone conclusion that he would call a second session to promote this very resolution which he was known to favor. The votes for tabling, by the very same majority that had previously voted for its passage, and then for postponement, were really moves in strategy and timing in favor of the resolution. Crockett was consistently to support this measure every time he had the opportunity to do so for the next four years.

West Tennesseans desired a constitutional convention for two important reasons. First, no provisions had been made, or were to be made for some time, to give the recently acquired territory of west Tennessee adequate representation in the legislature. The more rapidly people came into that territory, the more inadequately they were represented; and they naturally desired to correct this inequality by altering the state constitution. The second reason was a desire to correct inequitable land taxes. At this time all lands were taxed equally, so that the owner of stony hilltops in west Tennessee paid as much per acre for his scrapings as did the more fortunate plantation owner of rich loam in middle Tennessee. Since taxing the poor soil less meant taxing the rich land more, the proposal for tax reform involved a conflict in self-interest. The frontier had passed beyond middle Tennessee, which was composed mainly of large plantations and vested interests of various sorts; [2] while west Tennessee was a land of pioneers, small poor-land holders, and squatters.

There was strong resistance from middle Tennessee legislators against calling a convention to change the constitution. For a long time it was impossible to take any action. On the one hand, middle Tennessee was the most powerful section, and on the other, the western section was not adequately represented, nor could be until the constitution was amended by a two-thirds majority. The peculiar geographical position of middle Tennessee accounts for the fact that, from the point of view of the wealthy and more aristocratic East,

Jackson and his ideas could be regarded as the hatchings of a scurvy western democracy; at the same time west Tennessee squatters could view him as a greedy, plantation-owning aristocrat!

Crockett also voted against a bill to "suppress the vice of gaming," and against a motion to grant a divorce to James McMinn from his wife Nancy. This was in line with two of his generally consistent positions. He introduced an act to define the lines of Hickman County and to "fix the permanent seat of Justice therein," in connection with the Centerville-Vernon controversy. He sided with a negative majority in opposition to a bill that would authorize courts to hire out insolvent persons for costs accruing against them as a result of criminal prosecutions. The backwoodsmen were too intimate with poverty to allow them to support any such measure.

It was during the opening days of this session that Crockett won the honorable distinction of bearing the title "gentleman from the cane." Feeling ill at ease and awkward because of his ignorance of legislative procedure, Crockett rose to speak in behalf of some measure before the House. In the course of speaking against the position Crockett had taken, a Mr. M———l, alluded to David as "the gentleman from the cane." The remark brought a titter from some of the members. Crockett, seeing in this laughter an expression of snobbish contempt for himself and all "gentlemen from the cane" present in the chamber, responded immediately to the slur, but without receiving much satisfaction. Later, when he accosted Mr. M———l outside the chamber with the intention of pummeling an apology from him, that gentleman refused the encounter with a private statement that he had not had the courtesy to avow publicly: that in making his remark he had intended no personal invective or uncomplimentary innuendo whatsoever, but had only thoughtlessly employed the expression as a literal, descriptive term.

It chanced that later Crockett found in the dust a cambric ruffle of precisely the cut affected by Mr. M———l. This he pinned to his own coarse shirt. Choosing a dramatically propitious moment just after the House had attended informative remarks from Mr. M———l, he arose as though to express his own opinion on the matter. The cambric ruffle stood out on David's rough shirt like a light on a locomotive. Suddenly the humor of the situation burst upon all the members at once. Without a word's being uttered, the House burst into prolonged laughter. Mr. M——l hesitated for a single embarrassed moment, then precipitately withdrew from the chamber amid a rising roar. The moral victory assured David's popularity, and his backwoods friends, according to the story, often, thereafter, referred to him amicably as "the gentleman from the cane" in acknowledgement of his having won his spurs, and in recognition of that occasion as symbolic of their mutual understanding against the "quality folks" arising out of the conflict of interests between middle and west Tennessee. As far as I know, this story was first recorded in the 1833 anonymous *Life and Adventures of Colonel David Crockett of West Tennessee.*[3] James Parton repeats it from this source without verification.[4]

According to the rolls of the members of the Fourteenth General Assembly, the name of only one member fits the abridged version given by the author of the anonymous *Life:* Mr. James C. Mitchell, representing Rhea, Hamilton, and McMinn Counties. Twice later David used the phrase "gentleman from the cane" in his *Autobiography* with just the implications that phrase would entail if the story were true.

The House adjourned on November 17.[5] Immediately after returning home Crockett set out for west Tennessee to locate new land for his projected move. With him went John Wesley, his oldest son, and another young man named Abram Henry. Arriving at the Obion River in a wild and secluded country, he selected a spot of ground seven miles from the nearest inhabitant and fifteen from the next nearest, and set about getting it ready for his family. Around the new homestead was a complete wilderness, full of Indians and thick with many kinds of game. This region had undergone terrific earthquakes in 1811-12, and on the heels of the quakes there had been a number of destructive hurricanes. As a result, the area had been converted into a perfect game refuge by tangled windfalls and almost impenetrable morasses.

The Act of November 7, 1821, establishing new counties west of the Tennessee River had created Carroll County from a vast area stretching all the way from the Tennessee River to the Mississippi. Later, Gibson and Dyer Counties were formed from the western portions of Carroll County. The site which David selected was later to be included within Gibson County. At the time of his settlement there, and until 1823, it remained Carroll. He settled within a mile or so of Rutherford's Fork, the southernmost branch of the Obion River, on the east bank, a few miles northeast of the present city of Rutherford in the present Gibson County, or at a point in Gibson very near to the southwest corner of Weakley.[6]

After selecting a site for the cabin and making certain necessary accommodations, David's party set out to visit the nearest neighbor, Mr. Owens. According to the inaccurate map of the period, the Owens' homestead lay on the far side of the South Fork of the Obion some seven miles almost due north of David's site. It was early winter, the rivers were flooded, the water cold. By wading and swimming they made their way through and finally arrived to find Mr. Owens entertaining some travellers who had pushed up the Obion in the first boat ever to penetrate those waters. The owners of the boat were evidently engaged in some advertising "stunt," and they were determined to take their boat some distance further. They had passed up the South Fork above the Owens' place until stopped by a great windfall of trees blown into the river by a hurricane. Finding the water falling too rapidly to allow them to pass, they had dropped back opposite the Owens' cabin to await more rain (which fortunately came hard and heavy the next day). While they were awaiting the rise, David persuaded them to go out with him to his site. Along with them they took provisions of barrelled meat, salt, bacon, and whiskey. In a very little time they threw up a cabin for him. David also killed a deer. Then, leaving John Wesley to look after the place, he returned to the Obion to help the boatmen reach their destination—McLemore's Bluff on the South Fork. Back at the windfall that evening they found the water rising, but still too low to carry the boat over. Early next morning David set out hunting.

By nightfall he had shot six bucks, strung them up, and returned to the lower portion of the "harracane." However, the boat was gone. When he fired his gun, an answering shot came from above. David judged that the boat had gone through the fallen timber and was about two miles above him in the black night. Pushing with some difficulty through the tangle of vines, briars, and fallen timbers, he eventually came out at the point where he had killed his last deer, to find the boat nearby. Next day, after he and one of the boatmen had brought in the four deer nearest the mooring place, they all pushed off up the river. The weather was cold, and all out-of-doors was an ice box; presumably David intended to fetch home the other two deer after his return. On the eleventh day, the boat reached McLemore's Bluff and was unloaded there. The boatmen made David a present of the boat's skiff, and he and one of the young boatmen named Fluvius Harris, who had decided to live with him, turned back down the river to David's cabin.

Crockett's party now fell to work getting the homestead ready for occupation. Alternating work with hunting expeditions, they cleared a field and planted it to corn, but could not delay long enough to put up a rail fence. As David says, a fence was really not necessary, for there was no stock to be kept out, and no sort of fence invented could have kept out the "varments." Before the party returned to Lawrence County in the early spring of 1822, David killed ten bears and a great many deer but saw no white persons except the Owens family and "a very few passengers, who went out there, looking at the country." He stayed long enough to "lay by" his crop and then returned home, 150 miles east.

By the time of David's return, a number of suits had been brought against him for debt in connection with the loss of his mill. According to his account, they were brought on with his knowledge and consent against whatever possessions remained to satisfy the claims of his creditors. From a number of the judgments, however, he entered an appeal to a higher court. As this action may have been for legitimate contingent reasons, it does not necessarily imply a contradiction. Among these suits were the following: Pressley Ward vs David Crockett, for $71.70 plus $1.43 interest plus costs, awarded on October 5, 1821; John R. Crisp vs David Crockett, for $55.00 plus six per cent interest plus costs, awarded on the same day, appealed by Crockett; Burwell B. Quimby vs David Crockett, for $50.00 plus six per cent interest plus costs, awarded on the same day, appealed by Crockett. On January 12, while David was on the expedition in Carroll County, William F. Cunningham recovered of David and his securities $70.00 plus $1.40 interest and costs.

On April 1, 1822, a deed of gift of a piece of property from David to Nancy and Anna Musgrove was produced in open court. The deed must have been dated months earlier, prior to his trip to western Tennessee. On April 4, Pressley Ward had his judgment extended to include David's securities, Halford and King; and on the same day John Edmundson secured an execution order to sell David's land in order to satisfy an earlier judgment. The previous judgments were also executed on the same land, all locating and describing his homeplace, "160 acres of land lying on the head of Shoal Creek about 3 miles east of Lawrenceburg where Reubin Trip and Thomas Pryer now lives supposed to be the property of David Crockett." Finally, on April 5, 1822, the last entry about Crockett occurs in the *Lawrence County Court Minutes:* David's power of attorney given to Mansil Crisp, doubtless authorizing him to satisfy his debtors to the best interests of all.[7] One hundred and sixty acres of land at that location should have been more than sufficient to do this.

David did not move his family west until September, 1822. According to the records, Reubin Trip and Thomas Pryer were occupying David's homeplace as early as October 5, 1821. Where was David's family living during the intervening months? Evidently during his leave from the legislature, David had made arrangements for his family to vacate his property in preparation for satisfaction of his creditors' claims. He may have found a temporary place for them with one of his wife's sisters, who were by this time in his neighborhood, or with some of his own relatives who lived nearby. The fact of this temporary dislocation may explain why he went *immediately* to west Tennessee after adjournment of his first session, and prepared a place for his family.

Commenting upon his return to middle Tennessee from the Obion River homestead, David says: "I was met by an order to attend a call-session of our legislature. I attended it, and served out my time, and then returned, and took my family and what little plunder I had, and moved to where I had built my cabin, and made my crap." Since that is all he has to tell us about his second session, it is necessary to report on this second session from other sources—*before* he moved his family west. David's return must have been after April 22. On that date Governor Carroll issued his proclamation calling the Fourteenth General Assembly back into special session. The General Assembly reconvened on July 22.

Crockett was more active during this second session, in spite of its shorter duration. He was getting "to know the ropes." However, only a few of his activities concern us here. First among these was an early form of that particular Tennessee vacant-land bill which was eventually to become David's paramount issue. On Wednesday, August 21, 1822, the legislative Committee on Education made a detailed report and presented a resolution requesting Senators in Congress and Representatives to procure the passage of a law authorizing the Legislature of Tennessee "to dispose of the vacant and unappropriated lands, lying North and East of the Congressional reservation line, at such price as may be thought prudent by said legislature, for the purpose of education." [8] The House concurred, and it is probable that David here supported the resolution, as he probably did later when it was made applicable also to lands south and west of the line; for James K. Polk later charged in Congress that he did, and David did not deny it. He had not, at this time, become skeptical of the state political machine. It may have been that he did not see the full implications of the resolution, but assumed that the state would do justice to the interests of the "squatters" of west Tennessee. More details about this important and continuing resolution will appear later.

A second important matter arising in this session was a previously passed bill setting a definite date beyond which the Carolina land warrants would no longer be honored east of the Congressional line. On July 30, 1822, Crockett voted against a motion to extend that date. Had the motion passed, it would have thrown into consternation all holders of land in the east, by rendering their titles uncertain. Once more he presented petitions of various citizens to retain the county seat of Hickman at Vernon. On August 9 he was still voting with the simple majority for the call of a constitutional convention. Then, on August 20, he voted for a "bill more effectively to encourage the building of iron-works," a vote which may shed light on his later interests. He was also placed on the select committee to examine into the matter of a loan to Montgomery Bell for a "Manufactory and works."

Various records relate to David's efforts to relieve the needy, whose requests he nearly always supported. It is well to recall that these people had never fully recovered from the financial crisis of 1819. For example, he introduced a bill to provide for those settled on land south and west of the Congressional line since 1819. Its defeat in the Senate on the first reading gave David an object lesson he was soon to use concerning where the interests of the Senate lay. Another of his bills was "for the relief of Mathias, a free man of color." He opposed the bill to repeal redemption laws concerning slaves; opposed repeal of the act to provide for widows and children and to prevent fraud in the execution of last wills and testaments; voted for the relief of securities; and introduced bills for the relief of William and John M'Cann, Elisha C. Crisp, and Alexander Miller.

A final matter concerned a bill to restore certain fees formerly withdrawn from justices of the peace. Crockett opposed it, saying:

He hoped the bill would not pass: he hoped it would be killed in its tracks. There never had been a law repealed with so much propriety, or which resulted in so much good for the peace of society, as the repeal of the justices' out-of-doors fees. . . . I concur with the gentleman from Campbell, that there is no evil so great in society—among the poor people —as the management and intrigue of meddling justices and dirty constables. I have seen more peace and harmony among my constituents since the repeal of the fees, than I had seen for several years before. I do most earnestly hope that the house will be unanimous in putting the bill to instant death. [The bill was rejected.] [9]

This concluded the second session of his first legislature and left him free to move his family west.

Chapter 5

POLITICIAN FROM THE CANEBRAKES

CROCKETT had 80 miles to travel to his home, and another 150 miles to go to his new land in Carroll County. Yet by September 9, sixteen days after adjournment, he had reached home, packed "what little plunder" he had left, covered the distance to his new habitation, and done a bit of hunting into the bargain. On that date appears the first record of Crockett's career in west Tennessee: "David Crockett came into open court and made oathe to the killing of one wolf over the age of four months in the bounds of this county." [1] After the flood disaster, the cross-country trek, and setting up a new home, the three-dollar bounty for the wolf scalp was welcome—for the "sass" of the goose was undoubtedly already gone to settle the flood debts of the gander. This and similar entries are amusing in connection with David's boasts to his political opponent, Dr. Butler, that he would support his election campaign with the bounty he collected for wolf-scalps.

From now until his election to the next legislature, the records are scanty. [2] Running from December 9, 1822, to September 10, 1823, they include appointments to jury duty, [3] more bounties for wolf scalps, [4] a bill of indictment against him for assault, [5] and a suit for debt brought against him by Jessee West for $132.50 plus $3.40 damages plus court costs. In December, 1824, the court, concluding that it could not collect those costs, charged them up against West. [6] David, without moving, then resided in Gibson County. He had himself introduced the bill to create that county from Carroll. This had been effected on

October 21, 1823. This brief review of the records establishes that David had still not made his fortune.

Toward the last of October, after completing his corn harvest, David set out to fill his larder with meat for the winter. "Indeed, all sorts of game and wild varments, except Buffalo" were plentiful. As Christmas approached, he found that he had no powder left for firing the Christmas guns, or for further hunting. A brother-in-law, who had followed him to west Tennessee and settled about six miles west of him "on the opposite side of Rutherford's Fork," had brought along a keg of powder for him. David had failed to pick it up before the winter set in, and now the rivers were cold and swollen. Nevertheless, David decided to fetch the powder. Elizabeth strenuously objected to the undertaking, saying that meat or no meat they would as well starve as for David to freeze or drown trying to cross those expanses of flood waters. But David opined to Betsy that he didn't believe the half of it, wrapped himself up well, took an extra change of dry clothing, and set out through the four-inch snow under dark clouds. Perhaps he recalled pushing through that other snow, when, as a young boy, he had made his escape from Jacob Siler. He recounts at length his difficulties in crossing the flooded river, and the bitterness of the cold, saying that he had "not even smelt fire from the time" he started until he finally reached his destination.

His in-laws were both astonished and delighted to see him in such weather, and all hands took "horns" to drive out the storm. As the next day was piercing cold, he was persuaded to remain, especially since his companionable brother-in-law talked up the hunting they might do together. As a matter of fact, he shot two deer that day in spite of the bitter weather; and on the next, in the face of the same piercing cold, he spent the entire day following a large bear not yet gone into hibernation.

On the third day, knowing that his family was without meat, he decided, in spite of the continued cold, to return or to "die a-trying." Now he had the powder-keg to carry, as well as his tomahawk, rifle, and other equipment. He had hoped that by then the ice would be solid enough to bear his weight so that he might escape another soaking in ice water. Luck was against him. The ice soon crushed beneath his weight, and thereafter he broke his way through the crust with his tomahawk until he reached the swollen current itself. Arriving beyond the main stream, he saw freshly broken ice and concluded that it was the marks of a bear struggling about in the water. Though he was frozen through, he primed his gun and set out on the trail. Meat was meat. Strangely enough, the tracks led in the direction of his own path—in fact, led at last right up to his cabin door. Betsy, fearing his death, had sent out one of the young men living with them to search for him. This was the trail he had mistaken for bear tracks.

"When I got home," says David, "I wasn't quite dead, but mighty nigh it; but I had my powder, and that was what I went for." How characteristic of Crockett, this keeping his eye squarely on what he had determined to do, cost what it may, be it large or small; and this pride in undertaking and *performing* the difficult.

When the weather had warmed up a little bit his brother-in-law returned his visit. During the night there was a heavy rain turning to sleet. The next morning they again went hunting. David was after bear; his brother-in-law sought the more easily portable turkey. After travelling some six miles along Rutherford's Fork northwest, Crockett turned to cut across the angle to the main Obion. The sleet had grown increasingly worse, and the encasing ice had so interlocked the sagging trees and undergrowth that the ordinarily difficult task of getting through these wilds now approached the impossible. After a while, David flushed a gang of turkeys and bagged a couple of gobblers. Resting from his struggle through the icy passage, he heard his bear dogs strike a tune. Coming up to them, he found them barking up an empty tree. Off they went again, and again they treed, and once more the tree was empty. This happened three or four times. Enraged by their strange behavior, he determined that if he didn't soon shoot a bear he'd shoot an old hound dog. Finally, on the edge of what he calls an "open parara," he saw "in and about [7] the biggest bear that ever was seen in America. He looked, at the distance he was from me, like a large black bull." His dogs were afraid to attack, and this accounted, he thought, for their strange behavior in "barking up the wrong tree." The bear commenced to move away, and the race was on.

At last he treed in a large black oak. Crawling to within shooting distance, David shot twice before the bear fell. As he drew near, he saw that the fallen bear was clutching one of his dogs. He approached close to the bear and drew his attention so that he released the dog. Then he reloaded, shot again, and killed him. The bear was large indeed! (On his honor, about six hundred pounds, and the second largest he ever saw or killed.) There was now the problem of getting him home. Not knowing exactly where he was, David left the bear and began travelling east, apparently along the present northern boundary of Dyer County, from the point it leaves the Main Obion east to a point where it crosses Rutherford's Fork, or perhaps just south of that line, blazing his way as he went to mark out a return trail. The "open parara" on which he had shot the bear was evidently fifteen miles from his cabin.

Arriving home, he found his brother-in-law already back. David, the brother-in-law, and one of the young men set out at once, arriving at the scene just before dark. They began immediately to butcher the animal and finished after nightfall. Either that night or the next day they finally got the beast home; and for the rest of the winter he continued to get his family "aplenty" of both bear meat and venison.

David's recounting of this bear story is touched, perhaps jocularly and perhaps not, with superstition. Certainly it is touched with exaggeration—only Paul Bunyan himself could have covered those miles through ice-tangled wilderness within the daylight hours of a deep winter's day. He had undertaken to hunt bear that day instead of turkey as a result of dreaming the previous night of "a hard fight with a big black nigger, and I knowed it was a sign that I was to have a battle with a bear; for in a bear country, I never know'd such a dream to fail." Perhaps the dimensions of his dream and the alacrity of his imagination had also added something to the stature of this bear that looked like a bull!

As David was to do a good deal of hunting in the environs of Reelfoot Lake, the terrible tangle of windfalls and underbrush that made the place so fertile with game requires a brief explanation. In precisely this area there had occurred a tremendous succession of earthquakes, beginning on December 16, 1811, and running down to David's own time, though they had grown progressively milder after 1812. In 1811, 1812, and 1813 they had been so severe that the Mississippi, for awhile, reversed its current. According to the *National Geographic*, they were felt as far away as New Orleans, Detroit, and even Boston, "a great area throughout America ... [being] affected." These earthquakes created Reelfoot Lake,[8] and among the fallen and twisted timbers of this unfrequented wilderness the flora and fauna began to, thrive with unbelievable fertility. Crockett may stretch the reader's credulity with his account of killing 105 bears here in little less than a year, but it is probable that his story is accurate.

Much hunting means many skins. In February, 1823, David loaded up his horses with skins and set out with John Wesley on the forty-mile journey to Jackson, county seat of Madison County. There he sold his pelts and bought the staples he could not shoot—coffee, sugar, powder, lead, salt, and so on—and packed them preparatory to an early morning return. Before leaving the next day he dropped into the bar for a drink with some of his old friends from the Creek War whom he had run into in Jackson. While he was engaged in this pleasant occupation, he was introduced to three candidates for the next legislature. One of these was Dr. William E. Butler, nephew-in-law of Andrew Jackson, and town commissioner for Jackson. The other two were Major Joseph Lynn and Mr. Duncan McIver, both original members of the first court of Pleas and Quarter Sessions of Madison. McIver had been one of the earliest settlers in the area. All three were men of reputation and affairs. In the course of drinking and talking together, someone suggested, in what David thought was a humor reminiscent of the "gentleman from the cane" episode, that David himself should "offer" for the coming legislature from the district of his new home. Crockett blandly ignored the bait, however, replying that he lived forty miles from any white settlements and had no thought of getting back into politics at that time. Then he forgot the matter.

A week after this joking proposal, a visiting hunter congratulated David on the announcement of his candidacy and drew from his pocket, to substantiate his statement, a late February or early March, 1823, issue of the *Jackson Pioneer*, which carried the announcement.[9] This, David decided, was carrying a practical joke too far. He told his wife on the spot that he was going to "make it cost the man who put it there at least the value of the printing, and of the fun he wanted at my expense." He hired a hand to take his place on the "farm," and set out electioneering in earnest. It was not long before "people began to talk very much about the bear hunter, the man from the cane."

Faced with Crockett's voter-appeal, Butler, Lynn, and McIver decided to combine their total strength. To effect this purpose they held a caucus at the March term of court to choose from among them a single opponent to David. The final selection fell to Dr. Butler. Crockett says of Butler that he was the most talented man he ever ran against for any office; and of course the fact that Butler's wife was Jackson's niece did Butler's candidacy no harm. He was a man of education, refinement, and some wealth. David's campaign tactic was to present him as an aristocrat among backwoodsmen.

There was a mutual respect between Butler and Crockett. Both recognized that certain acrobatics were expected in elections, and neither held a grudge against the other for his electioneering antics. Hearing one day during the campaign that David was in town, Dr. Butler, in friendly fashion, invited him to visit his home and have dinner. Crockett accepted and shortly presented himself at the door. When he had stepped inside, he observed the most expensive furnishings and elaborate decorations he had ever seen. One rug especially caught his eye. In contrast to his own bear-skins, this rug was so luxurious that he felt guilty at the thought of stepping on it. He therefore made it a point to skirt around it, and all evening he refused to allow his feet to touch it. All of this he elaborately mimicked, of course, in his political speeches, concluding his account of the visit to the home of his wealthy opponent with some such climax as this: "Fellow citizens, my aristocratic competitor has a fine carpet, and every day he *walks* on truck finer than any gowns your wife or your daughters, in all their lives, ever *wore!*" [10]

It was a custom of the time for all candidates to travel in the same itinerary and speak in turn from the same platform to the same group. [11] On one such trip, it had become the habit for the other candidates (a Mr. Shaw and a Mr. Brown came out as candidates after Lynn and McIver withdrew) to speak first, David saving his remarks for a parting sally. After the group had been travelling together for sometime, Crockett requested that he might precede Dr. Butler, to vary the routine a bit. Dr. Butler gave ready assent. Thereupon, Crockett proceeded to speak Dr. Butler's usual speech word for word, having memorized it from previous occasions; and Dr. Butler was left wordless and speechless when his turn came to talk. In point of fact, Butler was an educated man, and it is hardly likely that such stealing of his thunder left him without any extempore lightning.

Crockett also records a street-meeting with Dr. Butler in the early days of this campaign. On this occasion, David had been attending some oratory being dispensed by Colonel Adam Alexander campaigning for the national Congress. After the oration, David walked up to where Colonel Alexander was treating the potential voters, and the colonel introduced him to several people, informing them that David too was out electioneering—for the state legislature. Just then Dr. Butler passed by without seeing, or noticing, David; but Crockett hailed him and he stopped. Then, referring to the caucus of the past March, when Lynn, Butler, and McIver had selected Butler to oppose him, Crockett jibed that he had thought the elections were to be in August, but that these three men had held their own election in March and seemed to think the matter was all settled. Butler, perhaps a trifle annoyed, replied, "Crockett, damn it, is that you?"

"Be sure it is," David answered, "but I don't want it understood that I have come electioneering. I have just crept out of the cane, to see what discoveries I could make among the white folks."

Doubtless there were those standing nearby who were familiar with the "gentleman from the cane" incident of the last legislature, as David's remark implies. Crockett went on to say that when he did go electioneering, he would be prepared to put every man on as good a footing when he left him as when he had found him. He would have a large buck-skin hunting-shirt made, with a couple of large pockets, in one of which he would carry a big twist of tobacco, and in the other a bottle of liquor. In this way, when he offered a man a dram, and the man threw out his quid to take one, he could bring out his twist when the drinker had finished and give him another chew, and thus leave him in the most jovial of humors.

Butler, laughing heartily, admitted that David had him beat in his methods. Crockett replied that he would give him better evidence of that before August, notwithstanding Butler's many advantages, particularly in the way of money. He would "go" on the products of the country. His children, being industrious, would coon hunt for him each night till midnight. When the coon fur wasn't good, he himself would "go a wolfing, and shoot down a wolf, and skin his head, and his scalp would be good to me for three dollars, in our state treasury money; and in this way I would get along on the big string."

At all this banter, the crowd, including Butler, were in an uproar. David left them at this point, being sure that he would "do a good business among them"—in any event being determined to "stand up to my lick-log, salt or no salt." With this David concludes his account of the electioneering, and announces that: "... when the election was over, it turned out that I beat them all by a majority of two hundred and forty-seven votes, and was again returned as a member of the Legislature from a new region of the country, without losing a session. This reminded me of the old saying—'A fool for luck, and a poor man for children.'" There are many evidences of David's pretended vanity, but his attribution of success on this occasion to luck is not among them. The voters were apparently well aware of the fact that during the previous legislature David had supported western interests. Certainly those who had announced his candidacy without his knowledge had been made to pay the value of the printing.

When the Fifteenth General Assembly met in Murfreesborough on September 15, 1823, David was present representing the counties of Humphreys, Perry, Henderson, Carroll, and Madison. This increase in the number of represented counties over the two he had represented in middle Tennessee indicates the rapid growth of the west. It also indicates the inadequacy of the representation there.

One gets the impression from the report of the early activities of this session that David had won a degree of recognition from the party machine, and that had he been willing to cooperate, the machine politicians might have been well content to make use of him. But this ill-starred alliance was destined to last about the usual fortnight of a honeymoon, after which it was forever doomed. Anyway, it was on Crockett's motion that five hundred copies of Governor Carroll's address to the legislature were printed for the use of the Senate and House, and that a Mr. V. P. Barry was ordered to be admitted to a seat at the Clerk's table. Immediately Crockett was placed on two important standing committees, as well as on the important select committee on Military Affairs. Crockett's resolution to consider no petitions or bills for divorce was immediately tabled, and when he called it up again shortly, it failed to carry by a vote of nineteen to eighteen. When he persisted, it was again tabled. In spite of the indicated unpopularity of the resolution, the bill passed twenty-five to thirteen on the next day. James K. Polk, almost a weather-vane for party winds at this time, voted with him twice, when his bill had failed and when it finally passed by an unusual switch in votes. All of this took place within the first legislative week.

An important event soon put an end to this dalliance, if indeed it ever existed. This incident was perhaps the most important single matter of the first session in terms of David's political future, and it is the only incident out of his whole legislative career that the *Autobiography* devotes much attention to. It concerned the election, at a joint session, of a United States Senator. It had important implications, for it was his first open break with Andrew Jackson.

The term of the incumbent, Colonel John Williams, had expired, and he was a candidate to succeed himself. However Williams had been a political enemy of Jackson's from the time of the Creek War and he had been critical of Jackson during his recently expired term —even though the political powers of the state were grooming Jackson for the Presidency. Consequently the enmity between Williams and Jackson was widely known. A victory for Williams, since it would be generally interpreted as an indication of popular opposition to Jackson in his own bailiwick, would seriously injure Jackson's prospects nationally. Williams was very popular with the legislators, and the Jackson forces had not been able to settle on another candidate whom they considered strong enough to defeat him. They were urging Jackson himself to run for the position, but Jackson balked at the idea of being "his own jockey." By October 1, the day for the vote, the Jackson men had still not agreed upon a candidate. When the Senate convened at seven o'clock in the morning, the Jackson forces, who were in control, immediately requested that the House postpone the election until the following Friday. The House, however, was not controlled by Jackson forces; and knowing the race, the horse, and the jockey, it promptly nonconcurred. The Senate re-emphasized its request, this time *insisting* upon a postponement. Again the House nonconcurred. In desperation, Jackson was forced to enter his own candidacy, and the two Houses met in a joint Session. There, after a hot contest, Jackson was elected Senator (he later withdrew) by a vote of thirty-five to twenty-five in a much hotter and closer contest than the final vote revealed.

The official records, do not, of course, contain the details of this election. However, a leader in the fight to prevent postponement of the elections, and a strong supporter of Williams, was David Crockett.[12] His motives may well have been mixed. Recollection of his resentful and face-saving account of the mutiny against Jackson in the Creek War suggests the possibility that even so early a burr lodged inside a hurt pride may have spurred David's action. Also, to the dispossessed of west Tennessee, the Jackson forces often had the appearance of unsympathetic enemies—hence the recalcitrance of the more representative body of the legislature in refusing to accede to Jackson's wishes for postponement of the election. Finally, David himself suggests another motive: "I thought the colonel had honestly discharged his duty [in his term then expiring], and even the mighty name of Jackson couldn't make me vote against him." He admits that the vote, in time, proved costly to him, but says that he was more certain than ever that he had done right. Whatever other motives he may have had, surely among them was a strong yeomanly determination to do what he thought was just, Jackson or no Jackson.

In his opposition to Felix Grundy's proposal to sell the remainder of the Hiawassee District lands for *cash only*, Crockett continued to keep faith with the poor, and anticipated his future opposition to a system of public land disposal that encouraged speculation. Commenting upon this proposal, Crockett said:

He was well convinced that if the sale was made for ready money, poor people would get but very little if any of the land; there were no ready money people settled in new countries, if they did, none of them had come into his country. He was decidedly in favor of selling on credit, or at least for the greatest part of the purchase money. He did not come here to legislate for ready-money men. . . .[13]

Several other important issues raised in the previous legislature continued to engage attention in this one. In early October a joint session met again to vote on calling a constitutional convention. The motion, as usual, failed to win a two-thirds majority. Crockett was still supporting it. In the same month a bill was introduced to extend the date for locating North Carolina land warrants, this time in *west* Tennessee lands. Crockett voted against extension, as he had when extension was proposed against the eastern lands. Though the eastern date had not been extended, the western date was. With reference to the franchise, David supported a bill on November 21 to reduce state taxes on free poles.

It was proposed during this session to use prison labor for promoting navigation of west Tennessee rivers. Crockett was in sympathy with the object of the labor, as later evidence will indicate. Nevertheless he voted against the bill, and later moved to table it, evidently because of its proposal to use prison labor. Many prisoners were debtors and in September he had introduced a bill to relieve honest debtors from imprisonment.

Because of David's later support of the Second Bank of the United States, his concern at this time with state banks is perhaps of interest. On October 2 he introduced a bill to continue the respective agencies of the Bank of Tennessee, withdrew it late in November, and then returned it with an amendment which was adopted. Most of the state banks had earlier had to suspend specie payments as a result of the panic of 1819. Crockett stated that he thought the whole earlier "Banking system [was] a species of swindling on a large scale." [14] However, he approved the new state banks, then being set up as a relief measure, because they would supply the settlers with money. He liked especially the provision whereby money was to be apportioned to counties, there to be "loaned and re-loaned." [15]

Two measures which seemed unimportant in 1823 took on important political implications at a later time. These were his bill to appoint the time for holding certain courts in west Tennessee, changing some established times, and another to regulate the militia west of the Tennessee River. J. M. Keating says that Judge John Overton, writing as "Aristides," achieved Crockett's defeat in his first campaign for Congress two years later by taking him to task in the papers for having neglected the interests of his constituents in the legislature with his bills to change the time of holding certain courts and to add an east Tennessee brigade to the militia of the Western District. [16]

Crockett seems consistently to have opposed a bill "to preserve the purity of elections," being one of a very small minority. Yet the same minority *favored* amending the bill so as to *prohibit* any person from selling spiritous liquors by retail in connection with an election. The majority favoring purity of elections overwhelmingly threw out this amendment! [17]

In view of the famous Carson-Vance duel that Crockett was to witness four years later, it is interesting that in November he introduced a bill to amend the 1817 act "more effectually to prevent duelling." The bill was rejected. David also opposed the bill against tippling houses. And since David himself had married a widow with children, it is amusing to see him introduce a bill on November 18 "for the relief of widows and orphans, and to encourage the intermarriage with widows."

Finally, near the end of this first session, the two Houses memorialized Congress, instructing Senators and requesting Congressmen to procure passage of a law allowing the State of Tennessee to dispose of vacant lands, this time south and west of the Congressional line, after June 1, 1825, "at such price as may be thought prudent by the legislature for the purpose of education." As there is no record of David's opposition, he evidently still supported the state's position. The first session adjourned on Saturday, November 29, 1823.[18]

Of the ten months between adjournment of the first session and the opening of the second, Crockett tells us nothing. Indeed, he records scarcely anything about the entire two-year period covered by this legislative term. "I now served two years," he says, "in that body from my new district, which was the years 1823 and '24." Adding a brief account of his vote supporting Colonel Williams against Jackson, he concludes: "During these two sessions of the Legislature, nothing else turned up which I think it worth while to mention"—and he is through with his state political career.

A few records do survive for those intervening ten months. On July 6, 1824, he served as a juror.[19] On September 14, evidently on his way to the second session of the legislature, he appeared in Carroll County court to take an oath as to the execution of a deed of "bargin and Sale."[20] An 1827 inventory of a deceased guardian, Olly Blakemore, reveals that several notes which David had made about this time had still not been paid: one for $9.37½ due on August 16, 1823; one for $23.00 due on November 1, 1823; and a third for $30.00 due December 25, 1823.[21] On April 14, 1824, David and several others signed a lease for a tract of land on the Obion River in Carroll County.[22] This may have been related to the establishment of a hunting preserve, which local legends still link to David's name. Presumably hunting, farming, and local politicking occupied his time between sessions.

In response to a call by Governor Carroll, the second session of the Fifteenth General Assembly met on September 20, 1824. The most significant action of this special session was the vote of the joint session finally presenting to the electorate the matter of calling a convention to amend and revise the constitution. The vote was finally carried by an exact two-thirds majority, David voting as ever in the affirmative. David was by now representing ten counties instead of five, four new ones having been created at the first session and the fifth at the present session. The ten counties were: Humphreys, Perry, Henderson, Carroll, Madison, Hardeman, Dyer, Haywood, Gibson, and Fayette.[23]

David introduced a bill to improve the navigation of the rivers of the Western District, this time without the objectionable feature of prison labor. On September 21 he introduced the bill to establish the Chancery Court of Gibson County, the very court into which he himself was to be hauled ten years later. Still interested in the issuance of certificates on land warrants, he submitted a joint resolution to investigate the actions of the register and the commissioner of west Tennessee on certain matters in this connection. He also presented the petitions of sundry persons in the Western District "praying that no more warrants may be sent upon them," and introduced a bill of instructions to the surveyors south and west of the Congressional line. He was opposed to tabling the resolution which would have required the Bank of Tennessee to publish annual financial statements in March, at Nashville and Knoxville.

On the recurring demand for internal improvements, Crockett took the position of the occupants rather than of the property owners. He said that "the people generally were willing to pay a small tax," probably 12½ cents on a hundred acres, though he realized very well that the absentee property owners would object even to that amount.[24] A further indication of his basic sympathies is revealed by his effort to prevent a land practice which he thought placed the settlers at the mercy of the speculators:

Mr. Crockett called up his resolution relative to land warrants. He observed that the practice which had been pursued under the act of the last session, of removing entries of long standing, entering them at twelve and a half cents per acre, and obtaining warrants for the removed entry, which they [the speculators] went over into the western district and sold for 1 and $2 per acre, was such a practice as would disgrace any country. He had heard much said here about frauds, &c., committed by North Carolina speculators; but it was time to quit talking about other people, and look to ourselves. This practice was more rascally, and a greater fraud than any he had yet heard of. . . . [Last session] he was . . . told that he would ruin the people; but it had not turned out so. The speculators then pretending to be great friends to the people in saving their land, had gone up one side of the creek and down another, like a *coon*, and pretended to grant the poor people great favors in securing them occupant claims—they gave them a credit of a year and promised to take cows, horses, &c., in payment. But when the year came around, the notes were in the hands of others; the people were sued, cows and horses not being sufficient to pay for securing it. He said again, that warrants obtained in this way, by the removal of entries for the purpose of speculation, should be as counterfeit bank notes in the hands of the person who obtained them, and die on their hands.[25]

The House adjourned *sine die* on Friday, October 22, 1824[26] and David's state political career was at an end.

Chapter 6

FROM CANEBRAKES TO CONGRESS

ALTHOUGH late in the summer of 1825, Crockett was defeated in his attempt to win a seat in the United States Congress, the entire record for the period, from the adjournment of the state legislature in October until his fateful venture in barrel staves, yields no more than a couple of pages of trustworthy biographical fact.[1]

Crockett's campaign for Congress was premature. Colonel Adam Alexander, the incumbent from the Western District, was a man of considerable means and influence. Among other things, he was the Surveyor General of the Tenth Surveyor's District in the "Jackson Purchase," as the Western District was called. A "high tariff" man, his vote in that connection in an earlier session of Congress had created dissatisfaction among constituents with few manufactures to benefit from a high tariff policy. David had been strongly urged, therefore, to enter the race for the new term, 1825-1827. For this reason he did not run again for the legislature. He had first resisted the urging of his friends that he run for Congress, saying: "I couldn't stand that; it was a step above my knowledge, and I knowed nothing about Congress matters." Nevertheless, he finally agreed to the undertaking and ran the campaign on the high tariff vote of Alexander during the previous term. A third candidate also entered the race.

David thus explains his defeat:

...Providence was a little against two of us this hunt, for it was the year that cotton brought twenty-five dollars a hundred; and so Colonel Alexander would get up and tell the people, it was all the good effect of this tariff law; that it had raised the price of their cotton, and that it would raise the price of everything else they made to sell. I might as well have sung *salms* over a dead horse, as to try to make the people believe otherwise; for they knowed their cotton had raised, sure enough, and if the colonel hadn't done it, they didn't know what had. So he rather made a mash of me this time as he beat me exactly *two* votes, as they counted the polls, though I have always believed that many other things had been as fairly done as that same count.

He went on, and served out his term, and at the end of it cotton was down to *six* or *eight* dollars a hundred again; and I concluded I would try him once more, and see how it would go with cotton at the common price, and so I became a candidate [again].

The election in which Crockett was defeated took place in August, 1825. Earlier (1824) he had issued a Circular Letter for the campaign in which he doubtless attempted to defend himself from Judge Overton's strictures concerning the bills he had sponsored during the previous legislature to change certain court times and to add an east Tennessee brigade to the militia of the Western District.[2] It is clear, therefore, that other considerations beside the price of cotton must have been involved in his defeat.

In the autumn of 1825 David decided to undertake a venture in the manufacture of pipe and barrel staves. For this purpose, he went to Obion Lake on the river of that name, some 25 miles almost due west of his home and south of Reelfoot, hired some hands to help him, and went to work. Some of the hands built the two boats he would need for shipping the staves to New Orleans while the others got out the staves. David worked with them until he got things going, but soon the rational pretext of a need for winter meat so worked on his passion for hunting that he set off in search of bear. The legitimate task was easily accomplished. He soon killed, took home, and salted down as much meat as the family would need. But before he finished salting the meat, a neighbor who lived on the Obion Lake tempted him to come back and hunt in his territory, representing that the bears were thick, fat, and easily followed. Of course Crockett succumbed. During two weeks of hunting, Crockett and his neighbor between them killed fifteen bears, more than enough for the neighbor's winter needs. Though David returned for a while to his hired hands and the boat-building and stave-getting, he could not for long resist the temptation of further hunting. Finally he took after bear again, this time taking along with him one of his younger sons (either Robert Patton, 9, or

William, about 16) and crossed over the lake. That very afternoon he killed three bears within a very short time in the area of Big and Little Clover Lick Creeks.

We need not follow in detail Crockett's account of the numerous bears they killed. One day he came across a "poor fellow" who "looked like the very picture of hard times," engaged in grubbing for another man in order to get money to buy meat for his family. "I was mighty sorry for the poor fellow," says David, "for [grubbing] was not only hard but a very slow way to get meat for a hungry family." So David took him off the job to go with them, promising to provide him with plenty of meat if he would only help pack and salt it. And David relates that when they closed their hunt he gave the man more than a thousand pounds of fine, fat bear meat. He saw him the next fall and learned from him that the meat had lasted the entire year.

This hunt was made between Christmas and December 31, 1825. Soon after the new year opened, David was again persuaded by a neighbor—this time by a man named McDaniel—to go back into the same territory. In his account David relates something of the art of hunting bears after they had gone into hibernation, though he imposes upon the reader's credulity by seriously affirming that after four months of hibernation these animals "come out...not an ounce lighter than when they went to house." After finding and killing a single bear "in house," they spent that night with a certain Davidson who lived near their camp. The next morning they started for the country between the Obion and Reelfoot Lake "as there had been a dreadful harricane, which passed between them, and I was sure there must be a heap of bears in the fallen timber." They had soon killed three more bears, salted and strung them up; then they pitched the night's camp.

On the morning of the third day David and McDaniel left the young boy in camp and set out for the "harricane . . . but we got along mighty slow on account of the cracks in the earth occasioned by the earthquakes." In fact, they were compelled to abandon their horses. In about the middle of the "harricane" they got their first bear. With butchering the animal and getting it back to their horses they consumed most of the remainder of the afternoon, arriving near their camp just about sunset. David called to his son in camp and got a reply; in the same instant he heard the dogs strike up a new trail. So entrusting his horse to the care of McDaniel, off he went on the heels of the hounds into the dusk.

He describes the difficulties through which he plunged after nightfall—the cold waters, the thick undergrowth, the fallen logs, the crevices left by the quakes. Finally the dogs treed. When he eventually reached them he perceived against the dim light of the moonless skies a lump in the fork of a poplar which he knew must be the bear. He fired twice in the dark and the bear tumbled down alive and angry into the midst of the dogs. David drew his large knife in case he should need to use it. He could not see well enough against the ground to shoot. At last the bear got down into an earthquake crack some four feet deep, and David, feeling about with the muzzle of his gun, fired at him again, but only wounded him and brought him again out of the crevice. David then put down his gun and drew his knife once more for defense. The dogs soon forced the bear back into the crevice, but David, searching around in the dark, could not locate his gun. He did find a pole, however, and with this he punched the bear in an effort to drive him out again. The bear, taking this patiently enough, David concluded:

it might be that he would lie still enough for me to get down in the crack, and feel slowly along till I could find the right place to give him a dig with my butcher. So I got down, and my dogs got in before him and kept his head towards them, till I got along easily up to him; and placing my hand on his rump, felt for his shoulder, just behind which I intended to stick him. I made a lounge with my long knife, and fortunately stuck him right through the heart; at which he just sank down, and I crawled out in a hurry. In a little time my dogs all come out too, and seemed satisfied, which was the way they always had of telling me that they had finished him.[3]

Now that the bear was dead, David faced the bitter cold of the January night. He built a fire, but could find no dry timber to keep it going. To keep from freezing, he tried jumping and hollering and going through bodily contortions. Finally, he resorted to climbing up a tree thirty feet to the first limb and sliding down again. He says he kept this up until daylight, after which he set to work, hung up the bear, and set out to hunt for the camp. When he had found his party and brought them back to the scene of the previous night's adventure, McDaniel examined the place and exclaimed that "he wouldn't have gone into [the crevice] ... for all the bears in the woods." The next morning they killed more bears, loaded up their five horses, and started for home about thirty miles east.

Crockett concludes his story by saying that during the fall and winter he had killed fifty-eight bears, and that when spring came, he hunted again for about a month, getting forty-seven more, or a total of 105 in seven months. This is a tremendous number of bears! However, included in the number "he" killed are all those killed by the various people who were with him on his hunts. It is also well to recall the wildness of this country and the recency of the white man's entry into it (bought from the Chickasaws on October 19, 1818). In all likelihood this area was as wild and full of game in 1824 as middle Tennessee had been half a century earlier. Hamer gives an account of a hunt in middle Tennessee in 1780 on which a group of twenty hunters, not in seven months but in one, five-day "drive" on Caney Fork, bagged 105 bear, 75 buffalo, and 87 deer.[4]

As for David's remarkable ability as a hunter, several reminiscences of his contemporaries establish that as fact. Stout gives various accounts he collected in 1843-44 from Crockett's old associates. He quotes a Mr. McLaurin, ex-sheriff of Gibson County, who claimed to have beaten David once at a shooting contest for a prize of $500. McLaurin freely asserted that David surpassed him as a hunter.[5] Colonel Chester testified to having slept on bear rugs upon the floor of David's house after David was a national Congressman.[6]

Returning to his barrel-stave enterprise about the middle of January, 1826, he found the boats almost completed and some thirty thousand staves manufactured. Sometime early in February, having loaded the staves aboard, all hands set "sail" down the Obion River for New Orleans and the market. Unfortunately, they were all landlubbers, and the unmanageable craft they had constructed testified to the fact. Once the boats were embarked into the Mississippi, they found they could neither maneuver the vessels nor disembark. When they attempted without success to land as the first dark fell, passing craft advised them to continue down the river through the night—advice which, against every instinct of landsmén, they, of necessity, followed to the letter. All night long they made futile attempts to land, as people at the landing places would run out with lanterns and shout directions which they were powerless to follow. They did, however, lash their two boats together so as to keep them from being parted in the dark night.

When they got through the difficult bends of the "Devil's Elbow," they gave up the idea of trying to land, and David went below decks. He wished he were hunting bears on hard ground rather than floating along the water where there was little relation between a will and a way. The boats were, at the moment, floating sidewise, David's boat behind. Suddenly there was a great commotion of feet overhead, and in the next instant he felt the sudden impact of the boat striking against an obstacle. He later found that the craft had struck "sawyers" (sunken trees gyrating in and parallel to the flow of the current) and other collected driftwood and debris lodged against the currentward end of an island. With a suddenness which prevented accommodation of action to events, the boat in which he lay sprawled began to capsize and turn under the forward boat and the debris. David arrived at the hatchway to find it at such a steep angle and water pouring in with such volume and force that it was impossible for him to get out.

High on the side of David's boat was a hole which had been made to allow those below deck to dip up water from the river. The boats were lashed together on that side, and David with difficulty made his way there seeking aid. He found the hole not large enough for him to get through, but he put his head and arms through anyway and bellowed as loud as his lungs could roar, for the water by now was shoulder high. The hands, now on the other boat, seized his arms and began to pull. David told them to tug till the arms came off, for it was his only chance, and never mind the hurt. By violent efforts they jerked him through, *sans* outer and nether garments and *sans* a good deal of flesh. David "was literally skin'd like a rabbit." Almost immediately the boat he had emerged from disappeared under the water, and all hands moved off the remaining boat onto the jam of logs and trash against which the crafts had foundered. There they sat all night, variously bareheaded and barefooted—with one, David, totally bare—a mile from shore on either side. But after his narrow escape from death, all such hardship seemed negligible, and he felt happy in his situation. At sunrise, according to David's version, a boat coming down the river sent out a skiff to pick them up and took them all down the river as far as Memphis. "Here," David reports, "I met with a friend, that I never can forget as long as I am able to go ahead at any thing;

it was a Major Winchester, a merchant of that place; he let us all have hats, and shoes, and some little money to go upon, and so we all parted."

This is all he has to say of Mr. Winchester, though he begins two chapters with a tribute to an unnamed "good friend" who lent him money for his Congressional campaign. From other evidence, this "good friend" seems to have been the Major Winchester he here "met with"—actually, met for the first time—when he arrived in the city of Memphis.

According to David's account, he afterwards took another man and went down the river as far as Natchez searching for his boats. Unsuccessful in this effort, he returned home and began to turn his attention to the August elections about which people were beginning to talk. This is all David tells us about this stave adventure, but other sources add additional information. First, however, it should be noted that David has left out a year of his life in this transition to the elections, for the boat episode occurred in the early part of *1826* and the August elections of which he speaks were not held until August, *1827*.

James D. Davis and J. M. Keating, in their histories of Memphis, tell this stave story.[7] Since they are often careless of facts, dates, and sources, it is impossible to tell from either author how much could have been substantiated from personal memory or documents, and how much derived from legend or perhaps from the *Autobiography* itself. Nevertheless, they give important additions, some factually verifiable. According to these sources, the accident took place within sight of the city of Memphis just above "Paddy's Hen-and-Chickens," and the rescue boat came up the river from Memphis, rather than from a vessel coming down, as David says. They go on to say that, after the rescue, Crockett became the hero of the hour and later capitalized on his notoriety to win his election through the good will of the people of Memphis. They relate how, after the boat-wrecked crew had been brought to Memphis, clothed, and given a "horn or two to restore their spirits," David began to tell stories and anecdotes with a humor so rare that Winchester was entranced and finally urged David to become a candidate for Congress. "It may be," says Davis, "that the misfortune at the head of the Old Hen was the starting point of his future importance and notoriety."[8] Without wishing to detract from the glory of Memphis, I think the reader will agree that we know too much about David's career up to this time—and about the lowered price of cotton—to give Memphis credit for more than a *helping* hand in his future.

It is my opinion that the Winchester whom Crockett, Davis, and Keating refer to as David's benefactor was M. B. Winchester, shortly to be postmaster of Memphis during Jackson's administration. He, and many others in Memphis, supported David even in 1831 after Crockett had broken with Jackson. Keating quotes a letter of complaint from Judge Overton to M. B. Winchester, postmaster, calling the people of Memphis to task for their continued support of Crockett. The letter was written from Rip Raps, Virginia, July 3, 1831. Davis is undoubtedly right in stating that this accident resulted in winning for David influential Memphis friends who were of great assistance to him in his future career.

The records show that David was home by the late spring of 1826. He may actually have returned sooner, for he himself has told us that he hunted for another month in this spring and killed forty-seven bears. It is the year 1826, ignored by him in his narrative, which we must now briefly consider. Few records of that year remain.

The disastrous venture in cypress staves caused Crockett serious monetary distress. Sympathy for his financial straits may be reflected in the entry on April 24, 1826, in which George W. Gibbs, who had been attempting to eject David from leased property, came into court and said "that he intends no further to prosecute" and paid the court costs to that point.[9]

Few records survive for this entire year, and these are widely scattered. Several of them relate to David's activities as a trail-blazer. On June 5, Crockett was placed on a jury of view "to run and mark out a road from the town of Trenton to Weakley County line in a direction to Dresden in said county. . . ." Some of David's neighbors along the line of the road were placed on the same jury: Andres Craig, David Crockett, Jr.,[10] Daniel Conlee, Squire Young, William Ferguson, John Gray, and Patterson Crockett. Those who lived along the routes were called on to "view" them as well as to build and keep them up. David must have been especially capable as a trail blazer. On the same day he was placed on another jury of view for a road to run from the town of Trenton to the Obion County line "in the direction of Martins Bluff on the Obion River."[11] And three months later, on

September 6 Crockett was overseer on the Martin Bluff road from Rutherford to Obion County.[12]

On the first Monday in September, 1826, among others summoned to appear later for jury duty were "David Crockett Colo. [and] David Crockett." A further reference to "David Crockett Senr." is followed by action making David foreman of the above grand jury.[13] Then on September 6 "David Crocket [and] Col. David Crockett" were included by the county court among veniremen to the next circuit court.[14] Thereafter the record is silent until the campaign for Congress got under way the following spring.

When, early in the spring of 1827, David opened his new campaign for election to the United States Congress as representative of the Ninth Congressional District, he was accompanied on his itinerary by his oldest son, John Wesley, at that time a lad of 19 or 20. From John's letter of March 6, 1827, to his friend "Charley," we see Crockett's electioneering through the eyes of a second generation backwoodsman as alert in his use of slang as a "modern":

Dear Charley.

I take the liberty of writing you these lines to inform you that I am well and in gunter; your father's family is well and all wish to see you very much [.] I am so loansome that I can scarcely live. Old Maj. Henry has cut out for Orleans in the hooks[.] T I Trice is gone to Kentucky and indeed every body else that has any life in them. I am ——— [excised word] for your father and am a whole hook—there are about a dozen candidates here and I heard them all speak yesterday. I heard my old father speak yesterday—for the first time. The old hook is a going ahead electioneering. I think the old fellow will come out in the gunter. He seemede to please the people very much in his speach. Your mother goes for him and you know she is a very good friend.

Yours respectfully—

John W. Crockett.[15]

This new phase of Crockett's career, like his entry into state politics, seems to have begun almost casually.

In the early portions of the last brief chapter of the *Autobiography*, in which he wraps up all the remainder of his life from 1827 to the time of writing in January, 1834, David gives a brief additional view of this campaign. As the newspapers verify, he was opposed by both General William Arnold and Colonel Adam Alexander, the incumbent and surveyor-general introduced previously. General Arnold had been one of the commissioners appointed for the city of Jackson by act of the legislature, on August 17, 1822; and as Colonel Arnold he had defeated, in 1824, the popular Colonel Robert H. Dyer, for the position of Major-General of the old Third Division.[16] Hence in Arnold, Crockett had an opponent of no mean proportions, to say nothing of the incumbent, Colonel Alexander. Arnold held his position of major-general of the Western District until he resigned it in 1833.[17] David says of him that he was not only a "major-general in the militia," but also "an attorney-general at the law." One understands Crockett's predicament, especially in view of his poverty, when he says he "had war work as well as law trick, to stand up under. Taking both together, they make a pretty considerable of a load for any one man to carry." These were probably the men in whose company David had spoken on March 5, 1827, when the son had heard his "old father . . . . the old hook" speak for the first time. The traditional story which attributes to David's campaigning only an ability to act the fool hardly suffices to explain his repeated victories over such candidates of long-proven popularity as these.

Of course, David had his own war record to go on; his own record in the legislature; the fall in the price of cotton, so far as Colonel Alexander was concerned; and the financial help, he tells us, of some friend, probably M. B. Winchester of Memphis,[18] who lent him $250.00 for the campaign and put in a good word for him while conducting his business at the different courts over the district. With this money, says the *Autobiography*, "I was able to buy a little of 'the *creature*,' to put my friends in a good humour, as well as the other gentlemen, for they all treat in that country; not to get elected, of course—for that would be against the law; but just, as I before said, to make themselves and their friends feel their keeping a little."

Until the creation of a new district in 1832, the Ninth Congressional District consisted of the nine counties of Carroll, Hardin, Henderson, Henry, Lawrence, Madison, Perry, Shelby, and Wayne, plus "all new counties west of the Tennessee River." [19] After 1824 there were nine of these "new counties"—Dyer, Fayette, Gibson, Hardeman, Haywood, McNairy, Obion, Tipton, and Weakley—or a total, from 1824 to 1832, of 18 counties. By 1830 the Ninth District was so large that, with the exception of Mr. Duncan of Illinois, its Congressman represented more voters than any other member of Congress—22,000 or more. The inadequate representation for the West, which David had been instrumental in correcting on the state level, was still apparent on the national scene. Throughout this large district, then, these three candidates were speaking.

During at least the early days of the campaign there was probably a fourth candidate—a Colonel Cook,[20] who attacked Crockett on the grounds of decency.[21] For every evil charge which his opponent made against him, David would make a worse one against his opponent. The adversary, knowing that Crockett's charges were completely false, shrewdly planned to trap him. He arranged to face David at the conclusion of one of his harangues with witnesses who would absolutely prove that he had been lying, and thus, by catching him in the act, humiliate him publicly and once and for all dispense with him politically. When, at the appointed hour, David arose and spoke, his opponent was delighted. On this occasion David seemed to outdo himself in making false charges. At the conclusion of his speech, Crockett hesitated as if prepared to take his seat. Then with a mild and smiling countenance added, as if by afterthought, that his opponent had planned to trap him and had brought witnesses to prove that he had been spreading lies. Now, said David, his opponent might have saved himself all the trouble by simply asking him, for he would have freely admitted that they were lies. However, he thought he had as much right to lie about his competitor as his competitor had to lie about him—for they had *both* been lying all the time.

How David had discovered the trap is not revealed. Anything his opponent and his witnesses might have had to say after that admission would have been an anticlimax drowned out in the roar of the crowd. His adversary, who had more justice than astuteness on his side, withdrew from the canvass in righteous indignation over the irrationality of the electorate, saying that he would not consent to represent people who would applaud an acknowledged liar.

Crockett's two remaining opponents, patently afraid of each other's influence, were undisturbed by David's prospects to the point of ignoring his candidacy. At one point as the three candidates were travelling through one of the eastern counties, speaking to the same group one after the other, General Arnold took great pains to reply to Alexander, but never once, even by implication, referred to Crockett's speech. It chanced that while the general was speaking a large flock of guineas came near the gathering with such a clatter that the general was compelled to stop until they could be driven away. At the conclusion of Arnold's remarks, David quickly arose, walked up to him, and cried out in a loud voice for all to hear that the general was the first man he ever saw, besides himself, who could understand the language of fowls. Being asked what he meant, Crockett replied that, since the general had not had the politeness to mention him in his speech, his little friends the guineas had come up and begun to cry "Crockett, Crockett, Crockett!" But the general had been ungenerous enough even to silence them by having them all driven away. This, reports David, "raised a universal shout among the people for me, and the general seemed mighty bad plagued. But he got more plagued than this at the polls in August."

And plagued indeed he was. Though reports of the exact figures vary, there is general agreement that David defeated his opponents by a substantial margin. David says the majority was 2,748.[22] Whatever it was, it was victory, and David had earned it.

Through the years David had remained on affectionate terms with his wife's people in western North Carolina; furthermore, he had lived throughout the state of Tennessee and had antecedents in North Carolina. It is not at all strange that once the election was over he should have decided to take a trip back through his old haunts. He had moved west without much prospect of attaining prominence, and pleasant must have been his journey to Swannanoa, North Carolina, for rest, celebration, and congratulations from friends and relations.[23]

Crockett set out shortly after October 1 for the North Carolina mountains, accompanied by his wife, Elizabeth Patton, and his son, John Wesley. About the middle of October he interrupted his trip for a visit with his old friend James Blackburn. On the day after resuming his journey, he was stricken with what he calls "billes feaver," probably a recurrence of the old ailment that we have previously called malaria. He travelled on to Swannanoa, but remained ill for some weeks after arriving there.

David was present at the famous Carson-Vance duel while on this vacation and established as fact the local legends concerning his presence there.[24] A brief résumé will suffice here. The duel was fought between Sam P. Carson and Robert B. Vance, both from influential families in western North Carolina. Carson's father, Colonel

John Carson, had represented the state in the legislature and was a man of influence and renown. Vance, superbly educated, had already been to the national Congress. His nephew, Zebulon Vance, was later to become Governor of North Carolina. Sam Carson, later to be first Secretary of the State of Texas, had defeated Vance for re-election to Congress in 1825. In August, 1827, when David Crockett had been campaigning against Alexander and Arnold back in west Tennessee, Carson ran against Vance in a race that began to get entirely too hot for safety as the elections drew near. For reasons relating mostly to his gentleness of nature and his slowness to anger, Sam Carson had gained a mistaken reputation in some quarters for cowardice. Dr. Robert Vance was a cripple. According to report, his whole ambition centered in the desire to return to Congress. Foolishly relying on the report of Carson's cowardice, Vance made the open charge in a speech when members of the Carson family were present that Sam Carson's grandfather had "taken protection"—had been a Tory and had sympathized with General Ferguson when that officer had invaded Burke County during Revolutionary times.

Colonel John Carson, Sam's father, demanded a retraction, evidently threatening a challenge in default of one, and Vance replied by letter: "I can have no altercation with a man of your age, and if I have aggrieved you, you certainly have some of your chivalrous sons that will protect you from insult." [25]

Vance wrote this letter on September 6. On September 12, Sam Carson (who had been again victorious in the elections just over) wrote a letter to Dr. Vance from Pleasant Gardens, some twenty-five miles east of Swannanoa. The following is an excerpt:

My friend Captn. Burgin is instructed to know of you distinctly before he hands you this whether I was the *"Chivalrous Son"* alluded to in your letter to my father dated the 6th instant.

If so this is my answer. Had you recollected my language to you at Morganton which was not equivocal and which gave you *distinctly* to *understand* what you were to expect at my hands—you would have spared yourself the trouble of writing or alluding to me in any way. However Sir, the malignant shafts of your *disappointed ambition* fall perfectly harmless at my feet....

You have been faithless to agreements *sacred* to *honor*, I will not therefore place myself in your power by violating the laws of my state.

Not to be misunderstood, you have received the votes of 2419 citizens of this District as a fit representative in Congress this gives you a claim which individually you are not entitled to. On my way to Congress I will pass through Asheville to meet some friends in East Tennessee. Your *course is open*. I will spend a week at Jones-borough on my route.[26]

There were Tennessee laws against duelling. Therefore, the duel was finally fought, not at Jonesboro, but just across the South Carolina line, near Saluda, North Carolina. As David tells it, the Pattons, the Carsons, and the Burgins were all his friends. Since David was on vacation not far from Sam's home when the duel took place on November 6, 1827, though barely recovered from his sickness, he was at the side of his friend as Sam Carson and Robert Vance marched off their paces. A letter from Sam Carson's daughter reports her memory of the event: "David Crockett was the first man who brought the news to Pleasant Gardens, he rode his horse almost to death, beat his hat to pieces & came dashing up yelling 'The Victory is Ours'...." [27] This is the last record of David before he arrived in Washington for the opening of his Congressional career.

Thus the pre-Congressional life of backwoodsman David Crockett concludes in violence and tragedy, a theme that runs its course in his life from beginning to end. From what he says in a letter of February 5, 1828, to James Blackburn, he had evidently planned to return with his wife and son to west Tennessee before going on to Congress, which convened on December 3, 1827. The delay occasioned by his illness made this impossible. About the middle of November David departed, probably in the company of Sam Carson, down the mountains by way of east Tennessee, through Virginia, toward Washington; and Elizabeth and John Wesley, now a strapping twenty-year-old, set out for home in far off Gibson County. About a month later, on December 17, 1827, David was in "Washington City."

The second step in his journey was finished, and Crockett was now launched, for better or for worse, upon the stage of national politics.

PART THREE

Up and Over

7

THE LAND BILL

D AVID arrived in Washington from Swannanoa still quite ill from the bloodletting the doctor had administered. He wrote a friend two months later, "I have thought that I was never to See my family any more tho thanks be to god I hope that I am Recovering as fast as I could expect I have a great hope that I am to Spend the ballance of the Session with much better health." In spite of his illness, he was probably present when Congress convened on December 3, 1827. His first surviving holograph reveals that he had immediately set about his Congressional duties.[1] By December 27 he had presented a petition for establishing a mail route from "Troy to Mills Pint and thence to dresden by Tottons wells" and had determined, once the route was established, to appoint Mr. Drabilbass and Mr. Totton postmasters. He had already appointed Mr. James Gibson postmaster at Fulton, discovering, with surprise, what prerogatives a Congressman had: "I find a representative have power to appoint who they pleas."

By December 6 he had already begun that undertaking which, first and last, lay closest to his heart—his work in behalf of his Tennessee Vacant Land Bill, about which, as always, he was optimistic: "I have

Started the Subject of our vacant land on the third day after we went into Session I have no doubt of the passage of the Bill this Session I have given it an erly Start."

This first letter betrays an ignorance of governmental processes even more startling than David's ignorance of grammar and orthography. He was very quick to learn, and his knowledge in both areas increased rapidly. In his next letter he reports to a friend: "I think I am getting along very well with the great men of the nation much better than I expected."

It will be recalled that Andrew Jackson had received a majority of the popular vote for the Presidency in 1824, but had failed to receive the necessary confirmation by the electoral college. In the consequent "run-off" in the House of Representatives, John Quincy Adams was elected President, perhaps by a "Coaletion" of forces with Henry Clay and by "bargain and management"—for Adams immediately made Clay Secretary of State after his election. So close a contest naturally resulted in high party feeling between the Jackson and Adams' forces. David's letters during February and March reveal that during the first session David was very decidedly a Jackson man, with a strong antipathy to the current administration:

the great party Spirit which exists on the great political question maks us progress very Slow with bussiness tho we are on the Strong Side our old patriot and friend to his Country Genl Jackson [has a] large majority of friends in both bra[nches] of congress and I can here from all quarters of the union and the Cry is that Jackson will be the next presidant I have no doubt but that he is gaining ground Every day our mighty adminestration that got into power by bargin and management and not according to the inlightened youmenry of the nation begins to look very much down in the mouth we have Elected Andw Stevenson from virginia a Jackson man for our Speaker and the Senate has appointed Genl Duff green public printer for that boday having choaked off Joseph Gails and Co. the treasury pap Sucking Editor imployed by the Coaletion by this you See that the adminestration is in the minority and I pray god that thare they may Remain thare is nothing to prevent our old Hero from Recieving the Reward of meret....[2]

"Joseph Gails and Co. the treasury pap Sucking Editor imployed by the Coaletion" was the Adamsite publisher of the *Congressional Debates*. David's antipathy for them, so strongly stated here, was to be quite short-lived.

Again, he expresses his unqualified admiration of Jackson:

we are progressing very Slow with bussiness owing to the great party Sperit that exists here on the great political question the old hickory is like the dimond in the hill of no vallue until it is Rubed and poliched So with Genl Jackson the harder they Rub him the brighter he Shines the adminestration party has made Several attacts on him and they all opporate in favour of Jackson we have all got entirely easy here it is given up from all quarters that I Can here from that the dye is cast and that Jackson will in a Short time begin to Recieve the Reward of his merit I can assure you that those heads of the Cabenet begins to treat the Jackson men with the utmost politeness.[3]

Finally, "I have no news except that old hickory is Rising thare is a great many of the adminestration party begins to give up the test."[4]

In another of his early letters, David complains to a constituent of the slowness with which the national legislature moved: ".... thare is no chance of hurrying bussiness here like in the legeslature of a State thare is Such a desposition here to Show Eloquence that this will be a long Session and do no good I will not tier your patience Reeding my Scrall."[5] The party spirit and the "desposition . . . to Show Eloquence" resulted in the accomplishment of very little during David's first session. Except for his land bill, only one or two matters are worthy of notice. Remembering that he had defeated Alexander on the tariff issue, we are not surprised to hear him say: "I Intend to vote against all amendments to the Tariff and finally I will vote against the bill."[6] He was also involved in a curious debate on legislative principle in connection with a bill proposing a pension for the widow of Major General Brown. Mrs. Brown was in indigent circumstances, but was not entitled, under the law, to a pension. A bill for her relief was introduced. It was contended that public funds should not be voted for private distress in particular circumstances. Only a general law applying generally to all cases of similar circumstances could be justified. Crockett, reversing his normal position of supporting any bill for the relief of anybody, sided with the opposition (evidently for technical reasons). He could not ignore, however, the need of Mrs. Brown and offered personally, with Thomas Chilton, to subscribe the proposed sum.[7]

His suggestion was turned down. The bill passed, and Mrs. Brown got her pension. What is more important for our purposes is the fact that in this very first record of David in the *Congressional Debates* his name is coupled with that of Thomas Chilton, Representative from Kentucky. Thomas Chilton was to collaborate closely with David in the writing of David's *Autobiography* in the winter of 1833-34.[8] It is historically fitting that these two names should be introduced into the *Debates* simultaneously.

The only really important matter to arise in David's first session was the Tennessee Vacant Land Bill. We have already observed his concern with that bill immediately upon his arrival in Washington. On February 11, 1828, he was still writing optimistically to a constituent: "I have the Subject of our vacant land under train and have but little doubt of obtaining a Relinquishment this Session I think in a few weeks you will find that I have been Successful I will gave the earliest infermation of the fate of the bill." A month later the optimism is still there, but a note of regret has crept in: "I did believ that I would have been abel to give infermation to my destrict that we had procured Relinquishment from the Genl Goverment for our vacant land tho I cannot give you this infermation as yet tho I have a Strong hope that I will give you this news as soon as we get Red of the Tariff."

The Vacant Land Bill proposed to relinquish all vacant federal lands in Tennessee, with the specific instructions that they be sold by the state of Tennessee for educational funds. David's primary interest was in the poor of west Tennessee, not in education. Up to this point he had assumed that if the land were relinquished, Tennessee would sell it cheaply to the poor. It is obvious that when David began to suspect the state wished to sell this land at prices beyond the ability of the poor to pay, he and the state machine would part company. Perhaps the first inkling of the state's intentions came to him during this first session. Crockett, at this time, attempted to get Polk to accept a stipulation that would protect his west Tennessee constituents, but Polk refused. Nevertheless, in this first session David still supported the state's version of the bill.

On April 24, 1828, Polk made a lengthy explanation of and justification for Tennessee's claim to the vacant Tennessee lands. The background of this claim is important for an understanding of this crucial bill. By act of April 18, 1806, Congress had authorized Tennessee to proceed to locate and grant the North Carolina land warrants, stipulating that out of every six square miles set off for those purposes,

640 acres should be appropriated by the state for the use of common schools, in accordance with the customary governmental policy relating to the public lands at that time. Had this provision been observed, Tennessee would have received as a gift from the government 444,444 acres. However, the Carolina warrants had been so numerous and so endless that only some 22,705 acres had been reserved for schools. Even then the warrants still had not been satisfied in the main portion of the state north and east of the Reservation Line.

To satisfy the remaining warrants, public lands west of the line were levied against. These lands, being poor, were quite cheap. According to Polk they were so cheap that it was not worth the expense to the Federal Government of setting up Federal Land Offices for making Federal Surveys and for selling it as public lands. Yet it was of value to Tennessee, inasmuch as the Tennessee Land Offices were already established. Since the state of Tennessee had been deprived of nearly all of the half-million acres to which she was entitled, and since, according to the figures issued by the bill's advocates, the total amount of public land left, both east and west of the line, was insufficient to satisfy Tennessee's legal claims, that state was requesting the government to give her all the scraps of public land remaining east and west of the line so that she could sell the whole to the highest bidder and apply the proceeds to education.[9]

While Tennessee's case appeared just, there were equally just points of disagreement. Many in Congress opposed establishing a precedent for giving away public lands which might lead to wholesale extinction of the public domains and to great corruption. Crockett at first supported Polk. Later he came into conflict with his state on this matter because many of these "land scraps" happened to be occupied by destitute squatters. Whereas the state was only interested in selling these lands for as *much* as possible, Crockett felt that the consequences to the destitute pioneers would be utter deprivation. Many of them would not possess the purchase price and the cost of the surveys which the state would demand.

Crockett regarded these "squatters" as the pioneering advance guard of the American nation. He felt that in return for their services they were entitled to the plot of land which they had improved, and on which they had made their homes. Most of them would never have a chance to "see the inside of the schools." The sale of these lands to the highest bidder would benefit only the people of east and middle Tennessee in an action that robbed Peter to pay Paul. Furthermore, though these people were a minority in *state* politics, they were, so far as the western lands were involved, David's *majority*. He was one of them, and he intended to represent their interests as well as his own. In David's position we see, in germinal form, the essence of the public land policy later to be developed under title of the Homestead Acts.

When Mr. Locke of Massachusetts objected to Polk's position, claiming that the real value and exact quantity of vacant lands was not known, Crockett rose to support Polk. He stated that he had been a resident of west Tennessee for ten years and knew it well. He affirmed that two hundred thousand acres of it was not worth one cent an acre—to say nothing of $12\frac{1}{2}$ cents an acre. City men might think its timber to be of value, but not people from that section. "For, sir, instead of wishing more timber on our land, we should gladly avail ourselves of some invention, to wish a considerable quantity of it off, with less labor." Much of the remainder was often flooded. A fact he knew personally, having rowed by boat from hill to hill. He referred to his own participation in the Creek War, and apologized for the "plain and unvarnished manner" in which he addressed them. He said he had never seen the inside of a college although "I thank heaven I know their worth, from having experienced the want of them." He was a farmer, destitute of educational advantages.

David recommended, to the House, a measure that would sell land cheaply to the poor, for, "to make of your citizen a landholder, you chain down his affections to your soil." He agreed with Mr. McHatton of Kentucky on the importance of reducing the price of public lands throughout the union. "The rich require but little legislation. We should, at least occasionally, legislate for the poor." Finally, he submitted the question for decision, "anxiously desiring that the bill may pass." [10]

On May 1, the land bill was tabled, awaiting an amendment by Mr. McLean of Ohio, over the opposition of the Tennessee delegation, including Crockett, by a vote of 131 to 64. Congress adjourned on May 26 before it came up again. From David's previous legislative record, his letters through March, and his position on the land bill as late as May 1, it is obvious that at the session's end he was still supporting the position of the state political machine, was still a Jackson man, was still "anxiously desiring that the bill may pass," and still had an antipathy for the Adams administration and for those who, like the "treasury pap Sucking Editor," Joseph Gales, supported it.

Further action on the land bill was postponed until the next year. On January 5, 1829, Mr. McLean arose and withdrew his amendment *in favor of one to be proposed by Mr. Crockett.* Crockett's amendment changed the purpose of the entire bill by proposing to give the land, not to the state for purposes of education, but directly to those living on and having improved their land in west Tennessee, no money to accrue to the state in the transaction. On January 15, Crockett put out a Circular Letter to his constituents, printed, and perhaps partially composed, by Gales and Seaton. The following account comes both from the *Debates* and from this source.[11]

To his constituents he admits that he had supported the state's version at the last session, "but not with the slightest hope that it would prove successful. I then believed, and still believe, that it would amount to an encroachment upon the rights of my constituents, to place it in the power of the Tennessee Legislature, or any other Legislature, to speculate upon the labor of the poor." He then justifies his distrust of the state with these questions:

Why, and how, did the Legislature of Tennessee interfere with your rights and interests, when, without a shadow of claim to the land, they compelled you to have your lands laid off, plotted, and registered, without your consent, and without the existence of the slightest necessity for it? Why, I ask, was this done? and what was the effect? The effect was, that it was placed in the power of a few deputy Surveyors to defraud you, by charging double prices for their labor, and often to sell the poor man's all to pay the [surveying] fee. Seeing what I have seen, and feeling what I have felt, on account of this legislative error, I was unwilling to trust your homes to their mercy. I moreover knew that the weight of the State Legislature would stand, in great measure, as the Tennessee delegation stands in Congress; that is, opposed to my proposition, which has been, and still is, dear to my heart. To make a short story of the whole affair, I wished you to have your homes directly from the hands of Congress, and then you could, with certainty, call them your own.

His belief, stated above, that the state's bill could not pass fails to agree with his repeated statement in letters of that period that "I have no doubt of the passage of the Bill this Session."

The important part of David's proposed amendment reads as follows:

Strike out all after the enacting words in the first section, and insert the following:

'That all persons who shall have made an improvement, and, on the 1st day of April next, shall be in actual occupation, or possession, of any of the vacant and unappropriated lands of the United States, within that part of the State of Tennessee lying South and West of the Congressional Reservation Line ... shall have the privilege of entering and obtaining a grant, in a manner hereinafter required, for a quantity of such vacant land, not exceeding, each, one hundred and sixty acres, which shall, in all cases, include their improvements: *Provided* such entry shall be made within one year from the said first day of April next.'

Other sections provided for the use of state surveying machinery and laws, proof by claimant of legitimate occupancy and legitimate acquisition, proof that it was public land and that claimant had made the improvements, and a deeding of all right, title, and claim of the United States to "the grantees, and their heirs forever...."

After the amendment was read, Crockett spoke in its behalf. Stating that he had to differ with his colleague, Mr. Polk, he explained that they were differently situated. It was true that they had received instructions from the legislature of Tennessee to ask Congress for the vacant lands for education. However, most of the land lay in his own district, and his constituents disagreed with the instructions of the legislature. He considered that he had "a higher authority, to which it was his duty and his pride ever to bow—his last instructions were from his own constituents, and these, in his estimation, took precedence of all others." He was proposing this amendment on behalf of the "hardy sons of the soil; men who had entered the country when it lay in cane, and opened in the wilderness a home for their wives and children." Many of them had once owned better homes with titles they thought were good. They had been pushed off their land, with all of the improvements they had made on it, by warrant holders with titles and warrants of older dates than their own. Some had suffered this cruel disappointment more than once. They had "been driven from improvement to improvement, and from home to home, till, in despair of ever realizing their early hopes, they had settled on lands that nobody would claim—on scraps and refuse fragments of the soil, which remained after all that was valuable had been first selected and occupied."

He then explained that though this portion of the country might be but a small part of the whole of Tennessee, embracing only a part of the district from which Mr. Polk came, the great mass of it was in the Congressional District from which he came, "and in fact made up the whole of that district." In the little scraps of land between the located tracts

the people for whom he was pleading had fixed their little homes. They had mingled the sweat of their brows with the soil they occupied, and by the hand of hard and perservering toil had earned the little comforts they possessed. Was it fair for the General Government to take away these humble cottages from them, and make a donation of the whole to the legislature of the State, for the purpose of raising up schools for the children of the rich. . . . Will you take away their little all and give it to the legislature to speculate upon? . . . Sir, my people think that those who live northeast of the dividing line have already made enough out of them. My district has already had to pay one hundred thousand dollars towards the erection of colleges in the northeast part of the State . . . but still more is now demanded, and I find myself under the necessity of defending one poor district against all the rest of the State of Tennessee. I shall do it; for I am dependent upon them for my station here; and so long as I hold a seat upon this floor I shall take their part against all who would exact upon them. Three hundred and five thousand acres of the best land in the district have already gone to satisfy warrants which I never believed to be just in principle . . . they had been issued to Revolutionary soldiers, who were dead, and had no heirs living, and I ever viewed the arrangements as unjust and oppressive.

When the measure was debated in the legislature of my State, I opposed it to the best of my poor ability, but we were overruled. . . . According to that arrangement, the Colleges got sixty thousand acres of our land. The University of North Carolina got one hundred and forty thousand acres more of it. After a little while, the demand for 96 thousand more was made. They demanded that this amount should be provided and secured: that I also opposed . . . . and in a little while the ninety six thousand acres had swelled to one hundred and five thousand. Yes, one hundred and five thousand acres taken out of one little district! You can readily believe that such a draft as that, made in 25-acre warrants, cut us up at an awful rate. The grant for the support of colleges drained us of fifty-two thousand five hundred dollars in cash. Ay, sir, in hard cash, wrung from the hands of the poor men, who live by the sweat of their brow. I repeat, that I was utterly opposed to this: not because I am the enemy of education, but because the benefits of education are not to be dispensed with an equal hand. This college system went into practice to draw a line of demarcation between the two classes of society—it separated the children of the rich from the children of the poor. The children of my people never saw the inside of a college in their lives, and never are likely to do so. Those who passed the act well knew that we never should derive any good from it: but they insisted that the land should be given up, and they sent State surveyors to survey it. The expenses of that survey pressed heavily on my constituents—it drove some of them to their wits end. Sir, I have seen the last blanket of a poor, but honest and industrious family, sold under the hammer of the sheriff, to pay for that survey.... Exactions like these were made on men whose whole worldly estate consisted of some twenty or thirty acres of the poorest land. Sir, it is for such men that I plead.... Will you not bestow it as a boon upon the unfortunate people who have nothing else in the world? There they are living in peace: they can there make shift to bring up their children. Some of them are widows, whose husbands fell while fighting your battles on the frontiers, None of them are rich; but they are an honest, industrious, hardy, persevering, kind-hearted people. I know them: I know their situation. I have shared the hospitality of their cottages, and been honored by their confidence with a seat in this assembly; and base and ungrateful, indeed, must I be, when I cease to remember it. No, sir, I cannot forget it: and if their little all is to be wrestled from them, for the purpose of State speculation; if a swindling machine is to be set up to strip them of what little the surveyors, and the colleges, and the warrant holders, have left them, it shall never be said that I sat by in silence, and refused, however humbly, to advocate their cause.

Whether David was writing his own speeches or not, the record shows that this statement of his position on the Western lands is accurate. This powerful speech no doubt left its mark in the minds of its hearers long after David had finished. His entire career testifies that his position was full-hearted, sincere, and honest—whatever the causes for the reversal of his position of a few months earlier, and whatever may be the judgment upon the simplicity of that position and the singleness of his motives. To call the state party a swindling machine on the floor of Congress took the sort of courage that could only have sprung from a deep feeling for those whom he was trying to defend.

Polk, in his reply to Crockett, tried to minimize the difference between them with the assertion that the state had already provided that the actual occupants should have a preference of entry, the first right to buy the land. Furthermore, he had prepared an amendment to make that stipulation more explicit. His amendment would have allowed the occupant first refusal of the land, provided he could match the highest bidder—a price magnified by the very improvements he had made on it. He said, hedging, that he was just as friendly to these settlers as anyone, but preferred leaving their interests to the state. He pointed out that the Federal Government had no surveyors or land offices or land records in Tennessee; that land could not be deeded without these aids; that inasmuch as the records of the state belonged to the state, the central government had no authority to take action requiring their use, and hence had no power, without going to the great expense of setting up land offices of its own, to deed land directly to these individuals or to order the state to do so, and that if the land were given to anyone, it *must* legally be given to the state.

Crockett answered that a mere right of preference of entry would be no protection to his constituents if the price which the land might command on the market, plus the cost of the survey, were more than the occupant could pay. As for the Federal Government's having no authority over the state surveyors—let the bill be passed; he would be the security that the surveyors would comply and do the surveying. "They love their fees and understand their interests too well to refuse," he said.

Mr. Wickliffe moved to amend Polk's amendment by inserting after the words *preference of entry* the words "without charge" (evidently meaning "without charge for the entry," not "without charge for the land"). He preferred Polk's amendment because it provided for the unoccupied as well as the occupied land. The Wickliffe amendment was then adopted. Crockett said that he would support Polk's amendment as amended, for the present, since it was better than the state's original bill, but that later he would move to strike out the whole and insert the amendment he had offered. Polk's amended amendment was then adopted.

When the question recurred on Crockett's amendment, the discussion definitely favored it, for no one knew exactly how much land Congress would be giving away under Polk's bill. David further scotched Polk by saying that whereas Polk had made it appear that the whole of the United States lands in Tennessee were settled upon, he, Crockett, did not believe that the one hundredth part was settled. Polk then took Crockett severely to task for "abandoning the whole delegation from the State, declaring openly that he would not obey the instructions from the Legislature, and going very far to impugn the purity and correctness of their Legislative proceedings." He continued that the lands were not for colleges, as David appeared to believe, but were for public schools and education of the poor, and that Crockett was embarrassing the whole issue and the whole charge by his amendment. With this the House adjourned on January 5.

According to David's Circular, Mr. Lea, of Tennessee, moved the postponement of the amendment, "alleging, indirectly, the death of Mrs. Jackson as the cause why he was not then prepared to discuss the subject." David was of the opinion that it would have passed had the question been then put, and that Lea's motion was only a maneuver to delay a vote. And he relates that when the question was taken up again on January 12, Mr. Lea opposed the Crockett amendment in a lengthy and able speech. Lea pointed out that Crockett's amendment took care of only a portion of the land and did nothing about education, whereas the state's version took care of all the public land and provided for education.

When Lea had finished, Mr. Samuel P. Carson, David's friend from North Carolina, rose to say that had the vote been taken on the fifth, he would have favored the amendment of "his honorable friend from Tennessee," Mr. Crockett, but that he had changed his mind (having no doubt heard from the North Carolina politicians in the meantime!). He said that he had drafted an amendment with the object of meeting the views "of his honorable friend from the Western District of Tennessee," his amendment being the same as David's own, except for an extra provision *reserving enough land to satisfy yet outstanding North Carolina warrant claims!*

In reply to Lea, Crockett explained why he had supported Polk's bill at the last session. He said that during the last session he had suggested to Polk, chairman of the committee reporting the bill out, the propriety of such a bill as he was now advocating (Polk did not deny it), but that Polk had not agreed and had presented the other bill. He, Crockett, had then supported Polk's bill, feeling certain that it would fail to pass and hoping thereby to gain the united support of his colleagues behind his own bill. He was sorry to find that he had been a very mistaken judge of policy. Now he was forced to face the delegation and the three best lawyers in the state alone. As for Mr. Sam Carson's amendment, he objected to it. There was plenty of good

land in Tennessee. If there were yet unsatisfied North Carolina warrants, let them be satisfied out of good land, not out of the little home-
steads of those who had titles, but not good titles, and who had been
already often uprooted. He pointed out, further, that both Tennessee
and North Carolina delegations had only last session acknowledged
that they knew of no more land warrants to be satisfied.

He said that if the state ever got its hands on this land it would set
a price upon it that would be too high. He saw plainly that his colleagues, rather than have his amendment pass, were trying to kill both
their own bill and his amendment. His own proposal was open and
honest, but the Polk amendment was a perfect trap which, under the
pretense of protecting the occupants, threatened them with loss of
their land. David said the North Carolina warrants were of a multi-
plying nature: they bred like rabbits; if gentlemen wished more to
come, they had only to give encouragement to the new demands.

His appeal was evidently a strong one. To judge from the remarks of
others in the debate, he aroused a great deal of spontaneous fellow
sympathy. In connection with Crockett's possible compact with forces
outside his own state, the conclusion of his Circular Letter is interesting: "I was utterly astonished at one thing. It was, that while
gentlemen from other states were aiding me in what I consider so
humane an attempt...my own colleagues were bending all their
powers against me. The measure met with no serious opposition (with
one exception) [The exception must have been his friend Carson.]
which did not come from them."

The bill was talked to death. On January 14, both bill and amendment were laid on the table indefinitely by a vote of 103 to 63. The
bill was not to be reconsidered until the next congressional session. The
tenor of the remarks in the debate strongly suggest that Crockett was
right in his opinion that had the bill come to a vote on January 5
it would have passed.

Crockett's defiance of the state machine naturally produced a strong
reaction within his party. The immediate party reaction is revealed
in a heretofore unpublished letter of January 16 from James K. Polk
to several of his constituents, two days after the indefinite postponement of the bill. One need not question what is reported in this letter
as fact; but one cannot accept, merely on the basis of the integrity of
Polk's character, his opinion as to what David's allegiances ought to

have been. When he says that Crockett had broken with the party machine, we know that he speaks the fact as far as he is properly informed. When he implies that Crockett *betrayed* the party machine, making his own allegiance the single measure of all proper allegiances, he is merely engaging in the venerable pastime of justifying himself by calling his opponent wrong. As Polk, a loyal party man, saw the issue, Crockett betrayed the party when he broke with it; as David saw it, he had merely relinquished a lesser allegiance that stood in conflict with a much greater one.

In his letter to Mr. Davison M. Millen of Fayetteville, Tennessee, Polk states that

the cause of its defeat is to be attributed in great degree to the course taken by our man *Crocket*. . . . He associated himself with our political enemies, and declared in presence of Mr. Blair of Ten. and others, that he would vote for any measure any member wished him to vote for, provided he would vote for his foolish amendment and against the original bill. . . . You may suppose that such a man under no circumstances could do us much harm . . . . but in this instance, many of the *Adams men*, not having forgotten the violence of the recent political struggle, and feeling more than willing to disappoint Tennessee and her delegation, seized upon the opportunity to use *Crockett*, and to operate upon him through his measure, for their own political purposes, and hence you see such men as *Buchner* of Ky. *Woods* of Ohio, Mallary of Vermont, Culpepper of N.C. making speeches for his proposition absurd as it was. . . . I forbear to comment in detail, on the disgraceful and disrespectful terms, in which Crockett was in the habit of speaking of his own State and her Legislature, further than to say that the whole delegation feel humiliated and can but regret that any one from our country, should have Cooperated with some of our bitterest and most vindictive political enemies, men, some of them of "Coffin handbill" and "six militiamen" memory, and joined them in denouncing the Legislature of his state on the floor of Congress. Gales and some of the *Adams*ites during the whole discussion, were nursing him, and dressing up and reporting speeches for him, which he never delivered as reported, & which all who know him, know he never did. Rely upon it he can be and has been opperated upon by our enemies. We cant trust him an inch. It is whispered that he intends to vote for *Gales* and *Seaton*, for public printers, against *Duff Green*. . . . If it shall hereafter become necessary . . . the balance of the delegation will notice him, under their own signatures. We do not wish in advance to do so, for that would give him consequence, and might have the appearance with those unacquainted with the facts, of an attack upon him, and thus excite a sympathy in his behalf which he does not deserve. This letter therefore is not written for publication in the newspapers:—but is addressed to you as a known friend, to furnish you with the facts, to meet any thing that may be said, until we can have an opportunity of meeting him personally, and exposing his conduct if necessary.[12]

Obviously, Polk protests too much about the absurdity of David's amendment, and the careful reader will observe that the letter does not aim at being meticulously fair. The great humiliation of the delegates at David's disaffection is amusing in light of the later disaffection of the rest of them—the loyal wheel-horse Polk excepted. Since there were squatters within Polk's district too, he could not afford to face his own constituents on a clear-cut issue of supporting the state's position as over against David's. His own remarks following the introduction of David's amendment are an indication of this fact, and Polk's very amendment of his own bill is a tribute to the justice of David's position. I believe Polk here tells the truth as he saw it—but not all of the truth as he knew it.

When the Twenty-first Congress convened early in December Crockett immediately began to maneuver in behalf of his land bill. On December 23 he arose on the floor to state that, though his bill had been rejected at the last session, a motion for its reconsideration had been laid on the table, and he now moved to consider that motion. The House promptly defeated the motion 86 to 74.[13] When, on December 5, he moved to appoint a *select* committee to consider the disposal of the Western Refuse Lands,[14] Polk promptly countered with a move to amend Crockett's motion and refer the matter instead to his *standing* committee on Public Lands. David's objection was sustained by a vote of 92 to 65 approving his amendment and rejecting Polk's. The vote seemed to augur well for David; unfortunately, whenever the vote turned on a really decisive point, his majority melted away.

On December 22 David's submission of an apparently innocuous resolution was the occasion for bitter wrangling with other Tennessee representatives. His resolution merely proposed that all the petitions and papers pertaining to Western Refuse Lands should be turned over to the Select Committee already established by his earlier motion. Blair of Tennessee opposed the resolution. Isaacs of Tennessee severely criticized Crockett for the phrase "to withdraw memorial" instead of "to discharge the Committee on Public Lands from Consideration of," and censured him for talking about having "personally . . . taken charge of the matter in Committee, as if he were the only member from the State of Tennessee interested in it." David replied that the purpose of the resolution was merely to make available for Eastern members of the new Committee not familiar with the case all the pertinent evidence. The reaction of the rest of the Tennessee delegation to his having "taken charge" of this special committee loaded by himself with Eastern members is significant. David's ineptness is revealed in such spontaneous exchanges. Gales and Seaton could not hide his mistakes of speech and strategy when these were the subject of the discussion.

This picayunish quarrelling with David, this quibbling over the very phrases he employed, must have struck Polk as a too obvious disclosure that the state machine was opposing Crockett's plan, not on its merits, but as a party policy. He must have sensed that such persecution might redound to Crockett's benefit, for he now rose to explain his former objection to turning the question of Refuse Lands over to a select committee. It had been based, he said, on the belief that a report from a standing committee would have a greater weight with the House than a report from a select one. He and Crockett's other colleagues had no desire to "interfere with his rights and privileges here." What he obviously meant was that they had no desire to *appear* to interfere. Nor had he told the whole truth about desiring to steer the question to the standing committee. That the acknowledged spokesman of Jackson and the Tennessee delegation felt it necessary to call a halt to this yapping at Crockett's heels reveals, as clearly as words can, the spirit of the House at this juncture, as sensed by Polk.

It is at this point that we reach the pinnacle of David's popularity in the House. Crockett's motion, modified by Isaacs' phrase, now passed 90 to 67. David had lost two votes from his previous majority.

Once more on December 31 "Mr. Crockett made an unsuccessful motion for the House to reconsider the Tennessee Land Bill. The House refused . . . 69 to 97." [15] Again, on January 6, 1831, "Mr. Crockett made another ineffectual attempt to get up the Tennessee land bill. He called for the yeas and nays on his motion, and they were ordered . . . ; and, being taken, it was decided in the negative— yeas 89, nays 92." [16]

Crockett's predicament was plain to see. With a new Congressional election only a few months away, it seemed impossible even to get his bill considered, much less passed. Yet, in a strategic effort to secure passage of the bill, he had alienated Jackson's friends. His call for the yeas and nays was for the record, and changed the vote, evidently, of some who had been voting against him. It constituted an admission of defeat for the duration of that Congress.

The Tennessee Land Bill came up again on April 26. Mr. Mallary, with a view to going into a committee of the Whole on the Tariff Bill, moved to postpone the intervening orders of the day, including David's land bill. "Mr. Crockett made an earnest effort to prevent [it] from being postponed; but Mr. Mallary's motion prevailed...." [17] A week later, Mallary again moved to postpone consideration of this bill: "Mr. Crockett expressed a hope that the bill would not be postponed. He would rather the bill were taken up and rejected, than that it should thus be sported with, as this would be the third time it had been postponed." [18] He went on to state a number of facts about the bill, and urged several reasons against its further postponement. The motion to postpone was then defeated 81 to 62, but Crockett's majority was slipping.

An amendment was now offered by Barringer and accepted by Crockett; George Grennell of Massachusetts opposed the bill in a long speech and "Crockett earnestly defended." Mr. Samuel F. Vinton of Ohio replied to Crockett. Mr. Vinton moved to lay it on the table and called for the yeas and nays. Thomas Chilton of Kentucky called for the previous question and was seconded. That motion was defeated 86 to 75. The main question was then put for the bill's ingrossment, and the bill was rejected 90 to 69.

On the next day, however, Grennell of Massachusetts, who had opposed it the day before, moved reconsideration of the third reading, stating that he did so at the request of Mr. Crockett. Crockett was willing to accept Vinton's amendment because he had become convinced that the state had no legal claims to the land. His great object was to secure the occupants in the possession of their lands. As he explained their condition and the necessity for their relief, he unwisely animadverted to the conduct of North Carolina and her University in relation to the land titles in Tennessee. At this point Mr. Bell of Tennessee submitted lengthy objections to reconsideration, and the

North Carolina representatives felt called upon to defend the unsullied reputation of their state. Mr. Sam Carson and Mr. Barringer denied Crockett's aspersion. Mr. Conner, not to be left out when this should be read back home, rushed warmly to the aid of his colleagues and his beleaguered state.

Mr. Cave Johnson of Tennessee, recently elected member from the West, now zealously supported the move for reconsideration and gave his entire support to the purpose of the bill. However, McCoy of Virginia moved to lay it on the table. Though Crockett opposed this move, McCoy persisted in his motion, and it finally carried "without a division." [19] Complete defeat was thus narrowly averted, and the bill was saved for consideration again at the next session. By his lack of aplomb, David had alienated some of his friends and, at least for the time being, lost a good cause. Henceforth, the battle was to be downhill, for the policy of his Eastern friends was not to give away public lands in small tracts to the poor, but to give it away in large tracts to the rich.

In a circular letter to his constituents on February 28, 1831, David reviewed his efforts, during the last four years, to secure action on the land bill. It speaks of Polk's having taken advantage of David's illness during the first session to put through a motion "to dispose of the government land in the District" by having it "referred to a Select Committee of which he was Chairman." In justifying his opposition to Polk's bill, David stresses the inequality of any struggle over the issue in the state legislature, where five Western members would be pitted against 35 opponents, and asks "what chance our five members ... would have to prevent a price being put upon that land, that would place it out of the reach of a large majority of the settlers, who have made valuable improvements on the land."

Because he proposed giving the land directly to the settlers, his colleagues opposed him *en masse* out of fear that his opposition might be successful. Against him in the House were pitted "six of the greatest lawyers of Tennessee," with another two "electioneering against" his proposal. He contends that after he had agreed, at a later session, to a compromise proposed by his colleagues (sale of the land for 12½ cents an acre for "the common school fund in the State of Tennessee") in return for their agreement to support the bill, every last one of them except Colonel Cave Johnson had opposed the bill, which was thereupon defeated by a few votes. Further, when as a result of this betrayal he prepared a substitute in place of the original bill designed to give a pre-emption right of "two hundred acres to each occupant at twelve and a half cents per acre" and two years to pay it off, this measure failed to pass only because, "the eastern members voting for it," his "colleagues made it a party question upon that ground and beat me three votes—with the whole delegation voting against me." He cried out in righteous indignation that:

instead of trying to aid me in procuring for the poor industrious occupant his home, they all united in running the influence of the Jackson party against me: it was the Jackson party that defeated the measure at the last session. When it has come to this, to defeat such a measure, merely to gratify the ambition of partizans, it is enough to make every lover of his country look down with indignation upon all such parties.

Actually, the vote which Crockett says above was on the land bill, was rather on his motion to reconsider the bill.

At this point David turns to review the relative expenses between the Jackson and Adams administrations, citing for his purpose more than five pages of figures (identical with those used in Chilton's Circular) from a communication which James Clark of Kentucky had made to his own constituents. This report tended to show that Jackson's expenses had been much greater, though he had paid less on the public debt, and jibed that "this is a startling attitude for public affairs to assume under the auspices of 'Reform and Retrenchment.' " Clark's explanation is that Jackson "has administered the Government, not on public but on party and personal principles." This oratory concludes the long excerpt from Clark.

In closing his Circular, David reverts to the land bill, a subject "near to my heart":

... since those remarks were penned, my attention has been called to it by letters ... received from gentlemen residing within the District. By them I am informed that a general alarm has been taken by the occupants; and that speculating warrant holders have taken advantage of that alarm, and in many instances practiced the grossest frauds and impositions upon them. This I heard with deep regret. For I call upon my conscience to bear me witness when I assert that no set of men on earth possess so great a share of my sympathetic regard, and my anxiety for their protection. It is asked why I have not done something to save them? Why I have not entered into some arrangement with my colleagues to secure the land to them? I can only reply that I thought I had done so. After it was ascertained that my first proposition would fail, I prepared a substitute for it, which I understood as being satisfactory—and which I again repeat I believe would have passed without difficulty, if they had not prevented me from getting the subject before the House. Heaven knows that I have done all that a mortal could do, to save the people, and the failure was not my fault, but the fault of others.

In order that the voters might decide whether he or his colleagues has been acting in good faith with them, he appended a copy of the bill. Its substance, in brief, provided: For anyone who by December 1, 1830, had "indicated a disposition to make a permanent settlement" on the public lands west of the line, 200 acres at 12½ cents per acre, with various stipulations: that previous State surveys should be held valid up to 200 acres, to include in every case the improvements of the occupants; that in the event 200 acres could not be secured in one tract, it could be allowed in two; that the state surveyors be responsible for making the surveys and legalizing them; that the fees of the surveyors, registers, and other officers should be the customary ones; that two years should be allowed for the occupant to observe the conditions, "during which time their improvements shall be secured against any and every other warrant, location, and entry made within the period"; and that two occupants having improvements contiguous in such a way as to prevent their getting two hundred acres each should have the available land divided equally between them, with due regard to quality as well as to quantity of land, so as to interfere with the improvements of neither.

David concludes his Circular with a warning against the designs of his enemies. Asserting that no one really in favor of securing the occupants in their lands could object to his bill, he brands as false the claim that only his "obstinacy defeated the measure." The motive behind this charge is obvious: "to break me down—and destroy your confidence in me." He warns that if they are successful in their goal, they "may get a man in my place who will suit their purposes better" —someone to "run at their bidding and do as they direct. This they know I wont do." Prophesying that "the party in power . . . are blowing up among themselves; and by another Congress will not be able to defeat anyone," he urged all occupants to "hold fast to your possessions, and the justice of your country will yet secure you. The party in power, like Jonah's gourd, grew up quickly, and will quickly fall." He vowed that if his constituents will only give him their support in the coming campaign,

I shall yet have the unspeakable pleasure, of seeing you seated by firesides which you can safely call your own. You know that I am a poor man; and that I am a plain man. I have served you long enough in peace, to enable you to judge whether I am honest or not—I never deceived you—I never will deceive you. I have fought with you and for you in war, and you know whether I love my country, and ought to be trusted. I thank you for what you have done for me, and I hope that you will not forsake me to gratify those who are my enemies and yours.

With best wishes for your prosperity and happiness, I am your friend and fellow citizen,

David Crockett

Chapter 8

FLOOD TIDE

ALTHOUGH the passage of the land bill remained foremost in Crockett's thinking during his congressional career, much about the man, his change in allegiance, and his political growth, may be ascertained from the role he played in other legislative considerations. An important area which was frequently discussed in one form or another was internal improvements.

On March 30, 1830, the Buffalo to New Orleans Road Bill was introduced, proposing to build a national road to connect Buffalo, N.Y., with New Orleans, La. Standifer and Blair of Tennessee favored it, provided it were located in or near their districts. North Carolina wanted it run "more centrally"—that is, closer to North Carolina. Polk revealed Jackson's thinking by opposing these proposals and internal improvements generally. His colleagues, however, contemplated the bill only as it addressed itself to their constituents. As Polk said, "This ... is the iniquity of this whole system of internal improvements; it does address itself to the local interests of sections; ... and whole masses are bought up ... with the prospect of local advantage...." He pointed out that ninety-nine hundredths of their constituents would think the bill wholly inexpedient if a route not favoring them were adopted. Here were the grounds of Jackson's approaching veto of the Maysville Road Bill.

Crockett submitted an amendment after, and despite, these remarks, providing that the road should run in a direct route from Washington and stop at Memphis, in his own district. He had, he said, given a pledge to his constituents to "oppose certain tariff measures" and to work towards lifting "duties from salt, sugar, coffee, and other articles" important to them "as well as the rich." He regretted that Congressmen "too often forget the interest of their employers"—the people whose servants they are. Crockett said he did "not mean to oppose internal improvements" altogether, though he could not go, "as the Kentuckian says, 'the whole hog.' " He would go only "so far as not to oppress." [1] He would support the bill with his amendment, but otherwise he would have to oppose it. He estimated that the adoption of his amendment would, by cutting off five hundred miles from the road's length, "save, in the outset, upwards of 750,000 dollars." Besides, he

would ... thank any man to show ... this committee the use of a road which will run parallel with the Mississippi for five or six hundred miles. Will any man say that the road would be preferred to the river...? And if the road should so terminate [that is, at Memphis], it would be on the direct route from this city to the province of Texas, which I hope will one day belong to the United States, and that at no great distance of time....

Furthermore, he pointed out that such a road would be impassable in winter, the very time when the frontiers would be attacked, if at all. The road would not serve the purpose for which it was intended, because in the entire eighteen counties of his district "there is not a spot of ground twenty-five miles from a navigable stream." Better to spend public funds on "clearing out those rivers, than in opening roads."

He was astonished that some of the representatives from the East were suddenly so solicitous of the South's need for roads. This eagerness to expend public money on the South was a startling change of Eastern policy. Unless he was deceived, it was "merely a bait to cover the hook.... We may bid farewell to all hopes of ever reducing duties on anything...." He himself could honestly support the bill only if he should "discover a determination to squander the public funds in some way," in which case he would "strive to 'come in for snacks.' " But he was firmly convinced that the proposed Bill was devised by "our Eastern brethren ... to place ... the South and West in" the dilemma of being "compelled to keep up the duties to their highest extent," in order to raise the fifty million dollars required to complete the road. It might even be necessary to "resort to a system of direct taxation."

The *Debates* reveal that on April 14 the bill was rejected, though David, after all, voted *for* it *without* his amendment. On the next day, when there was a move to reconsider, David delivered an interesting statement for a states' rights devotee:

> For his part, he had no opinion of this government's giving away power to the States. Suppose the States should turn round, and say, you shall not make a road? He would vote to go through any gentleman's state with a road or a canoe, that was for the good of the union. He did not believe that he should ever give up that doctrine.

The original speech appears too complex for David's reasoning, expressing as it does so clearly the relationship between huge expenditures for internal improvements and the inevitable consequences in high tariffs, which David opposed. Yet, when Jackson used precisely the same argument in vetoing the Maysville Road Bill and the whole system of Pork Barrel internal improvements, David violently opposed the Jackson position. This bill proposing to authorize a subscription of stock to the Maysville and Lexington Turnpike Road in Kentucky was debated on April 29. Crockett obtained the floor to state that he rose, not to make a speech—for he was convinced that if they spoke five days upon it not a vote would change—but to call for the previous question. The bill passed 102 to 86. Jackson vetoed it, using it as the occasion for proclaiming an anti-internal-improvements policy for the future.[2] There followed a motion to override Jackson's veto, which commanded only a simple majority, not the necessary two-thirds. David voted to override.[3]

Again when Jackson took much the same position with reference to Nullification which Crockett had taken on states' rights, David's sympathy was not with Jackson but rather with the Nineteenth Century Dixiecrats. On the other hand, if he had made a deal with certain men in the East on some matters, in the interests of his land bill, he certainly had not yet gone over to them in his general point of view. One should note, too, his interests both in navigable streams and in the annexation of Texas. Finally, his vote in favor of the Buffalo to New Orleans Road Bill, despite his vow to oppose it, is indicative of the complexity of the whole matter of internal improvements under the American system of splinter politics, which tends to emphasize immediate local gains to the exclusion of long-time national interests. In view of David's involvement in this system, a brief discussion of it is in order.

There were at least three sides to the question of internal improvements. The long-settled East had, under an old system of improvements, developed good roads and had good harbors, lighthouses, and so on. It could not, therefore, in splinter politics, be expected to show much interest in internal improvements elsewhere, except as a bait for the sake of enforcing tariffs. In the West, on the other hand, there were few and inadequate roads, the commerce of the country was largely dependent on the river systems. Where these were unimproved for navigation, the people were greatly handicapped. Inaccessible rivers tended to isolate them. Their country was new; they were planting a civilization in a wilderness; and they needed easy, quick ingress and egress for supplies, communication, and the locomotion that generally sustains life. In addition, their poverty precluded raising the large funds necessary for the needed improvements. Yet they were engaged in an undertaking from which the whole nation would benefit, in opening up new lands and conquering the wilds. They felt that internal improvements for them out of the general funds, especially in light of the enormous sums expended at an earlier date on the East and the Old South, was only a matter of justice.

From the point of view of the Chief Executive, whose responsibility was not to one section or another—not to a balancing of old grievances or injustices against new—but rather to the present and future state of the nation as a whole, there was still another side to the matter. He tended to see internal improvements as a pork barrel affair pyramiding the costs of government beyond all reason and out of all proportion to the good derived from the money spent, inasmuch as it was based primarily on sectional "grab" rather than on national need.

On May 1, 1830, the *Jackson Gazette* announced with pleasure that the Buffalo Road Bill had been defeated, listing those who had favored and those who had opposed. David wrote C. D. McLean, one of the editors, attempting to explain his vote. He said he believed that, had the bill passed, the road would have stopped at Memphis anyway, for he thought the engineers would have seen the wisdom of terminating it there when they came to survey. "My greatest object was to speak against duties on such articles as every poor man ... is compelled to consume in his family." ⁴

On the following February 24, 1831, the old matter of internal improvements arose again, in connection with the allocation of fifty thousand dollars to improve the navigation of the Ohio and Mississippi Rivers. Crockett advocated the appropriation at length, together with Mr. Wickliffe (Ky.), Mr. Verplanck (N.Y.), and Mr. Gilmore (Pa.). When a move to recommit the bill was made so that all analogous appropriations could be grouped and presented in separate bills, David opposed on several grounds. First, that the true object was to destroy the bill. It was late in the final session of this Congress and, if recommitted, the bill could not be acted on by this body. Second, it was no surprise to hear these sentiments from that gentleman who made the motion (Lea, Tenn.), for they had heard the same from him a year ago. For his own part, David had always supported internal improvements and expected to be consistent in his support of it, at least until he was better informed than he was at present. He stated:

Although our great man at the head of the nation, has changed his course, I will not change mine. I would rather be politically dead than hypocritically immortalized. ... Those State rights gentlemen who are opposed to appropriations by the General Government for purposes of internal improvement, may think that the navigation of those rivers ought to be improved by the States. I should like to know what State is to take charge of the Mississippi, and to clear the obstructions of that river.⁵

Polk's expressed hope that appropriations for certain surveys would be stricken from the bill was tantamount to a warning that, if they were not, Jackson might veto it under his new policy established with the Maysville Bill veto. Crockett hoped they would not be stricken out. He said that he had been a supporter of the administration, and that he still supported it:

I was also a supporter of this administration after it came into power, and until the Chief Magistrate changed the principles which he professed before his election. When he quitted those principles, I quit him. I am yet a Jackson man in principles, but not in name. ... I shall insist upon it that I am still a Jackson man, but General Jackson is not; he has become a Van Buren man. I hope the motion to recommit will not prevail.

That motion did not prevail, losing 62-107. When Polk then moved to strike out the $25,000 for surveys and Crockett and Buchanan advocated retaining them, the motion to strike them out was negatived 66-109, the Tennessee delegation splitting evenly. On this note of stubborn opposition to the Jackson party, Crockett's activities in his second Congress come to an end.

The two expressions that he would rather be "politically dead than hypocritically immortalized" and that he was "still a Jackson man but General Jackson is not" both occur also in the anonymous *Life* of 1833. We also find the former in Crockett's next letter in August, 1832. The remarks about Jackson's change of position referred to the fact that Jackson had earlier advocated the building of national roads. As a military man he had been made acutely aware of the inadequacy of the transportation facilities for troops and supplies. A national road, however, was a matter of "internal improvements." He had been in favor of roads; he must therefore have been in favor of internal improvements. Since he had now vetoed a road bill he must now be against them. There were also some other matters on which Jackson appeared to have changed his position.

David's essentially democratic spirit and his sympathy for the poor is again revealed in connection with the debate over appropriations for the Military Academy at West Point. A resolution was to be considered demanding statistical information on such matters as the distribution of patronage at the Academy in the past, the types of students expelled, the percentages of students from the richer and from the poorer classes, the percentages of fathers or guardians who were members of Congress or other officers of the General Government, the percentages of appointees by states, and so on.

Many amendments had been offered to cripple the resolution. On January 22, 1830, David rose to oppose these interferences with the intent of the resolution.[6] He was, he said, opposed to the whole idea of West Point, but it was possible his opposition resulted from want of information. Because of the views of his state on the subject, he labored under considerable responsibility. The Legislature had proposed to instruct the delegation to oppose West Point Academy; and though the instructions had not passed, his immediate constituents would expect him to promote the fullest inquiry into the matter. He hoped the resolution would be adopted as originally submitted. If anything were wrong with the operation of the Academy, the House should know it. Unless he could get full information, he would vote against every appropriation in its behalf. He demanded the yeas and nays on the adoption of the resolution. After further discussion, the resolution was referred back to the Committee on Military Affairs, obviously for emasculation, by a vote of 91 to 72.

Consequently, and true to his word, Crockett moved the following five resolutions on February 25:

That if the bounty of the government is to be at all bestowed, the destitute poor, and not the rich..., are the objects who most claim it....

That no one class of citizens...has an exclusive right to demand or receive...more than an equal and ratable proportion of the funds of the national treasury, which is replenished by a common contribution, and, in some instances, more at the cost of the poor man, who has but little to defend, than that of the rich man, who seldom fights to defend himself or his property.

That each and every institution, calculated at public expense, and under the patronage and sanction of the Government, to grant exclusive privileges except in consideration of public services, is not only aristocratic, but a downright invasion of the rights of citizens, and a violation of... "the Constitution."

further, That the Military Academy at West Point is subject to the foregoing objections, inasmuch as those who are educated there receive their instruction at the public expense, and are generally the sons of the rich and influential, who are able to educate their own children. While the sons of the poor...are often neglected, or if educated...are superseded in the service by cadets educated at the West Point Academy.

Resolved, therefore,...That said institution should be abolished, and the appropriations annually made for its support be discontinued.[7]

David spoke at some length in behalf of these resolutions, in line with the logic of the resolutions. He said:

A man could fight the battles of his country, and lead his country's armies, without being educated at West Point. Jackson never went to West Point School, nor Brown—No, nor Governor Carroll; nor did Colonel Cannon, under whom he had served...in defense of his country, though he mentioned it not to boast of it. He and thousands of other poor men had never been to West Point.

The truth was, he went on, that the academy did not suit the people of our country. Men who were raised there were "too nice to work; they are first educated there for nothing, and then they must have salaries to support them after they leave there"—for doing nothing.

A great deal had been said in the House about retrenchment, he continued, and the House had spent several weeks' time in trying to dismiss a poor little draftsman who all agreed had been useful. If they were going to retrench, let them do it so that they could feel it, on such a matter as this. He had intended, when the appropriation bill came up in Committee, to move to strike out this appropriation, and had waited until 3:00 o'clock when it was to have been taken up. It did not come up, and after he had left, the bills were taken up and passed through Committee. He wished, however, to see how the House stood, and requested the yeas and nays on his resolutions. McDuffie of South Carolina interposed that in view of the importance of the resolutions, they ought not to be acted on hastily. He moved that they be laid on the table until they could be printed for examination by the members. The motion carried.

On April 1, when the bill for appropriations for Fortifications was introduced, David moved to strike out that for erecting workshops at West Point.[8] The motion was emphatically rejected. By his peevishness and obstinacy even in small matters, by his growing unwillingness to play the game and take his defeats gracefully, David, it appears, was gradually losing the support of the House.

Crockett took a similar stand with reference to payment of Revolutionary War Pensions, but in this matter he stood shoulder to shoulder with the rest of the Tennessee delegation. In opposing these pensions, Crockett gave two reasons:

That by the proposed bill pensions were to be granted to those who had no more than a thousand dollars..., whereas in his country, a man with a thousand dollars was well off and did not require governmental aid....

That the bill provided for none but those of the continental ["regular" army] line and excluded all the volunteers and militia men who fought in the old war, who were old and who had been knocking at the door of Congress for years. He himself marched into the field in the last struggle with his gun and there discovered who had fought the bravest, the regulars or the volunteers and militia. When regular troops were living bountifully, the militia were in a state of starvation. I came here to do justice; and I will do justice, or I will do nothing. For God's sake, if you do extend charity to one class, do so to all. I voted against the old officers' bill last session, because you would not attach the soldiers to them, who fought with them side by side. Now, sir, if you cut off the volunteers and militia, I will vote against this bill.... If you do not adopt the amendment of the gentleman from North Carolina and attach the militia and volunteers as proposed by Mr. Chilton, of Kentucky, I will enter my protest against the bill, and believe that I have acted honestly.[9]

Here again, as in the West Point resolutions, is a clear illustration of Frederick Jackson Turner's thesis of the effect of the frontier in formation of the independent, democratic American spirit. When the amendment to make the bill also apply to the volunteers was defeated, James K. Polk spoke against the original bill. In the final vote *every single one of the Tennessee delegation from the West opposed it* —though the bill overwhelmingly carried, 122 to 56.

An important bill dealing with Indian rights came before the House during David's career. The *Debates* record no word he spoke for or against the Indian Bill from the time it was first introduced on February 24 until it finally passed on third reading on May 24, 1830. Yet, in that same year, a volume was published containing several pages entitled, "A Sketch of the Remarks of the Hon. David Crockett, Representative from Tennessee, On the Bill for the Removal of the Indians, Made in the House of Representatives, Wednesday, May 19, 1830." [10] Evidently someone wrote a speech for Crockett that he never got around to delivering.

Perhaps David's alliance with Eastern interests explains this discrepancy. There was much feeling in the East, from Pennsylvania north, strongly sympathetic to the Indians and opposed to the bill to move them all onto reservations west of the Mississippi. In view of what some of the states were doing to the Indians, there was some justice to this intervention by the Federal Government. In fact, at the time of the debate over the bill, the Society of Friends of America had a memorial before Congress advocating the Indians' cause. This volume of speeches was published in the East soon after the adjournment of Congress in order to exploit the great sympathy felt there for the Indians. Evidently the inclusion in that volume of a spurious speech by David was part of the Whig plan to build him into an anti-Jacksonite of national proportions.

Crockett states in his Circular Letter that he cast his vote against removal of the Indians. It is strange that he proclaimed that vote. It is not strange that he uttered no words which could be printed in the *Debates* and sent back to a constituency which had little love for Indians and much sympathy with those who wished to remove them from coveted land. One would gather from the facts of his biography that David's love for Indians was new-found and short-lived. The general environment out of which he had come influenced him: his participation in war against the Creeks, the Indian massacre of his grandparents, the general feelings about the Indians along the frontier, where, greedy for new land, the frontiersman lived amid continual skirmishes with the Indians, in constant fear of surprise attacks against his family. These conditions, which had existed in David's life at least as late as 1820, created in the backwoodsman an inhuman attitude toward Indians. Nor was there any evidence of the new sympathetic attitude in David's cold and hostile account of "killing them like dogs" in the war of 1812—an account written in late 1833. In fact, there is a remarkable discrepancy between the magnanimity of the 1830 "speech" and the cold realism of the 1833 narrative. When he came to explain his vote against the removal bill in the *Autobiography*, he slipped back into a role of tender sympathy at great odds with his point of view of a few weeks earlier. Whatever he may have thought his position was, I suspect it was in reality whatever it needed to be to oppose Jackson and to build David up in the East without *too* dangerously undermining him in the West. Jackson, of course, was in favor of the bill to move the Indians west.

The content of David's printed speech was slanted for an exclusively Eastern audience. It made excessive claims for the courage of his position; four times asserted a primary allegiance to the Deity rather than to his own constituents; repeatedly protested the clearness of his own conscience; gave a personal history of his legislative and educational careers, emphasizing the self-made backwoodsman legend in a sort of romantic Fenimore Cooper tradition of the noble savage; and referred to the "amicable" relations originally existing between the Indians and the Puritan Fathers. Especially does this ringing in of the Deity to justify opposition to his constituents seem completely out of character for Crockett.

On January 31 a small matter arose which perhaps softens the picture already drawn of David's attitude toward Indians or hardens the picture of his hatred of the Tennessee state machine. It is interesting to note David engaged in a difference of opinion with Clay. David presented the petition of three Cherokee Indians who were entitled to a reserve of 640 acres of land each, and moved its reference to the

Committee of Claims. Clay suggested that the proper committee for referral would be the Committee on Public Lands. David objected, emphasizing that these Indians had been dispossessed of their land by white men, had brought suit for its recovery, but were too poor to employ counsel. When they had thrown themselves on the mercy of Tennessee for benefit of the pauper law in order to be supplied with counsel, the benefit of that law had been refused them. He hoped that the petition would go to the Committee of Claims. Mr. Williams moved its reference to the Judiciary Committee. After conversation between Messrs. Clay, Williams, Whittlesey, and others, the petition was finally referred to the Committee of Claims, in accordance with David's request.[11]

On February 11 David joined in opposing the Jackson-supported bill for $100,000 to compensate Susan Decatur, wife of Stephen Decatur. The bill was defeated. David voted in the negative [12] against a motion for reconsideration, which also failed. In a letter written two days later, Crockett gave expression to open and violent anti-Jackson sentiments. As he had stated earlier to McClung, he estimated that Jackson's popularity was waning; he now felt that he could oppose him with impunity. The letter, written to A. M. Hughes on February 13, reads in part:

The Senate is handling the P M general with out gloves Mr Claton has laid that departmint open to the world in its true Coulers for refusing to answer the enquire made by the committee—Mr. Grundy has introduced a Resolution in the Senate to prohibit any man who has been reformed out of that office from giving testamony—This is Carrying proscription to the full extent that a man who has been proscribed for opinion Sake are not to be entitled to his oath this is high times in this bosted land of liberty the truth is Mr Barry has expended all the money that Mr McLean made for the Country and now we Cannot pass the post office & post Road Bill for want of money to Carry it into oppiration without Congriss make a large appropriation this is the effect of this glorious Sistom of retrenchment & reforme this is the effect of turning out men that knows their duty to accomodate a Set of Jackson worshipers what they lack in quality must be made up in quantity Can any honist people have the like of this put upon them I for one Cannot nor will not I would See the whole of them hung up at the devil before I will Submit to Such Carryings on as this I did not come to Cloke their extravigancy to let them make a Speculation of this government their partizens hire reminds me of Some large dogs I have Seen here with their Collers on with letters engraved on the Coller *My dog*—& the mans name on the Coller. I have not got a Coller Round my neck marked my dog with the name of Andrew Jackson on it—becaus I would not take the Coller Round my neck I was herld from their party

There will an explosion take place this week that will tare their party into a Sunder Mr Calhoun is Coming out with a Circular or a publication of the Correspondance betwen him & the President that will blow their little Red Fox or aleaus Martin van buren in to atoms—then you will See Genl Duff Green Come out upon thim with all of his powars this will Rais a fuss in the Camps....

P S you Can use this letter as you pleas I stand pledged to Sustain this to be a true fact [13]

John McLean, of Ohio, had been commissioned Postmaster General during the administration of James Monroe and retained this office under Adams. Shortly after Jackson's inauguration a new man, William T. Barry of Kentucky was commissioned Postmaster General. Under Barry, huge deficits were discovered in Post Office funds. Whether Barry or McLean was responsible has never been settled. Since Jackson had campaigned on a platform of noncorruption, "retrenchment, and reform" the shortage played into the hands of Jackson's enemies. Barry, however, retained office until May 1, 1835. "Claton" was Augustin Smith Clayton of Georgia, who had been a Presidential elector on the Democratic ticket of Jackson and Calhoun earlier and who was elected in 1831 as a States Rights Democrat to fill the unexpired term of Wilson Lumpkin.[14] Clayton was, in all probability, the author of Crockett's so-called "biography" of Martin Van Buren.

The reference to the Calhoun Circular has to do with the break which had developed between Jackson and his Vice-President, John C. Calhoun, following remarks Calhoun was reputed to have made years earlier about Jackson's conduct of military affairs in the field. As a result of this break and of Jackson's Nullification Proclamation, Calhoun was to resign the Vice-Pre idency on December 28, 1832. Already Duff Green and his paper had been replaced on December 30, 1830, by Francis P. Blair of Kentucky and the *Globe*, as the official Jackson party organ. As David's letter reveals, Green and his paper were already taking the side of Calhoun in this split.

The indignation in this letter is evidently David's own, but the stereotypy of some of the phrases suggests that they may have originated with others. The figure here employed of the dog collars with other men's names has in context all the homeliness of originality. Yet we cannot be sure that it was David's own. The same figure appears in Clarke's anonymous *Life*, and it was later twice employed by David in his *Autobiography*. It is possible that Clarke had already begun the *Life*, had first employed the expression there, and had caught David's fancy with it. Similarly when Chilton was helping David with the *Autobiography*, several expressions from that work crept for the first time into David's concurrent correspondence, and the testimony of the publisher is that the expressions there were not David's own. We will soon see two further expressions cropping up both in David's letters and in Clarke's *Life*, and I take it as circumstantial evidence that Clarke was now, by early 1831, well along with the writing of that anonymous account. At any rate, it is interesting to see a figure, which at least *appears* to be originating in this letter, show up again in the two volumes mentioned.

Chapter 9

NO CONGRESSMAN!

THE intervals during the congressional recesses of 1828, 1829, 1830, and 1831 were periods Crockett spent at home wooing his constituents in order that he might remain in public office.

The summer of 1828 was ominous with portents for Crockett's future. Yet the surface of his life during the months immediately following adjournment of Congress seems placid enough. Assuming that he left Washington the day after adjournment, he should have reached home about June 6 (the travelling time between Washington and west Tennessee was then about eleven days). He may have set out for home prior to adjournment, for on June 2 he signed the guardian's bond of one Wilson Brown in Gibson County.[1]

On July 14, having acquired land in Weakley County, he was placed on a jury of view there to "view and mark a road the nearest way and on the best ground from Dresden to meet a road at Gibson County Line on a direction to Trenton...." [2] This was the Weakley County portion of the Dresden-to-Trenton road, the Gibson County half of which he had helped to mark out in January, 1825. On October 14, the state brought suit for an affray against Joseph Sexton and fined him 12½ cents, with David as his security! [3] On December 5, probably after David had returned to Washington, for Congress convened that winter on December 1, Abraham P. Cantrell brought a suit for debt against David and Squire B. Partee; but the defense failed to appear, and the suit for $56.56 and costs was awarded the plaintiff.[4] Finally, a Weakley County delinquent tax list for 1824-1827 reveals that David owed taxes not only on the twenty-five acres he had purchased there, but on 200 additional contiguous acres which he had now somehow acquired.[5]

Beyond the noncommittal façade of these court records, David's break with Jackson was imminent. It is impossible to know exactly what did take place, but there are bits of evidence constituting interesting clues to the reality. When Crockett returned to Washington in December, 1828, he made an abrupt about-face on the land bill and split with the Jackson forces.

When historians have treated this reversal of David's position, they seemed to have erred as to the date of its occurrence and to have been confused as to its cause. Professor T. P. Abernethy and others have placed the date much too late—as late as 1830 or even later. This error arises, I think, because of David's political camouflaging. He knew that he could not be re-elected if he opposed Jackson openly in the campaign of 1829; he therefore pretended in that election to be a Jackson man, though he had, in fact, long before broken with him. This is clearly the face he puts upon the matter in the *Autobiography:*

> During my first two sessions in Congress, Mr. Adams was president, and *I worked along with what was called the Jackson party pretty well.* I was re-elected to Congress, in 1829, by an overwhelming majority; and *soon after the commencement of this second term,* I saw, or thought I did, that it was expected of me that I was to bow to the name of Andrew Jackson . . . even at the expense of my conscience and judgment. Such a thing was new to me, and a total stranger to my principles [italics added by Author].

David says that the break came in December, 1829, or early in 1830. The writing of this statement comes so close to the time mentioned, it is apparent that some subterfuge must have been involved. The break came during the summer of 1828. Evidently Jackson's animosity toward Crockett contained more justice than Abernethy allowed.

Charles and Mary Beard state that Crockett turned against Jackson "for reasons difficult to fathom," [6] strangely ignoring the natural conflict of interests between west Tennessee "squatters" and the landed gentry of middle Tennessee. In a sense the Beards are right, for such conflict of interest was evidently not David's only reason, though additional reasons stemmed from it. David's first allegiance was to the west Tennessee squatters, not to the state of Tennessee. When he became suspicious of the state's intentions with reference to the sale price of the vacant lands, he sought support for a proposal that the federal government give the land directly to the squatters rather than to the state. Obviously, he could not expect the state to support his proposal, so he had to look for aid elsewhere. There can be no question that, as far as his land bill was concerned, he made some sort of bargain with outside interests. It seems highly probable that he may have made this bargain during the summer of 1828.

Why the wealthy interests of the East should have been anxious to secure the name and courage of a backwoodsman as a weapon with which to fight Jackson is fairly obvious against the background of the political realities. Jackson's popularity and the increasing likelihood of his nomination to the Presidency predicated an approaching struggle between the government and the powerful Second United States Bank. It was Jackson's publicly stated belief that the influence of the bank had helped to pervert the previous election and deprive him of the Presidency. One should remember, too, the growing power of the new West and the fact that Tennessee was the power center of the West at this time. David's fame had passed local bounds and was rapidly becoming national. There was also the political consideration that if Jackson could be defeated in his own state, his reputation and candidacy would be destroyed nationally. History reveals a rather general agreement among the anti-Jacksonites that the best hope of defeating Jackson at home and turning the Jackson tide abroad was to oppose him with another popular Tennessean, a Western pioneer democrat. It was in this context that Crockett and the East got together—not later than 1832, possibly as early as 1828.

From evidence later to be presented, I suggest that sometime before Congress reconvened in 1828, Mathew St. Clair Clarke, friend of Nicholas Biddle, the president of the United States Bank, visited David Crockett in his backwoods home, and, without David's fully realizing all the political implications and affiliations involved, established personal ties which the Eastern Whigs came more and more to capitalize upon. The observation that the two men had been travelling together, recorded in the diary of Christopher Baldwin, Librarian of the American Antiquarian Society, cannot be dated later than 1832. Clarke wrote the anonymous *Life* of Crockett, which was finished before the end of 1832, and may have been started much earlier. The information

it contained came directly from David, and the narrative itself describes a visit by the author to David's home. Finally, for our consideration at this point, less than five months after Congress had
reconvened, David was writing a very friendly, personal, political
letter to the very Gales and Seaton whom he had contemptuously
described during the previous session as the "pap Sucking Editor imployed by the Coaletion." And in this letter of April 18, 1829, he
sends his regards to Clarke:

> Be So good as to answer this letter informe me how times is in the
> City and how You are Coming on and how every thing is working write
> Lenthy also Pleas to tender my Best Respects to Mr. Hyat and old friend
> Jessee Brown & M. St Clarke. I must Conclude & may god Bless You &
> faileys is the wishes of your friend   David Crockett.[7]

Evidently more than a mere break with Jackson was involved. David
wanted with all his heart to help his constituents of west Tennessee. However, he required support for that position beyond the
borders of the state. I believe Clarke promised him this support. His
sudden reversal seems to have been related not simply to Clarke, but
to Gales and Seaton, to Nicholas Biddle and the United States Bank,
and to the Eastern Whig forces generally opposed to Andrew Jackson. When Crockett returned to Congress in early December, the
compact had been made. From this point on his congressional speeches
were to be written for him, and little can be accepted at its face value.

The first indication of a compact is revealed in connection with
a Whig lampoon of Crockett a month before Congress reconvened.
Chapter XIII of the anonymous 1833 *Life* recounts Crockett's receipt
of a dinner invitation late in 1827 or early in 1828 to dine with President Adams. It describes how he attended that dinner in the company
of Mr. Gulian D. Verplanck of New York, and portrays him wittily
routing Adams' son when that young man attempted to ridicule him
after supper in the east wing of the White House. Though the banquet
had taken place months earlier, not until just about the time of David's
about-face did the newspapers print a distorted account of the occasion
in one more Whig lampoon of Crockett, the very last, I believe, pic-
turing him as having acted a complete boor, even drinking the water
from his finger bowl.[8] The false story was taken seriously by David's

constituents. To refute it, David secured the testimony of two Whigs that "the statement is destitute of every thing like the truth," and that "they observed nothing in your behavior but what was marked with strictest propriety." The two men who thus testified were James Clark, Whig governor of Kentucky in 1836, and Verplanck of New York. The original lampoon appeared in the *National Banner and Nashville Whig* for November 25, 1828,[9] and the denials were printed in the same paper for January 9 and 23, 1829. The denials came after David's break with Jackson was widely known; the original story before the break occurred. Evidently some good Whig newspaperman had blundered by discountenancing David, unaware of the compact; but he was quickly put right by Clark and Verplanck, once David had completed the bargain by breaking openly with Jackson. Immediately a revised Whig newspaper mould heroizing Crockett had to be cast—and was.

When Crockett returned to west Tennessee following the adjournment of Congress on March 3, 1829, there were a few political tangles to straighten out before election time, though in no sense was his political opposition dangerous. On April 18, 1829, he wrote the letter to Gales and Seaton, referred to above, containing the reference to Mathew St. Clair Clarke. The formerly unquoted portions of this letter give Crockett's estimate of the situation after having made a political canvass of his district:

I arived home Safe and found all well on the 15 of March. I am on my way home from a Journey of three weeks and am in Better health than I have been in for ten years past I have backed out three opponents and Colo Alexander has lately been entered against me tho my own oppinion is that he will back out before August if he does not I will beat him five thousand votes So Says the people

I was in Nashville a few days and a Circumstance tooke place last Saturday which created much exitement Our Governer Houston has parted with his wife and Resigned the governers appointment he told me that he was gouing to leave the Country and go up the arkensaw and live with the Indians as he Calls them his addopted Brothers the Ballance of his days [10] so I expect Wm Carroll will be our next governer with out opposition I hope the Chance is good for Lea and Polk both to be beat and Doct marable will be Badly Beaton So Sais the People of his district I have Just traveled through the Doctors destrict and Colo [Cave] Johnson has the voice of the people at this time I also traveled through Polks Destrict and done what little I could for him.

The content and tone of this letter indicate that Gales and Seaton had a definite interest in the outcome of these elections with reference to Jackson men. David's desire that Lea and Polk, both opposed to his amendment to the land bill, should be beaten, and his report to Gales and Seaton, may be significant. (His ambiguous statement a moment later that he "done what little I could" for Polk suggests that he had slipped back into his public pose of being a true Jackson man.) That Crockett was no longer a Jackson man, long before time for re-election had arrived in August, 1829, is abundantly clear—however he may have posed as such publicly for political reasons.

The earliest and (under whatever name) the only newspaper in west Tennessee for many years was the *Jackson Pioneer*, which had been founded in November, 1822. On May 20, 1824, Elijah Bigelow and Colonel Charles D. McLean took it over, re-christened it the *Jackson Gazette*, and used it belligerently in support of both Jackson and Crockett. McLean had been given the political plum of public printer for west Tennessee, but at about this time he was removed from this sinecure. The whisper in some quarters that Crockett had had something to do with McLean's removal was a matter, therefore, that disturbed Crockett, for it threatened to place him in the category of the anti-Jacksonites. He escaped the trap very neatly, however. As Keating records, David got support on this matter of the public printer from Felix Grundy, U. S. Senator from Tennessee: "This was the point on which he was very sore, and help from so distinguished a senator, in clearing himself of the charge, was very grateful to the old frontiersman." [11]

The *Gazette* published correspondence on this touchy subject between Crockett, McLean, and Polk. One spurious letter quoted by Keating from the *Gazette* shows David again in the dual role of the Jackson supporter in public and the Jackson opponent in private:

To General Jackson I am a firm and undeviating friend. I have fought under his command; I am proud to own that he has been my commander. I have loved him, and in the sincerety of my heart . . . I still love him; but to be compelled to love every one who for purposes of self-aggrandizement pretends to rally around the Jackson standard is what I can never submit to.[12]

The letter was undoubtedly written with David's knowledge and approval, for, in the language of the *Autobiography*, it is certainly "a huckleberry over his persimmon," and someone, perhaps the local editor, was composing his correspondence. It was this editor who came to David's defense when the Missouri *Republican* charged him with drunkenness and adultery.

When election time came round, Crockett's position, questionable as it might be to some, was not yet dangerously compromised among the voters at large. Quite naturally, his bill carried great weight among them. Hence Crockett won a strong victory over his old opponent, Colonel Alexander. Keating records the election returns as Alexander 4,330; Estes 132; Clark 9; Crockett 6,700. The *Autobiography* lists the majority as 3,585. Whatever the vote (notwithstanding David's earlier over-optimism, for Alexander had not dropped out, nor had David won by 5,000 votes), the re-election was decisive and put the Jackson forces on notice that work would have to be done before the next election if Crockett were to be eliminated from Congress. Both sides knew that if Crockett's land bill amendment were ever adopted, David's re-election was good for life if he wished it.

Following an election, a politician's celebration of victory must frequently be sobered by reflection upon his debts. As far back as April 28, Crockett and George Basinger had acknowledged in court indebtedness of $200 to Isaac Sellers; and William Spencer, one of the Sellers' securities, was accordingly released from further liability and was replaced as security by Crockett and Basinger.[13] Records for the interim, before the convening of the new Congress, again deal with that subject. On October 17, Francis Long brought a suit against him for debt which was to drag through the courts until April 12, 1832, to be finally ordered "stricken from the docket of this court for the want of Jurisdiction."[14] On the same day David C. Phillips brought suit for debt against Crockett.[15] As time went on, David's financial difficulties continued to grow.

The record of David's life between the two sessions of Congress in 1830 is a complete blank except for two brief court records.

On July 12 he was placed on another jury "to view and mark a road the nearest & best way from Beech Ridge on a direction to Dyersburg to the county line."[16] The tax list for David's land in Weakley County, reading, "David Crockett, 225 acres in Range 3, Section 5, District 13. Free Poll. $2.75,"[17] is the only other glimpse we get of him before he is found back in Washington active in the second session of the Twenty-First Congress.

The second session convened on December 6, 1830. David arrived late. He wrote in a letter to Henry McClung ("McLung") dated December 21:

> I arivid in the City on the 14th Inst but have neglected to write you until this time with a hope that I Could give you Some entilegence how the State of party was working on—I Still am of opinion that Mr Clay has as many frinds in Congress as Genl Jackson tho we have had no chance to try the test
>
> I here enclose you the five dollars which you was So kind as to loan me on my way which I Consider a particular favour....[18]

Henry McClung shared David's friendship with Sam Houston. McClung and Houston were from Rockbridge County, Virginia. McClung's wife, Elizabeth Alexander, was the sister of Phoebe Alexander whose son was the early Virginia romantic novelist, William Alexander Caruthers, also of Rockbridge County. Both McClung and Caruthers were Whigs. From this letter I infer that on his way to Congress David had visited in Staunton with McClung; that both were interested in the anti-Jackson strength of Henry Clay, McClung apparently being less sanguine about it than David; and that both were interested in some strategy supporting the Whig cause and opposing Jackson.

David began his campaign for re-election to the next Congress by issuing a long Circular Letter on February 28, 1831. Congress adjourned on March 3, 1831.

It is apparent that the speeches and Circular Letters issued under David's name during this period were superior in composition to his concurrent personal letters. Clearly he was receiving help in writing his public utterances, and Polk has suggested that this came from Gales and other Adamsites. David's letters establish that Thomas Chilton later helped to write the *Autobiography*. From 1828 on, Crockett and Chilton are to be found increasingly in one another's company as they join forces to support or attack many of the same measures. As Chilton was probably already among those helping to write David's speeches and Circular Letters, it is worth remark that David's Circular for February 28 followed by only one day a remarkably similar letter

Chilton wrote to his constituents on the same subject and for the same purpose.[19] They are too much alike not to have been written in collaboration.

David's sixteen-page Circular addressed to the "Citizens and Voters of the Ninth Congressional District," [20] opens with a severe attack on Jackson for extravagance. In spite of Jackson's criticism of Adams and Clay, the argument runs, government expenses have increased and the talk about economy "was a mere trap set for us." Whereas "when Mr. Adams was in power" clerks had been "too numerous and too lazy," the present cry is to raise their pay and increase their number, while "the Post Office ... instead of supporting its own expenses must now be supported by the Treasury." There follows an attack upon Jackson for his cruelty toward the Indians, ascribing it to Jackson's animus for Calhoun and friendship for Van Buren: Calhoun wishing to protect the Indians from the extreme cruelty with which Georgia was treating them; Van Buren, the bosom friend of Mr. Crawford of Georgia, inciting the President, in disregard of all treaty agreements and of "the voice of humanity, and the honour of his country," "[to flatter] the pride and views of Georgia" by giving them the choice of moving out or submitting to a Georgia now authorized to "wanton in her acts of wrong without fear of restraint from the President." In the same vein the letter surmises that nothing but the ballot box can now stop "this unfeeling career of treachery and cruelty."

The attack then shifts to internal improvements, accusing Jackson of opposing them only out of hate for Calhoun. Jackson and Calhoun had formerly supported internal improvements, but since Martin Van Buren is opposed, "General Jackson ... a western President" has abandoned his principles so "that Martin Van Buren may be his successor!" A fourth point of attack is against Jackson's appointment of members of Congress to high office, in flat violation of his earlier views: formerly Jackson had recommended an amendment to the Constitution to prohibit this practice, saying "that this was the means employed by the Presidents to corrupt Congress, and that its practice would ruin the Republic." Yet, in the face of this, Jackson had actually appointed to his cabinet from Congress Eaton, Ingham, Branch, and Berrien; and as foreign ministers Rives, M'Lane, and Randolph—Van Buren's friends almost to a man.

A fifth charge against Jackson is his unprincipled action of offering himself "again a candidate for re-election" in the face of his earlier declaration that a President should not serve longer than four years, which he had emphasized by urging Congress to recommend a constitutional amendment to enforce this principle of tenure. Here of course was a real rub for the Whigs and the Second United States Bank. The first section of the letter concludes with David's by now familiar claim that Jackson is no longer a Jackson man:

I thought with him, as he thought before he was President: he has altered his opinion—I have not changed mine. I have not left the principles which led me to support General Jackson: he has left them and *me;* and I will not surrender my independence to follow his *new opinions,* taught by interested and selfish advisers, and which may again be remoulded under the influence of passion and cunning

With this opening blast, the new election campaign was on. For the first time, Crockett was to electioneer in open opposition to Jackson.

Crockett's defeat in his campaign for re-election in the summer of 1831 raises the question of whether that defeat was due primarily to the determined opposition of the Jackson party. Such is the easy explanation—too easy, perhaps. It is possible that an even more important factor in Crockett's defeat may have been his loss of resilience to his opponents' blows.

In the words of Charles and Mary Beard, "the politics of the frontier was the politics of the backwoodsmen." Backwoods life was such that, if a candidate could not entertain a gathering, he would not command their votes. Practical needs of pioneer life required a healthy give and take: good sportsmanship was a fundamental requisite of the political candidate. He had to have the ability not only to deliver an opponent a fierce blow by fist or anecdote, but also to accept with a smile a similar blow in return. In his early career, David had this ability. Hate came to be his undoing, and it destroyed his resilience.

Political chicanery was at work on both sides. An anecdote from the anonymous *Life* (Chapter XI) suggests David's complicity in a Whig campaign to build him up as a legendary figure. Asked his reaction to the public jests which Whig newspapers were printing about him in the summer of 1831, David replied, "Oh, damn it, I don't care—those who publish them, don't intend to injure me." When he was further asked what he thought of his latest commission:

'What commission?' David asked
'The commission by Andrew Jackson, by which, according to the news-papers you are to climb the Alleghanies and wring the tail off the next comet to appear.'
David reportedly smiled, replying instantly, 'I'll be damned if I had a commission, if I didn't wring *his* tail off.'

The story illustrates the method by means of which the newspapers were contributing toward the creation of Crockett legend—a legend which, as V. L. Parrington commented, was to get out of hand and go much farther than its authors had contemplated. Nor is it surpris-ing that David did not object. He was by this time a party to the scheme for giving himself a national notoriety, though he drew a line between stories that were in fun and abetted his reputation, and those which were malicious and hurt it.

However, there were Jackson newspapers in the land too—and they were not handling him so grandiosely. In Crockett's words, his break with Jackson "was considered the unpardonable sin," and he "was hunted down like a wild varment" by all the little newspapers and "every little pin-hook lawyer." He was accused of wasting the gov-ernment's money by missing votes in Congress (though, he avers, he had missed only seventy) and swindling the government to the value of "five hundred and sixty dollars" (at eight dollars the vote). Even so, he said he would have triumphed had it not been for a dastardly plan concocted by the "little four-pence-ha'penny limbs of the law." "They agreed to spread out over the district, and make appointments for me to speak, almost everywhere, to clear up the Jackson question. They would give me no notice of these appointments, and the people would meet in great crowds to hear what excuse Crockett had to make for quitting Jackson." Instead, the "small-fry of lawyers" would ap-pear "with their saddlebags full of little newspapers and journals of Congress; and would get up and speak, and read their scurrilous attacks on me, and would then tell the people that I was afraid to attend." All of this was carried on secretly until "it was too late to counter-act it."

Had Crockett himself designed and used this device, it would have been good politics. The note of exasperation in his account of his opponents' putting to use a typically Crockett brand of wildfire is significant. There is a black note suggesting that his mellowness was

souring to gall, and that he no longer had at easy command that cheer-
ful sportsmanship and good humor which had earlier been his.

I believe it was this intangible loss which finally destroyed him. Of
course he had not secured passage of the land bill so urgently desired
by his constituents. He was now for the first time openly opposed to
Jackson. However, his loss of balance may have been in large part
responsible for his failure to succeed with his bill. If he had retained
his good humor, and had not developed a monomaniacal antipathy
toward all matters Jacksonian, I believe he might have differed quite
openly with Jackson without great political danger. The West loved
a man "who refused to sneeze when other men took snuff." It was the
new violence and the extremity of his position rather than the position itself which began to lose him friends and which at last led him
to take that intransigent stand resulting in death—and lasting fame!

This monomania we have already seen developing. It will increase
with mounting fury from this point on. There is evidence of it in an
anecdote, with substantial basis in fact, purporting to describe what
may have been the decisive event: an altercation between Crockett
and his political opponent William Fitzgerald at Paris, Tennessee, in
the summer of 1831. When Fitzgerald made certain charges against
Crockett, Crockett threatened to thrash Fitzgerald if he repeated them.
Fitzgerald's friends advised him of the danger of repetition and urged
him not to pursue the issue. When the hour for Fitzgerald's next
scheduled speech arrived, David was present amid a large gathering
composed largely of Crockett partisans:

> Fitzgerald came late, with but a few backers, and they of a class not
> fond of broils and difficulties. He was met before he reached the grounds,
> and begged to return, but he could not retreat without disgrace and de-
> feat. Fitzgerald spoke first. Upon mounting the stand he was noticed to
> lay something upon the pine table in front of him, wrapped in his hand-
> kerchief. He commenced his speech by an allusion to the reports that had
> been made, and when he said that he was here to re-assert and prove the
> charges, Crockett arose and stated that he was present to give them the lie,
> and whip the little lawyer that would repeat [them]. When Fitzgerald
> reached the objectionable point, Crockett arose from his seat in the audi-
> ence and advanced toward the stand. When [he was] within three or four
> feet of it, Fitzgerald suddenly removed a pistol from his handkerchief, and,
> covering Colonel Crockett's breast, warned him that a step further and
> he would fire. The move was so unexpected, the appearance of the speaker

so cool and deliberate, that Crockett hesitated a second, turned around, and resumed his seat.[21]

That incident, according to this account, "decided the election" of Fitzgerald to Congress. It is true that David later referred heatedly to Fitzgerald as "the thing that had the name of beating me." In the *Autobiography* Crockett says that "when the election came, I had a majority of seventeen counties, putting all their votes together, but the eighteenth beat me; and so I was left out of Congress during those two years." It was Madison County that had beat him, and the election was indeed close. *Niles Register* for October 22, 1831, records in its very first reference to David (it was eventually to become the central organ for a Crockett advertising campaign in Whiggery) that of "the enormous number of *sixteen thousand four hundred and eighty-two votes*... polled... Mr. Fitzgerald received the slim majority of 586 votes."[22] The *New York Evening Post* for August 27, 1831, gave the majority as 807 votes. Indeed, the election was so close that David contested it,[23] but without effect.

Immediately after the elections, before the official returns were in from all the counties, Crockett wrote a letter negotiating for a lease of twenty acres of land in Carroll County adjoining his land in Weakley. "I have been compelled," he said, "to Sel my land where I live to try to pay my debts," and he wanted to clear the new land and "build Comfortable Cabbens & Smoke house Corne Cribs & Stables and dig a well and Set out Some fruit trees." Noting that it was "verry heavy timbered and will take hard work to open a plantation" and that he might eventually want to buy the leased land, he turned abruptly to the recently concluded elections:

I have not herd the result of my election from all the Countys I expict I am beaton I have one Consolation I would rather be beaton and be a man than to be elected and be a little puppy dog I have always Supported measures and principles and not men I have acted fearless and independent and I never will regret my Course I would rather be politically buried than to be hypochriticalley imortalized I Contend that if the people of the western District elected me to fill the Station of an honourable Reprisentative I done my best to fill their expectations but if they elected me to be a little puppy dog to yelp after a party I have decived them and would again if elected I have always believed I was an honist man and if the world will do me Justice they will find it to be the Case.

Respectfully your obt Servt

David Crockett [24]

Clarke's *Life* of Crockett was deposited for copyright on January 5, 1833; it must therefore have been completed by the end of 1832. The repeated occurrence of such figures as the "puppy dog" figure in the letters and speeches and in the *Life* may indicate that the *Life* was already under way. The fact that *Niles Register*, at precisely this time, first takes note of his existence and the further fact that the Second United States Bank had already lent Crockett money, suggests a pattern of concerted action which increases the probability that Clarke's *Life* was already far along in the writing.[25] Certainly David could not have failed to know who was the author of his work. That he should pretend not to know its quite obviously Whig author is understandable. He could hardly have admitted having a part in the shrewd literary efforts of Eastern interests to elect him. Such an admission in the hands of Polk and other Jacksonites would have been fatal.

For January 7, 1833, there survives a heretofore unpublished Crockett letter to Mr. Richard Smith, cashier of the Washington, D. C., branch of the Second United States Bank. Since the question of the bank's use of financial power for political purposes is still much-debated, a word about this same Mr. Smith in another, but related, context is appropriate.

The subject of the Second United States Bank is one about which there will always be disagreement, for men of different ethical outlooks draw contrary conclusions from the same evidence. I personally fail to understand how the most authoritative student and defender of the bank to date, Mr. Ralph C. H. Catterall, in the face of the evidence before him, can say, "there has never been any evidence produced to show that the bank as a national bank ever spent a dollar corruptly."[26] There is the letter, for instance, by Mr. Smith to Nicholas Biddle, president of the bank, writing about a loan which seems to have been similar to that which David and other Congressmen and Senators received in Washington. The loan was being requested by Mr. Asbury Dickens, Chief Clerk in the Treasury Department, who already owed the bank $2,500 and who, though he was unable to pay and was not considered a good financial risk, had come to request $2,500 more, with Smith recommending approval. This letter is by a cashier to the president and marked "Private and Confidential." It does not indicate that hesitation one might expect from a subordinate

broaching to his superior a questionable proposal with which the
president could not be known to be in sympathy:

> ...the security which [Dickens] could give would not be adequate to
> cover this sum.... There are considerations of a delicate nature which
> would induce me [to] accede to this proposition. They cannot be com-
> municated to the Board of Directors, perhaps [where the government had
> representatives to protect the public interests, since all government monies
> were deposited in this private bank] but must readily occur to you. Mr.
> Dickens fills the confidential station in the Treasury, which has manage-
> ment of the bank accounts. He has already evinced the most friendly dis-
> position towards the Bank.... The report on the subjects of government
> deposits in the Bank, made to the Senate last winter by Gen. Smith [Sena-
> tor from Maryland] was in a great measure made from materials furnished
> by Mr. Dickins from suggestions obtained from me. This, of course, must
> not be talked of.... Such is my opinion of the services rendered by him,
> I should think it good policy to give up entirely the whole $5000, sooner
> than not to retain his friendly disposition.[27]

That was the course followed. In 1830 the remainder of Dickens'
indebtedness to the bank, about half the $5,000, was "given up entirely"
on the personal action of Nicholas Biddle, president. Catterall tries to
explain such cancellations as mere bookkeeping matters,[28] the writing
off of uncollectable accounts. It was bookkeeping of a kind which
a bank examiner, with this letter before him, would surely have found
highly "irregular," however profitable it may have proved in the
bookkeeping of politics. We find precisely the same thing happening
to David in exactly the same context. At this same time Richard Smith
made him a loan at the Washington Branch. Two years later, when
David was again back in Congress, the debt was stricken from the
books on the personal action of Biddle in the same kind of bookkeeping. It is also worth noting that David felt it necessary, when he
earlier applied for an extension of his loan, to state in his letter how
he had campaigned relative to the renewal of the bank's charter and
how he expected to be back in Congress before the matter came up
for a vote:

> I have wrote to my Securitys in Your Bank to try to indulge me until
> I Could make Some arangemint I hope you will extend all the liberalitys
> in your powar I did Come out in the late election in favour of the renewel
> of your Charter and the thing that had the name of beating me took the
> Jackson Ground against it I still hope to be in Congress again before there

is a vote taken on that Subject I have enclosed Some Blanks asigned with a hope that my Securitys would fill them and get them discounted for me times is hard in this Country I will do the best I can.[29]

Exactly when this loan was made it is impossible to say, but it must have been at least a year earlier.

The heading of this letter, "At home Weakley County Tennessee," is the only one identifying that county as *home*, though there are several others addressed from there. This is important in connection with some spurious Crockett letters published in the *Downing Gazette* of 1835 and with the authorship of the spurious *Texas Exploits* erroneously supposed by writers on Crockett to have been based on an authentic Crockett diary.

Congress had adjourned on March 3, 1831. Most of Crockett's activities during his enforced two year Congressional "recess" are irrecoverable. It is natural to assume that he divided his time between farming, hunting, and politicking—for he planned to be back in the next Congress. Of those two years, his *Autobiography* tells us nothing, and local records are extremely meager.

In April, 1831, John Shaw brought suit against Robert Powell and David for debt.[30] On May 19 David sold his twenty-five acres in Weakley and also a Negro girl "named Adaline" to his brother-in-law George Patton, of Buncombe County, North Carolina, in an effort to pay his creditors. Beneath both this deed and the bill of sale, immediately beneath Crockett's signature, and in each case spelled, phrased, and punctuated alike, are the words "Be allways sure you are right then Go, ahead." [31] This is the first positive link we have between David and that motto which has become so inseparably associated with his name, and it shows that by this date David was making the motto his own. A Crockett letter dated August 22, 1831, indicates that he continued to live in his Weakley cabin several months after the sale of the land.[32]

There is no further record of David Crockett until January, 1833. On January 9, 1833, two days after the letter to Richard Smith, Crockett and his brother-in-law Abner Burgin were appointed "commissioners" to view and mark a road "the nearest and best way from the Trenton Road between the middle and south fork of Obion Rivers and crossing the South fork at or near John Bradshaws; thence to Benjamine Tisons or to the County Line on that direction...." [33]

Three days later, David was appointed juror,[34] and late in the same year he was made executor of his father-in-law's estate, with the provision that he make a true account of his executorship within two years.[35] Naming his seven living children, Robert Patton first confirmed the gift of all property formerly donated them; then he bequeathed to his two daughters, "Sally Edmindson" and Ann Mc-Whorter, "ten dollars and no more." He provided for the selling of all his effects and the division of the proceeds of that and of all else he possessed among his other five living children and his two grandchildren by a deceased son (James), giving none of this to Sally and Ann. Finally, he appointed "my friend David Crockett & George Patton executors of this my last will and testament." Sally, Ann, and their husbands were later to attempt to break this will.

There is a possibility that David may have visited Washington, D. C., sometime in 1832. T. C. Richardson reproduces by photograph in *Farm and Ranch* a silver teapot which he asserts was given to David at Washington sometime in 1832.[36] With this final doubtful echo, the explicit record ends. There is another record implicit with much of importance to Crockett's future career. To this record we now turn.

PART FOUR

Down and Under

10

THE LAST LAP

CROCKETT'S defeat in 1831 had been close enough to warn both parties that the election of 1833 would not be won hands down by either. We have already seen some of the measures taken by "David and company" to get him re-elected. The fact that Clarke's *Life* was quite popular all along the Mississippi and throughout west Tennessee doubtless strengthened David's chances of victory. On the other hand, the Jackson forces were not idle. For one thing, they took up the exaggerated, bumptious backwoodsman role in which Clarke's narrative had cast Crockett, and used it against David, just as the Whig papers had done on an earlier occasion. They presented David in Congress as the proverbial bull in a china shop.

Another Jacksonian tactic was the use of "Black Hawk... (alias) Adam Huntsman, with all his talents for writing 'Chronicles.'" Adam Huntsman [1] was a west Tennessee lawyer and politician of considerable shrewdness, and a local political writer of ingenuity and wit. He was a Jacksonian and was finally to defeat David for Congress in 1835. In 1833 he did not compete with David directly, but he did have a shrewd hand in the determined effort to scotch David's political wagon. His "Chronicles" attacked David by impugning his political motives in his fight for the land bill. Done in biblical language to which the widespread use of Hebraic names in the backwoods gave great point, they combined genuine humor and solid information in a way that must have told heavily with David's backwoods constituents.

A brief selection from these "Chronicles" will indicate the flavor of Huntsman's wit and present the Jacksonian version of what was happening to David:

1. And it came to pass in those days when Andrew was chief Ruler over the Children of Columbia, that there arose a mighty man in the river country, whose name was David; he belonged to the tribe of Tennessee, which lay upon the border of the Mississippi and over against Kentucky.

6. And it came to pass in the 54th year after the Children of the Columbia had escaped British bondage, and on the first month, when Andrew and the wise men and rulers of the people were assembled in the great san hedrim, that David arose in the midst of them saying, men and brethren, wot ye not that there be many occupants in the river country on the west border of the tribe of Tennessee, who are settled down upon lands belonging to Columbia; now I beseech you give unto these men each a portion for his inheritance, so that his soul may be glad, and he will bless thee and thy posterity.

[But there were other "wise men" who objected, saying that the central government should give the land to Tennessee, who should in turn deal with the occupants—thus giving all Tennessee politicians, 'and, not just David, the glory for ever and ever. But David became angry at their resistance to his scheme and vowed vengeance.]

9. Now there were in these days wicked men, sons of Belial, to wit: the Claytonites, the Holmesites, the Burgessites, the Everettites, the Chiltonites, and the Bartonites, who were of the tribes of Maine, Massachusetts, Rhode Island, Kentucky, and Missouri, and who hated Andrew and his friends of old times, because the Children of Columbia had chosen him to rule over them instead of Henry whose surname was Clay, whom they desired for their chief ruler.

[These "Sons of Belial" saw that David was angry at his own group and made advances to this man who had fought against their great chiefs Henry and John Q. Then Daniel, surnamed Webster, a "prophet of the Order of Balaam"...]

12.... drew nigh unto David and said unto him, Wherefore... doth thou seem sad and sorrowful? .... And David lifted up his eyes and wept, and said, O Daniel! live forever. If the wise men and rulers had given my occupants the lands according to the manner I beseeched them, I could have been wise man and chief ruler in the river country for life. But if I join the wise men, and give it to the state of Tennessee, then they will share the honor with me, and the council of the State ... will give it to the occupants at twelve and one half cents per acre, and they will receive the honor instead of me; then the people of the river country will not have me for their wise man and chief ruler forever, and it grieveth me sore.

[Then Daniel had David swear to him that David and all the river people would come over to him and fight with him against Andrew and for Henry for chief ruler and in return promised to help David get the land for his occupants. "And David swore accordingly, and there is a league existing between them even unto this day."]

[David sent out a disciple who loved him and instructed him to be all things to all people. "As thou art a Baptist, they will put trust in thee." When he met those who were friendly to David he was to tell them to be strong and valiant. When amongst those opposed to David, he was to say that he, too, was opposed, but that he had been all through the river country, and that David "will be elected by a mighty host." Among the ignorant he was to say that Jackson was guilty of corruption. If a Jackson man should approach him, he should say that David had always been a Jackson man; if he should accost a Clay man, he should reveal secretly to him the bargain with Daniel, and so on.]

23. ... but the people were a stiff necked generation, and would not agree that David should bring Henry to be Chief ruler ... instead of Andrew; but with one accord said unto William, David hath beguiled us, we will desert him, and stick to Andrew, who has brought us out of British bondage—and we will vote for William, whose surname is Fitzgerald—and the people all said, Amen! [2]

Of course the "Chronicles" are biased: had the state been willing to specify the sale of land for 12½ cents an acre, Crockett might never have split with the Jackson forces. Yet there is truth in this excellent parody. It is entirely correct in making David's zeal to get his land bill passed central to all of his decisions and the determinant of his Congressional career. David grudgingly recognizes Huntsman's talents for " '*Chronicles*,' and such like foolish stuff," and they must have been broadly recognizable as caricature, or they would surely have been more disastrous. As it was, Crockett won the election by only a very thin margin.

The most practical effort designed by the Jackson party to defeat

Crockett was in so tailoring the new western Congressional District as to leave out those counties most enthusiastic for David and to include some where his opponent, Fitzgerald, was strongest. The *Autobiography* describes this move vividly:

When I last declared myself a candidate, I knew that the district would be divided by the Legislature ... and I moreover knew that from the geographical situation of the country, the county of Madison, which was very strong, and which ... had given the majority that had beat me in the former race, should be left off from my district.

But when the Legislature met ... Mr. Fitzgerald, my competitor, went up, and informed his friends in that body, that if Madison county was left off, he wouldn't run; for "that Crockett could beat Jackson himself in those [other] parts, in any way they could fix it."

The liberal Legislature you know, of course, gave him that county [included it in the district for which they were to compete]; and it is too clear to admit of dispute, that it was done to make a mash of me. In order to make my district in this way, they had to form the southern district of a string of counties around three sides of mine, or very nearly so. Had my old district been properly divided, it would have made two nice ones, in convenient nice form. But as it is, they are certainly the most unreasonably laid off of any in the state, or perhaps in the nation, or even in the te-total creation.

A glance at the map shows the truth of David's description. Crockett's new Twelfth District (the old one had been the Ninth) consisted of the counties of Haywood, Madison, Dyer, Obion, Gibson, Weakley, Henry, and Carroll. The other district created from the Ninth, the Thirteenth, started with Tipton on the west, dropped down below and south of Haywood and Madison to take in Shelby, Fayette, Hardeman, and McNairy, and then rose again to take in Henderson and Perry east and northeast, and on the other side, of Madison.[3] The ideal configuration would have thrown both Haywood and Madison into the Thirteenth District, and thus have rid David of the one county which had defeated him in the previous election. There was justice in his claim of "encirclement."

Thus David and Fitzgerald canvassed for the election in the Twelfth District including Madison. This too obvious manipulation of voters by an anti-western "liberal" legislature was apparently self-defeating, and so it is judged by Crockett in the concluding paragraphs of the *Autobiography*:

However, when the election came on, the people of the district, and of Madison county among the rest, seemed disposed to prove to Mr. Fitzgerald and the Jackson Legislature, that they were not to be transferred like hogs ... in the market; and they determined that I shouldn't be broke down. . . . I had Mr. Fitzgerald, it is true, for my open competitor, but he was helped along by all his little lawyers again, headed by old Black Hawk ... (alias) Adam Huntsman, with all his talents for writing *"Chronicles,"* and such like foolish stuff.

But one good thing was ... the papers ... were now beginning to say "fair play a little," and they would publish both sides of the question. The contest was a warm one, and the battle well-fought; but I gained the day, and the Jackson horse was left a little behind. When the polls were compared, it turned out I had beat Fitz just two hundred and two votes, having made a mash of all their intrigues. After all this, the reader will perceive that I am now here in Congress, this 28th day of January, in the year of our Lord one thousand eight hundred and thirty-four; and that, what is more agreeable to my feelings as a freeman, I am at liberty to vote as my conscience and judgment dictates to be right, without the yoke of any party on me. . . . Look at my arms, you will find no party hand-cuff on them. Look at my neck, you will not find there any collar, with the engraving "MY DOG. Andrew Jackson."

But you will find me standing up to my rack, as the people's faithful representative, and the public's most obedient, very humble servant,

DAVID CROCKETT.

Thus David concluded his *Autobiography* on January 28, 1834, concurrently with his last successful political campaign. With it he was beginning his canvass for the August, 1835, elections. In conjunction with the charge the "Chronicles" had made about a bargain between David and Daniel Webster, it is significant that immediately after Crockett's re-election, the Whig papers of the nation began outlandishly to propagandize David.

After the re-election of Jackson in 1832 the Whigs became desperate for a candidate, and as the Jackson forces began to build up Martin Van Buren for the Democratic succession, the Whigs cast about for a "White hope." Unable, finally, to decide on any one candidate, they attempted the strategy which had placed John Adams instead of Jackson in the White House in 1824—that is, of running a number of local favorites in the hope of throwing the election into the House, where they expected to be in a more favorable position to bargain. Perhaps it was such a policy adopted even so early as the end of 1833, or perhaps it was an early hope that David might be

built into a candidate, that led them to ask David to allow his name
to be offered as a Presidential candidate. In his letter of January 8,
1835, David reveals that they made this offer to him sometime before
December 1, 1833, through the medium of the Mississippi State Convention. "I am at prisent preparing an answer to Bentons letter to
the Convention of Mississippi I was asked by the Same State to run
for the Presidency and this gives me an excuse to answer him at
length." Little came of it, but it did offer a clever pretext for ridiculing Thomas Hart Benton's pro-Jackson refusal of the Convention's
offer in late 1834 of the Vice-Presidential nomination. The fact that
the offer was made explains David's repeated reference to himself in
his *Autobiography* (being written in December, 1833) as a Presidential
candidate, and to the possibility that he might be "forced to take
the 'white house.'"

On October 19, 1833, two months after the election and before
Congress convened, David, in his capacity as executor of the Patton
estate, sold an 18-year-old Negro girl, Sofia, "the property of Said
Robert Patton Decased [*sic*]," to L. K. "Tinckle" for $525.[4] When
the failure of the Whig campaign efforts in 1835 sent Crockett on his
fateful journey to Texas, "Tinckle" was one of his three companions.

The first session of Crockett's final Congress convened on December 2. By December 8, he was writing to reassure a constituent of his
support: "I go the whole hog for you against any person whatever
I never will have the Sin of ingrattitude to answer for."[5] After attacking Jackson on the grounds of the insolvency of the Post Office
and condemning him with reference to the U. S. Bank, he proceeds:

...the truth is I have no doubt but there is a Considerable majority in
both houses opposed to Jackson and his measurs
   The United States Bank has Come out in Self defence and Jackson and
the kitchen Cabnett out of measure I have but one Coppy or I would
Send it to you it is a large pamplet and Contains more than any thing I
ever Saw of its Size it will Sinque the adminestration in the mind of all
honist men it proves that the whole hostility of the president to that
instatution originated from the Cause that the bank refused to lend its aid
in keeping up the preasant power right or wronge when you See the
attempts to bring over the Bank to be Subservant to the preasant adminestration it will disgust you and every honist man the truth is I do
be lieve the old Chief is in a worse drive than he ever was before and
he is beginning to find it out

He then promised to "deliver your message to Mr. Clay and Everett with much pleasure relative to your two Sones their name-Sakes" and conveyed his respects to their mutual friends with the assurance that "from the [first!] Count [I am standing up] to the Rack fodder or [no fodder].... I will go a head I mus[t]...."

The use of the expression "[standing up] to the Rack fodder or [no fodder]" indicates that already Crockett and Chilton were at work on the *Autobiography* and had arrived at Chapter IV, where that expression first occurs. Its use here, and the phrase "I will go a head," reflecting his motto used on the title page, reveal matter going simultaneously into correspondence and into his life story. The intimate mention of the names of Clay and Everett is amusing in the light of the imputations of the "Chronicles." As for the Second U. S. Bank, a few additional words of explanation are necessary.

Important matters had arisen in Congress while David had been out of office, particularly the Tariff Bill, Nullification, the "Force" Bill, and the veto of the recharter of the bank. David's explanation of Jackson's anti-bank motives is quite .biased. Jackson, of course, had long been opposed to that institution, desiring not to bend it to his own purposes but to destroy it altogether as a dangerous monopoly institution. After his first inauguration he had become disarmingly quiet about this issue, but in occasional, but pertinent, references to it (such as those in his first two messages to Congress), he left the bank directors uneasy as to his intentions. With typical arrogance, urged on by Henry Clay, Nicholas Biddle decided to force the issue of the bank's recharter before the elections of 1832, and if Jackson opposed it, to use his opposition as a club with which to defeat Jackson for a second term. Hence bills for the recharter of the bank were introduced in both houses early in 1832, despite the fact that the bank charter was not to expire for four more years (on March 3, 1836). The normal time for its renewal would have come long after the elections of 1832. After it had passed the Senate on June 11 and the House on July 3, Jackson vetoed it with a ringing message on July 10, 1832, a few months before the Presidential election.

Biddle was delighted. With that incurable myopia so characteristic of wealthy ultraconservative Americans in politics, he thought he had created the issue that would defeat Jackson. Accordingly, he had many thousands of copies of the veto message printed and distributed all over the country. Nearly three-fourths of the beholden press defended the bank and attacked Jackson, as they have attacked every forceful President of either party before him or since, and the issue became heated. When election time came, Jackson was re-elected by a greater majority than ever. With his hand upon the pulse of financial power, and mistaking it for the pulse of the nation, Biddle only succeeded in forcing the hand of its conqueror to kill it in 1832 instead of in 1836.

To guarantee the decision reached in 1832, and to offset Biddle's sudden irresponsible manipulation of the currency in an effort to *force* the renewal of his charter, veto or no veto, Jackson ordered that no more monies of the United States Government be deposited with the United States Bank. This order was issued while Congress was in adjournment in the fall of 1833.

The deposits were removed in the absence of Congress. Biddle then deliberately attempted to create a money panic through a quick contraction of the credit of the state banks, still trying to blackmail the government and force a recharter. John C. Calhoun and his Nullifiers, who had broken with Jackson, joined forces with the Bank. In February, 1834, Congress found the reasons given to them by Secretary of the Treasury Roger B. Taney for removal of the *government* monies from the *private* bank "insufficient and unsatisfactory." [6]

Finally, Biddle's tactics became unbearable even to the money-interests—who were beginning to bleed from their purses. (In a letter to a friend, Biddle had written, "All the other Banks and all the merchants may break but the Bank of the United States shall not break. . . . Nothing but the evidence of suffering abroad will produce any effect in Congress." It was his purpose to produce that suffering and to manipulate Congress as he did Congressmen.) When a group of Boston merchants—of tea party inclinations when their economic interests were crossed—threatened to expose Biddle, he was forced to change his tactics and thereby reveal the game he had been playing. He had contracted credit violently on the pretext of preparing the bank for going out of business (four years later!), reducing its loans more than eighteen million dollars from August, 1833, to November, 1834. In the five months following his reversal of policy under threat of exposure by the merchants, he increased his loans by about fourteen and a half million dollars, and by June, 1835, nine months before the charter was to expire, the loans were as great as they had been formerly, while the note circulation was actually greater than it had ever been.

The Crockett holograph above reflects the indignation character-istic of many members of the new Congress friendly to the bank when, with the convening of Congress on December 2, they were confronted with the *fait accompli* of the already removed deposits, and when on the next day they were presented by Taney with his reasons for having removed the deposits during the absence of Congress.

The first record of Crockett in the Congressional proceedings char-acteristically relates to his Tennessee Land Bill.[7] On December 17, David introduced two motions: (1) that a Select Committee of the House, composed of seven members, be appointed to inquire into the most equitable mode of disposing of Federal lands south and west of the Congressional Reservation Line; (2) that all papers in the files of the House relative to this matter be referred to said committee, leave being granted the committee to report by bill or otherwise. Both motions passed. When in a letter to a constituent shortly thereafter Davids says optimistically, "My land Bill is among the first Bills re-ported to the house and I have but little doubt of its passage during the present Session," the historical pattern of his folly seems to be repeating itself: once more the dearly bought majorities support him in procedure but elude him when the issue itself is at stake.

In fact, the complete blindness of this simple, wayfaring man to the machinations of the Thieves of Jericho is amazing. In the letter referred to above, David's ignorant self-righteousness is apparent:

a delegation...from...New York...laid their memoreal before Con-gress and then waited on the President and he got into a perfect rage and told them that If every one of his party quit him that he never would agree for the deposits to be restored he Said that he had determined to put down the unitedStates Bank and By the Eternal he would effect his object By this you See we have the government of one man that he puts forward his will as the law of the land If the American people will Seanction this we may bid farwell to our Republican name it is nothing but a Shaddow our once happy government will become a despot I Consider the present time one that is marked with more dainger than any one period of our political history the South Carolina question was nothing to the present for the over throw of our once happy government You See our whole Circulating medium deranged and our whole Commercial Community destroyed all to grattify the ambetion of *King Andrew* the first becaus the united States Bank refused to lend its aid in upholding his Corrupt party the truth is he is Surrounded by a Set of *Imps* of famin that is willing to destroy the best intrest of the Country to promote their own Intrest I have Spoken free but I write the truth and the world will be convinsed I hope before it is two late

That the time was "marked with more dainger" for David than *he* was aware of is reflected in the postscript of this letter when, apparently referring to his Whig friends, he vowed that, though "it Costs me my Salary I will trust to an honist Comunity hereafter for reward I love my Country better than any party or Riches." [8]

The extent of his foolish trust in that "honist Comunity" is reflected in a letter, heretofore unpublished, that he wrote on January 10, 1834, to his son John Wesley:

I have waited for Several days to get a letter from you but I will wait no longer it is about three weeks Sence I received a line from you and in fact I have recieved but one Sence I left hom from you I must Charge you with neglect but I hop you will do better here after. . . .

We are Still engaged in debating the great question of Removing the deposits I have no doubt but that we are gaining ground and I do believe we will order the deposits back but the Jackson folks is beginning to Bost and Say that Jackson will veto any order that Congress will make . . . I must Confess that I have niver Saw Such times in my life. . . . I do believe in two years from this time that the man will be hard to find that will acknowledge that he ever was a Jackson man I have sent you a Coppy of my land Bill and report and I want you to Show it to the people It will relinquish upwards of Seven hundred thousands acres This will Secure every occupant in the district and that will effect the object that I have been So long and So anxious to effect my whole Delligation will go with me I have no doubt of effecting this object before this Session Closes my prospects is much brighter than ever it was at any former Session.

I am ingaged in writing a history of my life and I have Compleated one hundred and ten pages and I have Mr Chlton [*sic*] to Correct it as I write it I have had Several letters from Philadelphia and New York upon the Subject of publishing it and Several have wrote to me to buy the Coppy wright I have not yet Concluded yet to Sell it I expict it will Contain about two hundred pages and will fully meet all expectations.

I may take a trip through the eastern States during the resess of Congress and Sell the Book a great many have preswaded me to take a towar through the Eastern states that my presents will make thousands of people buy my book that would not by it and I intend never to go home until I am able to pay all my debts and I think I have a good prospect at present and I will do the best I Can. . . . [9]

Long before the *Autobiography* was completed, the tour to Boston and down East had already been planned, doubtless with the plausible argument, advanced by the Whigs to David, of increasing the sales of his book—an argument used to hide the real purposes which they intended the trip to serve. David's name was used early in the next year in publishing *Col. Crockett's Tour to the North and Down East*. It was a volume so obviously *not* composed by him and so pregnant with the propaganda and strategems of the Whigs and the Bank, that one sees in David's phrase, "many have preswaded me to take a towar through the Eastern states," a Whig design, formulated before the *Autobiography* was half completed, for yet another volume in this "literary" chain they were forging. Beyond that lay yet one more book to be issued under his name, the *Life of Martin Van Buren*. Then the Alamo intervened before he could be used any further. This part of David's story may be taken as a parable of the perpetual relationship between big money and the press.

It is possible that David was not revealing everything about his plans for the Eastern tour to his son. With regard to the land bill, he was speaking about a matter with which John was thoroughly familiar, and the latter part of the second paragraph attests to honest motives about the land bill in a way that is beyond argument. Its context, written to be read only by one who knew both him and the subject well, precludes any possible pretense.

The fact that he seemed to write to his children rather than to his wife (no letter to her has survived) and that when he was at home his letters were generally written from Weakley County, though his wife and children were living in Gibson County, is evidence that he maintained a dual residence and suggests unamicable relations between Crockett and his wife and a consequent dwelling under separate roofs. However, there is no positive evidence for this conclusion.

A letter written on January 20 about Post Office shortages and bank deposits reveals Crockett's growing fanaticism on the subject of Jackson:

I must Confess that I never Saw Such times in my life. . . . It is plainley to be discovered that old Jackson is determened to Carry his point or Sacrifise the nation It has been said by Some of his worshipers that he has been the Savior of the country. . . . the truth is If he had been dead and at the devil four years ago it would have been a harpy time for this

country. . . . I must Close and request you to excuse this rough letter as
the management here [is] enough to put any man out of tem [per] that
has any love for his Country [10]

It is a relief to find Crockett on February 24 (the day after Chilton
had accepted in David's name the publisher's offer for the *Autobiography*) discussing a matter that does not involve his monomania. On
that day Crockett and a Virginia Representative arose simultaneously
on the floor of Congress to comment upon a bill under consideration
to extend the pension laws providing for the survivors of the "regular-
army" troops of the Revolutionary War. An amendment had been
proposed to include also the survivors of the volunteers and militiamen
who had fought the Indians on the frontier from 1783 to 1795. There
had been bitter recriminations back and forth between East and West
on the relative merits of the volunteers and "regulars," a subject on
which we have already heard from David. The Chair recognized
Crockett. He stated that he did not rise to make a speech, for there
had been too many of those already, but to move the previous question.

Ruled out of order in deference to the Virginian, Crockett decided,
after all, to "make a little short speech" before relinquishing the floor.
"It was well known to this house and to the nation . . . that he had
always supported the pension system." In his opinion, the militia were
"even better entitled to pensions than regular troops," since the "regulars" sell themselves to the Government at a fixed price, whereas the
volunteer fights "for the love of his country." [11]

On the same day there was introduced into the House a Berks
County, Pennsylvania, memorial from farmers, mechanics, and manu-
facturers praying that the "deposites" might be restored to the U. S.
Bank. In the subsequent discussion concerning the wisdom of printing
it for distribution, Crockett was on his feet in righteous anger. Though
he was "the only person in the House from Tennessee opposed to the
administration," he was not to be prevented from speaking out against
the hypocrisy of spending "three or four thousand dollars" in talk to
save a few dollars in printing a matter so important. . . . "a matter that
perhaps, after all, will not be twenty dollars cost." He was familiar
with this talk of retrenchment as a disguise for frustrating the will of
the people: "It is something like loading a twenty-four pounder to
shoot a flea." For his part:

I love, sir, to see the petitioners come here, and my life on it, sir, they will come—ay, and from Indiana—from all that we hear to the contrary; and, from my own State, every day my letters tell me they wish this question settled. They know very well in my district the character of the man, who, when he takes anything into his head, will carry it into effect. They know how I should act in this bank business, for I told them before I was elected, how I should vote—that I would recharter the bank and restore the deposites.[12]

The real issue at debate, he said (and letters from his constituents show that they disapprove of the administration's actions) is "whether we shall continue to live and do well under the old and happy state of things, or have a despot." He forcefully maintained the right of the people to petition for remedy of grievances: "Sir, I tell you they must not be refused."

The *Globe's* account of this speech includes a final statement omitted by the *Debates:* "I can't stand it any longer—I won't." This excessively emotional remark, publicly delivered, discloses an ardent monomania all the more dangerous for being based upon honest conviction.

The imminence of the *Autobiography's* publication is at this time reflected in two unpublished Crockett letters for February 25 and March 8. In these he introduces a Rev. W. H. Bigham and a Mr. Lewis Levy to the publishers, with the suggestion that they might want to purchase a quantity of copies of the *Autobiography*.[13] By March 10 he is writing once more to a constituent some strictures about Jackson's removal of the deposits. In this letter he first refers to "Black Hawk," or Adam Huntsman, author of the "Chronicles":

... I am glad to see that you are a candidate for Convention I hope you will beat old Blackhawk to death I do hope the people of Madison will lay him away among the unfinished business.

I now see what occasioned him to come out so unprincipled against me in the two last Elections he thought I was so unppulat in that County that If he would come out against me that it would secure his present Election I have no confidence in him and I wish to see a man that Every Confidence can be placed in to fill that station.[14]

On March 14 an army appropriation bill was being discussed. A motion had been made to add a clause to the bill to provide $1,828 as partial reimbursement to Surgeon Beaumont who, while experimenting on the stomach in an effort to save the life of a wounded soldier, had spent $5,000 out of his own pocket. Beaumont had saved the soldier's life and also made certain important discoveries relative to the digestive process. After listening to numerous arguments pro and con, Crockett arose to insert his own brand of bitterness into the debate:

Gentlemen objected to paying for experiments; but in these days, when we were trying experiments on the currency, why not try experiments on the sciences. Though, for his part, he thought it hardly necessary to make appropriations at all for this or anything else. He had been almost ready to go against all appropriations until he knew where the government money was. If one man in the country could take all the money, what was the use of passing any bills about it? It was a mockery—it was childish to sit there and appropriate at all. If one man could take the money, and put it where the law had not placed it; how did the house know where it was? How could they tell but that it might be in his royal Majesty's pocket, or.in the pocket of that imp of famine, his fourth auditor. The money was not where the law put it, and who knew where it was? He would vote for one experiment, but he should for certain vote against the other.[15]

The motion carried.

To say the least, David was certainly being consistent, persistent, and insistent. One observes the House growing weary of his using every possible occasion to air his pet grievances, though there were undoubtedly some chuckles on this occasion. Still, a majority of the House were supporters of Jackson, and as time wore on, Crockett appears to have received less and less respect and attention there. On the other hand, his sentiments would have sat very well in the Senate.

On March 25, David wrote Carey and Hart for an advance of $150 or $200, explaining that "I was beaten the election before the last and it give me a back set in money matters an election costs a man a great deal in my Country." [16] He is also enthusiastic about the splendid sale of his book:

I was much grattifyed to hear that the first editions of my Book were entirely Sold out I hope it will sell agreable to your expectations there has been a great many Sold here Mr Thompson told me that it was the only Book that he Could Sell. . . I have no doubt of a great many Copies Selling on the Mississippi and ohio where that Spurious worke first made its appearance I wish to know if you have an agent in new orleans and in the towns on the Mississippi there it will sell better than any other place. . . .

On April 8 the general appropriations bill was read by sections. At one item providing $1,400 in salary for a clerk to be employed in arranging the archives of the State Department, David mounted his hobby-horse and rode indignantly off. It was not that he was particularly concerned "about the present item." However, he recalled the fuss made during the 1828 campaign about a "draftsman . . . not thought to be a friend of the administration," who therefore had to be "retrenched and 'reformed'" out of office—for economy's sake! "They reformed him out," but Crockett had voted against it, knowing that in the end it "would cost the government double what they gave this officer." In the sequel the House had "reinstated their draftsman by an overwhelming vote." David, too, favored genuine "retrenchment, against the extravagance of government."

But he had not known that they were going to behave like a parcel of little children on the bank of a branch, fishing for minnows with a pin hook. He had never thought to see expenses doubled in a few years. But he had lived now long enough in a civilized part of the country to find that when he was only a backwoodsman he knew little about matters. In short, what he had seen in this civilized part of the country had pretty much satisfied him that the whole of it was like . . . the little fellow who undertook to shave a hog—'great cry and little wool!' [17]

On the following day, Crockett returned to the attack. He objected to "talk of economy" while creating "a hundred new clerks." All that had been done was to reform "out all the old faithful servants of the new government, some with gray heads, to make room for partisans." Contrasting "the Prodigal's [Adams'] " budget of thirteen million with the Jackson budget of twenty-two million, he objected that "he could not stand such economy. There was no sense in it. In his part of the country it would not even be called good nonsense." For his part, he was against providing any more clerks. And the extravagance of this budget "was the consequence of letting one man wield the destinies of the government. That was not what our fathers shed their blood for." [18]

On April 10, the Globe (a Jackson organ) gives an interesting report not carried by the Debates (a Whig organ), bearing on a post mail route to Troy: [19] "On motion of Mr. Crockett it was Resolved that the Committee on the Post Office and Post Roads be instructed to inquire into the expediency of establishing a post route from Totton's

Wells, in Obion County, by Seth Bradford's, to Troy, Tennessee." [20]
There is a fuller explanation of what this resolution was about in the
Boston *Tour*, the next book to come out in David's name, in one of
the few parts that bears any close resemblance to an original Crockett
contribution. The passage records an amusing political blunder made
by Crockett's opponent Fitzgerald in the previous campaign:

Well, so after a while they have a coach from Reynoldsburg to Paris,
from Paris to Dresden, and thence straight to Mills Point. But they left out
Troy, and the people of Obion county began to talk about leaving out
Fitz. Mr. Barry immediately ordered his contractors to run anywhere
to get Fitz in: so he run the coach fifteen miles out of the way to Troy,
till the election was over, and then withdrew every stage from the district,
except one running straight through. Troy had not even a horse mail, and
I had to jog the postmaster-general's elbow and make him give them a
mail. [21]

On the same day (April 10) Crockett in another letter to his publishers refers indirectly to Chilton's equal partnership with him in the
Autobiography:

You propose to Sell 500 Copies of my Narrative provided I will agree
to have it accounted for at 50 Cents pr Copy I know mighty little about
Such matters But might this not end in a perminent reduction of the trade
price, So as to bring the Book down to little more in the end than the
mere Cost of printing & binding? I have the most implicit Confidence in
you, and that you will do nothing in the whole business with out an equal
eye to my entrest as well as your own If you think it advisable to make
the arrangement I do not oppose it So far as the 500 Copies Spoken of
are Concerned provided you will furnish two other lots of 500 Copies each
to myself and a friend on the Same terms if hereafter requested. [22]

Crockett also notes that he is "hard pressed in money matters," and
adds: "I hope to visit your City before the adjournmint" of Congress.
He planned to visit Philadelphia *before adjournment* as part of the
trip to Boston eventually described in the *Tour*. He had written John
Wesley that he might take such a trip *during the recess*. In view of
the fact that one of the serious charges which had helped defeat him
for Congress in 1831 had been his absences from roll calls, one concludes that he must have considered this trip important indeed to run
the risk of the same charges again. He had told his son that he might
take the trip to increase the sale of his book. Having sold out an edition
or so, this excuse scarcely holds water. In reply to a constituent a

little later on, he pled "a pain in my breast" and travelling for his health as the occasion for the trip. Obviously, a strenuous speaking trip could hardly fill this bill either. He gave a third reason on the flyleaf of the *Tour:* "His object being to examine the grand Manufacturing establishment of the country; and also to find out the condition of its literature and morals, the extent of its commerce, and the practical operation of 'THE EXPERIMENT,' " which must have referred to the deposits. In the light of all this and of what actually happened on the trip, we realize that the trip's real purpose was purely political—a part of the compact with his Eastern industrial friends, who had persuaded him not only to make the trip, but also to neglect his Congressional responsibilities in order to make it, whether David was fully aware of its real purpose or not.

A letter from Crockett to Jacob Dixon for April 14 is described as "a denunciation in matters of banking and faro dealing." [23] We have no evidence of David's gambling, other than tradition (though Captain William L. Foster's earlier letter denied that he gambled); but David had maintained in the Tennessee Legislature a consistent opposition to the bill "to suppress the vice of gaming." The story told in the previous letter of being "hard pressed in money matters" is but a new statement of an old and otherwise unsatisfactorily explained condition. This missing letter denouncing faro dealing may have had more to do with a smarting over a personal loss than with the zeal of a theoretical reformer, and might well offer a valuable insight from a vantage point we do not otherwise have. [24]

On April 25, 1834, David set forth on the "towar for his health" —his political health!

Chapter 11

"A TOWAR THROUGH THE
EASTERN STATES"

D AVID CROCKETT'S Eastern Tour extended over a period of
almost three weeks from April 25 to May 13 or 14. Morally
it was less to David's discredit than to the everlasting shame of those
who knowingly and cynically used this simple man for their own
selfish purposes. Politically, it was the blunder of Crockett's career.
While Congress was in full session, and with his itinerary advertised
in the Whig press, Crockett paraded himself before admiring throngs
at Baltimore, Philadelphia, New York, Jersey City, Newport, Boston,
Lowell, Providence, and Camden. He was banqueted, flattered, applauded, presented gifts, admired by exclusive clubs.

The document which registers the extent of the Whig exploitation
of David Crockett is the Boston *Tour* printed by the Whigs under
David's name. Its chief interest to us is as a schedule of David's itinerary, of the people he saw, and of his speeches and labors in behalf
of the Eastern Whigs. Parrington's estimate of the Boston *Tour* is
surprisingly accurate:

It is in the *Tour* . . . that the myth expands genially. A clever and amusing
campaign document, it is a masterpiece of Whig strategy to gull the
simple. The loquacious Davy joined heartily with his managers to cash in
on his reputation. . . . He was paraded at meetings with Daniel Webster,
given great dinners, applauded for his rustic wit and homespun honesty,
presented with a fine rifle; *and he seems never to have realized how grossly
he was being exploited.* . . . Wherever he went he was taken in charge by
the Whigs. Everything was carefully arranged beforehand. News was
sent forward that he was coming; crowds were gathered to greet him;

publicity was attended to; morning, noon, and night he was invited to speak, and the speeches were carefully reprinted—not authentic speeches, probably, but good campaign material nevertheless.[1]

David's alliance with the Whigs must be seen in terms of his efforts in behalf of his land bill, a matter Parrington never mentions, and not merely in terms of a stupid, loquacious fool desiring public attention. David was naive, but not an imbecile. His efforts to disguise the purely political purpose of the tour are naive too: the object of his trip was merely to increase the sale of his *Autobiography* (to John Wesley); he had a pain in his chest and was travelling for his health (to a constituent), and he even tried to minimize his absence from Congress by stating that the tour had lasted only two weeks.

David did not, of course, write the *Tour*, but merely helped to collect Whig notes and newspaper clippings recording ghostwritten speeches. Another man wrote the book from these "scissors and paste-pot" gleanings. A few portions bear his touch, but most is so inferior, so affectedly "backwoodsie," so full of sham vernacular and impossible harangue (though the views expressed are the anti-Jackson Whig ones of his letters and Congressional speeches) that the *Tour* richly deserved the oblivion that it promptly received.

Crockett left Washington on April 25 and spent that night at Barnum's Hotel in Baltimore, dining there with Whig friends. Next morning he crossed the Chesapeake on the steamer Carroll-of-Carrollton, boarded a train for Delaware City, re-embarked there for a trip up the Delaware River, and arrived in Philadelphia that evening, April 26. Here, as all along the route, he was "struck with astonishment" by the cheering throngs assembled to greet him. After making a short speech he was taken by friends to the United States Hotel on Chestnut Street, appropriately opposite the United States Bank. On the 28th he visited the waterworks, the mint, the asylum, the exchange (where he made the promised anti-Jackson harangue), the Navy Hospital, the Navy Yard, Schuylkill Bridge, the Girard School, the theatre in Walnut Street—all in the company of his new found Whig friends of Philadelphia. During this time he was presented with a watchchain seal engraved with his "go ahead" motto and was informed by Mr. James M. Sanderson [2] that the young Whigs of Philadelphia desired to make him a present of a gun, to be delivered later.

On April 29 he set sail up the Delaware River on the *New Phila-delphia*, took a train across northern New Jersey to Perth Amboy, and another from there to New York City. Here a committee of young Whigs came aboard to wait on him and conduct him to the American Hotel, where he lodged until the afternoon of May 2. In New York, the routine was repeated: he visited many places, hobnobbed with the influential Whigs, and made speeches voicing Whig sentiments. On April 30 he made a speech at the New York Stock Exchange, and thereafter on the same day dined with "the rale Major Jack Downing." Major Jack was a fictitious character created by Seba Smith of Port-land, Maine, whose political attitudes resembled those of Crockett himself. At first a loyal supporter of Jackson, Major Jack was about to turn against Jackson. Reputedly, Major Jack edited the *Downing Gazette*, and this organ was soon to publish so-called Crockett letters. David's *Tour*, in turn, published Downing letters. It is entirely pos-sible that David and Seba Smith may indeed have sat down to "cold turkey" on April 30, 1834, in New York City.

That evening Crockett dined with the young Whigs, along with Gulian C. Verplanck, who had defended Crockett's conduct at the Adams' dinner back in 1828. Augustin Smith Clayton, probable author of "Crockett's" *Life of Van Buren*, delivered a speech, and David spoke after him. On May 1, after visiting the newspaper offices, Crock-ett toured the Sixth Ward, stronghold of Martin Van Buren. The Big-Whigs had arranged on this day to hoist a new flag on the Battery. In the company of Mayor Gideon Lee and General Morton, the re-viewing officer, David participated vigorously in the "flag-waving."

His appearance that evening at the Bowery Theatre had been adver-tised by handbills, but evidently without prior consultation with David. He seemed to have had all his stomach could stand and it was only with difficulty that his managers could finally persuade him to attend as advertised. At last he put in a brief appearance, received the prearranged applause, and returned to his room. A good night's sleep must have re-lined his stomach, for on the next day, May 2, he went on to Jersey City for a public rifle shooting, and returned to New York in time to catch a three o'clock steamer for Boston.

On the way, Crockett's group stopped briefly at Newport and then landed at Providence, where Crockett was met by a cheering crowd. Proceeding by stage, they arrived at Boston in mid-afternoon of

May 3, David putting up at Tremont House. He now went through his paces at Boston, visiting a number of factories. Among these were the factories at Roxborough, where the proprietor gave him a hunting coat manufactured there—probably the coat about which he boasted to Colonel Robert I. Chester when the Colonel afterwards visited Crockett's cabin in west Tennessee. At eight o'clock he dined with the young Whigs and made a long anti-Jackson speech.[3]

On May 5 he continued to see sights and meet dignitaries. Rain interfered with plans on the 6th, but on May 7 he visited the mills at Lowell. In the *Tour* these factory visits are made the occasion for elaborate praising of Eastern industry. In fact Crockett experienced a revelation which made him change his entire position and become a thorough exponent of the beauty, the quality, the reliability of the manufactured materials and of the sweetness and light surrounding the employees in that town of the distinguished Brahmin name. He even included in his account a long table of statistics glorifying the Lowell mills. On the day of his visit, Mr. Lawrence, owner of one of the mills, presented him with a suit of wool bought from Mark Cockral of Mississippi, which "was as good cloth as the best I ever bought for best imported"—a neat tie-up of patriotism, Whiggery, industry, and the high tariffs that kept out the "best imported." That evening he dined with the usual "one hundred" Whigs of Lowell, and regaled them with his customary speech.

Returning to Boston on May 8, he spent that evening at the home of Lieutenant-Governor Armstrong where, to climax his trip, he met various notables. From the Lieutenant-Governor's he progressed to the theatre "to be looked at." When he went to pay his bill on the following morning, before setting out on his return trip to Washington, he was told that it had already been paid, a fact which the *Tour* attributed to the native generosity and hospitality of the people.

Proceeding by stagecoach to Providence on May 9, he declined invitations to dine (and speak), and went from there to New York, on May 10 or 11.[4] The party was greeted by a large audience at Camden, N. J., on May 11 or 12, and after a midday meal, David harangued them for "about half an hour," and caught the horseboat for Philadelphia, where he arrived later that day. When he arrived at Baltimore on May 12 or 13, he was greeted by a large gathering, proceeded to Barnum's and made another speech. And on the following day, he took a stage to Washington, arriving the same day, May 13 or 14. He continued his "towar" briefly after the House adjourned in June.

During this period, David had become an important figure in the Whig press. The space devoted to him in *Niles Register* and other Whig papers had gradually increased prior to the publication of the *Autobiography*. By March, 1834, these papers made frequent reports of his activities, and from that time on, he continued to occupy the pages of *Niles Register* until *after* his death. A single entry from that journal reporting Crockett's tour through the North is sufficient to indicate the tone of this news coverage:

The following is a sketch of the remarks of Col. Crockett, a member of the house of representatives ... delivered from the balcony of the City Hall, Boston, about two weeks ago.[5] The colonel returned and took his seat last week.[6]

He commenced by saying that he came here without the least expectation of making a speech; he came not as a politician, but at the suggestion of one of his most intelligent political friends, gen. Thomas, of Louisiana, to learn from personal observation, what could not be correctly known otherwise. He had no expectation of attracting any attention other than any private citizen, but for the kind of civilities he had received he considered it his duty to tender his most grateful thanks.

He then alluded to his political course. He said that when he first went to congress he was opposed to the protective system; he thought it his duty to oppose it; but since he had visited New England, he had changed his views on that subject; he only wished that some of the leading politicians of the southern states, would visit the New England manufacturies, and said that a single visit would do more to bring about peace, harmony and union between the different sections of the country than all the legislation in the world.

He said he had been one of the earliest friends and supporters of gen. Jackson; he had known him from his youth up; he had fought with him, and was one of the first who fired a gun in the battles in which gen. Jackson gained so much reknown. He had supported him for the Presidency because he believed him an honest man. He did not suppose, what he had since found to be the case, that he would consider the greatest sin a man could commit, would be to vote against Andrew Jackson.

He would refer back to the condition of the country only seven months ago. Then we had the best currency in the world, our commerce and manufactures were in the highest state of prosperity; now we see ruin and distress pervading all classes of the community. And for what purpose has all this misery been brought about? Merely to gratify the prejudices and will of a superannuated old man. He said we had arrived at a crisis such as we had never before known.

He had never apprehended any serious consequences from the troubles in South Carolina; he did not think the single state of Carolina could dissolve the union. But now things wore an alarming aspect, when we see neighborhood against neighborhood, city against city, and state against state; when the chief magistrate of the union seizes the sword of the nation with one hand, and the purse with the other, and bids defiance to Congress and to the whole country, we may with good reason tremble for the result. Look at the president's course. He first attacked the bank, and demolished that, and then levelled his gun and fired at the senate. But he was glad to say the senate was firm, that it was able to resist his assaults; that it *could* and *would* save the country; and when general Jackson discharged his gun at the senate, *he fired into the wrong flock.*

He said he was no man's follower; he belonged to no party; he had no interest but the good of the country at heart; he would not stoop to fawn or flatter to gain the favor of any of the political demagogues of the present time. Gen. Jackson's political conduct had disappointed him, and he turned the back of his hand towards him; and when he was reproached for deserting the party, "I told them I had rather be a *nigger's* man or a rackoon dog than belong to such a party."

He said he did not travel to make political speeches, he wished to travel as a private citizen. He trusted they would excuse his defects, for he was but a plain, unlearned man, as he had never had but six months schooling in his life, and it could hardly be expected that he was fitted to address the people of Boston, the most enlightened and accomplished city in the world. He concluded by tendering his most heart-felt thanks for the very kind attentions he had received in Boston, and indeed wherever he had been throughout New England.[7]

The Whigs had sent David North to test his popularity there, nor did they fail to keep the country informed of his travels. What must have been the bawdy laughter of the Whig politicians about the country at these earnest protestations of their marionette that "he was no man's follower," and that he wished to tender his "most heart-felt thanks" for their "very kind attentions"! David Crockett lived on physically until the Alamo. But the real David Crockett was here dying with his boots on in Washington, D. C., under the crushing weight of the aegis of the Second United States Bank and its minions —even as the integrity of Daniel Webster was being ground to dust by the same forces.

On his Eastern tour Crockett had spoken to Whig audiences marvellously receptive to his anti-Jackson sentiments. The apparent adulation of those audiences had the effect of causing him to abandon all restraint and to relax completely those proprieties which he had, at least in some degree, formerly exercised upon the floor of Congress. Now his hatred of Jackson grows dangerously hot, and soon upon the floor of the House he was to throw discretion to the winds.

In a letter of May 26 to Mr. Joseph Wallis, of Morgan County, Alabama, he spoke of "this political Judeas Martin Van Buren," and called him "a perfect Scoundral," one among "a Set of Imps of ... famin" so set upon "the Spoils of Victory" that they "would destroy the Country" and let Jackson go to the devil. To Crockett, Jackson was a "poor old man" so seduced by their "Singing glorification to him" that he had come to believe the people would support his destruction of the Constitution and the laws of the country. Jackson was the victim of the delusion that "until he mounted the throne" no man, "not even the men that formed the Constitution," understood it. David said:

In fact we may Say with propriety that we have the government of one man Andrew Jackson holds both the Sword and purse and Claims it by the Constitution as the Arms and amunition and other public property and he has tools and Slaves to his party enough to Sustain him in the house of representatives But we have one hope the Senate will Save the Constitution and laws in spite of King Andrew the first. ... we are gitting his poor lick Spittles almost ashamed of them selves [8]

On the following day in a letter to Colonel T. J. Dobings, he predicted the end of "our long and happy mode of government" and loss of "our republican libertys" under "the governmint of one man" whose "tools and Slaves ... Sustain him in his wild Carear," and whose purpose "is to promote the intrest of a Set of Scoundrals." He accused Jackson of taking "the government money out of the united States Bank" only to place it "whare he Could have the Controle of it" so as to make "that political Judeas Martin Vanburen our next prisedent." He was gratified "beyond measure" "that the people is well pleased with my Course," vowing that "I never did know any mode of legislating only to go and do what my Conscience dictated to me to be wright." Crockett predicted that should Jackson "once Conquer the Senate ... he will put his foot on the Constitution and tell the Judicial powar to go to hell. ...." He concluded with an ominously naive reference to the one political reality important to his public career: "I have been trying for Some time to get up my land Bill but we have not even passed the appropriation Bills and there is no chance to do any thing I know of no opposition to it if we Could get to act on it." [9]

The letters of this period are much like the speeches of his Boston *Tour*. How much of their content was his own, or how much of that content was composed of ideas and phraseology picked up from speeches written for him to play upon the gullibility of his ignorant but well-meaning patriotism, must be left to the reader's conjecture. However mistaken history may have proved David to be—however extreme and foolish are his statements about the sword and purse, the tyrant and king—there were many supporting his position at this time. Out of all his surviving correspondence, there is nothing that reveals real subterfuge or collusion. Compromise was represented over the long course. It must have taken place by such slow degrees and been so carefully coordinated by the Whigs to his growing hate for Jackson and to his increasing anger at the state party which blocked his land bill, that, as Parrington says, he "never . . . realized how grossly he was being exploited." Apparently it *was* a clear "Conscience" that aroused his indignation at the opposition as men without honor or principle!

His hatred of Jackson had driven him to a point beyond political sanity as evidenced by his attitude toward Polk's proposed adjournment date. Crockett was fully aware that his political future hinged on securing the passage of his land bill. Furthermore, by his own testimony to William Hack on June 9, that bill was in danger of being lost sight of among end-of-session pressures: "We will adjourn . . . on the 30 of June So I fear I will have a Bad Chance to get up my land Bill I have Been trying for some time and if I Could get it up I have no doubt of its passage [I] know of no opposition to it [the] whole delegation will go for it." [10] Hence it appears that his hate for Jackson had now become more important to him even than his land bill. To embarrass Jackson, he opposed Polk's proposal, on May 29, to extend the adjournment date from June 16 to June 30! Since Polk spoke for Jackson, David "was anxious for the 16th to be fixed upon"—even demanding "the yeas and nays." [11] He voted in the negative when the adjournment was extended 129–83. Crockett's animosity was now stronger than his interest in his constituents.

In the long letter to William Hack of Denmark, Tennessee, obviously a displeased constituent. David reveals his distraught mind caught in a web of self-righteous justification. In explaining his votes "against the Bank Committee being raised," he asserts that he has "never regreted it," because Congress, already having "voted the Bank to death," had no right "to Send a Committee to examin it." Crockett says it was "Just like taking a man up and hanging him and then examining a Jury to try whether he was gilty or not." The purpose of proposing the Bank Committee had been only to "rais an exitemint in the Country and prop up Jacksons Sinking popularity." He reminds his constituent that "in our Country whin a Juror once Sets and gives his opinion on a Case he is never more a Competent Juror in the Same Case." As for the supposed impartiality of the Committee, "Frances Thomas from Maryland" who "at the last Congress ... Said all he Could against it ... is now made Chairman." The Speaker had appointed "five Jackson men & two antiJackson men [to] Serve on the Committee you will get Both the reports and you Can Judge for your Self."

He then makes an ineffectual attempt to excuse his absence from Congress during the Eastern Tour:

> As for retrenchmint I have always wint for that I voted for it in Committee of the whole but when the final vote was taken I was not thare I had been for Some time labouring under a Complaint with a pain in my breast and I Concluded to take a travel a Couple of weeks for my health I knew they would do nothing more than to pass the appropriation Bill that was all the vote I regretted not being there at. . . .

He concludes in his by now familiar fire-and-brimstone manner, inveighing against Jackson's holding "[both the] Sword & purs and Claims it [from the] Constitution a powar never [heard] of by any other presedent."

Crockett's growing intransigence was reflected in his speech of June 13, in opposition to Polk's motion to table a joint resolution from the Senate censuring Jackson's removal of the deposits:

> Mr. Crockett rose and asked a call of the House He proceeded to say that his colleague [Polk] had been dodging around this question all the session, and now he asked that it be laid on the table. I had a hope, said Mr. C, that we had a chance to meet the question fairly, and let members stand up to the rack and say to their constituents that we have supported the laws and constitution. This question is to test that fact, and I hope to meet it upon its merits, and say to the country, by our votes, whether

we have a government or not. Mr. C. was called to order so repeatedly that we could not hear distinctly what he said, as it was not a debatable case. Mr. C concluded by asking for the yeas and nays on the call, which were ordered; and the roll having been gone through, 211 members answered to their names; and excuses having been made for some of the absent members—

Mr. Crockett moved that the Sergeant-at-arms should be dispatched to bring up those members for whom excuses had not been made.[12]

Polk's motion passed 114–101. Among those joining with David in opposition to the motion were Thomas Chilton, William Clark, and Augustin Smith Clayton, the authors or part-authors, respectively, of Crockett's *Autobiography*, Boston *Tour*, and *Life of Martin Van Buren*.

When thereafter Polk's motion to table another resolution (ordering all United States deposits to be again made with the Bank of the United States after July 1, 1834) carried 118–98, Crockett and his friends voted in the negative.[13]

On May 17 when the Harbor Bill had been under consideration in the House, Crockett had proposed an amendment to appropriate "$60,000 to improve the navigation of the Forked, Deer [*sic*—Forked Deer], Hatchie, and Obion Rivers, to be expended equally on each," and had spoken in defense of the amendment, but it had been rejected "without a division." [14] When in response to Polk's motion on June 19 for an amendment to strike out the provision for $100,000 to be spent to fortify Fort George's Island (this at the suggestion of the Secretary of War, provided cuts were necessary) there were patriotic clamorings from those whose district was deprived. Crockett rose to revive these May 17 proposals in a tone that aroused a hornet's nest of opposition:

Mr. Crockett said he had at all times supported internal improvements, and would now like to do so. He had [had] an amendment to offer to the harbor bill, for a small benefit for his district, which was to remove the obstructions out of the rivers Hatche [*sic*], Forked Deer, and Obion; but he unfortunately went home to his dinner, and, while absent, the bill was laid on the table. I now believe, said Mr. C, we ought to lay this bill on the table, too, and all other appropriation bills. Sir, it is useless to pass appropriation bills. A majority of this House has determined, by their votes, that Andrew Jackson shall be the Government. You say his will shall be the law of the land. . . . I have never seen but one honest countenance since I have been here, and he has just resigned. I suppose he cannot stand them any longer. And I am told that the other, the Secretary of the Treasury, is packing up to remove. . . . he is surrounded by a set of imps of famine, that are as hungry as the flies that we have read of in Aesop's Fables, that came after the fox and sucked his blood. . . . Let us all go home, and let the people live one year on glory, and it will bring them to their senses; and they will send us back here and teach us to make the gentleman in the white house take down his flag. Sir, the people will let him know that he is not the government. I hope to live to see better times.[15]

Such remarks, the most extreme to date spoken on the floor, could not go unchallenged by the Tennessee delegation. Mr. Dunlap, from the district next to David's, arose and castigated him. Crockett, he said, wanted all appropriations laid on the table merely because his own had been. Further, inasmuch as the states had never delegated power to the Federal Government "for internal improvements, . . . to vote for them was the sort of usurpation of power of which Crockett was accusing Jackson" falsely. He went on to demonstrate that to support these wasteful "improvements" necessitated high tariffs (as David had maintained in the debate over the Buffalo to New Orleans Road Bill) and said that those who voted for the one must of necessity support the other.

Crockett in his reply asserted that "he had no idea of warming his colleague," but he wished it distinctly understood that he took nothing back that he had said, but would reassert everything, and go further. He therefore now said we had no government at all, and God only knows what is to become of the country in these days of miserable misrule. David had clearly reached a point where, on matters relating to Jackson, his sanity may be questioned.

On June 23 during a renewed discussion of the Harbor Bill, Crockett again made an attempt to insert his amendment. He had by now decided to be content with a little "gravy" for his district, since he could not get more. He said: "that, as nobody knew where the money of the country was, he should not ask so much as he had done before; he would now be content with $30,000 instead of $60,000, and be glad to get even that." [16]

This amendment too was defeated, and Crockett's action for the session came to an end, except for one concluding act of spite against Polk. An account in the *Globe* and *Niles Register* discloses that on June 28 Crockett opposed R. M. Johnson's request "to submit a vote of thanks to the late Speaker Stevenson," saying, "I am not inclined to adopt a vote of thanks to any man, without knowing what for, or being satisfied they are deserved." [17] It was not possible to achieve a two-thirds majority for a suspension of the rules to allow the resolution to be submitted. On the evening of the same day, Crockett being absent, the same resolution was introduced again and passed 97–49, the chair having decided a two-thirds majority was not required.

David had already engaged passage on the stagecoach for Baltimore and Philadelphia for the next day, June 29. On that evening he was no doubt preparing for the journey and his return to Tennessee for the summer. As far back as June 15 he had planned to leave Congress before adjournment in line with plans to cooperate with Daniel Webster and others in a speech-making attack upon Jackson at Independence City on July 4. On that day (June 15) he had looked

forward to our adjournment with as much interest as ever did a poor convict in a penitentiary to see his last day come. We have done but one act, and that is that the will of Andrew, the first king, is to be the law of the land. He has tools and slaves enough in Congress to sustain him in anything he may wish to effect.

I thank God I am not one of them. I do consider him a greater tyrant than Cromwell, Caesar or Bonaparte....[18]

On the same day, in a letter to Mr. J. M. Sanderson of Philadelphia he reveals his July 4 plans. The young Whigs had commissioned Sanderson to have a gun made for David, to learn his desires in that connection, and to pass them on to the manufacturer.[19] David was to go to Philadelphia to receive it before Congress adjourned, and David's letter is written in contemplation of that trip:

Your favour enclosing the target of my fine guns first Shooting has Been Recd and I am much pleased to See that She Bunches her Balls She shoots two low but that will be altered by Raising the hind Sight

I have taken passage in the Stage for Baltimore on this day two weeks and expects to be in Philadelphia on monday the 30 and perhaps may Spend the 4 of July their

will you pleas to procure me Say a half Dozen or a whole dozen of Canisters Powder of the Best quality and See Mr Cary & Hart they are Sending me Some Boxes of Books to Pitts Burgh and get thim to Box it up with the Books and Send it on to Pittsburgh I will pay you the mony on Sight for it as there is no Chance to get the article in my Country I will also want Several Boxes of Caps of the Best quality these are articles Cannot be had in my Country....[20]

This simple request for powder to be boxed with his books led instead, according to Chapter VI of the Boston *Tour*, to an introduction on July 5 to "the great powdermaker, Mr. Dupont, who said to me, that he had been examining my fine gun, and that he wished to make me a present of half a dozen cannisters of his best sportsman's powder. I thanked him, and he went off, and in a short time returned with a dozen, nicely boxed up and directed to me." It is altogether fitting that Whigs, gunpowder, and Dupont, should tie up the knot to this little episode, with Nicholas Biddle and the United States Bank making the arrangements in the background.

David arrived in Baltimore on June 29. That evening, in conversation with friends, he remarked that he planned to write up his "tour," and if necessary, "do like members in the House—speak half a column and write [it up in the records as] two—or get it done." Reaching Philadelphia by boat on June 30, he was again put up at the United States Hotel on Chestnut Street. On the evening of July 1, the rifle was presented to him by Mr. Sanderson, and along with it were a tomahawk, a butcher-knife, and accoutrements for the gun. David made a speech in which he promised to use the rifle in defense of the country, if necessary, and to pass it on to his sons for the same purpose. On July 2 he went over to Camden, New Jersey, in the company of Mr. Sanderson and Colonel Pulaski to try out his gun. July 3 was devoted to an outing at the Fish House on the Schuylkill.

Finally the big day arrived for which David was waiting—Independence Day in Independence City, the Fourth of July in Philadelphia! In the company of Senators Daniel Webster, Poindexter, Mangum, Ewing, Robbins, and Representative Denny, he went early in the day to the Music Fund Hall, where, in the wake of the other speakers, he gave a rousing oration about tyranny, sword and purse, despotism, and independence. Later in the day David proceeded to a Whig gathering at the Hermitage in the First District, where he was greeted by loud cheers. The Declaration of Independence was read, and dinner was served. Crockett was then called upon to deliver his second speech of the day—about tyranny, sword and purse, despotism, and independence. Speeches followed by Webster, Robbins, and Denny. Afterwards the entire party proceeded to the Chestnut-Street Theatre where, to the large crowd assembled, Crockett once more spoke his piece—about tyranny, sword and purse, despotism, and independence. This concludes the day, and, doubtless, the purpose of the trip.

Poulson's American Daily Advertiser for Monday, July 7, 1834, describes one of these Fourth of July speeches: It was a proud day for the Whigs of Philadelphia on which so many distinguished members from both Houses of Congress spoke. Four hundred persons enjoyed the dinner at the Hermitage. Afterwards: "The President [Joseph R. Ingersoll] now announced a complimentary toast honoring Col. Crockett. The Hon. Member from Tennessee promptly presented himself before his delighted auditors, and in his usual unaffected and good humoured manner, contributed to the gratification of the day." [21] The editor adds, with the pious air of one sacrificing a victim on a political altar: "It is devoutly to be wished that every original friend of Gen. Jackson was as honest as Col. Crockett, and that he would abandon the President, when [the President] abandons those patriotic principles . . . he once owned."

On July 5 David rested, received Mr. Dupont's powder and an imported China pitcher, and made preparations for the trip home next day. On July 6 he took a train west, across Pennsylvania, toward Pittsburgh. A newspaper account gives a brief glimpse of him on that Sunday journey:

On Sunday evening last Col. David Crockett, the universally known Tennessean, passed through Columbia in the Rail Road cars on his way from Philadelphia, where he had spent the fourth inst., to the far west. He was invited to remain a day or two among us, but declined on account of his desire to reach home, from which he had been absent eight months. He said that he had spoken himself hoarse in Philadelphia, having made three addresses on the national anniversary of that city. Being persuaded to get out and take a social glass, by some of those who were present and gazing at the "lion," he gave us a toast, after his usual style: "God bless you, for I can't."

He talked warmly on politics, and did not seem pleased with the Jackson men of Lancaster, for putting up a hickory pole. He went "ahead," after a delay of fifteen minutes, and leaving persons who expected to see a wild man of the woods, clothed in a hunting shirt and covered with hair, a good deal surprised at having viewed a respectable looking personage, dressed decently and wearing his locks much after the fashion of our plain German farmers. [22]

At Pittsburgh, David embarked with Captain Stone on the *Hunter*, and travelled down the Ohio to Wheeling, West Virginia. Here David was compelled to refuse an invitation to speak, in order to catch his boat. The captain was prevailed upon, however, to return a piece back up the river and to come through again so that the crowd could send David off with a rousing cheer. At the mouth of the Guyandotte, the boat took on three Kentucky Congressmen—Tompkins, Beatty, and that other man so thoroughly intertwined with Crockett in the land of myth, BEN HARDIN.

In Cincinnati on Saturday, July 12, David was invited by a committee to "partake of a cold cut" and to make a speech. This he did, and on July 13 continued his trip to Louisville, where he remained for several days complying with invitations to speak. He followed his Louisville speech with another at Jeffersonville Springs, Indiana. He made a third speech at a dinner to which he was invited as a testimonial in favor of his political course. Finally he caught Captain Buckner's steamboat *Scotland*, and arrived, on July 22, at Mill's "Pinte," where William (his second son) met him for the thirty-five mile drive home to Gibson County.

Except for the chancery court suit, there is very little evidence concerning David's activities for the rest of this summer.²³ In the fall David's father died: he had moved across Tennessee in David's wake. On September 15 David Crockett, James Dean, and Daniel Conlee were made securities in the administration of John Crockett's estate, and David was made administrator.²⁴ There is also the record of an old court suit which David was at this time contesting. Some years earlier Robert Tinkle had brought suit against David, who was security for John Eubanks, for about thirty dollars. As Eubanks had property, Tinkle had agreed, upon condition that Crockett indemnify the officer in selling Eubanks' property to discharge the debt, that Crockett "should be exonerated and discharged from any liability as security to the said Eubanks." According to Crockett's plea of September 11, 1834, he had carried out his bargain, the property had been sold, and David had been discharged from liability. After six or seven years the original execution against David's own property was revived and the constable threatened to sell that property. On September 16 of this summer, David obtained a *supersedeas* writ to forestall that action until the former suit could be properly adjudicated.²⁵

Prior to his departure in November for Congress he signed a promissory note on October 11 to William Tucker:

One day after date I promis to pay or cause to be paid unto *William Tucker* just and full some of three hundred [twelve] and fortee nine and a quart. cent it being for value recd witness my hand and seal this 11 of Oct 1834

David Crockett [26]

Despite five years in Congress, his administration of two estates, and national fame, poverty continued to plague his steps.

The Boston *Tour* picks David up again with an account of his return trip to Washington, probably about the end of the second week in November. Having promised to spend a couple of days with Thomas Chilton, he arrived in Elizabethtown, Kentucky, on Saturday, November 18. There on November 22 Chilton and Crockett attended a dinner at Mr. H. G. Wintersmith's Hotel, and Crockett made his customary speech. After this, the Tour conducts him without more ado back to Washington.[27]

On December 8, David wrote the following letter to Nicholas Biddle, president of the Second United States Bank:

Washington City 8th Decr 1834

My Dear Sir

I have talked to Governer Poindexter upon the Subject that I was so much destressed about when I Saw You that was his being protected on the Bill which he endorsed for me with You and I informed him that You Stated to me that if he would indorse a note for me in the bank It Coul lie over awhile he Said he would do any thing he Could for me and I wish you to make out the account and enclose a note and Check for the amount and I will Get it endorsed and enclose it to You which I hope will keep matters easy until I Can pay It for Your friend-Ship to me You Shall never be forgotten by your friend & obt Servt

David Crockett

Nicholas Biddle

Ps write to Mr Poindexter that It is for the Same Bill that he endorsed for me as he may know that he is not decieved. DC [28]

Whether this indebtedness is the same as the one mentioned in David's letter to Richard Smith of January 7, 1832, I cannot positively state, though I believe that it was. At any rate, Nicholas Biddle was soon to write the note off as a loss.[29]

On December 9, "On motion of Mr. Crockett, the Tennessee Vacant Lands Bill was made the order of the day for tomorrow." [30] However, nothing came of it. On December 11, David submitted a resolution for improvement of the Western rivers:

Resolved, That the Committee on Roads and Canals be instructed to inquire and report to this House whether the improvements of the navigation of [the three] rivers, would be a national object; and if so, what would be the probable cost of removing the obstructions to the head of navigation of said rivers. [31]

Speaking in behalf of the resolution, Crockett said "he feared gentlemen did not understand the nature of his resolution." It is very probable that they understood too well. Re-election time was drawing on, and David had little to show for his efforts in behalf of the Western District, having squandered his energy in his fight against Jackson. Crockett claimed "it was a mere inquiry whether those rivers were of a national character or not." He pointed out that his request "for an appropriation to remove the obstructions out of those rivers" had been turned down as coming under the head of internal improvements. Since the President had more recently defined "national" rivers as rivers with a "port of entry," he was raising the point again. He could not "say there is a port of entry on either of those rivers":

but one thing I will say, if the French war should go on, and the French were to land an army at New Orleans, and it were to become necessary to meet them with an army, I have no doubt the district of country around those rivers would be the most convenient to call upon for supplies. It is a rich, fertile country, in general, on those rivers, and it might be considered a national object to improve them, although a port of entry may be lacking. I do hope . . . the House will indulge the inquiry, and adopt the resolution. I do not wish to put the chief magistrate to the painful necessity of vetoeing an appropriation, if I should be so happy as to get one for that object.

The fates continued unkind: "the resolution was rejected without a count." Although David had begun "to eat humble crow," having been reduced from asking for $60,000 to asking for $30,000, and finally to imploring administrative approval of his project—even that small request had been rejected "without a count." *Niles* elaborates upon his speech approvingly; the *Globe* mentions it only briefly.

On December 21, David wrote to his publishers concerning the Boston *Tour.* He had already "taken 31 pages to Mr. Clark to Correct" and has twelve more lying by ready. Clark "is well pleased" and "Sais he Can make you the most interesting Book you ever had." David hoped to have the book completed "by the first of January or earley in February," his only fear being that "Clark will not keep up with" him. The preface was already begun, and he was of the opinion that Clark "will pleas you well" and intended to let him write the preface to "Suit him Self." He was pushing to get "as much as posable" in their hands by January 1st so that they could begin setting the type. "Another reason that pushes" him was that he owed "three-hundred dollars . . . due the last of this month or the first of next," and he was hoping to be able to ask for an advance "to aid me in getting it out of the Bank . . . here" where it was payable:

I wish you to write to Mr—Clark how he likes what I have done and whin he thinks he Can have it ready I will asure you that I will do my part pleas to answer this and Say whether If we get on well next week with the work and I was to ask you for an acceptance If I Could get it for three hundred dollars I got a Check for the draft you give me I must Close in hast I remain your friend & obt Servt

David Crockett [32]

From this letter, one might get the impression that David was having a large part in writing the new book; yet such was not the case. A letter from Crockett to Charles Shultz, of Cincinnati, written on Christmas Day, gives an insight into his real part in writing the *Tour*. In a postscript to this letter, David asks:

will you get a paper from your editor that Contains the procedings of the day I Spent in your City last Summer on my way home [July 12] pleas to git and enclosce it to me as Soon as Convenient and obledge your friend

D.C—[33]

Shultz evidently was able to "obledge" his friend, for on pages 148-158 of the *Tour* is a quoted account from the Cincinnati *Gazette* of July 14 of David's visit there on July 12, including the long speech David delivered on that occasion. David had been busy gathering notes and newspaper accounts of his tour and that was about all he had to do with the writing of the *Tour*.

In the letter to Shultz, after a customary diatribe on Jackson, David had said:

I have almost give up the Ship as lost I have gone so far as to declare if he . . . martin vanburen is elected I will leave the united States for I never will live under his Kingdom before I will Submit to his government I will go to the wildes of Texas I will Consider that government a Paridice to what this will be. . . .

David's determination to leave the country if the forces he opposed should be successful attests to his utter sincerity. He failed to discount the political falsehoods with which the Whigs conducted their campaign. The Whigs who concocted the falsehoods—whether Biddle and his friends in the East, or Judge White and his supporters in the South— never certified the sincerity of their own charges of Jacksonian tyranny and their own claims to a love of liberty by a similar avowal to leave the country. Why should they have?

On December 27, Crockett repeated his resolution:

. . . I am not Certain that the people will object to being transfered by Jackson over to that Political Judeas little Van If So I have Sworn for the last four years that If Vanburen is our next President I will leave the united States I will not live under his kingdom and I See no chance to beat him. . . . I have Said for the last four years that I would vote for the devil against Van and any man under the Sun against Jackson and I have got no better yet [34]

In the same letter he showed, too, that he had "got no better yet" in his hollow optimism about the land bill or in his illusion that he still had political strength:

I expect in a few days to be able to Convey the good news to my District of the passage of my occupant land Bill it is the first Bill that will Come up and I have no fears of its passage every member from Tennessee that I have talked to Says it will pass if So it will Bless many a poor man with a home I See that they have got out A. Huntsman & McMeans Both and if they run Both I [am] of opinion [I wi]ll beat thim I Cannot tell [I am still dete?] rmened to do my duty if I Should niver See another Congress. . . .

Crockett clearly knew that his opposition to Jackson was costing him many votes and might, in fact, lose him once and for all times his seat in Congress. It did, for "A. Huntsman" defeated him in 1835. He was determined to play out his hand, not aware that it had been dealt off the bottom of the deck. "If So it will Bless many a poor man with a home" reveals David in the one domain where he had no superiors.

Chapter 12

CONGRESSIONAL FINALE

THE final act of the play had been carefully rehearsed and was ready to go on with the opening of 1835. During the between-scenes bustle we get a brief backstage glimpse of one of the "sets" being prepared for use. Adam Huntsman, peg-legged lawyer from Jackson, Tennessee, and loyal Jackson supporter, had long pestered David with his Chronicles "and such like foolish stuff." For example, back in March, 1831, in the Jackson *Southern Statesman,* he had depicted David as a rider of a broken-down nag named *Occupant* who couldn't make the journey, and had related how Crockett, astride him, had wandered off, lost, strayed, or *stolen,* from the Jackson wilderness trace. He was now to come out openly as a candidate against David.

Accordingly, on the first day of the new year, we see him making his preparations down in west Tennessee. On that day he wrote to James K. Polk in Washington:

My dear Sir,
I suppose you are all so tightly stuffed with Christmas pudding that you have but little time to write to any but your own constituents. Now as Davy of the River country does not honor me with a line I must claim it of some of my old acquaintances or do without. In fact I Should like to hear occasionally in relation to the actings and doings of your great folks at Washington and return for which I will give you some nonsense.
I begin to believe I can beat Davy and carry McMean's weight I have been in all the Counties but one in this District and Crockett is evidently loosing ground or otherwise he never was as strong as I supposed him to be—Perhaps it is both—If my friends take anything of a lively interest in it I think my prospects are as good as usual He is eternally sending

Anti Jackson documents here and it has its effects. If he carries his land Bill I will give him strength Otherwise the conflict will not be a difficult one

Accept my best wishes

A Huntsman [1]

One cannot miss the Huntsman humor of calling on another Congressman because his own would not write to him, or his allusion to his Chronicles in the phrase, "Davy of the River country." The sentence, "If he carries his land Bill I will give him strength. . . . Otherwise . . . ," passing between these two particular men, sounds like a death sentence. Indeed it was to reverberate like a death knell before the year was out. Although the Tennessee delegation had told David they would support his bill, those yet loyal to Jackson had little idea of favoring a measure whose adoption would mean the re-election of the bitter Jackson opponent from Tennessee. With this slight forecast of approaching events, we return to watch the curtain rise upon the last act.

On January 8, 1835, from Washington, David addressed the following letter to Carey & Hart:

Gentlemen Your favor enclosing the acceptance for two hundred dollars Came Safe to hand for which I feel under many obligations for I was with Mr Clark this morning and he red me what he had finished of the Book and I have no doubt of its filling your axpectation it must Sell

I am at prisent preparing an answer to Bentons letter to the Convention of Mississippi I was asked by the Same State to run for the Presidency and this gives me an excuse to answer him at length which will Compose part of the Book and I will try to make it as interesting as any part of it you Shall have it as Soon as posable

I am with respects your obt Servt

D Crockett [2]

PS excuse my Scrall I am in hast

We note from this letter that Crockett was *working on* his reply to Benton; that this was to make a part of the book; that a Mr. Clark was writing the book for which David was supplying the notes; and finally that the publishers were interested not only in its salability (for a belief in which they had advanced David two of the three hundred dollars he had requested), but also by implication in its purpose and contents— as Whig literature in the anti-Jackson and Van Buren campaign.

What infuriated Jackson above all else in this campaign was the secret letter that all of the Tennessee delegation in Congress (except Grundy, Polk, and Johnson) had addressed to Judge Hugh Lawson White of Tennessee, asking him to run for the Presidency. The Whigs and Nullifiers had agreed to unite around White in the South, in opposition to the candidate they felt sure the Democratic caucus would select in Baltimore on May 20, 1835—Martin Van Buren. The Whigs in general, and the Tennessee delegation in particular, had become convinced that Jackson had "stacked the convention cards" and picked his successor, and they had no desire to see a New Yorker in the Presidency. These Tennessee representatives, therefore, held a caucus of their own in a "smoke-filled" hotel room in Washington, agreed that White was their best hope, and issued him an invitation in a maneuver which only carried out, it seems, long and carefully laid plans. White had formerly been a Jackson man, but had now had a difference of opinion with him, real or fancied, and had finally gone over to the Whigs. Next to Jackson, he was perhaps the most popular man in Tennessee, and in truth there were many loyal Jackson men who were quite set against seeing the Easterner, Van Buren, in the White House. The Whig strategy with White was to carry all the Whig votes and enough of the Jackson votes to defeat Van Buren.

Jackson's fury was expressed in a number of personal letters written during 1835. To Alfred Balch he wrote:

You have been righly informed that all but those members which you have named from Tennessee with crockett their tool, with the exception of judge Grundy, Polk and Johnson have in secrete caucus brought out judge White as a candidate for the Presidency in opposition to a national convention, and has thrown him on the opposition for support.[3]

To James K. Polk, he addressed a note marked "Private," containing instructions as to the strategy Polk should employ on the floor of the House:

... If my hands were free, if I was a mere citizen of Tennessee again, and wanted everlasting fame, I would ask no other theatre to obtain it than before the people of Tennessee ... and Tennessee in 6 weeks would be ... erect upon her republican legs again, and Mr. Bell, Davy Crockett and Co., hurled, as they ought, from the confidence of the people. .... The Baltimore convention will be filled by high talents and more than ever attended any previous convention, and how degraded, and humuliated must Tennessee appear, and how emerge from her false position in which she has been placed by those apostates, Bell, Crockett and Co. ....[4]

"Crockett and Co." included not only the revolting clique in Tennessee, but as Jackson says, "the opposition," a national marriage of convenience with such other groups as the Clay supporters, the Nullifiers, the opponents of Martin Van Buren, and that powerful national coordinator of the entire resistance movement, Nicholas Biddle, egotistical and power-mad president of the Second Bank of the United States.

To Felix Grundy, one of the three from the Tennessee delegation who had refused to indorse White for the Presidency, Jackson wrote:

It has really appeared to me that Bell, Crockett and Co., with judge Whites flag had carried dismay throughout Tennessee that had paralised truth and patriotism.... Surely the conduct of Bell, Crockett and company, by usurping the sovereign power of the people has acted with more presumption and arrogance, than ever twelve men *dared* to usurp before ... it would give me more satisfaction to unmask the daring usurpation of the peoples sovereign rights by the selfcreated caucus of Mr. Bell, David Crockett and Co than any act of my life....[5]

To Andrew J. Hutchings he wrote a bit later:

Mr. Bell cries out against caucus [at Baltimore], but was there ever such a miserable caucus as his Crockett and Co. had, eleven members of Congress all from Tennessee. Still they cry out that judge White was brought out by the people when he was brought out by this miserable *little* caucus here.[6]

Finally, in another letter to the same person:

judge White has permitted himself to be used by Mr. Bell, Crockett and company, and like all others, who have abandoned the principles that gave them popularity, for sake of office, must *fall politically*, never to rise again in the affections of the people....[7]

Prior to this time, White had married an ambitious divorcee who kept a boarding house in Washington (Daniel kept her stirred up with ambition for her husband), and it is likely that the letter written by Crockett and the others, asking White to allow his name to be entered, was actually penned in White's own boarding house. *Niles Register* published a partially authentic Crockett letter of early January, 1835, which includes this statement:

I called last evening to see judge White. Mr. Luke Lea, Mr. Bunch and Mr. Standifer all board at the same house with the judge. My business was to see a letter that Mr. Lea had received from the judge, in answer to the one that the delegation from Tennessee had addressed to him....

The point to be made here is that the letter to White, sent by the Tennessee delegation, was dated December 29, 1834, and White's reply was dated the next day. Lea had undoubtedly written the letter, Lea had received the answer, Lea roomed with Judge White. The letter and White's reply were both reprinted in the *National Banner and Nashville Whig* for February 23, 1835, from the *Knoxville Register*. Suffice it to say that the Judge accepted the invitation, as planned.

From the contents of Crockett's letter in *Niles Register*, I date it January 10 (it speaks of having sent "yesterday" the "reply to" Benton's letter which his January 8 letter says he was still preparing). It leads back to January 1. *Niles* printed it, stating that it had been written to an editor in David's district, and following the portion already quoted, it reads in part:

The judge says, in his reply to us, as much as we could expect of him. He says the presidency is a place that in no time of his life he ever wanted —nor did he ever believe himself qualified for the office—but that his services have been long before the people, and that he was in the hands of his friends—they could, if they choose, run his name, and if he was successful, it was an office that he could not decline; but if his friends choose to withdraw him, they would have his hearty approbation. This was as much as we could expect him to say. I do believe him the only man in the nation able to contend against little Van.

The office holders have got their champion, Mr. Benton, to come out in a long letter, which I will send you, and I sent you the paper yesterday that contained my answer to it. The Van Buren party are sending off wagon loads of them printed in pamphlet form. I do hope the people will not be duped by it. My letter was intended for a burlesque on it, and I hope it may have the desired effect. I am satisfied that his letter was intended to alarm judge White and his friends, and drive them from the field; but I hope to see them stand firm—they cannot be beaten by the caucus system.[8]

The last paragraph will require some explanation, but first let me note either a contradiction or a revelation. Benton's letter to which Crockett refers had not been made public until January 2, 1835. But it had been *written* on December 16, 1834. If that letter had been aimed at driving Judge White's Presidential supporters from the field, Judge White's intentions must have been known long before his official acceptance on December 30, 1834.

Here is the situation out of which the reply-to-Benton letter arose.

We have seen the Whig strategy was to fix on a candidate strong enough to carry both the Whig votes and many Jackson votes. If they could get a strong Jacksonian on the Whig ticket, they thought they must surely succeed. Accordingly, sometime in the late fall of 1834, the Mississippi Convention wrote Benton, a popular Jacksonian from the Southwest, asking for the use of his name as a Vice-Presidential candidate on an anti-Van Buren ticket.[9] In a reply from Washington on December 16, to Major General Davis of Manchester, Mississippi, Benton expressed his appreciation of the honor, but stated that he could not be a candidate on the ticket proposed. He said he regarded the election as a very important one in terms of the outcome of the democratic struggle, which had been victorious once under Jefferson and twice under Jackson, and which was now facing perhaps its greatest climacteric. He recommended that the convention choose for its Presidential candidate—Martin Van Buren! Whereupon, at great lengths, he pointed out Van Buren's democratic philosophy, his wisdom, his strength, and his virtues generally.

Later his friends interrogated him as to the reasons for his negative decision and urged him to make them public. Whether this was a *bona fide* request, or whether, as David says, it was a political maneuver to circumvent the anti-Van Buren Mississippi Convention, which naturally had not seen fit to print Benton's letter, I cannot say. On January 1, 1835, Robert P. Lytle, of Ohio; Henry Hubbard, of New Hampshire; Ratcliffe Boone, of Indiana; and H. H. Muhlenberg, of Pennsylvania, drew up a letter requesting that Benton make public his reasons for refusing the candidacy. Benton replied, by letter of January 2, stating that the original letter had been meant for publication, and inclosing a copy of the earlier letter to the Mississippi Convention.

These three letters, the interrogation from "friends" dated January 1, Benton's reply and letter of transmittal of January 2, and the inclosure, the reply to Mississippi dated December 16, 1834, were widely printed in the pro-Van Buren papers. As David's reply of a year earlier to that same Convention had never been made public, he had made to order an excellent pretext for trumping up a series of letters superficially similar to those of Benton's in order to parody them. In preparation for this maneuver, it was first necessary to see that Benton's series should be printed in the Whig papers so that their readers would later know what was being parodied. Consequently, we see Crockett in the letter of January 10 sending the editor of the *National Banner and Nashville Whig* his own reply to Benton and promising to send a copy of Benton's letters shortly. These Benton letters were accordingly printed *first* in that paper on January 21, 1835,[10] and were followed on January 26 by David's own parody,[11] which had earlier been published by Gales and Seaton's *National Intelligencer* with many asseverations as to its authenticity. David, said the editors, had personally delivered it into their hands! The *Nashville Whig* republished it with similar testimonials.

The strategy of the letter was, of course, to reveal what the Whigs desired the public to think were the "real" political motives underlying Benton's correspondence by openly professing those motives in the series "written" by David. David actually had little to do with writing these except, as with the *Tour* and the *Van Buren*, allowing his name to be given to the whole. From the content of the two previous letters, I suspect that Judge White himself may have been the author or coauthor of this shrewd and humorous parody.

The first of the Crockett series was a letter of inquiry, dated January 7, 1835, from Nicholas Banks, of Pennsylvania; Andrew J. Bullion, of Indiana; Thos. B. Goldwire, of New Hampshire; and Martin V. Trashmoney, of New York, asking David to make public his letter to the Mississippi Convention:

We have learned, because you secretly informed us, that you have declined permitting your name to be used. . . . Upon a private understanding between you and ourselves, and a number of friends, held in a kind of caucus, it has been concluded that we should come out in seeming open application for a copy of your letter . . . but really to give you an occasion to play off upon the public one of your best efforts for effect, and to keep up the humbuggery of the bank, gold currency, and all that sort of thing, so necessary to blind the people, and keep our party together.

David's supposed reply, dated January 8, said he had refused the Presidency *now* so that a man from the North might be elected this time "that I may have a sort of plea to come in next time myself from the southwest. . . . But as we understand each other, I shan't say more, but just send the letter, and am glad you mean to publish it." Then follows the inclosure purporting to be David's letter of December

1, 1833, refusing the request of the Mississippi Convention. It is too long to reproduce here, but in affected Crockett language it cleverly insinuates the interpretation which the Whigs wished to put on Benton's motives. It refuses the Presidency, states that the "next election for president and vice goes ahead of all the elections that ever took place in America," insists that the "office-holders.... must hang together, like pitch plaster to a bald pate," if they are to win the election of 1836, and refers to the convention at Baltimore as having been "rigged" against the public interest.

It then proposes Martin Van Buren for the Presidency and under guise of complimenting him charges him with all kinds of political corruption. He has played both ends against the middle and been all things to all men. "He never was wrong in any dispute, if either side was right," for he had always taken all sides of every question. He opposed the "tariff of abominations" of 1828 in New York, next called the Harrisburg Convention and had them instruct him to vote for it, and then in Congress he had supported the measure. "This is the way he got the name of a MAGICIAN." There follows next a defense of John C. Calhoun, a former Jackson favorite, though of course in Van Buren's name. In a pretended defense, Van Buren is then ridiculed for his "rag" money and his "safety fund system" in New York. He is also charged with opposing the United States Bank abroad but with having favored establishing a branch of it in New York. This portion of the letter is then summarized:

They call him non-commital, too, and this is because he always looks before he leaps. They say he never gives the measure of his foot. Now how can this be, when it is shown that he speaks against the Tariff at home, and votes for it in Congress; goes for internal improvement... in New York, but against it out of it; goes against the Bank at Philadelphia, but in favour of it at Utica; goes for all the candidates for president in turn, Jackson last, notwithstanding which they say he is in higher favour there now than those that began before him. Went for the war, but went against Madison; wanted to turn out Madison and put in Clinton, and then turned Clinton out from the little office he held in New York. Goes for gold and hard money, and has more rag money in his state than all the other states put together. Call you this noncommital: As well may you call the fingers of a watch non-commital, that goes regular round to every figure on its face.

Then he states the purpose of his (*i.e.* of Benton's) letter:

the whole of this letter is just intended to keep the people from opening their eyes. Some very good, honest Jackson men are foolish enough to think they ought to have an opinion of their own. . . . Now Mr. Van and me, and the men that wrote to send 'em this letter to be published, and a good many of our folks, have all got together, and we think by making a great rush upon these free-thinkers, we can whip 'em back into the party, and make 'em stand up to their rack, fodder or no fodder. This letter is all for that purpose. I know, and we all know, that one-half of it isn't true, and the other half is trash. My friends said to me, your name sounds big, and if you come out and make believe that you don't want to be president, and talk about democracy, aristocracy, Jefferson, Madison, Crawford, persecution, the war, the bank, gold currency, hard money, but, above all, Jackson and the battle of New Orleans, and then hurra for union, harmony, concession, Van Buren, and the great state of New York; the seceders will tack and run back into the democratic republican fold, which means the Van Buren fold.

He thereafter ridicules a statement Jackson had made that he would be only an ordinary "voter" in the next election, which gave him "the right to dictate to the rest" at Baltimore. Saying that he (Benton, of course) did not want Judge White elected because that would interfere with his own ambitions, he concluded:

Let the next president come from the North; and then I go with all my heart for a Southwest president, the time after; and that president shall be myself.

Hoping that you will not forget me eight years hence, and that we can keep the people from thinking for themselves against a caucus nomination, I am, your fellow citizen,

David Crockett

David was no more capable of this long and complex letter than he was of writing a book without help. By now his reputation as the author of the *Autobiography* had been widely established and the Whigs were ready to cash in on their creation, not only in this parody with the editors' emphatic avowals that it was written by David himself, but in two more books soon to come. As David had advised his publishers, the above letters were to be included in the book then in progress, the Boston *Tour*, and the reader may find the whole of them there at pages 204-213 of the original edition. Contained in this parody, in embryo, is the second book that was yet to come out, the *Life of Mar-*

tin Van Buren. The book was to lack all the humor and restraint of this embryo and any pretense at simulating David's grammar and homely idiom. It was instead to be packed so full of vitriol and violence that Carey and Hart would not print it under their own name, though I am sure it was they who published it.

Attention has already been called to their evident interest in anti-Van Buren literature implied by Crockett's having informed them of his efforts in behalf of this parody and of the fact that it would make part of the *Tour*. Add to this the following facts: The Boston *Tour*, published openly by Carey and Hart, concludes with these lines: "There is one thing I had clean forgot: I have promised to write the Life of the *Magician of the North—Little Van;* and I'll do it; and if when you read it, you don't say I've used him up, I'm mistaken—that's all. The end." Further, the Crockett holograph below for January 22 (and also an unlocated one for January 16), written perhaps two months before the *Tour* was published, proposed to Carey and Hart that he write and they publish a life of Van Buren. This makes the above conclusion of the *Tour* a publisher's announcement to a Crockett public that Crockett and Carey and Hart would soon issue yet another book, the *Life of Van Buren* early in the summer of 1835 (supposedly published by Robert Wright of Philadelphia). Bound in with this book is a list of "New Works Lately published and Preparing for Publication by E. L. Carey and A. Hart, Philad." Included in that list of Carey and Hart books is the *Life of Martin Van Buren:*

This brings us to a consideration of the authorship of both of these volumes. In a letter to his publishers under the date of January 12, David wrote:

Gentle men Your favor & title page was recieved on yesterday I went imediately to Mr Clark and Showed it to him and he told me to Call this morning and he would have a package ready for me which I Send you and am Sorry there is not more of it done I intend to try and have my part done this week or in the earley part of naxt

Mr Clark has been engaged in the Post office Committee So that he Cannot keep pace with me But he Sais he will Soon be done and then he Can in a few days finish you have Stated that it is written by my Self I would rather if you think it Could Sell as well that you [the word *would* has been smeared through and replaced by *had*] had Stated that it was written from notes furnished by my Self But as to this I am not particular more than it will, perhaps give Some people a Chance to Cast reflections on me as to the Correctness of it and as the design of it will be to make it as amusing as posable I thought I wou[ld] Sugest this idea to you you Can think of it and do as you think best—I hope you will answer this and let me know what you think of it what is prepared I am with great respets your friend & obt Servt [12]

From the date of the *Tour's* publication as well as from his statement on January 8 that the Benton parody would make part of the book under discussion, we know that David was referring to the *Tour* in these letters. The publishers evidently thought little of the "notes furnished by Crockett" suggestion, for the title page as published made the claim, "Written by Himself." Had David's objection to this been based on meticulous ethical concern for accuracy, we should have to take more literally the claim in his letters to the part he had played in writing his *Autobiography*. It seems clear that David's concern was rather about the book's sale and about whether the claim that he wrote it might make it more liable to charges of inaccuracy and hence less effective Whig propaganda. For other considerations, he stated that he was "not particular."

The letters show that a Mr. Clark was doing the writing, that David had collected the notes, and that Mr. Clark was in some way connected with the Post Office Committee, as a result of which he was behind in the writing. The nature of the book itself demonstrates that this Clark was a Whig. First, it is clear that the Clark involved is not Mathew St. Clair Clarke, as some have suggested, because Clarke's services to the House had terminated on December 2, 1833, more than a year earlier, and he would have had no conceivable business in Congress in connection with the Post Office Committee. Furthermore, the one time David had mentioned St. Clair Clarke, he spelled the name properly with a final *e;* whereas all twelve times he names the Clark of this volume in his four letters of December 21, 1834, and January 8, 12, and 22, 1835, he spells the name without the final *e.* James Clark of Kentucky, the Whig governor of that state in 1836, had earlier been connected with Crockett, but for these particular years he was out of the House and in the Kentucky State Senate, so that it could not have been he.

A careful examination of all the Clarks and Clarkes in the *Biographical Directory of the American Congress* narrows the field to either Samuel Clark, Representative from New York, or William Clark, Representative from Pennsylvania. As we might suppose, our man is the Pennsylvania Representative. William Clark had been elected a Whig and so served from March 4, 1833, to March 3, 1837.[13] He voted with David and the Whigs on the indictment of the Post Office on February 14, 1835.[14] The *Debates* and the *Globe* fail to reveal that any member of either the Standing Committee on the Post Office and Post Roads or the Select Committee to investigate the Post Office (appointed on June 30, 1834, to sit through the recess of Congress[15]) was named *Clark*. But William Clark of Pennsylvania *was* a member of the Standing Committee on Public Expenditures for the session December 15, 1834, to March 3, 1835, the period in question, and as such he would have had occasion to work on expenditures relative to the Post Office and the salaries of Post Masters. He may well have had occasion, therefore, to consult "with the Post Office Committee." Samuel Clark of New York, on the other hand, was elected to this Congress as a Democrat, was so elected again later, and was finally defeated in 1855, still a Democrat.

Without question, then, William Clark, Representative from Pennsylvania, home of Nicholas Biddle, the United States Bank, Mathew St. Clair Clarke, and the publishers Carey and Hart, wrote the *Boston Tour*. The slight exceptions to this statement may be a passage or two actually contributed by David, such as the one quoted earlier about establishing a post mail route to Troy and the reply-to-Benton correspondence which Judge White himself probably took a hand in.

The *Tour* did not come from the press until late March, 1835—it includes material dated March 4. Yet less than three months later, the *Van Buren* was on the market. Though it goes somewhat ahead of our chronology, sufficient evidence for an explanation of the authorship of this work has been presented, and it is convenient to settle that matter here.

We have established that Carey and Hart published the *Van Buren* —one more link in a long chain that we have watched in the forming. David was connected with this work, and it came out in his name with his knowledge and consent. Somewhere there exists a Crockett letter of January 16, 1835, to Carey and Hart "proposing to write a Life of Martin Van Buren."[16] Furthermore, that subject is discussed in the following letter to them of six days later. Though David had not yet convinced them of the desirability of publishing it that winter (for they had evidently been misled into thinking that David himself was hurriedly preparing it), they obviously became convinced of the wisdom of bringing it out the next summer, once they had seen the manuscript itself and discovered its true author and the care with which it had been written:

Yours enclosing one to Mr Clark was recd and I will hasten to answer it I have finished my part of the Book and am truly Sorry that Mr Clark is hardley able to Set up This you know I Cannot help I Took my manuscripts to Mr Clark on Yesterday and he Said if he was able to Set up he could finish In a few days

I wrote on to Boston to Mr Abbot Lawrence to Send me a full Statement of one weeks work of all the maufactorys at Lowell I have recd a letter from him that he was preparing it for me and would Send it on in a few days It is one meterial that I want in the Book I regrit that Mr Clark has been taken down as bad as you Can I Just went a head until I fineshed my part I will write a Short article giving the Idea that I am going over to put things to rights with Lewis—Philips and the king of england this is all I lack Mr. Clark Sais he Can make as good a Book as you iver published out of the metirials that I have furnished to him

You Say that It will not do to write little vans life this winter I am not going to give him a chance at me for a libil what I write will be true we will Say nothing more on this I will write it and Bring it on as I go-home then you can read it and Judge for your Self and we can talk more about that matter I will hurrey Mr Clark all I can....[17]

The book referred to in the first two paragraphs was, of course, the *Tour*, in which was included that "full Statement of one weeks work of all the maufactorys at Lowell." The third paragraph connects David with the *Van Buren* and contains strong circumstantial evidence, despite David's statement that *he* was going to write it, that the manuscript was already either written or well under way.[18]

There is no question that David had less to do with this vitriolic, closely argued, legalistic, and finely dictioned work than with the *Tour*. This volume does not even make an occasional halfhearted attempt to affect a Crockett idiom or error. Its minute acquaintance with national political affairs removes it from any connection with Crockett authorship except for his eagerness in the Whig cause, his antipathy toward Van Buren, his suggestion for its publication under his name, and his cooperation in the subterfuge. In the light of all this, it must now be clear that the reply-to-Benton letters, as finally published in the *Tour* in March, had been intended not only to parody Benton's letter but to prepare the public for another book "written by David Crockett."

Claude G. Bowers misquoted Shepard when he attributed the authorship of the *Van Buren* to Judge White; [19] and Miss Rourke evidently followed Bowers' error in her speculation as to White's authorship. I believe we can dismiss the judge from responsibility for any of the writing. Shepard had actually said that White "was the man behind" it, not the man who wrote it:

> Soon *after* the Baltimore Convention [20] the most unconventional campaign biography . . . ever published in America was issued by a Philadelphia publishing house and given an extensive circulation. The present generation scarcely realizes that there were two Davy Crocketts—the man of the woods and the fight, and the less admirable creature who made a rather sorry figure in the Congress. It was the latter who was persuaded to write a part, and to father all, of this scurrilous biography of Van Buren, although it is generally accepted that Hugh Lawson White, the man of ponderous dignity and lofty ideals, *was the man behind* this questionable literary venture. The personal references to Van Buren are crudely and coarsely offensive throughout. [21]

I think Shepard is mistaken about David's having written any part of this work. His quick dismissal of him as a "sorry figure" we must view in the light of the fact that he was writing Martin Van Buren's life and that he lacked any creditable study of David to give him a thorough understanding of the man.

Unquestionably the book was written in Judge White's behalf; but the Judge did not write it. The only other serious contender for this questionable honor is Judge Augustin Smith Clayton, of Georgia, whom Crockett had been so glad to see on his tour, who had spoken from the same platform with David to a group of assembled Whigs on April 30, 1834. Professor John Donald Wade has reviewed some of the evidence for Clayton's authorship of this work in an article previously mentioned, [22] and it will be unnecessary to repeat that evidence at length here. *Appleton's Cyclopedia* and W. P. Trent in *Southern Writers* attributed the book to Clayton. To this must be added the statement of Judge Clayton's son that Judge Clayton: "Also wrote for Col. David Crockett, in his lifetime, a work entitled "The Life of David Crockett, Written by Himself." This was, for the most part, of a political character. I had a copy, but it has been lost." [23] The above statement cannot possibly be true, for we know that Chilton, and not Clayton, helped David write the *Autobiography*. Yet just as Mathew St. Clair Clarke, when pushed out by the evidence from the authorship of the *Autobiography*, remains prominently within the picture, so it is likely that this testimony by the son, though inapplicable to the *Autobiography*, must be accepted as the establishing link in the authorship of the *Life of Martin Van Buren*. How did the younger Clayton's error occur?

Two *Lives* were published in David Crockett's name (though only the *Autobiography* was so copyrighted), his own and that of Van Buren. During Judge Clayton's life, it was known in the home that he had written a *Life* which had been published in David's name. Judge Clayton died in 1839, almost twenty years before the son made this statement in 1858. The thing had become confused in the son's mind, without the aid of the father's knowledge for clarification, and so in 1858 he made what was a very understandable error, attributing to his father David's *Life* of Crockett instead of his *Life* of Van Buren. His statement that "this was, for the most part, of a political character," clearly removes the application from the *Autobiography* while precisely defining the *Van Buren*.

To these arguments we may add the further information that the surviving Crawford "machine" of Georgia was strongly behind the candidacy of Hugh Lawson White for President, that Georgia was the only other state in the Union besides Tennessee to give him its electoral votes in the general elections,[24] and that Judge Clayton had been sent to Congress at this time from Georgia and remained there through March 3, 1835. He would naturally have been an ardent Lawson White, anti-Van Buren man. Both the external and internal evidence appear sufficient to establish that the author of this penetrating, legalistically written *Life of Martin Van Buren* was David's friend and fellow-supporter of Hugh Lawson White, Judge Augustin Smith Clayton of Georgia.

It is time now to return to David Crockett in the last session of his last Congress, a forspent man.

Crockett's first recorded action during this session had been a motion on December 9 to make his land bill the order of business for the next day. But because of speech-making on preceding matters, his bill had never come up. On January 7, in the midst of long wrangling over the pay of navy officers, Crockett made one more valiant effort to have his land bill, "Occupant," considered. He explained that "his object

was to come to a determination on this subject some way or another."
The House had been engaged on the Pay bill for two weeks and "to
all appearance, were likely to spend two or three weeks more. . . . In
the mean time, there was much important private business on the
table, and among it, some that greatly concerned his constituents. He
therefore called for the previous question [so as to get rid of it and
take up the land bill]." But it would not be got rid of—"A majority of
the House . . . did not favor the motion." [25]

As time for legislative action rapidly dwindled, Crockett's rancorous
opposition to legislation taking precedence over his land bill continued.
It was proposed to amend a resolution giving members of the committee investigating the condition and proceedings of the Post Office
Department eight dollars a day for their work during the summer
when the rest of Congress had been at home, so as to pay their travelling time and expenses, since summer duties had necessitated trips
home and back by several members. Crockett opposed, saying he
thought the usual pay of eight dollars ample. "It was nonsense to talk
about its being a sacrifice to come there; for if it were, they would
not see so many grasping to be members of Congress. He considered,
eight dollars a day sufficient remuneration for any man, let his business
be what it may." [26]

His opposition to another proposal was less rancorous than shrewd.
A prime condition of good administration requires that key subordinate offices be held by men sympathetic to the point of view of him
who bears responsibility. A number of men who had been elected to
Congress as Jackson supporters were voting in opposition to the party's position in a defection similar to that of Southern Democrats today, especially the Dixiecrats. In order to force these mavericks into
line and so increase the efficiency of the party operation, the House
had been discussing a resolution to require that in all elections in the
House, "the votes shall be given *Viva Voce*, each member in his place
naming aloud the person for whom he votes." Naturally Crockett was
opposed, for the motion lessened the chances of getting a Whig elected
to a key office in a Jackson legislature. "Mr. Crockett moved that the
resolution be laid on the table. [He] said he hoped the House would
not proceed to vote on the resolution under consideration, without af-
fording to every member of the House an opportunity to record his

vote. It was a proposition to alter an old established principle of long standing." [27] David's motion to table was defeated 102 to 113.

Again on February 2, in connection with a member's pro-Jackson remarks, "Mr. *Crockett* inquired whether it was in order for gentlemen to be electioneering on that floor." [28] His feelings on the subject were rendered all the more bitter because opportunity for his own electioneering was denied. When he once more attempted, on February 4, to terminate discussion concerning the Alexandria Canal in order to bring up his land bill, there was a note of desperation in his effort:

Mr. Crockett said we were now within three weeks of the close of the session, and what had we done? Nothing. A great number of bills had been made special orders, and among them one of great interest to his constituents, but they could not be reached on account of the long speeches. Last session seven months were spent in talking, and two months more this session. He had therefore come to the conclusion that this was a better place to manufacture orators than to dispatch business. Believing that not one vote on this question would be changed if it were debated seven weeks longer, he moved the previous question. The motion was seconded by the House: yeas, 128.[29]

In fighting to get his land bill before the House, David was fighting for his very political life. When a member arose the next day, February 5, to offer a new resolution, "Mr. Crockett hoped [in vain] ... that the House would not change or postpone orders" of the day.[30] On February 13 he succeeded in speaking for the principle of his bill, but without getting that bill called up for consideration. On that day a bill was under debate for the relief of citizens of Arkansas, who had been dispossessed of land as a result of a treaty with the Choctaw Indians. It was proposed to reimburse them with more land. Vinton of Ohio opposed with vehemence, remonstrating against rewarding with a donation of one hundred and sixty acres men whose only merit lay in having trespassed on the public land and having refused to leave until compelled by military force. Mr. Sevier replied warmly, adverting to the policy of the government in granting pre-emption rights to those who had thus settled on the public domain. Mr. Ewing, of Indiana, reminded Mr. Vinton of the history of Ohio's settlement in the early days, and so on. This was a matter closely touching David's whole position and philosophy, though it did not directly concern his own constituents, and he was not content to remain silent. However, his Jackson grudge had to becloud the issue:

Mr. Crockett supported the bill, and was in favor of giving a home to every man who would pay for the survey. These were the men on whom the country could rely, and nothing would make them so love the country. A gentleman has said the country had two treasuries, one with a key, and the other with none; but he believed there was no key to either. There was nothing in the President's message pleased him so much as the recommendation of giving homes to poor settlers. He began to think the President was almost turning a Crockett man.[31]

Later, on February 14, Crockett was involved in Whig electioneering maneuvers in the House. Debate waged on a motion by Mr. Briggs of Massachusetts to print 25,000 extra copies of both the majority and minority reports of the committee which had investigated the Post Office, including all accompanying documents, a mass of material which would require three volumes of printing per copy. Though the arguments were phrased in altruistic terms, the Whigs were really attempting to get copies at government expense for propaganda against Jackson. The Van Buren-Jackson supporters, for ever so patriotic reasons, wished to print as few as possible: Mr. Beardsley of New York stated that 5,000 or even 2,000 would be sufficient, for to print 5,000 would cost from twenty-five to thirty thousand dollars and to print 25,000 would be prohibitive.

David was not to be outbid in this matter. Claiming that "it had already cost more than twenty-five thousand dollars to get this report" and pointing out that the report was useless "unless . . . sent out to the people," he claimed that the report "more than sustained" his former charges against the Post Office (for which he had been "almost hissed at").

Mr. Everett of Vermont expressed his surprise at David's arithmetic in saying it had cost 25 thousand dollars to get this report. Each member of the select committee had received $560.00, and their aggregate pay amounted to $4,920, the entire investigation not running above $7,000. Mr. Hamer of Ohio called attention to the fact that the entire procedure was wrong, that the reports had not even been received yet by the House and members did not know positively one word of their contents. "Congress would do well to hear before they strike," he said, in words eternally appropriate. Finally the original motion was amended and passed to print 3,000 of the reports with documents (the normal number being 2,000), and 20,000 without documents. James K. Polk opposed, Crockett favored.

On February 18 the bill to regulate the pay of officers in the Navy was taken up again for the third reading. The time for adjournment was rapidly approaching, and Crockett was desperate to get his land bill before the House. When the question recurred on the pay bill's final passage, several members arose. David obtained the floor to point out that the bill had already "consumed no less than three weeks in discussion," and, since he "had a bill made the order of the day, the day after this bill," and as he saw "a disposition to speak more on the subject, as speaking has become so fashionable here," he moved "the previous question." When Mr. Ben Hardin of Kentucky "hoped his friend from Tennessee would withdraw the motion," David replied, "I cannot do it, sir." [32] Crockett's motion failed to carry, 82 to 90.

Crockett's last recorded speech in the House, like his very first of any length, was in behalf of his land bill. On February 20, Mr. Dunlap of Tennessee, evidently at Crockett's instance, moved to suspend the rules and take up the Tennessee Land Bill. Crockett arose, desiring to make a few explanations on the subject of his bill. But "objections being made, Mr. Crockett resumed his seat." The House had apparently wearied of him, and his Eastern "friends" had deserted. Mr. Dunlap's motion to suspend failed to receive the necessary two-thirds majority. [33]

Crockett's opportunity on that subject, for one life time, was gone. This Moses of his people had not been sufficiently strong to overcome the temptations that stood in his way, and his was to be the lot of seeing the goal from afar. He was not able to attain it.

As David's last effort to speak was fittingly in behalf of the land bill, so his last recorded vote was appropriately cast against Jackson. On March 3, 1835, the Senate was in stubborn opposition to the position of the President with reference to the fortification bill, whereas the House refused to accede to the Senate's action. The question before the House was whether to reverse its stand and agree with the Senate in a final anti-Jackson vote before adjournment. In the eventual vote, the House continued to support Jackson 107 to 88. Among those eighty-eight opponents was recorded the name of David Crockett, the last vote ever recorded for him in the Congress of the United States. [34]

Adjournment came that day, and David set out for home to campaign for the summer elections. He was never again to return to Washington City. His political career was over. His life itself was drawing to a close. In almost one year to the day, March 6, 1836, David Crockett would be dead at the Alamo.

The sentence from Adam Huntsman's letter comes back to us ominously: "If he carries his land bill I will give him strength. . . . Otherwise. . . ."

PART FIVE

Out

13

A LATE SUMMER

DAVID had begun electioneering for the 1835 elections in February or March, 1834, with the publication of his *Autobiography*. He had won an election after the publication of the 1833 *Life*, and what works once in politics, as in Hollywood, must always be tried again. The Boston *Tour*, of March, 1835, was also aimed at Crockett's re-election, although it was designed even more to support the entire Whig cause. The *Life of Van Buren*, published only two or three months before the elections, seems to have lost sight entirely of David's own political interests in its pursuit of the larger Whig issues and, except indirectly, cannot be called Crockett campaign literature at all.

David did issue another Circular Letter to his constituents, giving his reasons for no longer being able to support Jackson and stressing his objections to the removal of the deposits, to the "Specie Circular," and to Jackson's preference for Martin Van Buren in the Presidency.[1] Though I have been unable to unearth a copy of this Circular Letter, I think we may be sure, from what we have seen of David's affairs, that it explained the failure of the Land Bill to pass and gave assurance once more that in another session it would. Surely it included an explanation of the "little caucus" held by all but three of the Tennessee delegation to choose White as Presidential candidate, for the Jackson forces had held this "little caucus" up to public scorn throughout the Western District.

The "Major Jack Downing" letters were also, in a sense, related to David's re-election efforts. Surviving Crockett correspondence does not once refer to "Major Jack Downing," the nationally famous and popular literary creation of Seba Smith, of Portland, Maine. Yet there grew up a peculiar relationship between Crockett and Smith. On January 18, 1830, Smith had published the first in his series of letters about this fictitious major. The character became widely popular, and had a strong influence on letters: Artemus Ward and Hosea Biglow were "descendants," and the influence on David's *Autobiography* is observable even in the long title; the volume itself makes specific reference to Downing in its opening chapter. So popular was the character that a number of imitations soon sprang up, and in an effort to protect himself from them, Smith collected and published the series in book form in 1833.[2] One significant thing about this entire series was that throughout its course the "Major" was a strong Jackson supporter, and in fact the volume in which the series was collected was "respectfully inscribed to General Jackson by his friend and humble servant, Major Jack Downing."

In recounting Crockett's Eastern tour, I called attention to David's statement that he had had an honest-to-goodness meeting with the real Major Jack at a dinner, and the suggestion was made that very possibly Crockett and Smith did meet and make arrangements there for a future junction of their forces. At any rate, on July 4, 1834, the day of David's hobnobbing in Philadelphia with Daniel Webster and the other Big-Whigs, Seba Smith issued the first copy of a *new* literary venture involving an *anti-Jackson* Major Jack Downing, which he continued to publish until the spring of 1836. This venture was a weekly news sheet entitled the *Downing Gazette*, published in Portland, Maine. The *Downing Gazette* was strongly opposed to Jackson, and in its columns were published spurious letters to and from David Crockett. Similar letters were published in Crockett's Boston *Tour*. Curiously enough, Seba Smith, on a very flimsy pretext, if taken literally, omitted all the *Gazette* materials from his later collected works of 1859, *My Thirty*

Years Out of the Senate (a take-off on Thomas Hart Benton's *Thirty Years View, i.e., within* the Senate).

Smith gave as his reason for this exclusion that the *Downing Gazette* papers "had been destroyed by fire," a reason which seems to have puzzled Miss Mary Alice Wyman in her study of Smith,[3] since that series was then, and is now, preserved in the original, not having been touched by a literal fire. The omission creates a large gap in the life and actions of Major Jack. They were deliberately passed over only for some carefully considered reason. That reason is to be discovered, I think, by reading Smith's language figuratively. The letters had been "destroyed" so far as his collected works were concerned because of the "fire" of passion which had led Smith too far in giving his support to what, in calmer hours of reflection, he decided he did not want to preserve under his final endorsement and name. I am suggesting that Smith was displeased at some of Jackson's policies, as were many other former pro-Jackson downeasters; and that he allowed, on a minor scale, something of the same sort of thing to happen to him temporarily that happened on a terrible scale and permanently to David Crockett. I think that he let Jackson's bitter enemies fan the fire of his temporary displeasure and use the generated heat for their own purposes against Jackson. A later recognition of what had happened led him to strike the whole work of this heat from his final edition.

There is one further elaboration of this hypothesis that ought to be broached. One of the most successful imitators of the original Major Jack series was Mr. Charles Augustus Davis, iron merchant of New York (where David said he dined with the real Major Jack), a director of the New York Branch of the Second Bank of the United States, and a close personal friend of Nicholas Biddle. *His* Downing letters, however, had always been presented with an anti-Jackson slant. We know that Daniel Webster, idol of the downeasters and strongly supported by Seba Smith in his anti-Jackson *Gazette* series, was a member of the group exploiting Crockett for political ends. I am suggesting the possibility that Seba Smith and Augustus Davis, after the proper maneuvers by Webster and Biddle, may have both sat down to dinner with David that April 30 in New York, either literally or figuratively, and that the influence of Davis on that anti-Jackson series which Seba Smith saw fit to eliminate from his collected works may have been quite strong. This is an idea which has not been intimated before, I believe, but it is a distinct possibility in view of the evidence presented. Mr. Arthur M. Schlesinger, Jr., in *The Age of Jackson,* attributed the "most famous series of Jack Downing papers" to Mr. Augustus Davis. I cannot discuss here which was the "most famous," but I think Mr. Schlesinger has given credit to Davis that should go to Smith. If the compact I have outlined actually took place, and if Davis had a strong influence on the *Downing Gazette* series, there may be some accidental truth in Mr. Schlesinger's estimate.

Six of the *Downing Gazette* issues lead off with references to David Crockett in column one, the first being for March 14, 1835, about the time of the publication of the *Tour* and of Crockett's campaigning for re-election. In August of that year, just prior to David's defeat, he was dropped from the series. Earlier than that, under date of February 6, 1835, David had included in the *Tour* a letter purportedly from Major Jack, not of New York City (Davis) but of Portland, Maine (Smith), and followed it by the reply he was supposed to have written Smith, dated March 4, 1835.[4] That some sort of an agreement took place between the Crockett-Whig-anti-Jackson forces and Seba Smith at this time seems obvious. Smith's elimination of this series from his collected works would tend to prove it. The Downing letters in the *Tour* are quite obviously spurious. I will not include them here as they are easily available, but I will include portions of the equally spurious letters from the *Downing Gazette,* since they are not of easy access.

The *Downing Gazette* was a single news sheet published weekly "at the office of the Daily Courier." It consisted of four columns topped by a masthead engraving representing Major Jack at work writing up the letters which, together with replies to them and items concerning him or his fictional relatives, mostly filled up the paper. These letters of course discussed many matters of contemporary political interest. Major Jack had written to David in the issue of February 28, and the first of the fictitious Crockett replies was carried at the head of column one in the issue for March 14:

Hoorah, if here isn't a letter from my old new friend Col Crockett, in answer to the one I sent him aweek or two ago to Washington. I'm so tickled I don't know what to do, to think he is going to write to me once in a while. I guess between us we shall keep matters pretty straight clear from here to Tennessee. The Col. asked me ... not to publish this [letter], because he was going to send me a larger ... one. ... But I couldn't wait:

I was in such a pucker to let folks know that I'd got a letter from the Col. that I thought I would publish it and ask his consent afterwards.[5]

Crockett's letter, addressed from Washington City and dated March 4, the day after Congress had adjourned, follows immediately:

My dear Major Jack Downing—
Your very polite note of the 26 Feb. was received this morning, and I will hasten to answer it, although I can add but little to what you can see in the papers relative to government matters. We broke up Congress last night, or rather this morning about three o'clock, in a *row*, and done nothing.

The dimocrats tried to give the Giniral three millions of dollars to make ready to go to war with France. But the Senate vetoed the proposition, and said we will wait a while before we will give the General that much of the people's money.

As for my part I have thought for near a year thet the Giniral has every dollar of the people's money at his disposal, and I considered it wholly useless to state any particular sum. I do not know where he keeps the money, but I reckon he keeps it in old Amos's [Kendall's] pocket. That is where I would go to hunt it, were I to set out to hunt the treasury. As for the balance of your enquiries I will answer you more fully hereafter.

I must now say something about how little Van and the dimocrats look since Judge White has come into the field. I think they are scared badly; and well they may be, for the Judge is one of the best men in the world, and it will not take long to make the people believe it. *He* is the only man in the General's government that can be looked upon to take charge of the deranged state of affairs, and make peace with our once happy country. I do believe he would put down the party strife and restore our country to peace and harmony.

I must close in haste, and remain... your obedient servant

David Crockett

This letter of March 4 from the *Gazette* is entirely different from a long letter of the same date and to the same person which David published in his Boston *Tour* at pages 222-228. Whereas David's letter to Downing in the *Tour* had been addressed from "Crocketts, Gibson County, Tennessee," the one in the *Gazette* for the same day was addressed from Washington City. Inasmuch as David voted in Washington on March 3, he could not have written a letter the next day from Tennessee. Since, in all probability, he left Washington for home immediately after adjournment on the 3rd, it is highly unlikely that he could have addressed a letter on the 4th from Washington either. The reference to Judge White as the "only man in the General's government" of any responsibility is similar to a statement in Crockett's speech in Congress on June 19, 1834, and suggests that possibly early plans had been laid to bring White out against Van Buren.

On May 23 another spurious Crockett letter appeared in the *Gazette*. It was dated April 20, 1835, and was addressed from "At Home, Weekly County." The form of this address is interesting for several reasons. First, though David continued to write letters off and on from Weakley County, he did not call that county home. The Downing letter in his own *Tour* had been addressed from "Crocketts, Gibson County," and his holograph to Joseph Wallis, of May 26, 1834, had in his own hand stated, "My Post office is Calld Crocketts P. O.–Gibson County." Smith's error was not in addressing the letter from Weakley, but in appending the phrase "At Home." Also, the spelling of *Weakley* in this heading contains two errors: *Weekly* instead of *Weakley*. Out of a bibliography of some sixty Crockett letters, every Crockett spelling of *Weakley* is correct. And finally, perhaps most interesting of all, the only surviving letter which David *ever* addressed from "At Home Weakley County" was the letter he had written on January 7, 1832, to Richard Smith, cashier of the Washington Branch of the Second United States Bank. Here again is suggestive evidence that the Bank and Seba Smith and perhaps Augustus Davis were working together.

I conclude, from his participation in the series in the *Tour*, that David was a party to these letters and that they were written with his consent by someone familiar with David's style in certain superficial ways, though not familiar with the facts of his immediate life. I am convinced that David himself had nothing to do with their actual writing. The April 20 Crockett letter included, among other things, the following:

... I wish to know what Judge White's prospects are in your section of the country–Please to inform me.–His prospects are brightening in every quarter that I hear from; and in this State he has been a favorite for the last twenty years. He can get a better vote in Tennessee than ever Jackson could in his brightest day of glory. President Jackson has made his will. I suppose he has willed his soul to God–if he has not, he ought to–and in the next place, he has willed the people to little Van in his letter to parson Gwin of Nashville. . . .

I have heard much complaint made by President Jackson against the United States Bank for meddling in elections. I was at a Post office a few

days ago in my District and I saw a number of packages in the office bearing the frank of Andrew Jackson on them, and I enquired what they
contained, and was answered they were Mr. Benton's speech on the ex-
punging resolution of the Senate of the last Session. I suppose his object
is either to electioneer against Judge White or myself. I do think when it
has come to this that the President of the United States will come down
from his high station to franking documents for the purpose of electioneering, I do believe it ought to be exposed and made known to every American citizen. . . . I happened to pick up one of the envelopes with the frank
of Andrew Jackson on it *that* I will keep for future purposes.[6]

An interesting item in the *Gazette* immediately following this "letter"
is the announcement that Van Buren had been nominated by the Baltimore Convention for the Presidency—a "Glorious triumph of Democracy!!"

In the next issue of May 30, Major Jack replied to David's inquiry
about White and said in part:

. . . I wish you could write to me oftner. My readers this way are a good
deal tickled whenever they can get hold of one of your letters. I think you
might tell us a great many things about the *great west* that would be very
interesting to us downeasters. Have you been out hunting any since you
got home? Is there a plenty of game this year? . . . .   '

You ask me what Judge White's prospects are for the Presidency in
this part of the country. Now I can tell you in three words how that matter
stans here. The people about here down east have got a considerable notion
in their heads that they want to have an honest man for President, and the
general run of em seem to want to have Daniel [Webster], but if they cant
get him they mean to pull for Judge White like two year olds; for they
say they will have an honest man if they have to go clear to Tennessee
after him.[7]

On June 13 the *Gazette* carried in its lead column what is called an
"extract from a speech lately delivered by Col. Crocket [*sic*] to his
constituents, at Trenton, Tennessee." It is almost two columns long
and has to do with proving that Crockett did not quit Jackson but that
Jackson quit his own principles; with Jackson's having willed the election to Van Buren through the Gwinn letter and the handpicked Baltimore Convention, the whole being blamed on the shrewdness of
Martin Van Buren. Significantly, the quotation ends with a whole sentence from the so-called Crockett-reply-to-Benton letter. The entire
issue, in fact, save about half of the last column, consists of an anti-
Jackson tirade. In this extract from a Crockett speech in Tennessee is

an anecdote that had already appeared some months before in Chapter II of the *Tour* as part of the speech David supposedly made to the Whigs in New York on that famous day of April 30 when Downing, Clayton, and Crockett all seem to have joined forces. The story, as told in the extract, is a better version, and includes biographical facts that the reader may recall with pleasure:

These changes have been produced by the magic of the little Kinder-hook intriguer. This reminds me of an anecdote of an old man in the barrens of Illinois; he took his boy out to plough, and there was no trees in the barrens, Says he, boy, do you see yon red heifer? Yes, says the boy. Well, do you plough straight to her. The old man left the boy. The boy he ploughed towards the heifer, and she moved and the boy followed, and so kept ploughing on all day. The old man in the evening came, and was astonished. Says he, you rascal, what sort of ploughing is this you have done? Why, says the boy, you told me to plough to the red heifer, and I have been ploughing after her all day. Sirs, I was among the first men that crossed the Tennessee river with General Jackson to fight the battles of our country. When he was at the battle of Tallahatchee, I was there—when he was at Talladago, I was there—When Gen. Jackson was behind the cotton bales at New Orleans I was starving in Florida; but when the General began to plough after the red heifer of Kinderhook, that was graz-ing in every direction, I quit him on account of his crooked rows, for I was learned to plough by an old Quaker, whose directions were to plough straight rows and go ahead.[8]

The two battles mentioned here, Tallahatchee and Talladago (*i.e.,* Tallussahatchee and Talladega) are the two battles which the records show David to have actually participated in. Not mentioned are the other two of the *Autobiography* (Emuckfau and Enotachopco Creeks) which the records won't support. Perhaps he did make this speech to the people of Trenton.

The final letter in the series, from Downing to Crockett, complain-ing that he had not heard from David in some time and asking about White's chances, and so on, need not be given here. The letter was undated, but appeared in the issue of August 1, 1835, not long before election day.[9] When David was defeated, the *Gazette* carried no more correspondence about him. The following spring the publication itself was discontinued. This is the series which Seba Smith omitted from his collected works with the statement that the Jack Downing letters in this journal "had been destroyed by fire."

During the summer of 1835 David was stump-speaking across his district against Adam Huntsman (Black Hawk), the peg-legged lawyer who had lost his leg in the Creek War but had never lost his sense of humor. Adam must have had to draw severely on the humor one particular night that summer if the following anecdote is true. It had such a widespread and persistent vitality among his contemporaries that perhaps it had at least a factual basis. The most nearly authentic source for the story is James D. Davis, who claimed to have been living in Memphis as a boy of sixteen at that time.[10] Huntsman, a wit and a man of judgment, had been popular for a long time in west Tennessee. He had been a town commissioner for Jackson when that town was yet called Alexandria, as well as a commissioner for the county of Madison. According to the story, his popularity with the ladies was not less than with the men. David knew that the race would be close, and out of that realization the event of this anecdote developed.

Crockett and Huntsman were travelling about the country together, speaking from the same stumps. On one particular evening they were both billeted with a well-to-do and politically influential farmer who, though quite hospitable to both, was generally known to be partial to Huntsman's cause. The household eventually retired for the night, and the contenders for Congress were quartered in the same room. Huntsman went soon to sleep and David lay reflecting on how he might win both the farmer and the farmer's influence to his own cause.

It happened that this farmer had an attractive, young, and unmarried daughter. The arrangement of the house and sleeping quarters was such that at one end of the back porch was her room and at the other end was the room shared by Crockett and Huntsman. At length, arising, David quietly took a straight-backed chair across the wooden porch to the young lady's door, and proceeded to make a noise as of one attempting to force an entrance. Soon frightened screams issued from beyond the portal, and David, placing one foot upon the rungs of the chair, hobbled rapidly back across the dark porch, softly closed the door, and jumped into bed. Fully attired for sleep as when he had arisen, he feigned deep slumber. Soon the farmer burst into the room and rudely rousted out Adam Huntsman, who seeming sheepishly to affect sleep, pretended complete ignorance of what the farmer was talking about and complete innocence of anything but sleeping in the proffered bed. The irate farmer would not be pacified, for he had dis-

tinctly heard with his own ears Adam's wooden stump beating a tat-
too back across the porch; and moreover he was perfectly well
acquainted with Adam's reputation where women were concerned.
David fortunately awakened just in time to prevent the indignant
father from doing bodily injury to the man who had violated the hospitality of his home! As it was, David restored a semblance of order,
and made himself security for Huntsman's better behavior for the remainder of the night—though the farmer roundly declared, in spite of
Crockett's generous efforts to appease him, that his voting intentions
had now been completely changed, and he vowed that he would
change as many of those of his friends as he could!

About this time Crockett wrote a letter to Carey and Hart. Miss
Constance Rourke mentioned it in her *Davy Crockett*, dated it July
8, 1835, and said that it expressed the desire to write one more book.[11]
I have discovered that the jist of that letter was put into the opening
pages of the completely spurious work which Carey and Hart pub-
lished in David's name months after his death at the Alamo, the *Texas
Exploits*. Here is my reconstruction of it from its paraphrase in the
Exploits:

Weakley County Tennessee
8 July 1835

Mrsrs Cary & Hart
   Gentlemen I have just returned from two weeks Canvass I have spoken
every day to many people with my Competitor I have him bad plagued
for he dont know as much as me about the Government his name is adam
Huntsman he lost a leg in an indian fight during the last war and the Government run him on his military Services—I tell him in my speech that I
have great hopes of writing one more book and that is the second fall of
Adam I handle the Administration without gloves and I do believe I will
double my competitor Jacksonism is dying here faster than it sprung up
I predict that the government will be the most unpopular man in one more
year that ever filled a high office four weeks from tomorrow will tell
and if I don't beat my competitor I will [go to texes?] I will write again
when the time comes I remain your obt Servt [12]

The context in which David expressed the wish to write one more
book is a mere jibe at Huntsman in his political speeches, not a serious
proposition to his publishers. Miss Rourke, taking that single sentence
out of context, used it to argue the plausibility of David's having contributed to the writing of the *Texas Exploits*.

According to this letter, the election would be held about August 6. It must have occurred at about that date, for on August 11 David kept his promise to "write again when the time comes." By then the elections were over and the votes had been counted. Crockett immediately notified his Whig friends, Gales and Seaton of the *National Intelligencer* [13] and the *Debates*, and Carey and Hart. As he seems instinctively to have realized, he was bidding then adieu. Here are portions of the letter to Carey and Hart:

...my Canvass is over and the result known I am beaton two hundred & thirty votes...I had Mr. Huntsman for my Competitor aided by all the popularity of both Andrew Jackson & Governer Carroll and the whole Strength of the Union Bank at Jackson I have been told by good men that Some of the managers of the Bank on the day of the Election was herd Say they would give 25 dollars a vote for votes enough to elect Mr Huntsman. . . . I have no doubt that I was Compleatly Raskeled out of my Election I do regret that duty to my Self & to my Country Compals me to expose Such viloney.

Well might Gov. Poindexter exclaim Ah my Country what degradation though hast fallen into Andrew Jackson was duren my election Canvass franking the entre Globe with a prospectus in it to every post office in this district and upon one ocasion he had my miledge and pay as a member drawn of and Sent to this distrect to one of his minions to have it published Just a few days before the election he Stated that I had Charged miledge for one thousand miles and that it was but Seven hundred & fifty miles and held out the Idea that I had taken pay for the Same miledge that Mr Fitzgerald had taken. when it was well known that he Charged thirteen hundred miles from here to Washington and him and my Self Both live in the Same County The Genls Pet Mr Grunday Charged for one thousand miles from nashville to Washington and it was Scanctened by the legislature I Suppose because he would Huzzaw for Jackson and because I would not the genl Come out openly to Electionaring against me I now Say that the oldest man living never herd of the presedent of a great nation to Come down to open Electionaring for his Successor We may truly Say the poor old Superanuated man is Surrounded by a poor Set of wretches using him to promote their own intrest in fact I do believe he is a perfect tool in their hands ready to be used to answer any purpose to either promote intrest or grattify ambetion—

...I am grattifyed that I have Spoken the truth to the people of my Distrect regardless of Consequences I would not be compeld to bow to the Idol for a Seat in Congress during life I have never knew what it was to Sacrafice my own Judgment to grattify any party and I have no doubt of the time being Close at hand when I will be rewarded for letting my tongue Speake what my hart thinks I have Suffered my Self to be politically Sacrafised to Save my Country from ruin & disgrace and if I am never a gain elected I will have the grattification to know that I have done my duty....

P S You may publish this letter it is the truth and I take the responsabilaty in Saying So—DC [14]

In reading this and other Crockett letters, we should not forget the historical milieu in which he lived. The dangers which he feared may sound ridiculous after so many generations of inherited "liberties," but they were not so farfetched to his generation. When David Crockett died at the Alamo there were still many people alive in the States who remembered when America had yet been under the rule of one king, some alive even who had fought to escape that condition. Democracy had not yet become the luxurious habit of long-accustomed freedom. Fears which may now sound preposterous to a platitudinous hindsight did not sound absurd at all in that day of surviving memories of English tyranny. Indeed, because that was so, men fierce in the jealousy of their independence were the more easily alarmed and thereby captured by such ominous warnings and oracular pronouncements on the threat of tyranny.

This brings us to David's holograph for October 31, 1835, and the whole matter of the Gibson Chancery Court Suit against him as administrator of the Patton estate. We have postponed this discussion in order to tell the whole story in connection with this letter.

The will by which Crockett and George Patton were made executors of the Patton estate has already been reviewed. As we learn from the ensuing suit, George Patton thought it unnecessary to come from North Carolina, and David became sole executor. To make the will binding, Robert Patton had left to two of his daughters ten dollars each, but no more; and they and their husbands had brought suit in an effort to break the will. The original bill was filed in the Chancery Court at Trenton, Gibson County, on May 8, 1834, ironically the day that climaxed David's Eastern tour, the evening of which he had spent in the Boston home of Lieutenant-Governor Armstrong. It was docketed as the case of William Edmundson and wife (Sally) and Hance McWhorter and wife (Ann) vs. David Crockett and wife (Elizabeth), Abner Burgin and wife (Margaret), Peter Trosper and wife (Matilda), James Emundson and wife (Rebecca), and George, William, and Sarah Patton.[15] As the case proceeds we learn that the six wives and George were children of Robert; and that another son of Robert's, James, had died leaving two children, William and Sarah, the last two named above, who would be entitled to a son's share. We learn that Peter Trosper may have been Peter *Hooper*.[16]

The William Edmundsons and the McWhorters stated that Robert Patton had died on November 11, 1832, at about 96 years of age. Shortly before his death he had executed a new will by which his estate of about four thousand dollars had been divided among his children, except that Sally and Ann had been left only ten dollars thereof. They continued:

Your Orators are informed and believe and charge the facts to be, that most of said legatees above named were around the said Robert Patton at and before the time of his making said will, and used means to influence said Patton in the deposition of said property, by which they imposed a fraud upon his age and infirmity, and prevented him from disposing of his property according to his own free will; and your Orators charge that said legatees prevented said Patton from giving your Orators anything except the ten dollars above mentioned by means of fraud in influencing the old man by fraudulent representations in regard to your Orators, and your Orators also charge that at the time the said Robert Patton executed his said will he was too much exhausted by age and disease to know what he was doing. . . .

They further charged that the legatees had the will proven in court without giving any notice to complainants that such was to be done, so that complainants had had no opportunity of contesting it at the proper time. They claimed that they had been "by the frauds of said legatees, deprived of their proportion of the estate" and prayed that the court would give them "the relief they are entitled to. . . ."

The reply of Crockett and the other defendants was filed on October 27, 1834, in which the matter of who has done what and to whom becomes amusing. David and the other respondents agreed as to the date of Mr. Patton's death, but affirmed that he was about 90 rather than 96. They also agreed that they had not notified complainants of the time of probating the will, but affirmed that complainants were "present in the Court at the time it was proven with full notice praying attention to it." As for Mr. Patton's faculties being exhausted or impaired more than other men of his age, they absolutely denied it:

on the contrary your respondents assert and say that they verily believe and think they can prove that he was a man of more than common understanding, and preserved in his intellects remarkably well to the last of his life. He transacted his own business and respondents are dearly of the opinion that he done so with more skill, judgement and prudence than the complainants transacted theirs.... and that the charge of imbecibility [*sic*], drunkenness, derangement or want of capacity in him is wholly untrue, and also the charge that your respondents by fraud, contrivance, circumvention, falsehood or by any other sort of under influence prevailed upon him to make a will any other than what his own [un]embarrassed pleasure and judgment dictated, whether to cheat complainants or any body else is entirely false, and wholly untrue.

They then gave Robert Patton's reason for leaving these two only ten dollars. They said that since he had paid and loaned Edmundson upward of $3,000 and had given him 200 acres of land, he had already received much more than an equal share "so that if all was equally divided he would have some to pay back, instead of receiving more than he has got." As for McWhorter, he had also received an equal share before Patton's death. For Mr. Patton had had a tract of land in which he thought there were about a thousand acres. This he had divided into 200-acre tracts to give to his children. The last 200 acres he had given to McWhorter in a deed worded "the ballance of the tract of about 200 acres." When surveyed, it proved to contain 500 acres instead of 200, and Mr. Patton had desired the return of the surplus 300 to live upon himself:

But the said McWhorter, when informed that he had the advantage by the way in which the deed was worded, held on to the whole amount, and by which he received that much more than the rest received, making about five hundred acres. And your respondents believe that these were the true reasons of his making his will in the manner he did, to try and equalize as much to the balance as near as he could.[17]

At this point something is missing from the records. The complainants took exceptions to this reply, but the exceptions are not recorded. However, David's reply to the exceptions is, and from it we can fairly well determine what the exceptions had been. The reply to the exceptions was filed on June 15, 1835, shortly before David's last election. It states that James Patton, Robert's son, had died in "the lower County Town" (Mississippi) at a date unknown to them and that "it is reported and believed that he left two children," William and Sarah

Patton, "whose residence is unknown to respondents, if they are living," who would be entitled to an inheritance if alive. The reply goes on to list the other heirs of Robert, to describe what his property consisted of, to state that the property had been divided in accordance with the provisions of the will, to deny positively that they had made "any threatenings to enduce said Patton to make a will in any way," and to reaffirm that "it was notorious when the will would be presented for probate and complainant McWhorter . . . was present, when it was proven in open court, and made no objection thereto."

From the foregoing, it is clear that matters concerning the children of the deceased James of Mississippi were up to this point quite vague. The final record in this cause shows that these heirs turned up to claim their inheritance, and David's letter on the subject, soon to follow, gives flesh and blood to the legal formalism of these documents. The John W. Crockett, Clerk and Master, before whom this and the former replies of defendants were sworn, was David's oldest son, John Wesley. The final court record is a statement dated October 28 by the children of the dead James (William Patton and George W. Harper, husband of Sarah Patton) accusing the complainants of "many untruths, uncertainties, and inafficiencies [sic]" and demanding that, if complainants have any evidence of "under means used to produce said will," they lay it before the court; otherwise, that the court dismiss the suit and "that they be permitted to receive their legacies. . . ." This statement was also sworn before John W. Crockett. Whether the suit was finally nolle prossed, whether David's demise put a permanent end to it, or whether it was settled out or thrown out of court the records do not reveal. A later letter from John Wesley refers to the executorship of the estate and its settlement, but makes no reference to the suit.

We are now prepared to understand that this was the last letter that David ever wrote from his native Tennessee, perhaps the next-to-last that he ever wrote at all. It was written three days after the last record mentioned above, and addressed to his brother-in-law, George Patton, in Swannanoa, North Carolina, and was mailed under the privilege of the Congressional frank. Though David had been more than two months defeated for re-election, he was legally entitled to the franking privilege until his official term should expire with the convocation of the new Congress in the succeeding December. Neither this letter nor anything in connection with the above suit has formerly been published in Crockett literature:

Weakley County Tennessee
Octr 31st 1835

Dear Brother

I have Concluded to drop you a line the whole Connection is well and I am on the eve of Starting to the Texes—on to morrow morning mySelf Abner Burgin and Lindsy K Tinkle & our Nephew William Patton from the Lowar Country this will make our Company we will go through Arkinsaw and I want to explore the Texes well before I return

I was Greatly in hopes that you would have Come out to Court this week So that you Could have Answered the Bill and Seen your friends from the lowar Country Both William Patton and his brother in law Mr George W Harper Came to my house on monday of Court and both went up and answered the Bill—and if you had Come or Sent on your answer the Answers would all have been Complete They will take yours as Confessed

I am not the least uneasy about their gaining it Mr Burgin let William have a horse at one hundred dollars and I have paid Mr Harper one hundred & 25 dollars—and I paid William a gun & Sadle and Some other things to the amount of Two hundred dollars—that I have paid them in all we have paid them three hundred They Brought Sufficient proof to Idintify them Selves—Mr George W. Harper is a first rate Blacksmith and a Clevever fellow you will be well pleased with him if you ever See him William will go with me and never return to that old woman again he is a fine fellow I am well pleased with them both I will leave a recept from the date your note Come due for the amount of $6.. 62 dollars or Credit your note with that amount You know if the will is not broke that there will be no difficulty They have never replyed to our answer as yet

George & Campbell has got a powar of attorny for that money ready to Send to you by Thos Foster G[eorge?] is in debt and wants hi[s] badly you will do him a good turn to Send it to him as Soon as posable I must Close in hast your obt Servt

David Crockett [18]

Several things need clarification. Tinkle, who was to accompany him to Texas, we earlier met buying a Negro girl from the Patton estate; Abner Burgin was a brother-in-law; and William Patton, nephew, was the son of Mrs. Crockett's dead brother James. "That old woman" to whom William would never return must have been William's mother. Since none of the family knew what had happened to William and Sarah, indeed, knew not whether they were alive until William and Sarah's husband showed up on the previous Monday,

George Patton could not have known whether William had a wife. If the expression "that old woman" had referred to William's wife, it would have made no sense to George in such a context. It is likely, however, that all of the family had known James' wife before he had gone to Mississippi. So the reference must have been to William's mother. David mentions that they came to his house on "monday of Court." The letter was dated on a Saturday. Since the date of their testimony was a Wednesday, they must have arrived the preceding Monday, October 26.

The arithmetic is a bit confused, but it seems to mean that $300 in all had been paid to the two, $100 of which was paid by Burgin, $200 by David. Of this amount, Harper seems to have received $125. William received $175, including a horse for $100, and a gun, a saddle, and some other things, totalling $75 more. Crockett and Burgin were obviously equipping William for his journey with them on the next day to Texas.

It is interesting that in this letter David uses the word *clever* to mean *friendly* or *sociable*. He employs it in the same meaning in the *Autobiography*, as for instance in his Chapter IV while describing his first prospective father-in-law, William Finley.

Finally, it is clear that David had no idea at this time of going to Texas to join the Texan forces and to fight for Texas independence. He went to explore the country, planning as he had threatened to do, to make one more move west to one more new frontier. His last letter verifies this intention. He did not live to make that last move with his whole family to a new horizon. After his death, his family made that move anyway, and settled on the Texas frontier.

This brings us to that day when three relatives and one neighbor set out to "explore the Texes," November 1, 1835.

Chapter 14

TEXAS–EXPLORED

CROCKETT, William Patton, Abner Burgin, and Lindsey K. Tinkle set out for Texas on November 1 and arrived soon afterwards in Memphis. James D. Davis, then sixteen, recording the occasion from memory, says that on the night of November 1, a group, presumably of these four and perhaps some Memphis friends, assembled in the bar of the Union Hotel, where they were stopping, and engaged in a farewell drinking party. Called upon during the course of the evening for a toast or a speech, David said something about the recent election. He commented on the fact that many who ought to have voted for him had instead voted for his opponent, and he concluded, "Since you have chosen to elect a man with a timber toe to succeed me, you may all go to hell and I will go to Texas." [1]

Before long they were all rather heavily "under the influence" and were driven first from this bar, and then from others in the town. According to Davis, throughout the night Crockett tried to play the peacemaker and to hold the carousers in check. The next day they set sail for Texas, and Davis says that he saw Crockett leave the hotel and, following him to the ferry landing, watched his departure: "He wore that same veritable coon-skin cap and hunting shirt, bearing upon his shoulder his ever faithful rifle. No other equipment, save his shot pouch and powder-horn, do I remember seeing." [2]

Briefly, here is the route they were to follow. They travelled down the Mississippi to the mouth of the Arkansas River, and ascended the Arkansas to Little Rock. Here they set out overland in a southwestwardly direction, following a path approximating what is today U. S.

Highway 67 from Little Rock to Fulton, Arkansas, on the Red River. They travelled up the Red River westwardly and passed through a place then called Lost Prairie, Arkansas, continuing along the northern boundary of Texas and exploring the Red River country. North of Clarksville, they crossed to the south side of the river and came into Clarksville, in north Texas. From here they went south to Nacogdoches and San Augustine, neighboring towns near the Louisiana line. Which town they entered first I am not sure. It is likely that two of them, Abner Burgin and Lindsey Tinkle, here turned back toward homes and families, while William Patton and David signed the oath of allegiance and moved on toward San Antonio. They passed through Washington-on-the-Brazos, Texas, and from there followed the route of the present U. S. Highway 73 and 90 to the Alamo.

Niles Register recorded David's departure from Memphis with his rifle and coon-skin cap. This organ, despite Crockett's defeat, still discussed him—was not Texas soon coming into the Union? The following prophetic words were published on December 5, 1835: "Col. *Crockett* has proceeded to *Texas*—to end his days there. A supper was given to him at Little Rock, Arkansas." [3] *Niles* must have been reporting the event several weeks late. Crockett's name was by now famous, and there is little doubt that the backwoodsman was entertained all along his route and that his journey was a pleasant one. The pioneer had returned to his own element, to activities in which he could excel, and to which he had of old been long accustomed. It must have been a satisfying experience to get back into the familiar clothes of his old ways and to set out once more to explore a new and wild country for one more move west, a nationally famous man doing what he liked to do.

Three weeks later *Niles* reported again:

> The emigration to *Arkansas* is very great—"with large droves of negroes"—says a *Little Rock* paper; exclusive of those who are about to join the people of Texas. Col. Crockett has left *Little Rock*, with his followers, for Texas. Many others had the same destination. [4]

I believe the party first struck the Red River at Fulton, Arkansas. Somewhere in the few miles between there and the Texas border was a town called Lost Prairie, where we catch our next glimpse of them. In a letter written from there in the spring of 1836, possibly the very letter which brought David's family the first *personal* news of his death, a Mr. Isaac N. Jones described to Mrs. Crockett David's visit to his home during the previous winter, as the party drew near to Texas. The portion describing the visit reads:

The object of this letter, is to beg that you will accept the watch which accompanies it.... as it has his name engraved on its surface, it will no doubt be the more acceptable to you.

As it will probably be gratifying to you to learn in what way I became possessed of it, permit me to state, that, last winter (the precise date not recollected by me), col. Crockett, in company with several other gentlemen, passed through Lost Prairie, on Red River, (where I live). The company, excepting the colonel, who was a little behind, rode up to my house and asked accomodations for the night. My family being so situated, from the indisposition of my wife, that I could not accomodate them, they got quarters at one of my neighbors' houses. The colonel visited me the next day and spent the day with me. He observed, whilst here, that his funds were getting short and proposed to me to exchange watches—he priced his at $30 more than mine, which sum I paid him, and we accordingly exchanged.

With his open frankness, his natural honesty of expression, his perfect want of concealment, I could not but be very much pleased. And with a hope that it might be an accomodation to him, I was gratified at the exchange, as it gave me a *keepsake* which would often remind me of an honest man, a good citizen and a pioneer in the cause of liberty, amongst his suffering brethren in Texas.[5]

Here I must repeat that this watch is now one of the heirlooms owned by Mrs. A. Sidney Holderness; I wonder if its owner knows this story of how it was sold and, through the generosity of a stranger, was returned into the keeping of the family.

David's last surviving letter, though written later, reviews his explorations and the purpose thereof along the Red River, and a part of it reads:

It's not required here to pay down for your League of land. Every man is entitled to his head right of 400–428 [4,428] acres. They may make the money to pay for it on the land. I expect in all probability to settle on the Border or Chactaw Bro of Red River that I have no doubt is the richest country in the world. Good land and plenty of timber and the best springs and will [wild] mill streams, good range, clear water and every appearance of good health and game aplenty. It is the pass where the buffalo passes from north to south and back twice a year, and bees and honey plenty. I have a great hope of getting the agency to settle that country and I would be glad to see every friend I have settled thare.[6]

Having explored the Red River Country, David and his companions turned south. The next reliable reminiscence of their journey comes from a family who resided near and gave its name to the present Clarksville, Texas. The account coincides interestingly with David's remark above about "bees and honey plenty." Still exploring, Crockett was passing south through Red River County of which Clarksville is now the county seat, travelling in a southwestwardly direction:

Mrs. Clark hearing of Crockett's itinerary and knowing the risk he was incurring mounted her horse in company with a daughter of Russel Latimer, overtook Crockett and his party on Becknell's Prairie five miles west of Clarksville, warned him of the danger of traveling to the southwest, and prevailed upon him to wait for a guide and recruits to pursue a course bearing towards the east. While thus waiting at the Becknell home Crockett's party went on a hunting trip to the southwest under Henry Stout as guide.[7] The party when near the headwaters of the Trinity River met James Clark. Crockett told him of the woman who halted his journey and changed his course. This statement called forth from James Clark the remark, "That was my wife, for no other woman would do a thing like that." Clark advised the hunting party to turn back, as the Comanches were at that time on the warpath. While on this trip the party rode on until it reached a grove alive with bees. The place was given the name of Honey Grove by Crockett as a descriptive of the place. This was the sight of what afterwards was known as the city of Honey Grove, in Fanin [sic—Fannin] County.[8]

This name it bears today.

Whether Crockett ultimately turned east, or whether he continued southwest is not clear. Miss Rourke, probably on the above evidence, says they went east in a sort of parabola from Clarksville toward Marshall to San Augustine, but found the undergrowth impenetrable and turned back to the Red River and followed a route that brought them in from Natchitoches, Louisiana, to San Augustine. However, David's letter of January 9 was written from "Saint Agusteen," and refers to his having "taken the oath of government and enrolled my name as a volunteer," which the evidence indicates that he did in Nacogdoches. That, in turn, appears to indicate that he may have come down through the interior of Texas· arriving first at Nacogdoches and taking the oath, and then going on to San Augustine. Whatever the route he followed, sometime before January 9 the band arrived in San Augustine, where David wrote his last surviving letter to his oldest daughter, Margaret, and to her husband, Wiley Flowers. (The portion already quoted is indicated here by asterisks):

Crockett P.O.
Gibson County, Tennessee
My Dear Sone and daughter
    This is the first I have had an opertunity to write you with convenience. I am now blessed with excellent health and am in high spirits, although I have had many difficulties to encounter. I have got through safe and have been received by everyone with open cerimony of friendship. I am hailed with hearty welcome to this country. A dinner and a party of ladys have honored me with an invitation to partisapate both at Nacing docher [Nacogdoches] and at this place. The cannon was fired here on my arrival and I must say as to what I have seen of Texas it is the garden spot of the world. The best land and the best prospects for health I ever saw, and I do believe it is a fortune to any man to come here. There is a world of country here to settle.
    ************** I [it?] would be a fortune to them all. I have taken the oath of government and have enrolled my name as a volunteer and will set out for the Rio Grand in a few days with the volunteers from the United States. But all volunteers is entitled to vote for a member of the convention or to be voted for, and I have but little doubt of being elected a member to form a constitution for this province. I am rejoiced at my fate. I had rather be in my present situation than to be elected to a seat in Congress for life. I am in hopes of making a fortune yet for myself and family, bad as my prospect has been.
    I have not written to William but have requested John to direct him what to do. I hope you will show him this letter and also Brother John as it is not convenient at this time for me to write to them. I hope you will all do the best you can and I will do the same. Do not be uneasy about me. I am among friends. I will close with great respects. Your affectionate father. Farewell.[9]

    It seems clear from David's last two letters that his journey to the Alamo was determined after he signed the allegiance oath. Since the names of Abner Burgin and Lindsey Tinkle are not among those subscribing to the oath with David, I assume that, at this point, they separated from William Patton and David, returning to their families rather than signing the oath of allegiance and joining the army. Both of these letters establish quite clearly what David's objectives were. He planned to move his family to Texas. He hoped to become land agent and to acquire that affluence which he had for so long tried but failed to acquire. He took the oath of allegiance in order to vote and be voted for, as well as to take a leading political, which is to say military, part in securing Texan independency. He planned ultimately, I believe, to enter again into national politics when Texas should come into the Union. The political forces of the nation, once removed, were engaged in the same power struggle in Texas as in the states. Though David had lost a battle, I think he had not given up the war. The conclusion of his letter, "Farwell," sounds in retrospect dramatic and might appear to reflect apprehensions. Such was probably not the case, as the expression occurs occasionally in his writings and he had signed a letter similarly as early as the one of January 27, 1829, to George Patton.

The letter speaks of leaving for the Rio Grand in a few days. Before we turn to that matter, there is another connected with his signing of the oath of allegiance, that involves a Crockett anecdote which I think is authentic beyond a doubt. Properly interpreted it is more than an anecdote, for it is instinct with tragedy and lays bare David's Achilles' heel. On June 23, 1838, *Niles Register* carried the following account from the *Texas Telegraph*, which had cited for its authority Judge John Forbes, the official who had administered to David the oath of allegiance to Texas:

Col. Forbes has recently related to us an interesting anecdote of the celebrated Crockett. At the commencement of the war the latter arrived at Nacogdoches accompanied by several volunteers. Soon after their arrival they proceeded to the office of col. Forbes (who was then first judge of the municipality), to take the oath of allegiance. The colonel immediately wrote out the following form:

"I do solemnly swear that I will bear true allegiance to the provisional government of Texas, or any future government that may be hereafter declared, and that I will serve her honestly and faithfully against all her enemies and oppressors whatsoever, and observe and obey the orders of the governor of Texas, the orders and decrees of the present and future authorities, and the orders of the officers appointed over me according to the rules and articles for the government of Texas so help me God."

Upon offering it to Crockett he refused to sign it, saying that he was willing to take an oath to support any future *republican* government, but could not subscribe his name to this form, as the future government might be despotic; the colonel therefore inserted the word republican between the words future and government, and Crockett signed the instrument.

The original has lately been deposited in the office of the secretary of War, in which the word republican appears *interlined*, and beneath it is the autograph of David Crockett.

Texas Telegraph.[10]

Since at this time Texas had not come into the union, the secretary of war referred to would be of the state of Texas. A letter from the War Department in Washington confirms this.[11] The Texas Adjutant General informs me, however, that the original records were destroyed when the Texas State Capitol burned in 1855. Fortunately Judge John Forbes himself made a "true copy" of the original record in question, probably at the time the original was forwarded to the secretary of war of Texas, and this certified copy has survived. It may be found at page 114 of the *Texas Mobilization Records*. According to the letter from the Texas Adjutant General the oath as there recorded, included the word *republican*, reads:

I do solemnly swear that I will bear true allegiance to the Provisional Government of Texas or any future republican Government that may be hereafter declared, and that I will serve her honestly and faithfully against all her enemies and opposers whatsoever, and observe and obey the orders of the Governors of Texas, the orders and decrees of the present or future authorities and the orders of the officers appointed over me according to the rules and articles for the government of Texas. 'So help me God.' [12]

Nineteenth on the list of names subscribing thereto is the name of David Crockett.

The oath transcribed by Judge John Forbes differs so slightly from that published in 1838 by *Niles*, that the one tends to authenticate the other. Its publication at such an early date by *Niles*, the Texas *Telegraph*, and no doubt other papers, when if untrue it could easily have been refuted by others who may have been present at the swearing in, also tends to corroborate it. In addition, the crediting of the story to Judge Forbes himself, who had administered the oath and who made the transcription above, adds to the probability of its accuracy. But the fact which seems to me completely to clinch the matter is that the name of William Patton, David's nephew from the "lower country," occurs on the list subscribing to the above oath *three names below that of David Crockett*. For it is only the Chancery suit and David's letter of October 31, 1835, which informs us about William or that he was a member of David's party. That suit and that letter have never before been published. William Patton's name has never been included among those who fell at the Alamo, though I think it ought now to be. Its occurrence on this list of subscribers to the oath of allegiance to Texas could only mean a corroboration of the reliability of the list and the oath as transcribed above.

The one thing that gives trouble here is the dating of the oath, January 14, 1836. David's letter of January 9 spoke of having already taken the oath of allegiance. Miss Rourke referred to this document as being dated January 5,[13] on what authority I cannot say—but if without authority, that only artificially delivers one from the dilemma. There seem to me to be three possible explanations. David's letter of January 9 may have been misdated (I have been unable to see the original letter); the document made by Judge Forbes may have been misdated (or in the copy he may have inserted the date of his copying rather than that of the original; or he may have consolidated a number of affidavits, putting on the consolidated list the date of the last one or the date of the consolidation—surely not all sixty-four of the signers here listed were in David's small party); or David may have taken an earlier oath orally and for some reason have taken it again, this time in writing. I cannot tell which answer is the proper one, but have concluded that the instrument of the oath is unquestionably authentic with the possible exception of the date.

David's objection to signing an oath of allegiance except to a government which he himself could specifically designate republican is amusing in terms of his old apprehensions about Jackson's regime back in the States. Was this a mere theoretical fear of Crockett's, a hangover from out of the past, or did it have application to an immediate situation which had already developed in the Texas he was now joining? Though it may destroy all of the humor of the anecdote for us, I think nevertheless that the answer is, the latter. David had hopes of going to the Constitutional Assembly. He did not get there. Why?

From November 14, 1835, until March 11, 1836, the General Council of the Republic of Texas was in session at San Felipe De Austin,[14] and its proceedings clearly reveal that already by the date of David's oath-taking two forces had developed in Texas, evidently the same ones which were active back in the states—the Jackson and the anti-

Jackson forces. This Council, from about the end of 1835, spent most of its time quarrelling with the formerly established government and fighting with Governor Henry Smith. In fact, they finally impeached him as a "tyrant" on January 13, electing a new governor. Smith, who had charged them with being more concerned about drawing big salaries for themselves than about settling the dire problems of Texas, refused to be deposed. From then until March 11, the vital period for this study, there were two governors of Texas: Smith elected by the earlier Consultation Convention; and James Robinson, Lt. Governor and ex-officio President of the General Council, elected by the General Council.

Nor was this all. A similar situation split the military authority as formerly set up by the Consultation Convention and as now set up by the General Council. In a speech in the summer of 1845, Sam Houston said that he had been made commander-in-chief of the Texas forces by the earlier convention; but that the General Council, above, set up another commander-in-chief, just as they had set up another governor.[15] There were two factions at odds, and the cleavage ran from top to bottom. "I very soon discovered that I was a General without an army, serving under and by authority of a pretended government, that had no head, and no loyal subjects to obey its commands," Houston said. He considered himself superseded in command of the army *by an illegal act* of the General Council, *at the solicitation of his inferior officers*, and consequently he asked for a parole and set about securing a new Convention of the people for the purpose of organizing a permanent government. This new convention was in session, and had again made Sam Houston Commander-in-Chief of the Texan Forces, when the Alamo was besieged.

Now the point here is that Sam Houston seems to have been generally understood, correctly or incorrectly, to be a representative of Andrew Jackson and his philosophy in Texas.[16] Powerful forces in the General Council, which was setting up a provisional government, were bitterly opposed to him. This situation had already developed before David took his oath of allegiance to Texas and insisted on the insertion of the word "republican." Those in command at the Alamo were among those subordinates who had urged the replacement of Houston as commander-in-chief. They were men who refused to accept the authority of Houston and who were in fact guilty, as we shall see, of absolute and complete insubordination in remaining at the Alamo after January. David and Sam Houston had been friends earlier; perhaps, where politics were not concerned, were friends still. David's feeling about Jackson had come to be his guiding passion. If Houston represented Jackson and the Jackson concept of "liberty," there was no question on which side David would take his stand. In the light of these facts, of which David could not possibly have been ignorant, his refusal to sign the oath until the insertion of "republican" had allowed him the privilege of deciding which of the Texas governments he would choose to support was no idle gesture about an abstraction. It expressed an exception he was taking to one of the then-contending governments of Texas.

In short, I believe we see in this anecdote an epitome of the great forces whose involvement was to be the undoing of David Crockett at the Alamo, the very kernel of his life in one little shell. It reflects the consummation of all of his past political struggles, the determinations and sentiments which had long been developing and which were now to take him to the Alamo, to make him support the anti-Houston and anti-Jackson forces in military insubordination, and finally to cause him to lay down his life. In it we see the violent hate for Jackson which not only had been the cause of his political undoing, but was soon to become the proximate cause of his death. A grim anecdote it becomes, then, in the light of these facts. Houston's own explanation of the Alamo, and of the actions of its defenders, we reserve for the next chapter. This much was necessary here for an understanding of the deeper implications of this "anecdote."

"I . . . will set out for the Rio Grand in a few days with the volunteers from the United States," David wrote on January 9. The final surviving Crockett holograph reveals that he did so. By January 23 he had arrived in Washington-on-the-Brazos, Texas, about one hundred and fifty miles to the southwest. I think that nephew William Patton, unmarried, far from home, and determined not to return "to that old woman" again, having taken the oath of allegiance with his uncle, remained with him and made one of the small party to which the holograph pertains. In David's familiar writing, which we here see for the very last time, the brief "I.O.U." reads:

Washington 23rd January 1836

This is to Certify that John Lott
furnished my Self and four others
Volunteers on our way to the—
army with accomodations for our
Selves & horses The Government
will pay him $7.–50 cts—

David Crockett [17]

This concludes the holographic evidence relating to David Crockett. The rest is general and often contradictory evidence, a great deal of fabrication, guess—and silence. Having reached, and departed from Washington, Texas, the volunteers proceeded directly to San Antonio De Bexar. David arrived there early in February, 1836.

Chapter 15

AN END–AND A BEGINNING

WE come now to that event which was to terminate the life of the historical figure, *David* Crockett, but which was at the same time to immortalize the mythological character known as *Davy*. Judging the responsibility of the biographer to be historical rather than dramatic, mythological, or fictional, we must conclude our account where history ends and legend begins. An explanation of the origins of the legend and a cursory account of its development fall within the scope of history, and we have reserved for an epilogue the factual explanation of the inception of Crockett's new career upon the grave of his old.

I suppose no event in recent historical times, with a basis in fact, has been more conducive to the creation of legend, fiction, gossip, error, and falsehood than the destruction of the fortress at San Antonio De Bexar and the massacre of all military forces therein by the troops of the Mexican General, Santa Anna. A few among the defending forces survived that battle—Negroes, women, a child—but none who participated, none who was not in hiding, none whose fright was temperate enough to allow him to be a reliable witness. Except for the date and the fact of its fall, there is almost no single point about the Alamo upon which the testimony of the few survivors does not disagree. The absence of verifiable fact, the contradiction of testimonies, has left without bounds the zeal of the patriot and the imagination of the fictionalizer. Fiction and romance have done with the Alamo what they would, ingenuity what it could, and more particularly with David and Davy at the Alamo. If the interest of the reader is in a "good story," dramatic or odiously melodramatic, and if he calls such erroneous accounts of historical events good, there are numerous sources easily available in which he may satisfy that interest. In keeping with the purpose of this volume, the story recounted here will be brief, for such is the evidence. To say that is to say that none of the conventional accounts of David Crockett at the Alamo come within our range, other than by way of brief mention for the purpose of refutation.

Returning to Crockett and his volunteers, it would be well to make clear exactly what the military situation at the Alamo was when David arrived there in early February, 1836. On January 17 Sam Houston, Commander-in-Chief of the Texas Military Forces, had sent James Bowie to the Alamo with orders for its commander, Colonel Neill, to blow up that fort and retreat to the interior to join him. By the time these orders reached the Alamo, Colonel Travis, who belonged to the forces refusing to acknowledge Houston's authority, had relieved Neill. Travis refused to obey orders: refused to blow up the fort, refused to retreat. Travis determined to remain where he was. The disaster which followed, like the similar disaster a bit later at Goliad under Colonel Fannin, was directly consequent to the refusal to obey the orders of the commander-in-chief. As noted, Houston asked for a parole when his position became untenable, and aided in the formation of a convention for the establishment of a permanent government, in which he took his seat as a member on March 2. In the meantime, the fortification of the Alamo had been surrounded and Colonel Travis had sent urgent messages for relief to Colonel Fannin at Goliad, and to the President of the Convention in which Houston was seated—but none to the commander-in-chief himself. On March 3 that message arrived at the Convention, and on that same day Sam Houston was confirmed again as Commander-in-Chief of the Texas Military Forces. In the previously cited speech at Houston, Texas, in 1845, Houston stated that he left the next day for Gonzales to recruit troops and to go to the aid of the Alamo defenders. In a later speech before the United States Senate in 1859, he stated that he left on March 6, and this seems to have been the correct date for his departure.[1]

Perhaps it was this delay, plus the fact that the forces surrounded there were known to be antagonistic to him, which gave rise to the rumor that Houston had deliberately allowed his intransigent subordinates to be destroyed and which constituted the reason for his speech-making in explanation and self-defense. At any rate, when he arrived at Gonzales on March 11, some seventy-odd miles east of San Antonio and a little less due north of Goliad, in what appears to have been a perfectly *bona fide* expedition to rescue the Alamo forces, word was brought him by those claiming to have been eyewitnesses that the Alamo had fallen and all of his defenders destroyed. Immediately, Houston sent orders to Colonel Fannin to blow up La Bahia, the fortress he occupied, and to fall back with a general convocation of troops to Victoria. In a personal note to Captain P. Dimmett, on the next day, Houston said: "I am induced to believe from all the facts communicated to me that the Alamo, has fallen, and all our men are *murdered!* We must not depend upon Forts; The woods, and ravines suit us best." [2]

Fannin's reply to Houston's order makes interesting, albeit tragic, reading. It is an insulting bit of insubordination in which he still refuses to accept Houston's authority and in which he appears to me to employ Jacksonian language tauntingly: "I will take the responsibility" for absolute disobedience of orders. Fannin, like the defenders of the Alamo, hesitated too long where he was. Changing his mind, he began to retreat toward Victoria in broad daylight across open and arid terrain away from water, instead of by foothills and at night. He was cut off by the Mexican forces, surrounded, and before long, with no water for the troops, was forced to capitulate "on terms." The Mexicans did not respect the terms; the troops were returned to Goliad, lined up against a wall, and shot in groups, save for a few who jumped over the wall and escaped to tell the story. Colonel Fannin lost his life consequent to a refusal to take orders, even after Houston had for the second time been made Commander-in-Chief of the military forces. This is doubtless what Colonel Robert I. Chester had in mind when, in his reminiscences of David Crockett, he replied to H. S. Turner's mention of the Alamo with: "The fight at the Alamo was a blunder. What did a man shut himself up in a fort, and allow Santa Anna to surround him for? It was downright folly!" [3] Of course Colonel Chester as a Jacksonian could not know the extent to which hatred for Jackson could derange the minds of men.

With this insubordination and its tragic consequences clearly before us, we must seek an answer to this important question: Is there anything to connect David Crockett personally with these subordinates of Houston who refused to obey his commands, or was he merely an unwitting victim of the circumstances? Two things, I think, establish that he was a participant in the insubordination. One is the history of Crockett's growing hate for Jackson, which we have followed.[4] We have witnessed the ravages of that hate, and we have pointed out the continuation in Texas of the same political and philosophical struggles which were being waged in the States. When we add to this a reference by Houston himself, slight, but definitely coupling the name of David Crockett with those of Travis, Fannin, and Bowie as being in opposition to his own policies, the matter seems to be removed from any reasonable doubt. It is the only reference I could find in all of Houston's published writings to David Crockett.

To understand its implications correctly one must know the context of the speech in which it was made. Houston had been accused of deliberately allowing men to be destroyed who had become national heroes since their destruction. He was attempting to defend himself from that charge. He could not use any defense based upon, or even remotely implying, a defamation of these men. To do so would supply evidence of that assumed malice on his part upon which the original charge had been based—would, in other words, defeat the whole purpose of his defense. His was the ticklish job of attempting to refurbish his own reputation without blemishing theirs in any way. He had to handle the matter of their insubordination in such a way as to make it appear, if not glorious, at least unblameworthy. Here is the way he put it under those circumstances:

Travis, Fannin, Crockett, Bowie, were all brave and gallant spirits; they never, while living employed falsehood and slander to carry a point or injure a character; their acts were open and bold; *their policy of warfare was to divide, advance and conquer. My policy was to concentrate, retreat and conquer,* and at this very moment could the veil be drawn that divides the earth from heaven, I cannot but imagine that these brave and manly heroes, bending from their exalted position, would look down upon my insignificant and wicked slanderers with withering scorn and contempt.[5]

De mortuis nil nisi bonum—especially if the dead be nationally enshrined heroes. What he did *not* say was: "That was their policy, but this was mine. I was their commander-in-chief and had ordered them to blow up the Alamo and to retreat." To have done so would have been to call down upon himself a good deal more wrath than such an explanation could possibly generate in our own day.

Nevertheless, in that speech he revealed that David Crockett was one with those who opposed themselves to his authority. Though this may not allow so glorious an ending to the story, it makes that ending much more consistent and lifelike. David's hate for Andrew Jackson was his undoing. The tragic drama of his life must be understood in terms of that weakness. There were other motives, of course, nor would I detract from them. Some of them were not without grandeur. I believe that a number of these men hoped for Jacksonian-like military fame by success at the Alamo, on which, like Jackson, they might rise to important state, and later national, office. In the light of David's emphasis in the *Autobiography* on the importance of military fame to political advancement and in the light of the reason he gave in his last letter for having joined the Texas forces, I surmise that such a consideration was not entirely alien to his own mind. And yet—a man does not jeopardize his life lightly for purely worldly considerations. These men believed that they fought for a great cause. Perhaps from the point of view of strict military strategy, they made the mistake of identifying one particular piece of land and one battle with Texan victory or defeat, or errors of judgment of other sorts. Yet what military strategist can properly evaluate the extent of the credit for Texan Independence which ultimately may have stemmed from "Remember the Alamo!" and from the inspiration which the stand of the men there gave to the remainder of the army; and from the fact of the slaughter there of so many of the flower of the enemy's troops? Whatever history may say as to their errors, that they faced with courage and paid with their lives for what they evidently held to be dearer than life, there can be no mistaking. The decision was theirs, in the face of gun and sword; not ours, in armchairs. Just as it behooves us not to approve their judgments automatically merely because of the price of their sacrifice, so it also is not for us to deny them the right of arriving at their own convictions and of defending them wisely or foolishly, with all that they had. Truth is a many-colored dolphin.

Santa Anna arrived with his forces at the Medina River, a few miles south of San Antonio, on February 20. On the 23rd he sent a demand for surrender of the fortress which was refused. It seems clear that the men inside could easily have escaped had that been their desire.

On the 24th the bombardment began, and that night Travis sent to Gonzales his first call for aid. About March 3, some thirty volunteers arrived from that place and crept into the Alamo. The letter written by Travis to the President of the Convention noted that "Col. J. B. Bonham, a courier from Gonzales, got in this morning at 11 o'clock, without molestation." [6] Many of the men at the Alamo were unfit for service; and as the bombardment continued with no substantial help arriving from any direction (Colonel Fannin started out, but turned back), the situation became acute.

The rest of the story for our purposes may be gathered from the evidence presented by the witnesses below. In his order to Fannin to retreat from La Bahia, Houston wrote, on March 11, that the tidings he had just received had been brought to him by a "Mexican supposed to be friendly, which however was contradicted in some parts by another who arrived with him; it is therefore only given to you as rumor, though I fear a melancholy portion of it will be found true." He told Fannin that "the Alamo was attacked on Sunday morning [March 6] at dawn of day, by about 2,300 Mexicans, and was carried a short time before sunrise, with a loss of 520 Mexicans killed and as many wounded. Col. Travis had only 150 effective men out of his whole force of 187. After the fort was carried, seven men surrendered and called for Gen. Santa Anna for quarter—they were murdered by his orders. Col. Bowie, was sick in bed, and also murdered." [7] A number of Houston's facts here, which he had got from Mexican runners, are now known to be in error. There is no question that the Alamo fell on that Sunday morning, and that the size of Travis' forces was more or less correctly stated. The Mexican forces were much larger and suffered more disastrously. Subsequently, Houston reported in a letter to James Collinsworth on March 15 that the survivors, Mrs. Dickerson (usually misspelled *Dickinson*), wife of an officer at the Alamo, and two Negroes, one the servant of Colonel Travis, the other of Colonel Almonte, had arrived at his headquarters and corroborated most of the earlier reports. [8]

With this we turn to the testimony of the survivors, or of those claiming to be survivors or witnesses, of that battle: Ramon Martinez Caro, private secretary to General Santa Anna; Madam Candelaria, who claimed to have been nursing the sick Bowie inside at the time of the fall; and Mrs. Dickerson, who was positively there. The emotional strain of having lost her husband and having endured the imminent danger of losing her own life and the life of her little daughter doubtless explains the inconsistency in Mrs. Dickerson's testimony as reported at the time by Houston and later by herself. Such details as whether Bowie shot himself and Travis stabbed himself, or whether they were slain by the Mexicans, or whether they were among those who surrendered and then were killed in cold blood, we leave to the dispute of historians. Our interest here must be limited primarily to David Crockett.

The editors of *Houston's Writings* say that historians have accepted as accurate Ramon Martinez Caro's statements of the number of Mexican troops present and slain at the Alamo.[9] The number has been variously given from five to seven for those who surrendered; and fictionalizers, craving the final dramatic act, have made Crockett one of them. In this version, seeing the death signal given, David lunged at Santa Anna in a final fierce surge, to be cut down by swords inches short of the throat of his target. Patriots would not have it so, seeing in surrender a possible impugning of Crockett's intrepidity. What evidence remains suggests that, in fact, David's death was quite undramatic, that he was one of the first to fall, and that he died unarmed.

The figure for the size of the Mexican troops has ranged from 2,000 to 9,000 with the same virtuosity of all other matters relating to this battle. Caro's estimate that there were 5,000 Mexican troops present and that 1,544 of the flower of them were killed [10] probably is close to the facts. Santa Anna himself had to lead the final surge in order to inspire the men who were ready to withdraw and retreat after several repulses and the loss of so many troops.

It is known that Mrs. Dickerson was present during the battle of the Alamo. Yet what appears to be the most reliable information comes from a Madam Candelaria, who claimed also to have been there. It will be necessary briefly to examine the bases of her claim. For more than half a century she had continued to maintain her story before the state of Texas undertook to hear testimony and to investigate its accuracy. After due deliberations, however, a bill was introduced into the Texas House of Representatives for her relief, based solely upon the acceptance of her claim. This passed the Texas House 72 to 5 and the Senate 21 to 9, becoming law on April 13, 1891. The pension rewarded "Mrs. Andrea Castanon de Villanueva, alias 'Madam Candelaria' " for rendering "efficient service to said cause as a nurse to the sick during the siege of the Alamo, in the year 1836," and suspended "the constitutional rule requiring bills to be read on three several days" so that it could become effective immediately.[11]

Three years earlier, on March 17, 1888, a historian, Mr. William Corner, had had an interview with her, and published the results in his *San Antonio De Bexar: A Guide and History* in 1890. That interview appears to have been conducted with circumspection and parts of it are therefore worth quoting here:

I asked her . . . a few questions that I thought would elucidate what some deemed to be obscure pretensions. The result of this and other later interviews are here given, and the reader must judge for himself the value of the statements and evidence. She is at least a very old and interesting person, lively and full of the recollection and reminiscences of the men and the stirring times of the Texan Revolution.

I asked her was she inside the fortifications of the Alamo during the fight? She answered unhesitatingly "Yes." Was she in the Alamo Church building during the last stand? She replied as before without reflection that she was, in those moments she was nursing Colonel James Bowie who was in bed very ill of typhoid fever, and that as she was in the act of giving him a drink of water the Mexican soldiery rushed in, wounding her in the chin—showing an old scar—and killing Bowie in her arms. She demonstrated this scene in quite an active fashion and showed us exactly how she was holding Bowie, her left arm around his shoulders and a drinking cup in her right hand.

I next asked her what was done with the bodies of the Texans? She said all were cremated. With the bodies of the dead Mexicans? All were cremated. Were there many American families living in San Antonio then? Some, but they all fled or the men took refuge within the Alamo. Did she know Mrs. Dickinson [*sic*]? Yes, but not well. She adopted an expression of considerable repugnance at this question, and said with some snap that Mrs. Dickinson hated Mexicans. . . . I was particular to ask her about a child of Mrs. Dickinson and she said that the husband of Mrs. Dickinson was fighting as one of the defenders of the Alamo and that when he saw the cause was lost he hastened down from the walls and took his son, a little child, and tied him around his waist in front of him, got to the top of the wall at the front of the Church and jumped down among the fighting Mexicans below and both were killed. This is very dramatic but it is not I believe elsewhere recorded.[12] Being anxious to know about the daughter of Mrs. Dickinson I asked her if she had not heard that such a child had escaped the massacre with her mother. She believed she said, that Mrs. Dickinson had taken a daughter with her in her flight, she had been told so at any rate.

She said that she recollected David Crockett before the fight.[13]

The author goes on to describe her very old, withered, wrinkled, and toothless face, and to give her age.[14] He continues:

I then asked her a question upon a matter which had puzzled me and which puzzles me still, though she had a ready answer to it as she had for any other asked. She informed me that the water from the acequia was used constantly by the defenders of the Alamo during the siege. I naturally asked why the besiegers did not cut off the water or divert it and so distress those within? She said the Indians at the Missions would not have allowed this! .... She mentioned Mr. John Twohig, saying that she knew him "Como mis manos"—"Like my hands," which is a favorite idiom of the old woman. ...

Returning to the subject of David Crockett, the old Senora said he was one of the first to fall; that he advanced from the Church building towards the wall or rampart running from the end of the stockade, slowly and with great deliberation, without arms, when suddenly a volley was fired by the Mexicans causing him to fall forward on his face, dead.

Corner gives more details about other matters which need not detain us here, yet the pains he took for accuracy and his warning of moderation to the reader are important as evidence of the reliability of his interview and his report of it. I give his conclusion:

Such are her recollections; the reader must make many allowances. So long and active a life as hers must be crowded—more—overcrowded, and jumbled with the multitude of things to remember.

On other occasions, in April of this year [1890] I revisited her twice with a good interpreter as a companion, and she said: "My maiden name was Andrea Castanon. I was born on St. Andrew's day in November, 1785, at Larodo. I am 105 years old. I have been twice married; my first husband was Silberio Flores y Abrigo; my second was Candelario Villanueva, but I am called familiarly Senora Candelaria."

I may add that I read to my companions these interviews at the dates of our visits. I wrote them from notes taken at the time upon arriving home, and my companions subscribed to every particular.

So much for her testimony on David Crockett, as recorded by someone who seemed to be a very careful reporter. Corner appends to the above account a record he found, of the same Senora Candelaria, definitely proving that at least she was of age and living in Bexar as early as 1837, and certifying even so early that she was then claiming to have remained in the country at the time of the Alamo. The source which he cites is the "County Records," which would be the Bexar County Records:

> I do solemnly swear that I was a resident citizen of Texas at the date of the Declaration of Independence. That I did not leave the country during the campaign of the spring of 1836 to avoid participation in the War, and that I did not aid nor assist the Enemy; that I have not previously received a title for my quantum of land, and that I conceived myself to be justly entitled under the Constitution and laws to the quantity for which I now apply. April 29th, 1837.
>
> Candelaria Villanueva.

Nor is it necessarily strange that this oath does not make the claim that she had actually served in the Alamo, inasmuch as it was obviously a stereotyped legal form to which she, among many, affixed her signature.

We have reviewed Corner's reports of Madam Candelaria's testimony at some length both because it appears to have all the earmarks of reliability and because other "reports" of so-called interviews with her are so completely different and attribute to her such radically different testimony. The others are newspaper stories, and they are apparently guilty of the very worst practices of American yellow journalism. Mr. Maurice Elfer, in a small volume in 1933,[15] uncritically based his entire account upon two newspaper articles *written at the time of Madam Candelaria's death in 1899.*[16] The articles were based upon supposed interviews prior to her death. From their content it is evident instead that they were post-mortems. They have the usual newspaper preoccupation with the sensational, the "human-interest *angle*," and the fabrication aimed at headlines and sales promotion. In view of the care with which Corner's report was made, I think we can only attribute the vast discrepancies between them to such journalistic considerations.

According to Corner's interview, Crockett had been one of the first to fall, unarmed, undramatically, alone. What journalist would be satisfied with such "news"? Citing the newspaper reporter's "quotation" of Madam Candelaria, Elfer records:

Crockett ... was one of the strangest men I ever saw. He had the face of a woman, and his manner was that of a girl. I could never regard him as a hero until I saw him die. He looked grand and terrible, shouting at the front door and fighting a whole column of Mexican Infantry. He had fired his last shot, and had not time to reload. The cannon balls had knocked away the sandbags and the infantry was pouring through the breach. Crockett stood there, swinging something over his head. The place was full of smoke and I could not tell whether he was using a gun or a sword. A heap of dead was piled at his feet, and the Mexicans were lunging at him with Bayonets, but he would not retreat an inch. Poor Bowie could see it all, but he could not raise himself from his cot.[17]

The report states, "quoting" Madam Candelaria, that Crockett had earlier loaded Bowie's rifle and a brace of pistols and laid them by Bowie's side, assuring the sick man that:

he [Crockett] could stop a whole regiment from entering.... It looked as though 100 bayonets were thrust into the door at the same time, and a great sheet of flame lit up the Alamo.
Every man at the door fell but Crockett. I could see him struggling at the head of the column, and Bowie raised up and fired his rifle. I saw Crockett fall backward. The enraged Mexicans then streamed into the buildings, firing and yelling like madmen....

And so on and so on. There is much more, but it is unworthy of further citation. It is obvious that the newspaper "reports" had simply commenced where Richard Penn Smith had stopped his "diary" and added to his last entry for March 6! Furthermore, Elfer gives evidence of a lack of care, and it is sometimes not clear whether he is reporting a reporter's report of Madam Candelaria's reminiscences or whether he is merely reminiscing on his own.

Mr. Elfer attempts to explain why Madam Candelaria happened to be inside the Alamo nursing Bowie. He stated that her grandson, James Villanueva, chief clerk in the county assessor's office at San Antonio, had personally told him, in 1933, of a letter which Sam Houston had written his grandmother. The letter suggests that if she wished to prove herself a true friend of his, she would personally go into the Alamo and "nurse his friend Bowie," who was ill there. Two considerations make it impossible for us to accept such unsupported testimony. First is the relationship which existed between Bowie and Houston at the time, plus the fact that Sam Houston labored for years under the stigma of a charge that he had deliberately allowed Bowie and the others to be destroyed, yet never mentioned as evidence in his own behalf any such request that Madam Candelaria go into the Alamo and "nurse his friend Bowie." Second is the further fact that, though Madam Candelaria was striving to establish her presence at the Alamo, she seems never to have produced or referred to such a letter from Houston. That Elfer would put such implicit faith in two newspaper articles of 34 years earlier, without checking them or their statements against other evidence, inclines one to the belief that his credulity was too easily imposed upon.

Whether Senora Candelaria was actually inside the Alamo or not we shall probably never know. But inasmuch as a bit of the testimony of the person who without question was there (Mrs. Dickerson) tends to corroborate her account as reported by Corner (the location of David's body when he fell), her version is the one which I am inclined to accept. Even the most meticulous search of the evidence still leaves any final conclusion a matter of probability rather than of established fact.

The testimony of Mrs. Dickerson conflicts at some points with that of Madam Candelaria, with that of Houston (who of course was not there), and even in different versions with itself. Furthermore, by her own account, she had remained "in her room" after her husband came and told her goodbye, and she was in no position or condition to receive or to bear accurate information.[18] Here, nevertheless, is her testimony relating to David Crockett:

> As we passed through the enclosed ground in front of the Church, I saw heaps of dead and dying. The Texans on an average killed between eight and nine Mexicans each—182 Texans and 1600 Mexicans were killed.
> I recognized Col. Crockett lying dead and mutilated between the church and the two story barrack building, and even remember seeing his peculiar cap lying by his side.[19]

Even this testimony is compromised, of course, for it is quite obvious that it fails to distinguish between what she saw at the time and what she later discovered, or thought, or was told. She could not have seen that 1,600 Mexicans had been destroyed or arrived at the average number of Mexicans killed by each of the defenders. The intrusion of these matters into her testimony tends to bear out Senora Candelaria's remark as to her hatred for Mexicans. The cap to which she refers was undoubtedly the coon-skin cap which he was supposed to have been wearing. This corroborates the statement of Davis that he had seen Crockett leave Memphis wearing such a cap.

Though a very great deal more has been written on this subject, I believe this is the essential material which, more nearly than any other, deserves presentation as "the evidence." According to this evidence, David was not among the five who surrendered. Nor was he one of the last to die, inside the fortress, in the doorway, fighting off a whole regiment. Instead, he died on the outside, one of the earliest to fall, with no gun on him, going on some mission which apparently made him oblivious of danger. Such tales of melodrama as have been told are not necessary to establish David Crockett's courage, for that is indelibly imprinted upon his whole conduct throughout his life; they but tend to cheapen, by gilding, a very real and quiet luster which requires no such tawdry aids.

Houston's letter to Fannin on March 11, describing the fall of the Alamo, was in the newspapers by early April, as were the accounts of that battle given by others. On April 16 *Niles Register*, quoting a dispatch from the *New Orleans True American*, identified Crockett as among those slain there: "We regret to say that Colonel *David Crockett*, his companion *Jesse Benton*, and Colonel *Bonham*, of South Carolina, were among the number slain." [20] David's family must, therefore, have gotten the news within a month after the event, if not earlier, by this means. The first personal communication to that effect, however, may well have been the earlier quoted letter from Isaac N. Jones of Lost Prairie, Arkansas, returning David's watch. At any rate, sometime after its receipt the letter was given to the local Jackson *Truth Teller* for publication. It was at about this time that John Wesley Crockett first wrote in July to his mother's people in North Carolina, verifying the newspaper reports that his father had been killed at the Alamo. One sentence in this undated letter from Jones, "We hope that the day is not far distant when his adopted country will be freed from a savage enemy," suggests that the letter was written fairly soon after the Alamo, before the Battle of San Jacinto on April 21, 1836, when Santa Anna was finally defeated. Portions of the Jones letter read:

Lost Prarie [*sic*], Ark's, 1836

Mrs. David Crockett:

Dear Madam: Permit me to introduce myself to you as one of the acquaintances of your much respected husband, col. Crockett. With his fate in the fortress San Antonio, Texas, your are doubtless long since advised. With sincere feelings of sympathy, I regret his untimely loss to your family and self. For if amongst strangers, he constituted the most agreeable companion, he, doubtless, to his beloved wife and children, must have been a favorite *peculiarly* prized. In his loss, freedom has been deprived of one of her bravest sons, in whose bosom universal philanthropy glowed with as genial warmth as ever animated the heart of an American citizen. When he fell, a soldier died. To bemoan his fate, is to pay tribute of greatful respect to nature—he seemed to be her son.

* * * * * *

His military career was short. But though I deeply lament his death, I cannot restrain my American smile at the recollection of the fact that he died as a United States soldier should die, covered with his slain enemy, and, even in death presenting to them in his clenched hands, the weapons of their destruction.

We hope that the day is not far distant when his adopted country will be freed from a savage enemy, and afford to yourself and children, a home, rendered in every way comfortable, by the liberal donations of her government.

Accept, dear madam, for yourself and family, the most sincere wishes for your future happiness, of

Your most obedient servant and friend. . . .

This admirer of the "grand style" and of Shakespeare's version of Mark Antony's final soliloquy, who had evidently already heard some of the more grandiloquent reports of David's death, was not wrong in prophesying that Texas would invite David's family to come there. It is fitting for our saga of this westward migration to note that in 1854 Elizabeth Patton Crockett, her son Robert and daughter Rebeckah ("Sissy"), David's children, and George Patton, son of her first marriage, and his wife Rhoda, made the move David had contemplated for them from Gibson County, Tennessee, to Texas in one final migration of that generation west. Some further details about the family beyond this point may be found in the cited volume of Crockett genealogy.[21]

Since we have reviewed David's part as executor of the Robert

Patton estate, perhaps the following bare and cryptic court entry from the *Gibson County Wills and Bonds Book II* will be meaningful to the reader: "John W. Crockett made executor of Robert Patton." [22] It is with this matter that John Wesley's letter to his uncle about David's death deals. To compare John's efficiency in this letter—his "laying down the law" to his Uncle George Patton—with David's leniency in his letter of October 31, 1835, to the same man, is to come closer to the personality of David. George's refusal to come to Tennessee, his inclination to procrastinate, and the difficulty which that was causing David as executor can be read between David's lines, especially after reading John's letter. David's gentleness, his self-denying lenience with his friend, and his easygoing inattention to "business matters" is doubtless a part of the explanation both of his lifelong poverty and of his friends' love for him. John was more the positive man of action and affairs, a teacher and a lawyer. These two letters throw a very mellow light on our backwoodsman.

This is the letter John wrote to his Uncle George Patton four months after David Crockett's death:

Trenton 9th July 1836

Dear Sir:

You have doubtless seen the account of my father's fall at the Alamo in Texas. He is gone from among us, and is no more to be seen in the walks of men, but in his death like Sampson, he slew more of his enemies than in all his life. [For] Even his most bitter enemies here, I believe, have buried all animosity, and joined the general lamentation over his untimely end.

I have been appointed administrator of your father with his will annexed, since my father's death. And the object of this communication is to inform you that it will be necessary for me to bring the business of the estate to an immediate close, and consequently it will be necessary for you to come or send out as soon as you possibly can, and attend to settling up your interest in the estate—Your note is here with Uncle's [*sic*] Peter and Abner as securities, and is entitled to sundry credits if you will come out & have them allowed. Your own legacy & mother's are both to come out of it, but If you dont attend to it in the course of two or three months, I shall be compelled, however it may conflict with my feelings to proceed against your securities—This would be very far from my wish or feelings, as you must know, but the law points out my duties and I am compelled to go by it—We have no news, of any importance. We are going ahead here for *Judge White*, and I hope you North Carolinians will join and assist

us in resisting executive dictation. Please present me kindly to your family
and permit me in conclusion to subscribe myself as ever

Yr devoted friend & obt servt.

John W. Crockett [23]

The boy who, at 19, had spoken of his father as "the old hook" and
thought he was "in the gunter" had sharpened his faculties considerably in nine years. It is interesting to see him using his father's expression "going ahead" and so fully sharing his father's point of view on
"executive dictation."

This brings us to the end of the story of the life of the historical
figure, David Crockett. We conclude that story with the testimony
of one of his contemporaries as to how the news of his death affected
not merely his family, but his acquaintances, those who had known
him boy and man, neighbor and friend or enemy, for many a year.
The writer is Dr. S. H. Stout, who at the time was a grown boy almost out of his teens and fully capable of observation and of memory:

> When the news of the massacre in the Alamo reached Nashville, Ten-
> nessee, the writer well remembers seing adult men and women shed tears
> on account of the death of David Crockett. None ever knew him per-
> sonally, who did not love him; none who were familiar with his public
> career, that did not admire him. The whole people of the state were then,
> as now, proud of him.[24]

There were personal qualities about the man which led those who
knew him to love him: the humorous, gentle, human traits partially
revealed in the contrast between the two letters of father and son to
George Patton, as well as in numerous other places throughout this
volume—qualities with which his political partisanship began to play
havoc, until he became something which was not his essential nature
at all.

Too much has been made over the details of *how* David died at the
Alamo. Such details are not important. What is important is that he
died as he had lived. His life was one of indomitable bravery; his death
was a death of intrepid courage. His life was one of wholehearted
dedication to his own concepts of liberty. He died staking his life
against what he regarded as intolerable tyranny. A poor man who
had long known the devastating consequences of poverty and who all
his life had fought a dedicated fight for the right of the dispossessed
to a new opportunity, he died defending a poor and insecure people

and proclaiming their rights to participate in the arts of self-government. A pioneer who had helped to spread a new civilization across the vast stretches of the backwoods died in a last valiant stand to establish one final frontier. The simplicities of backwoods life had not prepared him to comprehend all of the intricacies of political machinations. In the death of this pioneer of geographical boundaries was born the hardy pioneer fighter for the rights of all men to liberty and opportunity. This is the true significance of the death and rebirth of David Crockett.

Significant is the fact that his very death helped to achieve that for which he had given his life. David had implanted his ideals in the son who loved him. In 1839 and again in 1841 John Wesley Crockett went to the United States Congress for the purpose of securing passage of David's land bill. In February of the latter year, John saw his father's bill, in modified form, become law.[25] The land was finally given to the state of Tennessee, but with the stipulation that it should sell for 12½ cents an acre and that the occupants should have pre-emption purchase rights, the very compromise which David had first accepted from Polk in committee back in December, 1829. Had the Tennessee delegation stuck to its agreement then and voted for this compromise, it is possible that David would have repaired the breach with Jackson and that his present position in history might be unbelievably different.

Interestingly enough *Niles Register* printed, toward the climax of the battle for the land bill, a "rumor" that David Crockett was still alive. I have not seen it elsewhere recorded. Perhaps it formed the factual basis for the legend that grew up that "the spirit of Davy Crockett yet roams the land." In April, 1840, *Niles* ran this item:

The Boston Traveller has been informed that the son of Col. Crockett (a member of Congress from Tennessee) has received information inducing him to believe that the report in relation to his father being in one of the mines of Mexico, is correct. Steps will be immediately taken to ascertain its truth, and procure his liberation.[26]

This announcement was followed on June 6 with the following comment in the same journal: "The Texas Sentinel pronounces the story of Col. Crockett's being alive and a prisoner in the Mexican mines, to be a hoax. The rumor never received any credit at Austin." [27]

David was gone. But the ideals and aims of the father, invested in the love of the son, could not be denied. However David was battered and destroyed by his abusers, through his oldest son he finally achieved, for the destitute poor of west Tennessee, his neighbors and his friends, the aim to which he had dedicated his political life.

In no sense was the struggle of David Crockett in vain.

Chapter 16

EPILOGUE: DAVID, THE LEGEND AND THE SYMBOL

THE explanation for Crockett's becoming and remaining a national legendary figure has six primary facets: the imaginative temper of the unsettled West; the imaginative temper of the settled East; the qualities of the man himself with reference to the tempers of the time; the political culture of the period; the use of David as a symbol by both political parties, and their employment of a *national press* to establish that symbol clearly in the minds and thoughts of a whole nation; Crockett's dramatic death at the Alamo, which raised him to the level of national martyr; and the pursuit by latter-day writers of "Davy of the typescript."

What we may call the *imaginative* temper of the backwoods, as distinct from its economic, political, pragmatic aspects, may perhaps best be viewed by looking at the "tall tale" of Western literature. Those who go with life and limb into the unknown wildernesses of a strange and forbidding land, necessarily develop both elastic horizons and elastic imaginations. Strange sights, strange animals, unaccustomed noises, unforeseen experiences, and completely novel combinations of life continually confront this social creature in his solitary backwoods fastness. His imagination must be prepared to face anything, he must be able to believe in the possibility of all things.

Counterbalancing that credulous imagination is a trait characteristic of the thinking animal, a sense of play, of funning—an anchor and a balance which pulls him back toward center when he moves too far forward on the peripheral extreme. The physical basis for this lies perhaps in the tension and reflex of the neuron itself.

The unsocial situation of separation and isolation in which the backwoods family spent its nights and days stimulated this sense of play by making special demands upon it. Entertainment was scarce, opportunities for convivial get-togethers infrequent. Necessarily, therefore, every harvest or house-raising became a social and playful occasion, and ordinary prosaic affairs were cast in the entertaining form of the "tall tale." Political speeches in the backwoods were no more to be divorced from entertainment, from tall tales, from picnic, frolic, barbecue, stomp-down, than freckles from a boy who lives in the sun. Woe be to the political candidate who did not know this need for entertainment or who, knowing it, could not cater to it naturally. This urgent need for social entertainment is also a partial explanation of the fact that the tall tale was *so* tall. Yet, though the imagination had to be elastic so as to be prepared for any danger, it was necessary also to guard against magnifying minor danger to the proportions of major peril—against making a bear of a rat, a lion of a bob cat, and thus creating fear and paralysis in place of courage and action.

It was necessary to preserve balance and sanity by joking about danger, to prick the taut nerve and thus return bursting tensions to normal. And so the wonders were made *ridiculously* wonderful. Each hunter must outlie every other about the nature of the marvels which had personally befallen him, until one bestrides a tornado and is immediately outclassed by another who makes a perambulator of the sun, in a sharpening of those faculties in play which, in the backwoods, must ever be sharp in dead earnest. Hence that strange array of "varments" in backwoods folklore: the creature so curiously adapted to the steepest mountains, with legs shorter on one side than on the other, to be caught only on one of its infrequent visits into the lowlands, where it could only run in circles; or that other, even more difficult to catch, that could dig a hole in a flash, plop into it, and pull it in after him.

I feel sure that this temper characterized our backwoods at a very early time in our history. It lived for a long time only in the unwritten cultural heritage of the isolated Southern and Western wonderlands of the forests, and up and down the rivers, the highways of that day. About 1830 it began to become literate and vocal, and to get into the quick-freeze mediums of print. Two of the very earliest products of this new literacy were David Crockett's *Autobiography*, by a real backwoodsman himself; and Augustus Longstreet's *Georgia Scenes*, by a literary man making use of those materials for his own literary purposes. It developed through a long line of humorists, and finally culminated in Mark Twain. The original strain at last petered out as the primitive conditions of life out of which it had grown disappeared.

What was there about David Crockett that tended to typify those qualities characteristic of the imaginative, tall-tale temper of the backwoods? First of all, he was one of them. To use one of their own expressions, appropriately modified for print, he was "common as coon spore in a barley patch." He was a "gentleman from the cane." He had a keen sense of humor in the Western tradition—the broad and exaggerated, the hyperbolic and vast, or the same in reverse, the sly and dry understatement, as revealed in numerous incidents ("he beat me exactly *two* votes . . . though I have always believed that many other things had been as fairly done as that same count.") Further, he had certain characteristics which were strange, different—which made people talk. I think of his unusual determination to cross that swollen river in midwinter to get his keg of powder, his going after the bear at night alone and not turning back until he had got it, his setting out as a child through knee-deep snow in the dark to walk miles in order to escape from his employer. Society today may look upon such adventures as more foolhardy than wise. In the backwoods the qualities of unusual strength, unusual perseverance, extraordinary courage, unbelievable determination, even in connection with what may *now* appear to be relatively trivial matters, were the measures of a man because they were in a very real sense the measures of life. Crockett so excelled in these qualities that when an incredible story was to be told, the fixing on Crockett about whom to tell it lent it that air of reality and credibility which made the story delicious to its hearers.

Also, there were other qualities about the man which simply made him a "character"—the relation of his life as early as 1833 had been titled "The Eccentricities of," and incidentally had been quite popular; and the defense of him by a paper in his own district had granted his "eccentricities."

There were the lovable qualities of good sportsmanship and good showmanship (the occasion when S. H. Stout as a small boy stared at him in church) which made it *fun* to tell a story "on him" because of his reaction to the stories ("I'd wring *his* tail off!"), or because of the titillation of the listener in his imagining of David's reactions, either to the story or to the situation in which the imaginary story placed him. Yet these were not qualities which tended to make him a butt of a joke, for not of such is a lovable legend made.

In brief, Crockett possessed in the extreme many of those abilities which the backwoods required and admired, and in terms of which it judged a man. He possessed also the personable qualities which led tall tellers to make him the center of their tales. There was that in the man which tended to make him a *local* tradition and character long before literature or the press began to catch him up. Being, in his person, the essence of the backwoods of his locale, since his locale was the nucleus of the whole tradition he was the apt representative and symbol of the whole Western culture.

The imaginative temper of the East, however different from that of the West, was in a sense complementary and easily capable of accepting David Crockett, *properly spruced up*, as the symbol of its concept of the Westerner. The age was romantic. Eastern society, as compared with the West, was relatively settled and uneventful. The backwoods was almost as far, in spirit, from the drawing rooms of New York society as from the ball rooms of London. Yet it was close enough geographically and in the pages of the newspaper, to be especially piquant to jaded but uncritical imaginations. James Fenimore Cooper picked up the tales of a romantic age, transferred them to a local setting, and supplied pabulum for the hungry maw of a romantic East. His *Spy* (1821), *Pioneers* (1823), *Last of the Mohicans* (1826), and *Prairie* (1827) not only fed the romantic appetite, but helped to set the pattern for and to stimulate avid interest in a highly romanticized picture of the backwoods where David was actually living. We have never been able to erase from our literature, and I suppose now we never shall, this romantic young girl's dream of all the beauties and glories of the backwoods and of backwoodsmen who talk like little Lord Fauntleroys in buckskin, though any three words from the real vocabulary of an actual backwoodsman would send the blood to her cheeks and cruelly shock her artificial modesty.

The *literary* versions of the backwoods, then, had come into being as a delightful new and stimulating toy with which to escape the "vapours" of a settled society. As the backwoods flowed into print, the gentleman and the lady became adventurers-on-their-own-terms in a backwoods the more real because physically closer than Irving's halls of the Alhambra in lands beyond the sea. There resulted an orgiastic revelling in the romantic backwoods. Into the literature of the East went this local legend, this David Crockett of the West, out of ephemeral tradition into solid print. This was the situation, the imaginative temper in which the legend grew. Other factors, of course, helped it to grow—helped an historical figure, David Crockeit, to replace, so to speak, the literary creation, Natty Bumppo, as the national symbol of the backwoodsman.

The next most important factor, I believe, aside from the historical juncture which made the backwoods play such a dominant theme and occupy such an essential role in the affairs of the moment, was David's rise to prominence in politics and the consequent manipulations by the press of his "public person." This aspect of the fable has been developed by Professor Walter Blair in his article "Six Davy Crockets." [1] Four of the six Crockett's that he discusses—the two Crocketts produced by the Jackson papers, one while David was pro-Jackson, the other when he became anti-Jackson; and the two produced similarly by the Whig papers before and after his "switch"—are the political Crockett of fiction produced by the press. In the light of the story that lies behind us, elaboration on that point is unnecessary here. Simply stated, while Crockett was a Jacksonian, the Democratic press polished him up with little reference to the true man, and the Whig papers, with just as little regard for fact, tried to laugh him out of Congress as a blundering bull in the sanctified halls of gentlemen. When David changed his allegiances, the Democratic papers were prone to take up the old line initiated by the Whigs and enlarge upon that, while the Whigs refined upon the earlier tradition which the Democrats had so carefully built up.

The point of our explanation here is that through all of this, coming as it did at a time when the American press had just vanquished all barriers, extending itself even into the far reaches of the backwoods, the name of David Crockett, scattered to the four corners of the America of that day, slipped willy nilly into that image which Western and Eastern minds alike, Whig as well as Democrat, carried about in their realistic or romantic imaginations—the idea or *ideaform* of the American backwoodsman. David became the body. He fitted into the realistic Western concept as he was. He was dressed up, first by the Democrats and then by the Whigs, to fit into the romantic concepts of the East. The whole tradition was furiously stirred by Charles Brockden Brown, by Fenimore Cooper, by many others, in fact, by history itself. The speeches which Easterners carefully wrote for him on his Eastern tour, speeches peppered with the condiments of backwoods vernacular, humor, and homeliness, yet smooth enough not to offend any romantic sensibility, were but one of the more obvious and conscious exploitations of a popular public taste. The theoretical backwoodsman was present in the minds of all, East and West. David won his right to represent his class in his own neighborhoods in a succession of localities as he moved across the state. The exploitation on a national scale of the public taste, and of Crockett to satisfy that taste, had a tremendous effect in establishing him in the minds, thoughts, and conversations of people all over America. It played, that is, a tremendous part in fixing him as the symbol in the cultural tradition that lives in a people's talk and memories. In that early exploitation of a national taste, the early Crockett books and such a play as the *Lion of the West* contributed their significant parts.

To attempt to say which factor was of greatest importance is meaningless. Without the newspapers David would have been a local legend, and would doubtless have survived as such for a time. Whether that tradition would have grown or dwindled one cannot positively state. Watching what has happened to it, even with the help of the press, I suspect that it would not have survived to our day, except in the most isolated and occasional instances. The historical man would have survived for his *Autobiography*—if for no other reasons because he symbolizes aspects of our history. On the other hand, the newspapers could not pick up just any man as a symbol of the West. Without David's personification of the backwoods, without the man himself, his experience, his slow rise to the point where he had become, with all his native endowments, *capable* politically and personally of *being exploitable* as the national symbol of the type, the mere universality of the press unaided would not alone have sufficed to initiate a legend. He had to be authentic to be acceptable to the West. Given David and what he was, the press did create a temporary, more or less homogeneous national tradition of the backwoods, with David as its central figure. Yet its success was predicated upon the imaginative tempers of both East and West, nor could it have occurred at any very far-removed juncture of our history.

Finally, David's death at the Alamo at approximately the height of his greatest renown in a fight that itself seemed to symbolize the growing, expanding, liberating destiny of America, a death that seemed to be the final bravest act of which a brave man was capable, the giving of all material things even unto his own body and blood in defense of a spiritual idea—so fired the imagination of America as to bring to volcanic heat the miscellaneous sediments of the times and to fuse the softer and rather evanescent materials of a local age into the granite or obsidian which appears for awhile to outwear time itself. The peculiar circumstances of that battle likewise allowed the imagination free play, for no reliable witness of much of what happened there survived, and history was incapable of cluttering up the event with fact. History, indeed, came to the aid of the imagination in its record of the pass of Thermopylae, and helped to glorify the Alamo in similes as grand as the records of man could supply.

These seem to be the most important factors which have created and kept alive the mythological "Davy," so far as he is alive. There is another type of mythological "Davy" who seems to live principally in the carols of folklore romanticizers. He lives in literature mainly at the expense of the historical Crockett, and in recent years he has crowded the *Autobiography* out of anthologies and the historical person out of literary histories. This contemporary literary romanticism is, I think, a variety of sentimental romanticism indulged in by sedentary folk to escape dull reality. The exciting and untempered zeal of rediscovering our origins all clothed in the quaintness and charm of time and distance stimulates imaginations dulled by the prose of fact. Such "rediscovery" also appeals to the self-interest of the conventional patriot of my town, my state, my section, my nation, and all of the other multitudinous ramifications of *me*. In an age which combines the loss of a physical backwoods (or even of a simple rural life that would accord with the nature and instincts of man) with a nationalism in which self-interest is stretched tight by powerful national rivalries, I suppose it was, and is, in a sense, inevitable. I will not, therefore, say more about it here. It is only necessary to trace briefly the path of the literary myth for those who may wish to pursue their folklore in literary adaptations.

We have noted in the appendix the initial play which helped to fuse a backwoods tradition, both real and literary, with the person of David, *The Lion of the West*. We have noted the excessive tall-tale elements of an exaggerated literary sort which were incorporated into the first *Life* of Crockett, in its original issue and in its reissue as the *Eccentricities*, and which partially created and partially helped to perpetuate the literary legend. We have further cited the various newspaper creations, and such novels as those of William Alexander Caruthers and James Strange French which also helped to give sustenance to the literary figure. We have pointed out in appendix three the creation of spurious lore in the *Texas Exploits* of Richard Penn Smith, guessing that this was perhaps the first purely literary exploitation, completely unconcerned with politics. One very important early medium, probably only slightly related to political motives, we have not heretofore discussed—the "Davy" Crockett Almanacs.

Miss Rourke's bibliographical chapter devotes a great deal of space to giving an almost complete list of these "Davy" almanacs, and I will not repeat the list here. The first Almanac issued, Volume 1, Number 1, published in Nashville, Tennessee, was *not* copyrighted in the name of the man whose life we have undertaken to tell, the *David* Crockett in whose name the *Autobiography* was copyrighted: rather, it was copyrighted in the name of that hallmark of the myth, "Davy" Crockett. The masthead motto read, "Go ahead, or Davy Crockett's Almanac of Wild Sports of the West and Life in the Backwoods." It was published by Snag and Sawyer! This Almanac is a veritable mare's nest of fictional tall tales coupling the names of Davy, Ben Hardin, Black Hawk (Adam Huntsman), and others. It is as disrespectful of or indifferent to fact as the fabricators of children's bedtime stories. Indeed, it is their very power to create gargantuan hoax that has so endeared the Almanacs to lovers of the tall-tale and patriot ferreters after the Great American Epic.

Huntsman's wooden leg has taken on flesh and blood in the Almanac woodcuts. The "autobiographical" details of Davy snub David's own account which had come off the press six or seven months earlier—but that is fitting, seeing that David had just as completely ignored, in his correspondence or in anything else he wrote or said, the "Davy" almanacs. The first issue had been copyrighted late in 1834 for 1835; the second, copyrighted in late 1835 for 1836, was printed this time not *by* "Davy," but *for* him, inasmuch as all the world knew that David had been gone from Tennessee since the preceding November. The third issue I have not seen, but the fourth, published in late 1837 for 1838, was printed, according to the title page which for some reason the lovers of the almanac tall tales suddenly decided to take quite literally, by "his heirs." The fifth (Number 1 of Volume 2), was published by "Ben Harding," as was the next issue. By 1842 (Volume 2, Number 4), the publication had moved to "New York and Philadelphia," though fortunately Ben Harding had now learned the correct spelling of his own name and writes it *Hardin*. For some reason this native Kentuckian copyrighted it in the eastern district of *Pennsylvania!* The Davy myth was now widespread, especially had the seed been sown in Pennsylvania, and it afforded a plentiful harvest in many places.

From this point on, it had not even the identity of geographical locale to connect it with David, and I refer the interested reader to Miss Rourke for further bibliography on the subject. Yet I must point out one fact: even so recently as the middle of the Twentieth Century, Mr. Joseph Leach, in a published adaptation from a book he is writing, could say: "These [almanac] sketches may indeed represent a kind of collaboration because, before leaving for Texas, Crockett himself *reportedly* had prepared enough material to fill six full issues." And: "The [almanac] sketches faithfully transcribe the backwoodsman's realistic vernacular." [2] I have pointed out to Mr. Leach the total error of both statements, as well as the "slanting" in his use of the word "reportedly." For I have not found even the slightest suspicion of a trace of a connection between David Crockett and the Davy almanacs, except of course in the claims of the almanacs themselves. As for the vernacular, its realism is as spurious and artificial as the faked Crockett vernacular in the 1833 *Life*.

In my opinion, David neither sponsored nor in any way contributed to these almanacs, nor were they issued for David or by or for his heirs. They were part of the exploitation of his renown which yet goes on; and they represented that point, I think, at which a low type of literary exploitation joined hands with the economic need of inferior literary ability. It was a sort of shot-gun marriage of the economic and literary motives, and could hardly be expected to be of a very high quality, though some folklorists profess to see in it pristine specimens of the native American Legend out of which the Great National Epic *almost* arose.[3] Perhaps my own taste is at fault. Fine or poor, as history they were completely false and spurious, and as such here deserve, at the very most, a questionably honorable mention. However, in the creation and perpetuation of the literary "Davy," they were one among a number of important mediums.

This is the field which the Twentieth Century Scholar has chosen to pitch upon and to cultivate to the exclusion of the real Crockett. If one cares to pursue the literary mythological figure in the present century, he may add such names to those I have given him as Vance Randolph, John A. and Alan Lomax, B. A. Botkin, Julia Beazley, Carl Sandburg, Irwin Shapiro, V. L. O. Chittick, Edwin Justice Mayer, Franklin J. Meine, and Walter Blair. Peace be to them. But let them be reminded that the historical David and his classic *Autobiography* need, and strongly deserve, their interest in history. Let them recall V. L. Parrington's observation that the best joke David and his exploiters ever played, they "played upon posterity that has swallowed the myth whole and persists in setting a romantic halo on his coonskin cap."[4]

Our narrative began with the ending of the old, old story of man's long migration westward from his cradle somewhere in central Asia a million years ago. Slowly and feebly he moved outward. Millennia by millennia he crept onward. Finally, only in the last century and on our own North American continent, he at length completed, in a dramatic burst of speed, his thousands-of-years-old transmigration of a planet, and conquered the final geographical boundaries of this globe. One frame for David Crockett's biography is the vanishing frontier— the frontier vanishing not simply from America, but from the world; not merely from the scene of a nation or of a time, but from the scene of all mundane nations and of all earthly time.

David Crockett is a significant figure in terms of that old story. To follow his career from North Carolina across that great Appalachian barrier to east Tennessee, then to middle Tennessee, thence to the mighty Mississippi, and finally to Texas is to follow the last far-flinging lines of the frontier in its concluding marches back to the Pacific. To follow his life is to see repeated therein much of the history of the old kind of man and his old frontiers—the barbarous rudiments of his beginnings, where brute force hewed roughly at the inimical environments; his quenchless wanderlust for new, and ever new physical horizons; his slow and tedious advance in knowledge, in understanding, and in the creation of a primitive culture; his gradual rise out of a blind wilderness into elementary forms of social living and law; and finally his subduing all physical boundaries until the continents had been reduced into national constitutions and governments. David Crockett is the archetype of the age-old pioneer, slowly mastering the world's physical frontiers.

In another real sense this narrative concludes with the beginning of a new story and so is pitched within a new frame. By the very act of conquering geographical barriers, man created a different sort of world and set himself upon a new and entirely different sort of quest. Having learned to live with, then to master, all physical frontiers until he reduced the world and the nations to one small demesne, man must now learn to live with and to master the frontiers of the human mind, heart, and spirit until he reduces that demesne to one home. Man's new frontier is the spiritual frontier of universal brotherhood where all men are their brothers' keepers. Not until he masters this frontier will man make a home of his narrowed world.

David Crockett's greatest value is as a symbol of the new man striking into this new and spiritual frontier. His life and career depict the great formative struggles in the birth of this new philosophy on this new continent. Crockett did not espouse the philosophy of the old physical man who judged people in terms of externals—ancestry, caste, riches, or fame—holding some men of value and some worthless and setting one group to war against another. Instead, he grasped the philosophy of the new spiritual man who judges a people intrinsically in terms of their inherent worth and their divine potential in a universe where all are the sons of God and where all before God are of inalienable value and entitled to equal dignity and justice. This passionate spiritual faith in the worth of all personality, extending beyond religious shibboleths to legal, social, political, and economic areas, is the faith of the new and spiritual frontier—and the only faith which can make man's shrunken world his home. This faith is so new that to date it has prevailed only among small groups and for limited periods. The furthest advance along this new frontier on any grand scale in all history is the story of the rise of the American civilization. Even that civilization has fallen far below its aim, and sometimes seems to prefer its own destruction to a radical reaffirmation of that new faith. David Crockett symbolizes the essential man, that vital "common stock," that has played a most important part in this new land in the shaping of that philosophy of the new spiritual frontier.

Here, then, is Crockett: symbol both of the pioneer of that old world of physical frontiers, just ended; and of the pioneer of the new spiritual frontier just beginning, attacking those barriers that separate man from his fellows and that threaten to make of his world a Buchenwald. To our own generation has been bequeathed the decision as to whether we shall follow David Crockett into this new and unconquered spiritual wilderness, master it, and make of our world a home; or shall violently explode back into barbarism and begin anew that weary, age-old pioneering of the old physical man along the blind, physical boundaries of a creature existence.

Appendices

WILDFIRE AND THE *LIFE*

In 1833 the anonymous Crockett *Life* was published to aid David's campaign for election to Congress. The complete title is *"The Life and Adventures of Colonel David Crockett of West Tennessee,* Cincinnati: published for the Proprietor, 1833. It was entered for copyright by J. S. French, in the Clerk's Office of the District Court of Ohio on January 5, 1833." [1] Before undertaking to unravel the problem of the book's authorship, it is necessary to review briefly the context in which the book was written.

It is necessary to recall the following items already touched upon: the Crockett letter of April 18, 1829, with its friendly reference to Mathew St. Clair Clarke; the Polk letter; the sudden shift in Crockett's Congressional position on the Land Bill between May, 1828, and January, 1829; the Christopher Baldwin reference to David's travelling with St. Clair Clarke at this period; the loan to David at this time by Jackson's bitterest enemy, the U. S. Bank; David's increasing hatred for Jackson; David's being glorified and gentlemanized after 1831 by the Whig press; the publication in the East of a so-called Indian Bill Speech which he never made; and related matters. This evidence seems sufficient to suggest the existence of a working alliance between David, the Eastern Whigs, and the Second United States Bank. I have placed the alliance as early as January, 1829, and have attributed it to David's passion in behalf of the poor in west Tennessee. If this judgment is accurate, a close examination of every public literary venture involving David after January, 1829, is called for.

In 1830, James Kirke Paulding wrote a stage play called the *Lion of the West*. Its central character, the "Lion" or *Colonel* Nimrod Wildfire, was immediately associated, under peculiar circumstances, with the name of *Colonel* David Crockett.

According to Paulding's son, William I. Paulding, Mr. James H. Hackett "sometime in the year of 1830" offered a prize for an American comedy, and "*induced* Mr. Paulding to compete, *suggesting, as I learn from himself, the title of drama and hero:* viz: 'The Lion of the West' and 'Nimrod Wildfire.' " [2] How much more Mr. Hackett suggested we are not told. When we find, a year before the play had been produced, possibly even before it had been written, that the leading character-to-be was coupled in the press of the country with the name of David Crockett, we are justified in looking upon the matter with more than ordinary interest.

The play itself has unfortunately been lost,* and there is not a great deal known about the details of its content. It was first produced on three evenings in mid-November 1831.[3] Almost a year earlier Crockett's name had been widely associated with it. The New York *Mirror* for December 18, 1830, ostensibly at Paulding's request, denied that Wildfire was Crockett.[4] There had been an earlier "denial" on December 15 by the *Morning Courier and New York Enquirer*.[5] These denials must have followed the linking of David's name with the play. In fact, we cannot be positive that the names of Crockett and Wildfire were not coupled before the play was ever written, or from the time, even, of the play's initial conception in the mind of Hackett or others, as the similarity to Crockett of Wildfire's title and his descriptive cognomen both suggest.

W. I. Paulding relates how James Kirke went even further in denying his intention of portraying Crockett in Wildfire by writing David to that effect in December, 1830. In his memoirs of his father, Paulding innocently publishes David's "reply" of December 22, 1830, as *bona fide:*

Sir: Your letter of the 15 inst. was handed to me this day by my friend Mr. Wilde—the newspaper publications to which you refer I have never seen; and if I had, I should not have taken the references to myself in exclusion of many who fill the offices and who are as untaught as I am. I thank you however for your civility in assuring me that you had no reference to my peculiarities. The frankness of your letter induces me to say a declaration from you to that effect was not necessary to convince me that you were incapable of wounding the feelings of a strainger and unlettered man who had never injured you. Your character for letters and as a gentleman is not altogather unknown to me.
I have the honour with great respect &c
David Crockett [6]

* The play was thought to be irretrievably lost until J. H. Tidwell found a copy in the British Museum. The following edition has recently been published: James K. Paulding, *The Lion of the West*, ed. J. N. Tidwell (Stanford: Stanford University Press, 1954).

This letter, so patently spurious, is obviously designed to "dress Crockett up" while retaining sufficient literary illiteracy (*strainger, altogather*) to gull a romance-reading, sentimental public. One concludes that W. I. Paulding was the dupe of a literary hoax which may have been an essential part of the whole Whig campaign to make David a more powerful anti-Jackson weapon in the hands of the friends of the U. S. Bank.

I do not essay a guess as to whether Paulding was a witting participant. It seems highly probable that there was more than accident behind this national advertising of Crockett's name by means of this play, beginning perhaps with the play's conception and extending throughout its long and popular run in America and England. Mr. Adkins is surely wrong in ascribing the association of the play and Crockett to accident. He says, "*at last* an ingenious scandal-monger *hit upon* David Crockett." [7] The point is that it was not "at last," but *at very first;* nor does it seem to have been "hit upon." It is a fact that this stage play tremendously nationalized and pictorialized the name and reputation of David Crockett, and precipitated about his name much of the current tall-tale legend of the West. Considering that the next great step in that same direction was the anonymous *Life* by Clarke, and noting how similar were the materials which entered into both, we become increasingly convinced that the tie-up of the *Lion of the West* with David Crockett could not have been merely accidental. Indeed, the very content of the play itself indicates that, whatever the denials, *David was obviously meant from the first to be its central character*, and that all these contrary protestations were merely a clever means for identifying the two and advertising both.

There are a number of evidences of the similarity between the play and the 1833 *Life* of Crockett. For instance, the reviews show that the play contained comments by Colonel Wildfire to the effect that he was "primed for anything, from a possum hunt to a nigger funeral," that he hadn't had "a fight for ten days, and he felt mighty wolfy about the head and shoulders." [8] Lt. Coke, an English soldier on furlough, noted that the play was popular in the East but its performance in the West in 1832 was such "as to excite a strong feeling against [Hackett]; and so incensed the 'half-horse, half-Aligator [*sic*] boys' 'the yellow flowers of the forest,' as the [*sic*] call themselves, that they threatened 'to row him up Salt river' if he ventured a repetition of the objectionable performance." [9] The West was evidently objecting to what it recognized as an Eastern caricature of itself, as Crockett pretended to object to the same thing in Clarke's handling of him in the *Life* (though earlier he had cooperated in the caricature—and in truth was never averse to public applause, even by such a route).

Evidently David was not so squeamish. When he visited the Washington Theatre to view the play on December 30, 1833, far from objecting, he took bows from Hackett playing Wildfire and applause from the audience! [10]

The play was performed in Covent Garden in April, 1833, under the title of *A Kentuckian's Trip to New York in 1815*. The London *Times* review referred to one of Colonel Wildfire's speeches containing the boast that he had "the fastest horse, prettiest sister, the quickest rifle, and the ugliest dog in the states." Again, that he could "jump higher, squat lower, dive deeper, come up drier than any other fellow in the world." [11] W. I. Paulding quotes a description Hackett sent him from the London *Times* concerning the character of Wildfire that hits uncomfortably close to a description of David:

It is a pleasing one. He may be compared to an open-hearted, childish giant, *whom anyone might deceive but none could* daunt. His whimsical extravagance of speech and his ignorance of the conventional restraints of society he over-balances by a heart that would scorn to do a mean or dishonest action.[12]

Finally, the *Times* is also authority for an account of a fight in the play between Colonel Wildfire and a river boatman whom the colonel bests so completely that the boatman, in admiration, promises to *vote for him next election*.[13]

To summarize: the character of the play is a Westerner recognizably similar to the Crockett of fact and decidedly similar to the Crockett of legend; he is a colonel; he is running for election—all of this in a play coupled with David's name a year before the play was produced. In addition, much of the same material was in the 1833 *Life*, self-proclaimedly a literary venture in behalf of David, and obviously directed toward helping re-elect him to Congress in 1833. Even the significant detail of the fight between the colonel (in the *Life*, Crockett by name) and the boatman, with the latter promising, upon being drubbed by David, to vote for the colonel at the next election is included. The play and the *Life*, then, appear to be two of several coordinate steps leading up to the same eminence.

In the 1833 *Life* there is an abundance of such expressions as the "wolfish about the head and ears, and thought I'd spile if I wasn't kivered in salt, for I hadn't had a fight in ten days" talk; the "yaller flower of the forest" boast; and the "go down deeper, come up drier" brag. I therefore conclude that the *Life* drew heavily on the Paulding play. Take for example the account of the fight between Crockett and the boatmen in the *Life* (p. 132):

Said I [Crockett], 'Ain't I the yallur-flower of the forest? And I am all brimstone but the head and ears, and that's aquifortis.' Said he [boatman], 'Stranger, you are a beauty: and if I know'd your name I'd vote for you next election.' Said I, 'I'm that same David Crockett. You know what I'm made of. I've got the closest shootin rifle, the best coon dog, the biggest ticlur, and the ruffest racking horse, in the district. I can kill more lickur, fool more varmints, and cool out more men, than any man you can find in old Kentuck. . . .

They part, and David calls after him, "Don't forget that vote." The author says that he has heard this story attributed to a Colonel Wildfire, but is unwilling that the hard earnings of Crockett should be given to another. Two chapters later we are regaled plentifully with the Crockett mythology of the half-horse, half-alligator, touched-with-the-snapping-turtle, wader-of-the-Mississippi, rider-of-the-streak-of-lightning type which has recently become so popular in the library carols of the mid-West.

In connection with the above association of Crockett and "old Kentuck," the following series of coincidences is interesting: the Paulding play identified its central character as a Kentuckian; many a legend of the period made Crockett a Kentuckian; W. A. Caruthers, in an 1834 novel with almost the same title as the London version of Paulding's play, *The Kentuckian in New York*, uses Crockett as the titular character; David had several Whig friends from Kentucky; David's homeplace back in Franklin County in 1813 was, according to the Gowan notes, called "Kentuck." As the West moved into Kentucky, the typical Western figure became a "Kentuckian." In falling heir to the whole Western lore, David, who lived in Tennessee a few miles from the Kentucky line, fell heir to this designation also.

There is a remarkable similarity between the *Life* and David's own *Autobiography*. Except for an elaboration of the Creek War chapters (good campaign material), there is very little in the *Autobiography* which was not, in some form, in the earlier *Life*, including the general organization. There were, however, a great many things in the *Life* which David chose to omit from the *Autobiography*, in particular the half-horse, half-alligator, yallur-flower-of-the-forest bombast, the legend and tall tale which had characterized the earlier work, and the unsympathetic treatment of David's own father which the *Life* contained. David added more political and autobiographical details, more realistic language and restraint, more homely expressions, and more typically backwoods idiom. There are a number of minor factual inaccuracies in the *Life* of the sort one would expect from a reporter who got his story orally and wrote it down later from memory and inadequate notes. Place names are misspelled; events are misdated; locales are sometimes confused. Nevertheless a great deal of the matter of the *Life* is verifiable by authentic records.

The following conclusions are, therefore, unavoidable, despite David's protest in his preface and correspondence to the contrary: Someone who knew David well wrote the 1833 *Life;* he was a literary man; he was a Whig; he was interested in the re-election of David to Congress as a Whig; only David himself could have furnished such minute information about himself for the period of his whole life; it would have been impossible for Crockett not to have known who that author was.

A further fact is obvious: David, while professing to repudiate the earlier *Life*, leaned heavily on it in his own *Autobiography* for many matters of content, organization, format, and occasionally (sometimes for considerable passages) even for phraseology. A chapter-by-chapter analysis of each reveals, with the exceptions noted, a similarity startling to one who had originally put credence in David's profession that he did not know who wrote the *Life* and that he resented the manner in which the author treated him. The truth probably was that David's enemies (Jackson men) were using the outlandish material to persuade his constituents that he was not suited to serve their best interests in the decorous and stately halls of Congress. Crockett found it necessary to try to lay a ghost he had helped to raise. Thanks to this rather complex situation, we have that classic in American realistic literature, David Crockett's *Autobiography*.

To date, the author of the 1833 *Life* has been recorded as unknown, except for occasional tentative attributions to James Strange French, the man in whose name it was copyrighted. In 1835 French wrote the novel *Elkswatawa, or, The Prophet of the West*, containing a Kentucky character named "Earthquake," whose prototype is clearly Crockett. Even a casual reader would affirm that the twenty-eight years old author of that loose, unaccomplished work of 1835 could not possibly have written, at 25, the much more finished, mature, informed, and literary work of three years earlier.[14]

I have proposed as author of the *Life* Mathew St. Clair Clarke, Clerk of the House of Representatives from December 3, 1822, to December 2, 1833, friend of Nicholas Biddle of the United States Bank, literary man, author, and historian. I offer the following data to support the claim.

Christopher Baldwin, Librarian of the American Antiquarian Society in the '30's, associates Clarke and Crockett together in the only portion of his diary mentioning either of them. Among other things, the entry informs us that during the summer of 1833 Clarke was travelling with Peter Force through the Atlantic States searching the state records and gathering material for their historical volumes, *American Archives*. They arrived back in Washington on October 7 (the day prior to the diary entry), where they attended a party at which Baldwin had also been present. It continues:

Clarke is a prodigy at story telling. We left the party at 12 and as soon as we reached the hotel where I board, he called for a cigar and a tumbler of brandy and Good God! how his tongue went! He kept me up till nearly four in the morning. I dare not undertake to repeat any of the pleasant accounts he gave me. He had a most discriminating perception of the ridiculous, which is, after all, the true meaning of the word "wit." *He gave a most ludicrous account of his travelling with David Crockett, the famous member of Congress from Tennessee,* and I know not where his talking would have ended, had he not been interrupted by the stage which came to carry him to Hartford. He is a native of Pennsylvania.

I must not leave him without attempting to tell one of his stories, though it will be utterly impossible to do it justice. *He said he was travelling in the western part of Virginia and Crockett was with him. David had been entertaining him with his hunter's stories and amusing adventures that had happened to him.*[15]

We interrupt the quotation to suggest two things. First, Force and Clarke were engaged in serious historical research throughout the summer of 1833; and Clarke was of necessity in attendance upon the House from December, 1832, to its adjournment in March. Since the *Life,* copyrighted by January 5, 1833, would have had to be completed in December, 1832, the travelling with Crockett in western Virginia must have been prior to December, 1832. Second, the "hunter's stories and amusing adventures that had happened to him" sounds remarkably like the material that went into the *Life.* Proceeding with the quotation, we find in fact that the very anecdote related by Clarke to Baldwin was likewise recorded in the *Life:*

They stopped at a public house overnight, and in the morning they found a travelling menagerie halting in the village . . . nearby. . . . David at once decided that he must have a peep at the *criturs.* Clarke accordingly accompanied, but without any expectation of the curious scene that followed. . . . no sooner had David reached the center of the tent, than tipping his hat on one side of his head, sung out in a loud voice, "where's the keeper of these ere varments." Upon this the proprietor, *seeing David to be well dressed,* went up and acknowledged himself to be the owner of them. "Is that are hyena for sale," said David, "no," replied the keeper. "Well, mister, what would be the damage if I should happen to kill him?" The keeper told him that no money would purchase him. "But damme, Mr. Keeper," said David, "I want to try his bottom." "Why what do you mean by that?" asked the keeper, "Nothing," said David, "only I want to grin at him jist to let you see the hair fly." And then placing his back to the centre post that sustained the tent, and going through with many manoevres of the arms and contortions of the face, the keeper seeing him, began to be alarmed lest the fellow should really slay his Hyena, entreated of him not to do any mischief. David, however, swore and went on with his preparations and making up horrible faces, insisted on having one fair grin at the Hyena before he quit. The keeper manifested so much concern for the safety of the animal, that his anxiety extended itself to the spectators & a general panic began to prevail. David was now persuaded to let the poor beast alone, but immediately began to trump up the Lion. "You d----d cowardly varmunt, come out here. Keeper open his box and let him out. I must fight him. Out with him; O you cowardly varmunt." And at the same time walking toward his cage, with such an appearance of earnestness, that the people supposing him to be really going to encounter the Lion, made such a rush to escape from the tent that they carried away some twenty feet of the canvas. Crockett was as serious in this farce as though he had been in the honest discharge of his duty. So eccentric is the man.

Baldwin was too modest about his attempt to do Clarke justice. A comparison of this account with the same story in the 1833 *Life* establishes the similarity of the two. Clarke's powers of story-telling must have been prodigious indeed to enable him to induce a historian to accept this farce as a veracious account of a true experience. The story appears in the following form in the *Life*:

During the Colonel's first winter in Washington, a Caravan of wild animals was brought to the city to be exhibited. Large crowds attended the exhibition; and prompted by common curiosity, one evening Colonel Crockett attended.

"I had just got in," said he: "the house was very much crowded, and the first thing I noticed was two wild cats in a cage. Some acquaintance asked me 'if they were like the wild cats in the backwoods?' And I was looking at them, when one turned over and died. The keeper ran up and threw some water on it. Said I, 'Stranger, you are wasting time. My looks kill them things; and you had better hire me to get out [of] here, or I will kill every varmint you've got in your caravan.' While I and he were talking, the lions began to roar. Said I, 'I wont trouble the American lion, because he is some kin to me, but turn out the English lion—turn him out— kick him out—I can whip him for a ten dollar bill and the Zebra may kick occasionally during the fight.' This created some fun; and I then went to another part of the room, where a monkey was riding a pony. . . .

Of course, the *Life* had been published early in 1833, and it is possible that Clarke had merely read the story therein, or heard it told as part of the legend, and that he was elaborating on it, giving it as a part of a personal experience. However, we cannot forget that Crockett was sending personal regards to Clarke as early as April 18, 1829. In light of all the evidence presented, the interpretation of Clarke's merely having read it appears far-fetched. Clarke knew the story and could elaborate on it because he had himself composed it in the 1833 *Life*.

The *Life* affords much internal evidence to support the assumption of Clarke's authorship: numerous jokes relating to the Dutch, which would have been natural and familiar to a Pennsylvanian; an anecdote about Sam Slick, a Yankee clock peddler entirely Eastern in its content, outlook, and humor; and much evidence that the writer was a man with an astute knowledge of history (Clarke assisted in editing *American Archives* and *American State Papers*), of Indian Affairs (he wrote *A Faithful History of the Cherokee Tribe*), of the geography of the country, of national affairs (he wrote a *Legislative and Documentary History of the Bank of the U. S.*). (*See* the Preface and the Billy Buck Allegory bound in with the *Life*.) There are expressions which reveal an idiom foreign to the Westerner altogether, such as the one in the quotation above, "While *I and he* were talking," or the one introducing the chapter full of Dutch anecdotes (Chapter VII): "Reader! let you and I hold a small confab." The internal evidence profusely demonstrates that it could well have been written by Clarke, the literary historian and prodigious storyteller. Let us proceed with the external evidence.

Miss Constance Rourke dismissed as rumor a story told by Mr. J. S. Derby about the authorship of David's own *Autobiography*. Since she had evidence leading her to believe that the story was incorrect, she was careless in examining the Derby source. Had she begun reading Derby a page earlier, and been interested in finding out the source of his story, she could certainly not have dismissed it as merely a current tradition in the trade. Derby relates that he had this story directly from Mr. Hart, a member of the firm of Carey and Hart, who published David's *Autobiography*. He had been told the story by Mr. Hart not long before the publication of Derby's book in 1884. Beginning "During a recent visit to Philadelphia, Mr. Hart related to me some interesting incidents of his book-publishing career," [16] Derby relates several stories, one of which goes thus:

At an earlier day they [Carey & Hart] published the "Life of David Crockett" written by himself (according to the title page). This book became famous all over the country. Col. Crockett, it will be remembered, was at the time a member of Congress from Tennessee, an eccentric backwoodsman. The fact was, that the book was not actually written by David

Crockett, but for him, by Matthew [sic] St. Clair Clarke, then Secretary of the Senate [sic].

In this book originated the well-known expressions attributed to David Crockett, "Stand up to the rack, fodder or no fodder," "Be sure you're right, then go ahead," and other sayings, which became household words. Col. Crockett was interested in the copyright, and enjoyed his fame as an author very much. Tens of thousands of copies have been sold, and the sale continues.[17]

Now there is irrefutable evidence in holographic form (to be presented later) showing that Mathew St. Clair Clarke did *not* write or *help* to write David's *Autobiography*, which Mr. Hart had evidently confused with the earlier *Life*. Considering that Mr. Hart was recounting this story after fifty years, I think we are justified in concluding that though it may contain some inaccuracies (such as placing Clarke in the Senate instead of in the House), it is not without the substance of truth. Both books dealt with the same subject; both were remarkably similar in many ways; and in one sense the author of the earlier volume *was* at least partial author of the later one. These similarities would certainly account for Mr. Hart's confusion of the two after the lapse of fifty years. The very fact that the statement cannot possibly apply to the *Autobiography* is, in my opinion, very strong corroborative evidence that it *does* apply to the anonymous *Life* of Crockett of a year earlier. This, taken in conjunction with the other evidence presented, should establish once and for all that Clarke wrote that work. However, two matters in this connection should be considered briefly: the very slight contrary evidence, and the reason for copyrighting the book in a name other than Clarke's own.

The contrary evidence is not really evidence at all. It simply consists of two casual statements by Edgar Allan Poe that he thought James Strange French was the author, though he disclaimed any real knowledge about it. He evidently made this attribution of authorship on the mere basis of copyright; just as he picked up the location given at the close of the Preface to *Elkswatawa* (Jerusalem, South Hampton County, Virginia), the volume he was reviewing, and listed it as French's residence. Certainly, if Poe had read the *Life*, his sense of style would have prevented him from attributing this earlier and better work to the author of *Elkswatawa*. Here is Poe's statement: "This novel [*Elkswatawa*] is written by Mr. James S. French of Jerusalem, Virginia—the author, we believe of "Eccentricities of David Crockett,' a book of which we know nothing beyond the fact of its publication."[18]

The *Eccentricities* was the title given to a re-edition, with very few changes, of the *Life* under a new copyright in November, 1833.[19] His other reference is equally casual: "Mr. French is the author of a 'Life of David Crockett,' and also of a novel called Elkswatawa." [20]

If Clarke was the author, why did he copyright the book in the name of another? The answer is evident. The volume was composed as part of an effort to re-elect David Crockett to Congress as an anti-Jacksonian and supporter of the Second United States Bank, and to increase his usefulness through a multiplication of his fame. For the volume to have appeared under the name of a well-known Whig, who because of his political affiliation lost his position as Clerk of the House under Jackson, would have been to reveal the purpose and defeat the strategy. Perhaps he disliked having his reputation associated with a book containing much that was trivial and buffoonish.

Since the *Life* had to be copyrighted by another, the fact that it was issued in the name of the Virginian James Strange French may even be corroborative evidence for Clarke's authorship. Information on French is exceedingly scarce. It is known that his family had been intimately associated for three generations with a family of Stranges (first cousins of J. S. French) who owned "a country place of near Natural Bridge, Virginia," in Rockbridge County, where French visited them. David had friends in Rockbridge County, and it is probable that he and Mathew St. Clair Clarke were there together between 1828 and 1832. A letter from David on December 21, 1839 was addressed to Henry McClung, uncle of William Alexander Caruthers, of Rockbridge County. Caruthers was a graduate of Washington College (now Washington and Lee), where McClung was a trustee. These individuals and the school itself were at this time strongly Whig. This evidence is only circumstantial. However, the fact is significant that we have at the same place, at about the same period, and in a positive or highly probable relation of acquaintanceship David Crockett, Henry McClung, Mathew St. Clair Clarke, William Alexander Caruthers, and James Strange French.

The following facts should be noted: the mutual interest in literature shared by Clarke, Caruthers, and French; the fact that all three wrote works in which one of the characters was David Crockett (Clarke, the *Life;* Caruthers, *The Kentuckian in New York;* and French, *Elkswatawa,* the Crockettean character being "Earthquake," an obvious allusion to the territory of the "shakes" where David lived); and the fact that all three can be traced to Rockbridge County, Virginia, at about the same time, the time of the writing of the *Life.* This evidence supplies a plausible background for the copyrighting of a book by Clarke about David in the name of James Strange French, a young man of literary aspirations whose literary reputation it could not hurt and might help to establish. I believe that the fairest interpretation of all the evidence presented is that Clarke was the author of the first book about Crockett to be printed, the anonymous *Life* of 1833.

There are other suggestive matters concerning Caruthers which in a work of this sort should not be omitted. His 1834 novel, *The Kentuckian in New York*, recounts a trip by three southern aristocratic boys and one Crockettean backwoodsman to New York. Though Clarke was not a Southerner, it is possible that Clarke, Caruthers, French, and Crockett may have made such a trip in 1832 while David sat out his defeat by Fitzgerald. Though it is conjectural, one notes that in this work of Caruthers the name of one of the young ladies is a Miss Frances (French?) St. Clair (Mathew?), and that the girl with whom the rough Kentuckian, Damon (David), was in love and whom he married was "Betsy," diminutive of Elizabeth, the name of David's wife, as well as the name which the 1833 *Life* had given to David's hunting rifle.

Another work which, like Caruthers' *Kentuckian*, seems to reflect in its title the earlier Paulding play, is a long, anonymous poem called "Davy Crocket; or, the Nimrod of the West" (Colonel *Nimrod* Wildfire). It is possible that this, too, may have come from the pen of Caruthers. I cannot yet affirm it, but there is some internal evidence to suggest it—evidence relating to Washington (and Lee) College, which Caruthers had attended; a knowledge of medical terms (Caruthers was a medical doctor); the opposition therein to mesmerism (Caruthers was vehemently opposed to it); the knowledge of literature revealed (Caruthers was an educated writer); and the fact of its publication privately in New York at about the time Caruthers was in that city (1837); together with the author's claim of personal acquaintance with David Crockett. This first canto of a poem, evidently never completed, may be found in the Library of Congress. Also, the central character of Caruthers' *Kentuckian* was immediately identified as Crockett by the newspapers, and the identification has continued down through Parrington.[21]

APPENDIX 2

THE AUTOBIOGRAPHY

In a letter to G. W. McLean written on January 17, 1834, among a spate of complaints about the deposits, "Jacksons Kingley powar," and a hope that "Congress will teach him a lesson that will be of use to the next Tyrant that fills that Chair," Crockett goes on to discuss his *Autobiography*.

I am ingaged in prepareing a worke that may be of little prophit to me but I Consider that Justice demands of me to make a Statement of facts to the amirican people I have no doubt but you have Saw a Book purporting to be the life and adventers of my Self that Book was written without my knowledge and widley Circulated and in fact the person that took the first liberty to write the Book have published a Second addition and I thought one inposition was enough to put on the Country and I have put down the Imposition and have promised to give the people a Correct Statement of faicts relative to my life as I Consider no man on earth able to give a true history of my life I have undertaken it my Self and will Compleat it by the last of next week ready for the press and it will Contain about two hundred pages and I hope it will fill expectations I give the truth and I will venture to Say it will be as interesting as the Imposition that has been imposed on the people [1]

The "Second addition" of Clarke's *Life* of David refers, of course, to the previously noted *Sketches and Eccentricities*. Crockett's protestations of an imposition and his statement that the *Life* was written without his knowledge—the same pretensions which, properly improved by Chilton, went into the Preface of the *Autobiography*—cannot be accepted at face value. Like his statement that he was writing his own life, it was a necessary camouflage for a political strategy which, if revealed, would have been self-defeating. Clarke may have originally issued the book without David's knowledge; but David had continued to pretend ignorance as to its author after it was published. Indeed, without such a pretext, he would have had little excuse for issuing yet another book on his own life for the new campaign of 1835.

David's first letter to Carey and Hart (publishers of the *Autobiography*) was written on January 28, 1834, and it is undoubtedly an important one. I have not been able to trace it.[2] If and when it comes to light, it will be found to be in the handwriting, not of David Crockett, but of Thomas Chilton. David's letter to Carey and Hart on February 23, 1834, states that all previous communications from him to them were written by Chilton. A photostat of the following letter of February 3 verifies his statement that that one at least was not in David's hand, and must therefore be in Chilton's. Any other Crockett letters to Carey and Hart written prior to February 23, if such survive, will doubtless be found to be in the same Chilton hand. The February 3 letter, accepting in David's name the publishers' terms for printing the autobiography, is obviously far beyond David's ability in punctuation, paragraphing, spelling, grammar, diction and information:

Gentlemen.

Your favour of the 31st Jany came to hand by yesterdays mail; and having duly considered its contents, I have determined to accept your proposition to publish my Narrative. I enclose the Manuscript by to days mail, and I hope it may reach you safely—as I have preserved no copy of it—nor indeed have I time to have it copied. The Copyright, certified by the clerk is attached to the Preface—and I am too ignorant of the business of printing, to pretend to give you any instructions about the manner of executing it—except barely in relation to one thing. I wish it, printed in *large* type, and so leaded, as to make it very open and plain. Please do not neglect this—as in that way it will easily spread over more than two hundred pages—which I have ascertained by counting the number of words on an average page of the manuscript, and several printed books that I have also examined and counted. It has been hastily passed over for correction, and some small words may have been omitted. If so you will supply them. It needs no corrections of *spelling* or *grammar*, as I make no literary pretensions.

The sale of the work, I am satisfied will exceed any calculation you have made. All along the Mississippi, where the counterfeit work sold rapidly, I have been urged by the people generally, to publish. There, very many copies will sell. I have also recd a letter from a Bookseller in Louisville Ky—assuring me, that it will sell rapidly there. That more than 500 copies of the other work, had been sold at his single house in that place; and that many more of the genuine work would find ready market. In this place, I should be glad to receive 500 copies, at your price to the trade, instead of selling to them. I however mean, that number of the first copies that you send off. The very first moment that you can do so—please send me 10 copies—with a Bill of the cost of printing & binding *per copy* that I may know what the profit for *division* is to be.

Like yourselves, I hope and believe, that we will have no difficulty in managing the ultimate settlement of the concern. All I can or do expect, is—that the work will be executed by you as cheap as it could be procured to be done by any other printer—And that a faithful account of the number of copies printed, will be rendered by you. Your high standing is a satisfactory guarrantee, though I am personally unacquainted with you. I reserve your letter, of the date alluded to, as your contract—and you will consider this, as my acceptance of it.

Please inform me immediately, on the reception of this, whether you have safely recd the manuscript, and when I shall get my 10 copies—and such other matters as you may deem important. Respectfully Gentlemen I am Yrs.   David Crockett [3]

Since this is the only Chilton manuscript of whose existence I am positive, it may be more important than if it had been written by David (as it was quite obviously written with his knowledge and probably in his presence). It can be used for comparison with the composition of the *Autobiography*. Several things about it should be emphasized. First is the significance of the statement that no copy of the manuscript had been preserved, that a single copy of the manuscript existed. We learn from a later Crockett holography *that this single copy was entirely in the handwriting of Thomas Chilton*. Next, the specifications as to the large type, open printing, 200 pages (the book actually ended on page 211), and so on, were aimed, I judge, at duplicating the format of the 1833 *Life* which had already demonstrated its popularity.

The instructions not to change the *spelling* and *grammar* (Chilton's italics) are unusual directions to give a publisher. I suspect that the errors had been intentionally made. A comparison of them with David's own letters proves that they are not characteristic of Crockett's writing. Since the above letter is proof that they were not characteristic of Chilton's either, we see that they are only literary illiteracies. Here was another small literary hoax.

In order to proceed to a summation of matters concerning the authorship of the *Autobiography*, I quote here, in its entirety, David's letter to Carey and Hart of three weeks later, February 23:

Gentlemen

For Some days I have been anxiously expecting the arivel of a Copy of my book which you had the goodness to promis to Send me So Soon it was finished. But as you were mistaken in its length when you Stipulated the time at which I would recieve a Copy I Suppose its completion has been probably delayed by that Circumstance I desire it early as may Suit your Convenience—not for the purpose of indiscriminate use but for my own private Satisfaction until the time Shall arive at which you may open a Sale of them at the different points to which you may think proper to Send them in my former letters I Spoke of you Sending me (500) Copies to this place. As the trade is to be Supplied here, and as my public engagements Consume all my time I have Concluded that it will be unessacery to do So—and you will therefore decline it unless I Should make Some Subsequent arrangement with you on the Subject pleas however Send me ten *Copies* as I wish that number for distribution among my imediate friends I wish you also to understand that the Hon Thos Chilton of Kentucky is entitled to one equl half of the Sixty two and a half *per cent* of the entire profits of the work as by the agreemint betwen you and my Self—and also to half the Copy right in any Subsequent use or disposition which may be made of that I have thought proper to advise you of this fact and to request that you will drop him a memorandum recognizing his right as a foresaid that half the Said profits, which would otherwise be due to my

Self may be Subject to his order and control at all times here after Enclose Such a memorandum to me and I will hand it over to Mr Chilton It is more over proper that this Should be done in order that if either or any of us Should die our heirs may understand the arrangement This will therefore be my relinquishment to Mr Chilton of the intirest aforesaid one half of which you are duly notified The manuscript of the Book is in his hand writing though the entire Substance of it is truly my own The aid which I needed was to Classify the matter but the Style was not altered

The letters which you have heretofor[e] recieved from me were also in his hand writing as I was unwell and not able to write at their dates I deem it necessary to give you this infermation that you may hereafter know my hand writing and his, as it may be necessary that each of *us* Should correspond with you when absent *from each other*

Several Gentlemen from London in Great Britain have urged me to Secure the Copy right of my Book in that Country I wish to Consult you on the Subject A Mr Jno Barry who is a Strainger to me *but* who has the appearance of a gentleman is anxious to attend to it for me and proposes to do it with our Charge he will probably Call on you—and you are author-ised to make any arrangement Concerning it which you may think advis-able I Suppose you have agents in London and if So you Could if you think it would be profitable make the arrangement through them this letter will always answer you as a guide in Judging my hand writing as it is written by my own hand Pleas let me here from you on recept of this, and afford me a bill of Cost *per Copy* of printing the Book

This whole arrangement as to the interest of my friend Mr Chilton is Committed to yourselves as Confidential—and So will your memorandum to him be Considered I am gentlemen Sincearly your friend and obt Servt

David Crockett [4]

Beyond all peradventure, Mathew St. Clair Clarke's authorship of the *Autobiography*, save to the extent that it patterned itself after the 1833 *Life,* is absolutely disproved.

The salutation, heading, and close of the letter, as well as its employment of the comma, italics, and dashes, and its request for the costs of printing, are obvious indications that David had seen Chilton's earlier letters, and had learned from them. Chilton may have dictated as David penned the letter but was not spelling the words for him.

We defer a moment to emphasize that this is a *confidential* letter, and to remark that David's claim of sickness as an excuse for Chilton's having written his letters was probably not his real reason. He had obviously be-lieved that he would get better terms and attention if the initial contact with the publisher presented the author as a man of shrewdness as well as of learning. Further, he probably did not know enough about such matters to initiate the proceedings. The fact that he had not copied Chilton's letters in his own hand, or taken them from dictation, may indeed have resulted from a sickness beginning near the end of January and extending beyond February 3.

Who, then, was the real author of the *Autobiography?* How much should Chilton be credited with and how much should David Crockett? [5] The evidence only verifies the immediate impression gained by a reading of any page of the *Autobiography* in comparison with any page of David's holographs, I here summarize briefly the rather exhaustive comparisons I have made between the two. First of all, the diction of the *Autobiography* does not appear to be typically the diction of Crockett's letters (there is some overlapping, as in *deposits, Jackson, Kitchen Cabinet*). Taking the top ten characteristic expressions, from a compiled list of more than fifty which occur most frequently in the *Autobiography* and a list of several hundred from the letters, I find in the *Autobiography* forty-two examples, in one form or another, of "go ahead"; thirty-nine of "cut out"; thirteen of "harricane"; nine each of "butcher," "deposites," and "horn"; seven of "plenty" and "varmints"; and five each for "frolic" in connection with the "Presidency," and for "wrath" or "wrathy." In the letters I find only one or possibly two usages of "go ahead" (and that while the book was being written), quite a few to "deposits," and a single reference to himself in connection with the "Presidency." The other eight expressions used most frequently in the *Autobiography* are not found in his correspondence. This of course is not a thorough test of diction, but it represents exactly what a more thorough study revealed. Though the complete study of the diction would not be conclusive by itself, it becomes so in the total picture.

The *Autobiography* is marvelously free of misspellings as compared to Crockett's holographs. This is as it should be if he had it "run over" for spelling. Even more interesting is the fact that words which David typically misspells in his letters (*whare, thare, becaus, collers, determened, pleas, powar, preasant, pint* [for *point*], *rout, sone* [for *son* or *sonny*], *betwen*) are not misspelled in the *Autobiography*, or not misspelled in that way. For instance, the *Autobiography* misspells *Christmass* in that fashion four times, nine times it spells *deposite* or *deposites* thus; whereas David spells *deposits* without the "e" in every one of his many usages of that word, and misspells *Chrisemas* thus instead of *Christmass*. Another instance of the use of the same word a few times by both is the dog collar David refused to wear for Jackson. The *Autobiography* always spells it correctly and David's letters misspell it in every usage (some five times) *collers*. These matters are of particular note in consideration of the fact that the manuscript was all in Chilton's hand and that the publisher had been instructed not to correct the spelling and grammar.

On the matter of grammar, we find precisely the same thing: the errors most frequent in Crockett's letters are not those that characterize the *Autobiography*. David's most frequent errors are, first, a failure in agreement between subject and verb and, second, the misuse of an adjective for an adverb (get them *regular*, write me *lenthy*). The use of the past participle, or past participle corrupted, without auxiliary in lieu of the past tense, or of the past tense in lieu of the past participle (I *knowed;* I *seen;* had *flew*), while occurring in David's letters, are *relatively* very rare. The most characteristic grammatical error of the *Autobiography* is of this type (I *know'd;* had *flew*), a type easy to affect and easy to adopt in superficial simulation of grammatical ineptness. David's typical grammatical errors are almost nonexistent in the *Autobiography*. Taking a dozen samples of Crockett's letters at random, I find in them a total of about 193 misspelled words, 16 errors of subject-verb agreement, and 12 errors in the use of adjectives for adverbs. *None of these errors is characteristic of the Autobiography.*

As for capitalization, punctuation, redundancy, sentence structure, paragraphing, and the like, the differences between the *Autobiography* and the Crockett letters written at the very time when the *Autobiography* was being composed are so numerous, so vast, and so obvious that comment on them here is considered superfluous (though we should note the excessive use of commas both in the Chilton holograph given above and in the *Autobiography*). They merely corroborate what we have already seen. We must conclude, therefore, that so far as the manuscript, spelling, grammar, punctuation, and the mechanical portions—the form generally —of the *Autobiography* is concerned, even perhaps including much of the diction, the work was the contribution of Thomas Chilton. What about the *content* of the work?

I have made a careful annotation of the entire *Autobiography*, and I find that the evidence here is precisely the reverse of that on matters of form. Much of the evidence as to the factual events of David's life has already been laid before the reader. When one compares the authentic records about Crockett with the *Autobiographical* account of them, he finds only two sorts of discrepancies: first, a few additions, and slight, seemingly deliberate alterations which I have attributed to the fact that David was still in politics and intended the *Autobiography* partially as campaign literature; and second, errors not in fact but in the accuracy of dating fact, attributable obviously to its having been written entirely from memory. However the rest of it is so meticulously accurate, as established by parallel surviving records, as to prove quite conclusively that in content the work is all David's own. Let me summarize my judgment of what took place, and of what credit belongs to each.

Crockett was running for re-election locally and was being viewed by the Whigs nationally as a valuable tool against Jackson, possibly as a candidate with whom to defeat him. Eastern financial interests had for some time been ballyhooing him. In return for their promised support of his land bill and for perhaps even more significant promises, he was being persuaded to move further and further away from Jackson. Thomas Chilton had also fallen into this Whig alliance, and he undertook to further the whole cause by writing David's *Autobiography*. Leaning very heavily on Mathew St. Clair Clarke's earlier *Life* for form and arrangement of factual matter and for a touchstone of what factual episodes to treat and what to omit or telescope, Crockett and Chilton began the undertaking in early December, 1833. Both men were from the West and knew the point of view, the language, and the legend of the area. Under these circumstances, and in view of the minute factual accuracy of most of the *Autobiography*, and the personal minutiae with which much of it deals, it is not conceivable that that work would fail to partake, in large part, of the spirit of David. Add to this the fact that Chilton had known David well for at least six years. From David's laconic statement in a letter to his son that Chilton was helping him, with no explanation of who Chilton was, it seems that he was also a friend of the family. How, then, could Chilton have written this narrative of facts and events furnished him by David orally or by notes (the accuracy of the end product leads me to suspect notes) without consciously or unconsciously catching the very spirit of the man who had lived that narrative?

Moreover, behind the demand that the fabulous and tall tale qualities included in Clarke's *Life* be omitted from the *Autobiography* was David Crockett himself. David is therefore responsible for the racy realism without bombast and exaggeration, the very quality that makes the work highly valuable. He was anxious to tone down that "bull in a china shop" caricature which, though he himself had cooperated in forming it, had boomeranged to the advantage of his political enemies. The holographs indicated that the *spirit* of the *Autobiography* is largely David's own. However, we cannot take seriously the claim that he did not know the author of the earlier *Life* or that Chilton's only share in producing the *Autobiography* was looking it over for arrangement of material, spelling, and grammar. It was not "looked over," it was *written*, by Chilton.

The guiding spirit, the realism, the humorous adventure, the historical fact, the rude but real heroism—these are largely David's. The language and the telling of the narrative were mostly the work of his silent partner, Thomas Chilton, who—knowing the Western backwoods even as David knew them—was a great deal more familiar with the written heritage, including the Bible, grammar and punctuation, and the refinements of "education." The work was copyrighted in David's name (NOT "Davy's" as were the spurious Crockett Almanacs), the only book of all those bearing his name which was so copyrighted, and so far as the law was concerned, all of the rights of ownership were vested in him. Because the help in the actual writing was considerable, the agreement was that he and Chilton should divide the proceeds—share and share alike. To protect Chilton in case of accident or death, David wrote the confidential letter of February 23 as a supplement to their oral agreement. Thus the true nature of their joint project in authorship is revealed.

I conclude that their division of the proceeds pretty accurately reflects the proportion of their respective contributions. The Autobiography probably comes as close to being autobiography as it is possible for biography to become. Unquestionably it is the only acceptably accurate, though very incomplete, story of David's life that has appeared since the Crockett literary deluge began with the Lion of the West in 1831.

Crockett and Chilton were writing for contemporary consumption: in all likelihood, they had not the faintest idea that posterity would find an interest in their work. Yet the work they produced was a frontier classic which, except for a recent twenty-year-old fad in the mythological "Davy" of the tall tale, has stood the test of time. It has maintained its position of value and popularity for almost a century and a quarter.

Twentieth-century critical opinions have unanimously praised its qualities. The Southern scholars Edwin Mims and Bruce R. Payne wrote: "[Crockett] better than any other, gives adequate expression to the life and times of the real pioneer in the South." [6] The historians Charles and Mary Beard likewise judged it in superlatives: "So the politics of the frontier was the politics of backwoodsmen, and if a type of the age is needed for illustration, it may well be David Crockett, whose autobiography is one of the prime human documents for the American epic yet to be written." [7] Two passages from V. L. Parrington develop this claim in some detail:

In Longstreet's Georgia Scenes, Joseph G. Baldwin's Flush Times in Alabama and Mississippi, and Davy Crockett's Autobiography, the frontier is painted in homely colors that time cannot fade.... By far the most significant of them is the braggart but naively truthful Narrative of the Life of canebrake Davy who in his several removals followed the advancing frontier the length of the state of Tennessee. Davy would seem to have been the authentic backwoodsman, and the life of the individual may be taken as the description of the genus. . . . As a full-length portrait of the Jacksonian leveler, in the days when the great social revolution was establishing the principle of an equalitarian democracy, the picture is of vast significance.

The Narrative of the Life of David Crockett of the State of Tennessee was woven from the same stuff that Longstreet made use of, but the fabric is of far better texture. It is the great classic of the Southern Frontier, far more significant than *Georgia Scenes*, far more human and vital. . . . It is an extraordinary document, done so skillfully from life that homespun becomes a noble fabric, and the crudest materials achieve the dignity of an epic.[8]

In the words of Russell Blankenship, "This is a book that no student of American life can afford to miss."[9]

Had these writers known just how historically accurate the *Autobiography* is, their praise might have been even more lavish. The work is a classic of American history as well as of American literature. The book and the man together constitute the outstanding authentic archetypes of *frontier America* and the *pioneer American*.

APPENDIX 3

TEXAS—EXPLOITED

It is appropriate to discuss a book which supposedly traced Crockett's westward trek, and to examine its credentials. The volume claimed to be based upon a diary David kept on that trip, and was, in fact, published in his name after his death. "*Col. Crockett's Exploits and Adventures in Texas*, Written by Himself," was published in Philadelphia in 1836 by T. K. and P. G. Collins. It has long been the source of so many errors, fabrications, and misrepresentations that for once it deserves—and we hope may here receive—its final refutation.

Briefly, here is a description of the paraphernalia which set up this long-lived hoax. The preface to the volume, purportedly written by one Alex. J. Dumas, contained a so-called "letter" supposedly from Charles T. Beale, written from San Jacinto, Texas, on May 3, 1836, two months after David's death. The "letter" claimed that its writer was present at the Alamo shortly after the battle and that he somehow "came into possession of" an authentic *diary* which Crockett had kept, from which he had written up the transmitted manuscript of the *Exploits*. The letter and the manuscript, it said, were being sent to Alex. J. Dumas, who was to publish it if he saw fit. Dumas wrote a preface, included this letter in it, and with appropriate flourishes dated the preface June, 1836. Here, then, is what we will see to be the single source for all the fictionalizing which has gone on for so long about a so-called Crockett diary.

First, let us consider the evidence as to the real publishers of the volume. Printed as a frontispiece to it is a photograph of Crockett, the one published as a frontispiece in the Boston *Tour*, which bore Carey and Hart's imprint. Also, in fine letters and *as a part of the photograph* are the same words that had appeared on the photograph as they had published it: "Published by E. L. Carey and A. Hart, Philadelphia." Further, on the verso of the title page occur the identical words which had occurred on both of the volumes which had openly borne their imprint (the *Tour* and the *Autobiography*): "Stereotyped by L. Johnson, Philadelphia." This is not conclusive evidence, but it prepares us to receive the admission of Mr. Hart himself that his firm actually published the volume, as he does in the following quotation completing his statement partially given in connection with the authorship of the 1833 *Life*. This was a statement which Mr. Hart had made to Mr. J. S. Derby shortly before the latter, in 1884, published his book, *Fifty Years Among Authors, Books, and Publishers*. The remainder reads:

The late Richard Penn Smith was in Carey & Hart's one day, when Edward L. Carey told him that they had a large number of copies of Crockett's "Tour Down East" which didn't sell. Crockett had just then been executed by the Mexican authorities at the Alamo, and Mr. Carey suggested to Mr. Smith, that if they could get up a book of Crockett's adventures in Texas, it would not only itself sell, but get them clear of the other books. They secured all the works on Texas they could lay their hands on, and Smith undertook the work. Mr. Carey said he wanted it done in great haste, and asked him when it would be ready for the printer; his reply was, "Tomorrow morning." Smith came up to the contract, and never kept the printer waiting. The result was that a great many thousands of copies of the book were sold and all the balance of the edition of the "Tour Down East." [1]

Miss Rourke, in *Davy Crockett*, attempted to refute that quotation in several ways. First, unaware of the source of her cited story (Mr. Hart), she mistakenly said that Derby's statement "seems to rest on an assertion in an article on Smith appearing in *Burton's Gentleman's Magazine* for September, 1839, which states that Smith wrote the book." [2] Another point in her refutation rests on a semantic misunderstanding. The entire book, she says, could not possibly have been written in one night. The quoted passage does not say that it was. If it is not clear in the passage above, it is crystal clear in the passage she cited from *Burton's Gentleman's Magazine*, that Smith composed enough the first night to be ready for the printer, and that he continued to write fast enough so that he "never kept the printer waiting," *i.e.*, the stereotyper, L. Johnson:

In the same year [1836, the year of publication of *The Forsaken*] ... he [Richard Penn Smith] produced a work which has been the subject of much grave speculation. We allude to "Colonel Crockett's Tour in Texas," a pseudo-autobiography, or memoir, which purported to have been written by the gallant Tennessean, prior to the fatal field of the Alamo. This work which was published anonymously [as to Smith], and of course, without any view to reputation, was prepared in great haste, but it contains nevertheless much that is worthy of admiration. As an evidence of Mr. Smith's facility in composition it may be mentioned *that on the day succeeding that on which the idea was first suggested by the booksellers, for whom it was written, a portion of this volume was actually in press, and the remainder was supplied from time to time, so as to keep even pace with the stereotype founder.* Few books have gained equal popularity. In the course of a single year, upwards of ten thousand copies were sold in the United States, and the demand for it still continues active [in 1839]. Soon after its appearance here, it was reprinted in London, where it was reviewed by the principal critical journals in terms of the most flattering approval. Frazer's magazine commends it for its quaint humor and graphic description; the London Monthly Review compares it to Goldsmith for pathos, and to Swift for satire, and Chambers' Edinburgh Journal, completely deceived by its air of sincerity, quotes from it as the best account of the then existing state of affairs in Texas. Indeed, although Mr. S never visited our sister republic, it is not unlikely that his descriptions of her agricultural demesne, and his strictures on her civil polity may be to the full as true as most of the accounts of "travelled history" which in this bookmaking age are so abundant.[3]

This article was anonymous. Let us consider the implications of what the quotation says: it was published in Philadelphia in 1839; the sale of the *Exploits* was still tremendous; the publishers of the volume were located in Philadelphia; Richard Penn Smith was living in that city; this long and conspicuous attribution of authorship was made in a reputable and popular magazine, under the editorship of the critically gifted Edgar Allan Poe. Could this have happened and, if in error, never be retracted either at the request of the publishers, of the "real" author, Richard Penn Smith, or of anybody else who might have had the true information—such as Beale or Dumas?

In seeking the author of this anonymous sketch of Smith, I discovered that Poe himself gave some interesting corroboration to this story. Writing several years later in *Graham's Magazine* for January, 1842, he said:

> Mr. Richard Penn Smith, although, perhaps, better known in Philadelphia than elsewhere, has acquired much literary reputation. His chief works are "The Forsaken," a novel; a pseudo-auto-biography called "Colonel Crocket's Tour in Texas".... We are not sufficiently cognizant of any of these works to speak with decision respecting their merits. In a biography of Mr. Smith, however, well written by his friend Mr. Mc-Michael of this city, we are informed... of the "Tour in Texas" that few books attained an equal popularity.[4]

From this passage alone, both in phrasing and in content, we recognize that Poe has given us the name of the author of that anonymous article on Smith for which we are seeking. There are other phrases in Poe's discussion, omitted above, which were also drawn from Mr. McMichael's "anonymous" biography of Smith. Fortunately, among other things, McMichael had confused the name of the *Texas Exploits* with that of the Boston *Tour*, writing "Colonel Crockett's Tour in Texas," and Poe's repeated employment of this error completely clinches the matter. Poe was writing from, or remembering, the article McMichael had written for him when he had been editing *Burton's*. The anonymous author of Smith's biography was a personal friend of Smith's, another Philadelphian, who had every reason to know the author of the *Exploits*. Furthermore we have this testimony from Poe as to Mr. McMichael's reliability: "We have only to add that we have the highest respect for the judgment of Mr. McMichael."

In addition, I think Poe's statement independently corroborative of Smith's authorship of the *Exploits*. Though he undoubtedly first learned of it from McMichael, Poe was, at the time as well as later, well known at Carey and Hart's, visited there, and corresponded with the firm. Considering his ease of checking the McMichael statement with the publishers, one doubts that he would have accepted such an attribution without knowing of the authority with which McMichael spoke.

Earlier Poe had referred to Richard Penn Smith, and once again he had connected his name with that of David Crockett. In November, 1841, in his article on "Autobiography: Part I," for *Graham's Magazine*, he had written: "[Smith's] Ms. is legible, and has much simplicity about it. At times it vascillates, and appears unformed. Upon the whole, it is just such a Ms. as David Crockett wrote, and precisely such a one as we might imagine would be written by a *veritable* Jack Downing...."[5] His underscoring of *veritable* indicates that he was fully aware that Major Downing was one of the hoaxes of that hoax-full literary age (though with tongue in cheek he goes on to give the handwriting of the original and only Jack himself!) His pairing of Smith's handwriting with that of Crockett, and both with that of a fictitious character, must have been an allusion to Smith's authorship of the *Exploits* and possibly to the Crockett-Seba Smith alliance with Downing. I suspect that Poe had not in fact the slightest idea of what Crockett's manuscript looked like—unless, perhaps, he had been shown one of David's letters at Carey and Hart's.

We see, then, that instead of having to deal with a trade legend based on an earlier anonymous account, we have two entirely authoritative statements by people in positions to know: one a personal friend of Penn Smith; the other, the publisher of the book. The statements are completely independent of one another and are mutually corroborative. In fact, if we count Poe, we have three independent statements all alleging the same thing. This sort of evidence cannot be ignored or lightly brushed away.

Another argument must be considered, if this ghost of a diary is to be once and for all laid: the contention that it is quite possible that Crockett kept a diary, inasmuch as he expressed a wish "to write one more book," and that Beale might have found it. Also, that "it seems highly probable that Crockett wrote a number of letters on the journey to Texas," from which material could have been drawn for the book. This is merely wishful thinking directly opposed to the evidence. There is one letter surviving from the Texas period, which lasted, after all, only a few days over two months.[6] The only other remaining holographic material surviving is an order David drew on the Texas government to John Lott. Other things being equal, it must be true that the nearer Crockett's letters were written to March 6, 1836, the day on which his name became famous for history, the greater the probability of their survival. The truth is, that Crockett did not do a great deal of writing except while he was in Congress answering the letters of his constituents or writing his publishers about his books. The year by far the most copious for his surviving letters is 1834. As far as I have discovered, for the entire two years during which he sat out an election defeat, 1831-33, only one brief letter has survived. We have not a single letter for the whole of his life prior to his election to Congress in 1827, though one survives from his 19-year-old son. For 1834 there are no less than 28 surviving holographs. There are at least ten for 1835. When David was defeated, and had passed that information on in letters which survive, it seems clear that his letter writing days were, for the most part, over.

Indeed, an examination of the single surviving letter from the Texas trip corroborates what common sense ought to tell us—that under the circumstances letter writing was difficult for a man who had never gotten very far in that art to begin with. He was exploring and travelling through the wilds of an unsettled country. He couldn't have written many letters. The one letter says, for instance, "This is the first I have had an opertunity to write you with convenience." It also says, "I have not written William but have requested John to direct him what to do. I hope you will show him this letter and also Brother John as it is not convenient at this time for me to write to them." There are possibly a few letters of those few weeks never yet, perhaps never to be, discovered. There could not have been many. To state that it "seems highly probable that Crockett wrote a number of letters on the journey to Texas" is to ignore Crockett's inclinations, habits, and circumstances, as well as the evidence of his one surviving letter.

Since the theoretical author of these *Exploits* had composed the book within two months of the Alamo, all of which time he had remained in Texas, how could letters which Crockett mailed home to Tennessee have come into possession of "Beale" in Texas, as the "diary" so conveniently did? It is highly unlikely that any papers which Crockett might have had on him, including the preposterous diary, might have survived, inasmuch as all the bodies at the Alamo were, in all probability, immediately cremated, before any Texas troops could arrive. We dismiss this statement as not only contrary to all evidence and reason, but as having nothing whatsoever to do with the authenticity of the *Exploits*. The letters, regardless of numbers, could not have been available to Beale.

What is the evidence supporting the existence of a Crockett diary? We pass over the suspicious peculiarity of the two names connected with it, Beale and Alexander Dumas. Mr. "Beale," whose letter was printed in the Preface, claimed not only to have found the diary but expressed his profound sense of awareness of the importance of such a document. How could it happen that such a valuable document should be preserved *after* the Alamo in the hands of one aware of its importance, and yet should so completely vanish from the face of the earth? Mrs. A. Sidney Holderness, inheritor in the primogeniture line of descent of various Crockett relics, replied to my inquiry (based on the statement of the authors of a Crockett book that she had such a diary): "I do not have nor have ever had a diary of Davy," adding that she knew of none.[7] I once was startled, having reflected on all the above evidence, by a line from a letter of David's grandson, Ashley W. Crockett: "I have heard of unsupported stories that he wrote letters home after he entered the Alamo in February, 1836, but I doubt the truth of these stories. Of course, we have his brief diary covering his *last week* before the Alamo fell, of which you doubtless have read."[8] To my immediate inquiry, he answered, running into the ground another fiction, by saying: "Referring to your letter of 26th inst., I wish to say that the diary of David Crockett's I mentioned in my letter was a printed copy added to a reprint autobiography." [9] None of the other relatives nor anyone else, so far as I have been able to discover, or any authentic record of any place or time, was ever able to produce a shred of evidence that such a diary existed or ever had existed. There was only the melodramatic sequence of the *single final week* of events (to which Mr. Ashley Crockett had referred) in which the playwright Penn Smith had arranged his fictional *Exploits*, as he recounted the imaginary tale. I think enough evidence has been produced already to prove to a reasonable person that this work was completely spurious. Nevertheless, we are dealing with a myth as long-lived as a Phoenix, and I want to scatter its ashes lest it make of them a new flesh.

Upon examination of the contents of the *Exploits*, we note this peculiar fact: that the volume begins with a diary entry for chapter one, and with a second diary entry for chapter two—but thereafter no other diary entry occurs in the entire volume until the final chapter is reached. In the final chapter a number of entries for the final week are recorded in quick succession, carefully and melodramatically arranged in heightening order. (Smith was also a dramatist of the melodramatic variety. *See The Sentinels and Other Plays*, ed. R. H. Ware and H. W. Shoenberger, 1941.) Having made a collection of Crockett's letters, I discovered the basis for these first two diary entries of the first two chapters—they were two authentic Crockett letters to Carey and Hart that Mr. Carey had turned over to Richard Penn Smith when he commenced writing the *Exploits!* Both of these letters survive in the original, though I have found the owner and secured photostats of only the second, on which the second chapter of the *Exploits* is based. That was the letter, partially transcribed in chapter thirteen, dated August 11, 1835, from Weakley County—though not "at home." Chapter two of the *Exploits* begins: "August 11, 1835. I am now at home in Weakly County. My canvass is over," and so on, the entire letter in content and phraseology being reproduced there as a "diary entry," though Smith inserted comments from time to time and made some minor alterations. This single fact not only disproves the "diary" story, but also absolutely proves that Smith wrote the book for Carey and Hart. How else could the author of the *Exploits* have come into possession of two letters written to Carey and Hart? This evidence seems irrefutable.

As for the first chapter of the *Exploits*, and the first "diary" entry, chapter one begins thus: "I begin this book on the 8th day of July, 1835, at Home, Weakly county, Tennessee"; and it contains the statement that: "I tell him [Adam Huntsman] in my speech that I have great hopes of writing one more book, and that shall be the second fall of Adam, for he is on the Eve of an almighty thrashing." The letter David wrote Carey and Hart on July 8, 1835, contained a statement about writing one more book. In the light of chapter two and the Crockett letter on which it was based, I am sure that chapter one was based on an earlier letter from David, and that chapter one gives us the true context in which David desired to write one more book. It was not a serious expression to his publishers to write another book at all. The occurrence of that sentence, the date of the letter, and its place of writing both in the letter and in chapter one of the *Exploits*, when examined in the light of what was done and proven in chapter two with David's letter of August 11, certifies to the accuracy of the discovery. The first chapter was also based on a Crockett letter in the possession of, and addressed to, Carey and Hart.

It is apparent that the two Crockett holographs were the bases for these two "diary entries." By examining the holograph available to us and studying what Smith did with that in chapter two, it it possible to reconstruct from his chapter one a fairly reliable text for the other authentic holograph which exists but which I have not located. Smith's misspelling of Weakley twice, and his gratuitous designation of that county as David's home, would further disprove that David had made any such diary entries, if such proof were yet necessary. It reveals instead that Smith was careless and also that he had still other materials (such as the *Tour* or the Downing Letters or that single letter from Richard Smith of the U.S. Bank, addressed "at home Weakley County") from which to draw.

If this scatters the ashes, let us finally dynamite the spot. Here is some internal evidence taken from a letter which Dr. Alex Dienst, of Temple, Texas, wrote to Dr. John Donald Wade, commenting on Dr. Wade's article on the authorship of the *Autobiography*.[10] Dr. Dienst did not fully agree with Dr. Wade's article because he was inclined to believe too implicitly in David's claims of authorship. However, on the subject of the *Exploits* his critical faculties were perfectly sound:

... it is *fiction* pure and simple. It is a compilation made from current historical books published concerning the war in Texas. *There is not one word in that entire mess written by Crockett.* I analyzed the book when I recd. it years ago. . . . It exasperated me to see a man attempt to palm such stuff off as history or diary by Crockett the Martyr.[11]

Dr. Dienst was correct in intent, though technically in error, for two modified letters of David's were included in that volume. Dienst proceeded to give an illustration or two of the factual errors, including the statement of the opening pages of Chapter III that: "I . . . took hold of my rifle, Betsey, which all the world knows was presented to me by the patriotic citi-

zens of Philadelphia... and thus equipped I started off [to Texas]...."
Dr. Dienst remarks: "He did *not* take the Philadelphia rifle, it was left at
home." We know that this is true. Finally, he quoted again from the melodramatic last chapter, Chapter XIII, the entry dated February 23, describing the flag which flew over the Alamo: "thirteen stripes, red and white,
alternately, on a blue ground with a large white star, of five points, in the
centre, and between the points the letters TEXAS." About that he said:

This is a description given by several of the first monograph writers and
even a few careless historians and copied verbatim by this *diary imposter!*
Every student of Texas history knows absolutely that the flag flying over
the Alamo at this time was the Mexican Constitution flag of 1824 with the
numerals in large letters—1824—on the flag. No *stars*, stripes, or TEXAS.
The Martyrs of the Alamo did not even know that the Texans Declaration
of Independence was on March 2 four days previously [they were besieged inside]. This one absolute *lie proven* will convince any historian
that the entire *Texas diary* is a pure fiction as Crockett certainly would
have described the real flag, 1824, had he *written the diary.* [Dr. Dienst's
italics]

But to make the mistake even more preposterous, Dr. Dienst should have
pointed out that the "diary" entry describing the Texas flag was dated,
not March 3, 4, 5, or 6, *after* the Texas Declaration of Independence, but
February 23, eight days prior to that event!

There is, of course, multitudinous internal evidence which could be ad-
duced, but surely this is sufficient. I hope it concludes for good the myth
of the diary of David Crockett which has for so long bemused the public,
or of any relation between David and that work, except for his two pur-
loined letters. The *Texas Exploits* was not in any way related to the *political* exploitation of Crockett, popular in the early days, but was instead a
publisher's exploitation of his name and fame in a literary type of sham
which has become more popular of late.

APPENDIX 4

PORTRAIT OF DAVID CROCKETT

No reminiscences or portraits describing Crockett before his entry into
the national Congress survive. Those that depict him fall into three distinct
categories: those of his honest friends; those of his honest enemies; and
those of the thieves of Jericho who cared nothing for him but would use

or abuse him in accordance with how it served their purposes. As for his visual image, there is little enough to go on at any date, except for his later portraits, and some of these are not reliable. Verbal descriptions of him, too, are blurred by a mass of deliberate fiction. From all this chaff, the truth is difficult to winnow.

Robert Patton Crockett, David's youngest son (oldest child of his second marriage) was born sometime in 1816. In 1947 and thereafter, when I corresponded with the family, three of the children of this Robert Patton were yet living: Ashley W. Crockett; a sister in Illinois, no longer able to correspond; and Mrs. T. H. Hiner. Since Robert Patton was almost twenty at David's death, I had hoped to obtain, through his children, authentic descriptions of David. Both grandchildren, obviously without prior consultation, wrote the same disclaimer and the same guess. Mr. Ashley W. Crockett, under date of Nov. 12, 1947, wrote: "I do not remember of hearing my father speak of David Crockett's physical make up, his size or his weight. I would think, as he spent his life mostly outdoors that he must have been in very robust health and of very compact build. I imagine he was of average height, say 5 ft. 8 inches." Mrs. Hiner, writing from Fort Worth on Nov. 14, 1947, replied similarly: "I never heard my father speak of his personal appearance, He was not a large man his hight I imagine was five feet 8 or ten inches was not a fleshy man at all. Had dark blue eyes & broun hair was not bald at all." In giving his coloring Mrs. Hiner may have been describing the paintings with which she grew up.

Had David been of unusual proportions, "Six feet four in his stocking feet," as some fictional accounts have it, that unusual fact would have been a matter of comment both by his family and contemporaries whose reminiscences survive. He was probably of average height, of muscular build, had thick brown hair and blue eyes, and wore red roses in his cheeks. A previously cited letter from Crockett to James Blackburn for Feb. 5, 1828, remarks: "the last attact was the pluricy the doctor took two quarts of Blood from me at one time I am much Reduced in flesh and have lost all my Red Rosy Cheeks that I have carryed So many years." His constitution must have been formidable before sickness struck him, and even then he must have retained a remarkable physique to have been able, at forty-nine, to set out for the wilds of Texas.

Dr. S. H. Stout, partially prejudiced in David's behalf, saw him for the first time in 1829 as Crockett stopped in Nashville for a visit on his way to his second term in Congress. His inadequate description (in "David Crockett," pp. 3-21) is:

When he arrived ... everybody wanted to see him, shake hands with him and congratulate him, save a few, who, more learned than he, thought they should be sent to Congress. My boyish curiosity to see him was gratified ... in Nashville in the Presbyterian Church.... in the family pew of Mr. George Crockett, one of the leading merchants and a respected citizen of the city.... [He was] of Scotch-Irish descent, and the clan of the Crocketts in the old country. I was in the pew immediately in front. My admiration of his character engendered by what I had heard of him, and my childish curiosity, got the better of my politeness ... and I turned around and looked at him steadily until with a nod and a smile, he indicated that he was more amused than offended. I have never forgotten his face and that smile on that occasion. In the *Confederate Veteran*, published in Nashville ... of June, 1894, appeared a beautifully printed engraving of a photographic copy of a portrait of Crockett, that must have been painted about that time, for it recalls his features, his dress, the high collared coat, fashionable then, his handsome face, high forehead, moderately long hair —then also fashionable, and that benevolent, good humored expression, that those who ever saw him can never forget. I often saw him afterward at church and on the street.

From this testimony, Crockett's reputation had already spread widely and was perhaps even beginning to reach the proportions of legend. Stout's reference to his fashionable dress is part of a theme he argues more explicitly, that David never affected clothes in Congress or in town other than those in customary good taste. Partial verification comes from Ashley Crockett, who comments in the previously cited letter: "There are some pictures of grandfather printed in newspapers and magazines that are imaginary, showing him in hunting costume and wearing a coon skin cap. I don't think he ever had a picture made of him while in hunting uniform." There is no question that David wore various rough clothes for hunting and living in the woods. However, those portraits showing him in backwoods garb in urban scenes are only sentimental fictions.

Stout (pp. 18-19) verified his recollection of David's dress by interrogating Captain William L. Foster, whose father, Senator Ephraim H. Foster, had been an intimate friend and associate of David's. Captain Foster, five years Stout's senior, replied:

I remember David Crockett well and always with pleasure. He was very often a guest of my father, always a pleasant, courteous, and interesting man, who, though uneducated in books, was a man of fine instincts and intellect, and entertained a laudable ambition to make his mark in the world. He was a man of a high sense of honor, of good morals, not intemperate, nor a gambler. I never saw him attired in a garb that could be regarded as differing from that worn by gentlemen of his day—never in coon skin cap or hunting shirt. He acquired his reputation as a successful hunter after he removed to West Tennessee, where for several years the settlers had to depend upon wild game for their chief article of food.

Crockett's *Autobiography* disputes Foster's last sentence, saying his reputation as hunter began when he moved to middle Tennessee. In 1843-44 Stout lived in west Tennessee and became acquainted with David's neighbors and with his eldest son, John Wesley. He reports on the basis of that experience that all who had known him loved to talk about him and about his noble qualities of head and heart, giving evidence again of those indefinable qualities which tended to make David, even during his lifetime, a legend.

On the subject of David's oratorical appeal, as evidenced by his success in various elections, Stout says that he was the most popular politician in the Congressional district, that he could get together larger crowds and hold them longer than anyone else, that as a stump-speaker he was first-rate.

The father of Marcus J. Wright, though politically opposed to David, seems to have thought well of him. In the Johns Hopkins Library is a letter addressed from the War Department, on November 3, 1888, to James R. Gilmore who, under the pseudonym of Richard Kirke, wrote history and fiction from 1863 to 1888 about the post-Revolutionary, the Civil, and the post-Civil War periods of American History. Wright himself had published an account of David in 1883, republished in 1897. Unfortunately instead of giving us his actual memories, he draws from the *Autobiography*, with the exception of a very few remarks about David's stand on national politics and a half-page close, not reliable, on the fall of the Alamo. The following is an excerpt from this letter:

It occurred to me, that you ought to write an authentic life of Col. David Crockett, *I think* he was a *great man*, There are some half dozen *so called* lives of him, some or all of them contain many truths, and many falsehoods. . . . I as a six year old boy heard him speak as a candidate for Congress against Judge Fitzgerald, He represented West Tenn the district I was born in, My father an old officer of the Army & a fast friend of Genl Jackson, was opposed to him, yet he was my fathers guest when at our County town. . . .

Marcus J. Wright

Finally, John Wesley, in an unpublished letter owned by the Tennessee Historical Society, announced his father's death to his Uncle George Patton, saying: "on his death like Sampson, he slew more of his enemies than in all of his life. [For] even his most biter enemies here, I believe, have buried all animosity, and joined the general lamentation. . . ."

These are reminiscences from honest friends of Crockett. Among his honest enemies must be included James K. Polk, Colonel Robert I. Chester, Andrew Jackson, and others. Recent scholarship has tended to place President Polk at a much higher level than that of a Jackson "yes-man," a reevaluation that is unquestionably deserved. It remains true, nevertheless, that as a younger and developing politician, he was a very regular party man. One cannot follow the legislative and Congressional careers of his early years without seeing very clearly that, if one wished to know how Jackson was blowing, he would best cast an eye in the direction of Polk.

Some of the very qualities which lent great strength of character to Jackson were the same qualities which sometimes made him follow courses neither fair nor just: for accentuation can be achieved only at some expense to impartiality. Impetuosity and quick decisiveness enabled him to be a forceful leader. Such daring, predicated on a lack of hesitation and patience, of necessity often missed many considerations which a more deliberate and discriminating care would have seen. His iron determination, backed by an overpowering will, forced him to pursue without quarter what his deepest conviction told him was right, and to carry it against heavily unequal odds to a successful conclusion—whether against Indians, mutiny, the English, Secession (Nullification), or a Second United States Bank. The same will, coupled with unhesitating certainty that his honesty of motives was a guarantee of the correctness of his opinions, led him to fight to the end more than one man as fair and as honest as he was himself, but whose difference of opinions he could only comprehend as disloyalty or treachery. No more than with Polk can we accept the judgments of Jackson merely on the basis of his fame or on that of his integrity.

Jackson doesn't give extended views of Crockett. From a number of occasional references in his personal letters, his judgment is crystal clear. These references have already been quoted in the body of the text.

Another honest enemy was Robert I. Chester, whose reminiscences need be discounted little if at all because of his family ties with Jackson. Turner, who transcribed the reminiscences in his "Reminiscences of Colonel Chester" (pp. 385-87), had remarked that some people had placed Crockett and Jackson in the same rank: "They stood on a very different plane. Jackson was a wonderful man. Crockett was a backwoodsman only." Later returning to the same subject, he added:

David Crockett was a backwoodsman, strong, keen eyed, observant. On the stump he told anecdotes that pleased the people, but in Congress he was without influence. Crockett's cabin on the Obion River, was open to all. I once crossed that river in a canoe—my horse swimming by me—and slept in his house on a bear-skin, and ate bear-meat with a bowie knife and a cane fork.... Crockett boasted a great deal about a coat made from American wool sent him from New England.

He went on to insist that Crockett was not comparable to Jackson as a soldier or as a statesman, though he was partially wrong that Crockett had little influence in Congress. He came to have little; but, from whatever exigencies, he had influence there in his first years. Chester's reminiscences, as reported by Turner, were corroborated by Colyar (*Life and Times of Andrew Jackson*, pp. 178-79).

The date of Chester's visit is definitely established by the coat of wool given David by one of the New England mills. This could only have occurred after his Eastern tour during his last Congress, late in 1834. The bearskins, the dirt floors, though he had been for five years a member of Congress, his pride in this flimsy gift as evidence of a friendship which more and more he came to need, his simple ambition and his childlike naïveté which allowed him to brag in open innocence to a friend and relative of Jackson's about what a Jackson man could only have looked on as one more bribe for his joining with the Eastern forces against Jackson, his standing welcome in his impoverished cabin to all comers—these make a picture which forbids one absolutely to see in him a cunning, an ambition-dominated, an evil man. "Crockett boasted a great deal about a coat made from American wool sent him from New England" contains, for one who knows *all* of the implications of that statement, a terrible pathos.

Polk, Chester, and Jackson had legitimate reasons for regarding Crockett as an adversary. If they were prejudiced, their prejudices were honest ones. Their remarks concealed no ulterior motives and, when taken in the context of their points of view, are not difficult to square with the facts. There was another group who did not love or hate David but who were willing to use and if necessary destroy him if his use or destruction could serve their purposes. They were the men whose kind remarks about him were calculated to make of him a national figure so that, as a weapon in their hands, he would be more effective in their war upon Jackson. These were the thieves of Jericho who fell upon him. Of all of those who have used him to their own purposes (politicians, financiers, publishers, writers, historians, native sons, descendants, genealogists), those who waylaid him at Jericho were the most heartless, the least interested in the man as man, and the least worthy of tolerant indulgence. Among this group were leading Whig publishers of the time, some of whom were subsidized by the Second United States Bank. Two brief quotations from these sources will suffice.

The editor of *Niles Register* first took note of David about the time of his defeat for Congress in 1831. Once he was re-elected with Whig help, *Niles Register* set the lead in putting him to Whig music. Gales and Seaton, publishers of the *Congressional Debates* and of the *National Intelligencer*, cooperated, even writing many of his speeches. Only a few days after Crockett's re-election in August, 1833, but three months before he was to return to Washington after an absence of two years, *Niles* published this reminiscence of him on September 7 (XLV, 21):

A great deal has been said in the newspapers concerning Col. Crockett, who has been again elected a member of Congress from Tennessee. It was the misfortune of the colonel to have received no school education in his youth, and since to have had but little opportunity to retrieve that defect; but he is a man of a strong mind, and of great goodness of heart. The *manner* of his remarks are [*sic*] so peculiar that they excite much attention, and are repeated because of their originality; but there is a soundness, or point, in some of them which shews the exercise of a well disciplined judgment—and we think it not easy for an unprejudiced man to communicate with the colonel without feeling that he is honest. We have had some opportunity of knowing the calibre of many members of Congress for 25 or 30 years past, and have met with many, very many, far less capable of ascertaining the truth than Col. C.—much less attentive to the duties of their place.... But the colonel does not thus [like an automoton] say a ye or no—for, whether right or wrong, *the vote is his own.*
We have been oftentimes asked, "What sort of a man is Colonel Crockett?" and the general reply was—"just such a one as you would desire to meet with, if any accident or misfortune happened to you on the highway!"

The editor's italicized words are important. It was necessary that Crockett in particular and the public in general *believe* that David's vote was his own if the Whig strategy was to be successful with either.
Another sample from the same journal for May 3, 1834, was attributed to the correspondent of the Portland, Maine, *Advertiser* (in *Niles Register*, XLVI, 148), who was describing a long and excitable debate on the House floor on the proposition to abolish the office of the draftsman of the House, as an economy measure. Crockett opposed it on the grounds that it made a show of economy to camouflage the lack of honest administrative intent to effect real retrenchment:

And so the debate run on, as water runs down hill... but there was not much in it—till Col. *Crockett* arose. Now every pen was dropped—every nerve aroused—every eye was fixed—every whisper hushed! None but orators can throw such a calm over the stormy waters—and, therefore, the colonel must be an orator; Friends and enemies rallied around. The galleries hurried to the balustrades—and the colonel began. There is some men whom you cannot report. The colonel is one. His leer you cannot put upon paper—his curious drawl—the odd cant of his body and his self-congratulation. He is an original in everything, in the tone and structure of his sentences, in the force and novelty of metaphors, and in his range of ideas. "I thought," said the colonel, "when in 1826 the gentleman from New York (Mr. Cambreleng), was for cutting down the office of draftsman, it was for reforming a little to get more. [But] It was like the children on the branch of a great tree hanging over the river, sitting there and fishing with pin hooks to catch minnows. It was like shearing a hog—great squeal and little wool."

McDuffie's most potent thunder, Burges' wit, Binney's logic, could not have won such a burst of applause from the magnates of the land. The colonel sat down with delight—and the members here and there gave him a shake of the hand, as they often do when a man does a wonderful thing.

Were the account true it would be more interesting. Crockett had not been in Congress in 1826, nor had the economy measure been passed then. Furthermore, in 1834, David was no longer capable of inspiring such a demonstration. This is all a part of the Crockett abuse by a Whig press. The official record indicates that he did employ the metaphors cited, though in a somewhat different and clearer context. It is just possible that the description of his mannerisms and physical appearance is accurate. The metaphors have the earmarks of spontaneity and of Crockett thinking and talking.

Having sampled brief opinions from his admirers, his enemies, and his exploiters, we turn now to a brief discussion of David's oil portraits. I have found a record of eight or nine, at least two of which no longer survive.

The first hung for years in the home of Robert Patton Crockett, David's youngest son, who gave it eventually to the state of Texas. This was destroyed when the Texas Capitol burned. It seems reasonable to assume that Robert would have allowed to hang in his home for years, and then would have passed on to the state as the recognized official likeness of his father, only a portrait which he considered highly authentic. Robert's son, Ashley Crockett, remembered that portrait which hung in his father's home. Of the painting destroyed by fire, Ashley wrote me in November, 1947:

The picture of him that was in my father's home in Texas and was destroyed in the burning of the Texas State Capitol was an oil painting, large size, and showed him sitting at a table, while in Congress at Washington.

It presented a full face view, depicting a ruddy countenance, with his hair parted in the middle, as he always wore it. He wore the dress of a member of Congress, with a high standing collar.

The second portrait, which may or may not be one of those listed separately below, is one discussed by a Crockett holograph of May 5, 1830, which had been lost and which David was trying to recover. (He had rolled it up and marked it "a map of Florida.") He states there that the painting had been done by Hincley. This may have been the earliest portrait ever made of him, and so far as I know it was never recovered.

A third is one "painted by John L. Chapman when Crockett was a member of Congress in 1834. [It] ... is now in the Alamo, cared for by the 'Daughters of the Republic of Texas.' " From the print I have seen, David's hair is tightly plastered to his head, his nose is beaked, and his face appears flat, his clothes informal, though urban, with open Byronic collar. I think it a "romanticized hunter" portrait, having more of the type than of the individual in the face. A letter of June 12, 1878, of an earlier grandson, Robert H. Crockett (son of David's oldest son, John Wesley), states that John Wesley had not considered the Chapman portrait to be the best likeness of his father (letter owned by Tennessee Historical Society, Nashville).

Two portraits which I have never seen in original or reliable copy are owned by Mrs. A. Sidney Holderness, great-great-grand-daughter of David, who inherited them through the primogeniture line of descent (by way of John Wesley and Robert H. above). One is a small aquatint and crayon likeness done by James Hamilton Shegoyne in 1833. The other, a half-length full-size portrait by Rembrandt Peale, is one which at least one grandson endorses. Robert H. Crockett, in a letter of February 4, 1879, refers to this one as being "the best likeness, or at least was so considered, by my father and others." (Owned by Tennessee Historical Society. I believe this may be the portrait from which was made the photograph which S. H. Stout said resembled Crockett as he looked in 1829, the photograph appearing in the *Confederate Veteran* [II, 167] for June, 1894.) Mrs. Holderness writes that this portrait is unfortunately no longer legible.

I have said that David's hair was brown and his eyes blue. A contradictory report should be noted which comes from the owner of this portrait. In describing the two portraits, Mrs. Holderness writes on July 13, 1950:

I do not know that I can be of a great deal of assistance to you in the matter of old Davy's coloring. The Peale portrait which I own has so darkened with age that it is difficult to even see the figure itself, and one must stand at a certain angle and have the light just right to do even this. The hair and the complexion in the oil portrait, therefore, are necessarily all rather dark.

The crayon and aqua tint picture . . . 1833 is in somewhat better condition. From this picture I would judge that his hair and heavy brows were black, his eyes a dark brown, and his complexion highcolored or ruddy. He was clean-shaven, but from the darkish appearance of his cheeks and chin, he looked as if he might have had a heavy beard, had he not shaved often.

A poor replica of this Peale portrait is owned by the Tennessee Historical Society, which in 1878 borrowed the original from Robert H. Crockett for copying. The copy was made by Louise Goodwin of Nashville, but Robert H. was so displeased with the photograph of it sent him that he urged the destruction of the negative. In this copy David appears as a gentlemanly young pickwickian Englishman rather than a Tennessee backwoodsman. The features appear to have been shortened, the face rounded. The nose is abbreviated and slightly retrousse. I regard it as highly romanticized and unreliable.

The New-York Historical Society owns a water color portrait of Crockett on paper, 9¾ x 7¾ inches, painted by Anthony Lewis DeRose.

Another portrait is one painted about 1834 by Samuel Stillman Osgood. I do not know who now owns the original, or whether it survives, but reproductions of it exist in two forms.

T. B. Welch made an engraving from this portrait, and this is the form of the Osgood painting which seems to have been most widely employed. This particular reproduction contains beneath it an authentic signature of Crockett and, whether he affixed it to the Welch engraving or not, the signature seems to be reliable.

The other impression of this Osgood painting is a lithograph by Childs and Lehman, the lithograph itself having been copyrighted by the painter, Osgood, in 1834. This fact establishes the lithographic likeness as being near enough the original to satisfy the artistic tastes of the painter himself, as the Welch engraving does not, and recommends it for that additional reason. On March 16, 1948, Mr. Ashley W. Crockett wrote me about this photograph:

After careful examination of the picture of David Crockett you sent me, I am inclined to believe it is nearer like the original one which my father had in his home [than is the Welch engraving]. . . . If you were to place a table in front of this picture you sent me, and put a goose quill pen in his hand, it would be almost exactly like the one that hung in my father's home. . . . I would appreciate a copy of this picture of grandfather, if you can send it. I can have it framed for my home.

I regard this testimony of the grandson as satisfactory evidence of the reliability of this photograph. It should be noted, however, as I pointed out to Mr. Ashley Crockett, that the superscription appearing on this photograph may be in David's hand but the signature itself is not. Among the more obvious dissimilarities between David's usual autograph and this are the addition here of the final *e*, the formation of the double *t*, the design of the flourish for crossing it, the separation of the *o* from the *r*, and the lack of separation at the right juncture of the *c* and the *k*. The statement above the signature is either a much more careful forgery, or else is authentic David script. I believe that the superscription was probably written by David, who perhaps unintentionally failed to add his signature; and that the signature was added by another, possibly Osgood, for whom David had written the inscription.

Finally, in Chapter III of *An Account of Col. Crockett's Tour to the North and Down East* David says that on May 4, 1834, he sat for his portrait for a Mr. Harding, in Boston. It is not clear in context whether Mr. Harding is the patron or the artist. This portrait, therefore, may be one of those listed above, or it may be another.

Notes

(Only short titles have been employed in these notes. Immediately following is a complete alphabetical list of all works cited, with fuller bibliographical information.)

Chapter 1

1. Crockett's paternal ancestry was Norman-French and Irish, his maternal English. Great great great grandfather, Antoine de Crocketagne, agent for salt and wine merchants in southern France, was converted by them to Protestantism before third quarter of 17th century. Then Louis XIV ordered Huguenots to leave the south of France; and Antoine fled with his family to England, then to Ireland, settling at Bantry Bay. His third son, Joseph Louis, presumably arrived at the age of discretion, took to wife Sarah Stewart and joined the migration of Irish folk to America about 1708, fleeing from economic distress and religious persecution. They settled first at New Rochelle, New York, but soon moved to Pennsylvania, then to Virginia, appearing in the South prior to that trans-Appalachian leap for the Pacific. David's *Autobiography* says that his father (John) was, *he thought*, born either in Ireland or on the way over. His childhood recollections were confused. His great grandfather, son of Joseph Louis and Sarah Stewart, was born on the final part of the voyage or shortly after arrival, for the records list his birth as 1709 in New Rochelle, his name being William. William, with his father, Joseph Louis, arrived in Virginia between 1716 and 1718.

The English forbears of Crockett's mother, Rebecca Hawkins, arrived in Gloucester or Matthew County, Virginia, in 1658. Her father was Joseph, born about 1712 and married in 1739 to the Quakeress, Anneke Jane Edwards. Of the nine children of this marriage, Rebecca was one; another was Sarah, who was to marry John Sevier, of King's Mountain fame and first governor of Tennessee. For the most complete work on Crockett genealogy see J. S. French and Z. Armstrong, pp. 1-9, 203-4, 327-29, and especially p. 538, the "Maury Letter." For the genealogy of David's brothers and sisters, and his children, see also pp. 341-81.

2. J. S. French and Z. Armstrong, *The Crockett Family and* ...., pp. 372, 543-44.

3. W. L. Saunders, *Colonial Records of North Carolina*, X, 708-11.

4. *Ibid.*, XI, 458.

5. J. S. French and Z. Armstrong, *The Crockett Family and* ...., pp. 372-73, citing *First Minute Book Court Records*, Washington County, Virginia. The reader will recall that not until two years later, in 1779, was it discovered that this extreme territory belonged to North Carolina instead of to Virginia, hence the recording of the event in Virginia.

6. It reads: "Here lie the bodies of David Crockett and his wife, Grandparents of 'Davy' Crockett, who were massacred near this spot by Indians in 1777. Division of History, State of Tenn. 1927."

7. *Washington County* (North Carolina, now Tennessee) *Court of Pleas and Quarter Sessions, 1778-98*, I, 46. John came from the western side of the mountains to fight at the Battle of King's Mountain, Oct. 7, 1780.

8. L. W. Reynolds, "The Pioneer Crockett...," *D.A.R. Magazine*, LV., 188-89; *Greene County Minutes of Court of Pleas and Quarter Sessions, 1783-96*, pp. 40, 139. John's brother Robert was also a constable in Greene.

9. L. W. Reynolds, "The Pioneer Crockett...," *D.A.R. Magazine*, LV, pp. 188-89.

10. *Green County Minutes of Pleas and Quarter Sessions, 1783-90*, p. 468.

11. *Sullivan County Deed Book, 1775-90*, I, 196, 218.

12. *North Carolina Land Grants* (State Land Office, Nashville, Tennessee, Book No. 2), p. 490.

13. Original record in *Jefferson County Deed Record Book "CD," 1792-99*, pp. 159-60, item 89,—later transferred with errors to *Deed Book "Q", 1797-1802*, pp. 94-95, both at County Court House, Dandridge, Tennessee.

14. Some have placed it east rather than north of Dandridge. But early maps show that prior to 1800 there was only one road running through the county to Washington, D. C., the "Main Holston road" of the cited document. John's tavern was on this road. Not until 1814 do maps record a second road running south through Dandridge, then east, and finally turning north and coming into the earlier road at about the Virginia line. The Tavern was about ten to twelve miles north, not east, of Dandridge on the earlier Knoxville to Washington Road, in the neighborhood of the present Jefferson City, then called Mossy Creek.

15. *Jefferson County Book No. One, 1792-1810*, pp. 176, 354.

16. Most records of him to his nineteenth year are contained herein. For two reasons we think this account of his early years reliable. First, what few parallel documents do exist for the early period corroborate the story. Second, the many independent documents for the later years demonstrate the exceeding accuracy of the latter portions of the *Autobiography* and lead to the conclusion that the earlier portions are equally trustworthy. Another volume, an anonymous "biography" of 1833, though disavowed by Crockett, was certainly written from his own recounting, with or without his knowledge that it was to be published. It needs, however, to be carefully discounted with reference both to its political discolorations and its romanticizing and mythologizing tendencies. The biographical data it gives are not strictly reliable where they diverge, infrequently, from David's own account. But the date and circumstances of its composition and its author's knowledge of frontier life give it an authenticity of atmosphere worthy a reader's attention. This biography, however, has drawn on it sparingly, and always with a citation to it as the source.

17. He had four older brothers, the oldest not known by name. The others, in the order of their ages, were James, William, and Wilson.

18. According to the 1833 anonymous *Life* of Crockett, the reunion between David and his father was not as amicable as David's *Autobiography* indicates. Perhaps the most serious *unintentional* errors David makes in his account of his life (he deliberately inserted a few war experiences from the whole cloth) are chronological ones, and this is hardly surprising inasmuch as he wrote the story as a man of forty-eight looking back upon a very eventful life, with no notes and a not-to-finical memory. He says that he returned home from this trip when he was almost *fifteen*, instead of almost sixteen, as a bit later he tells us that he was about *eighteen* when he took out his first marriage license, though the surviving document itself shows that he was nineteen. But the facts are accurate, only the time of their occurrence slightly in error.

19. *Jefferson County Marriage and Bond Book, 1792-1840*, p. 53.

20. That instrument itself seems not to have survived, but the fact of its issuance and the date are recorded in the *Jefferson County Marriage and Bond Book, 1792-1940*, and reads: "David Crockett to Polly Finley Aug 12 1806." But another document, perhaps as interesting, does survive and hangs in a sealed frame on the wall of the county

clerk's office in Dandridge. It is the cited bond which all applicants had to post to certify that a proposed marriage was in good faith.

It is well to note here the fact that David could at this time at least write his own name. I have personally examined the document.

21. *Jefferson County Will Book*, II, 237-39.

22. *Margaret* Crockett appears twice in the *Dumplin Baptist Church Minutes* cited above.

23. This is one of the few dates he gives in his *Autobiography*. Previous accounts of David's removal to middle Tennessee have erred in drawing on this, as well as on other dates calculated from this, such as the dates for the birth of his children. On September 11, 1811, David Crockett appeared in Jefferson County as a juror in the case of Jenken Whitesides *vs.* Alexander Outlaw (*Jefferson County Court Minute Book No. 5, 1810-11*, p. 191. Dandridge is the county seat of Jefferson, which is in east Tennessee.). Had David not still been a resident of the county he would not have been subject to jury duty. It will be remembered that David has told us that he *first* settled in Lincoln County, "on the head of Mulberry fork of Elk River." There are no records of him in Lincoln County prior to 1812, and the record existing of him there at that time is for land at the spot where he says he first settled: "Surveyed. David Crockett . . . —enters 5 acres of land in Lincoln County and on the head waters of the East fork of Mulberry Creek a North Branch of Elk River. BEGINNING at a Beech Marked D.C. Standing about 60 or 70 yards north eastwardly from S'd Crocketts house running thence West in Oblong and South for quantity, 25th., April 1812, including Sd Crocketts house and improvement,

David Crockett."

(From *Surveyors Entry Book C, Surveyors District II*, Entry No. 3944, p. 414, Tennessee State Archives.)

24. In 1871 a new county, Moore, was made from parts of Lincoln and Franklin Counties. The spot where David lived is about a mile and a half within the Moore County boundary line, northeast of Fayetteville.

Chapter 2

1. Settlement of this territory, then a wilderness, had begun about 1800. The county was created on December 3, 1807, the first court convened at the home of Major Russell, one of the first settlers, early in 1808, and in 1810 the town of Winchester was laid out.

2. J. A. Henderson, "Unmarked Historic Spots of . . . ," *Tennessee Historical Magazine*, pp. 111-20. The article also contains accounts and photographs of the spot where Crockett's house once stood. The name of his homeplace, "Kentuck," I accept from some unpublished notes which Mr. Charlie E. Gowen took in the summer of 1904 from an 84-year-old "Uncle" William Floyd, who got them from Mr. Charlie Gowen's grandfather, a personal friend of Crockett's in middle Tennessee. The notes were brought to my attention by Mr. F. W. Motlow of Tullahoma, Tennessee.

3. H. S. Halbert and T. H. Ball, *The Creek War*, pp. 147-48.

4. David says that the recruits met once, and again "a day or two after this," and that both meetings were more than a week before they started south. "We then received orders to start on the next Monday week." Since the day of rendezvous in Huntsville was Friday, September 24, and David says they started from Winchester on a Monday, the starting date must have been September 20, and the days of the original musters in Winchester more than a week earlier at least as early as Thursday and Saturday, September 9 and 11, ten and twelve days after the massacre at Mimms.

David's account of the organization to which he belonged and the men under whom he served prove to be remarkably accurate. He relates that when they first paraded in Winchester, a local lawyer there, a Mr. Jones, later in Congress from Tennessee, raised a company which David joined, and that at the second meeting this Jones was elected captain of the company. This is corroborated by the *Congressional Directory*, which reveals that a Francis Jones, Captain, local lawyer from Winchester, represented Tennessee in the National Congress from 1817 to 1821. It is also a fact that military officers in the local militia were then elective, for military and civil duties, like military and civil districts, overlapped.

From the muster and payroll records we learn that David (number 18 on the muster roll) was a private in Captain Francis Jones's company of Tennessee Volunteer Mounted Riflemen in the regiment of Colonel Newton Cannon. They marched from Winchester, Franklin County, forty miles to Huntsville, then Mississippi territory, where they were mustered in on Friday, September 24, 1813, for a period of three months, or until December 24 of that year. See *Creek Indian War Muster and Payroll Records*, War Records Division, National Archives, Washington, D. C. Photostatic copies of all those pertaining to the Tennessee troops are bound in unpaginated volumes in the State Capitol Library, Nashville, Tennessee. For this entry see photostats thereunder title of *War of 1812*, Vol. 3, Photostat No.11-c-1(3).

5. Creek War Records give his complete name as Major John H. Gibson, second major under Colonel Coffee. Coffee was soon to be promoted to Brigadier General on October 29, 1813, and placed also over the regiment which Colonel Cannon was commanding. Hence Coffee was to become Crockett's commanding general. During these early days Cannon, who had not yet arrived, was a captain. Coffee was a colonel and all the troops at Beaty's Spring were under his temporary command.

6. "Major" was a courtesy title. His real rank was captain.

7. S. P. Waldo, *Memoirs of Jackson*, p. 72.

8. Augustus De Morgan, *The Book of Almanacs*, p. 59.

9. S. P. Waldo, *Memoirs of Jackson*, p. 76-78.

10. David may be in error when he states that a Lieutenant Moore was killed. Jackson's account reported no officer lost.

11. A. S. Colyar, in *Life and Times of Andrew Jackson*, pp. 82-83, records it. He makes General Moore, of Lincoln County, from whom he got the story, captain at the time of David's company, an obvious error. Did the story not fit so neatly into attempts to reconcile two irreconcilable Tennessee native sons, one might entertain it longer. But to off-set its probability is Dr. S. H. Stout's statement (young Tennessee contemporary of David's) that the expression was general and that David's fame was responsible for making it exclusively his in later years; the fact that David never had a captain named Moore; and the fact that we find no documentary association of David with this motto until May 19, 1831, on a deed and bill of sale to his brother-in-law, George Patton, where it reads, "Be allways sure you are right then Go, ahead."

12. Here is the background for the following mutiny. In 1812 Congress authorized the raising of a Volunteer Corps of 50,000 men because of the unsettled relations with the British. They were to give *one year of service within a two-year period from the date of muster in.* Jackson raised 2,500 men, offered them to the government, and was accepted into the national forces in November, being mustered in on December 10, 1812. With Jackson in command, they were ordered down the Ohio and Mississippi for defense of the lower states, and they left their rendezvous on January 7, 1813, starting south. Upon reaching Natchez (Feb. 15) they were ordered to halt and await further instructions. There was then a keen rivalry between the local militias and the regular army, the latter finding it difficult to recruit men. When Jackson received further orders "to dismiss his Volunteers, and deliver all public property in his possession to Major-General Wilkinson," the regular-army commander of that district (with whom Jackson was on unfriendly terms), he "smelled a rat." To dismiss recruits far from their place of enlistment without pay, food, or clothing was contrary to

army policy (though it may have been a *bona fide* blunder of the two-day-appointed new Secretary of War Armstrong). Anyway, Jackson interpreted the order (especially since it was dated prior to his departure from Nashville, yet was not delivered until some time after his arrival in Natchez) as an attempt to force his Volunteers, by deprivation and hardship, into involuntarily joining the regular army. He indignantly refused to obey and set out at once with his men on foot for Tennessee, living under and suffering equally with them the difficult and trying conditions of the return journey. (His iron determination and toughness of physique earned him on this journey the name of "Hickory," later to become "Old Hickory." Incidentally, so suspicious were the circumstances which led to his disobedience, that the administration in Washington finally "approbated his conduct" and paid his men.)

Arriving back in Nashville, the troops were not yet entitled to a discharge for their year of service was not up. Yet the infantry needed their rifles, and the cavalry wished to retain their swords and pistols, which they were authorized to do only upon "discharge." Jackson with implicit trust gave them an *unofficial* discharge and allowed them to return to their homes and retain their arms, with the "gentleman's agreement" that they would return upon call. He seems to have assumed their realization of the fact that he would regard the time spent under this "discharge" as furlough time to be added on to their year's service. When Governor Blount in October issued the order calling out 2,000 militia to prosecute the Creek War, many of these earlier volunteers were called back to finish out their service. But according to official War Department records, these men had been in continuous service and their year would be up about December 10, 1813. Whether the troops confused the matter, or whether two months of fighting and of absence from home argued more strongly with them than a hazy understanding of almost a year earlier, the fact was that a dangerous situation had been created and that legally Jackson did not have a leg to stand on.

When late November arrived, and Jackson had the Indians on the run and was anxious to pursue his advantage and end the war quickly, but found himself faced with adamant soldiers who maintained that their time would be out on December 10, his wrath was boundless. This is the background for the mutiny and for Jackson's action with reference to it.

13. The account is worked into an elaborate figure comparing Jackson's highhandedness on that occasion with that of his removal of the deposits from the U. S. Bank (a controversy in full swing at the time of the writing of the *Autobiography*) such as David could not conceivably have concocted without a great deal of help.

14. *War of 1812*, Vol. 3, Photostat No. 11-c-2(1).

15. This Crockett had previously served under Colonel Thomas Benton, but at the time of his desertion was in the company of Captain James McFerrin under command of Colonel William Pillow. He deserted on November 19, 1813. This was during his period of enlistment from September 26, 1813, to December 10, 1813. The dates, periods, and names are all quite similar, but the periods of enlistment are not concurrent and establish quite as clearly as if one had been named Smith and the other Jones that this was not the David Crockett of our story. Furthermore the David who deserted had come into service at Murfreesboro rather than at Huntsville-via-Winchester, as had the David of this biography. This information may be verified in the *War of 1812* records, Vols. 2 and 7, in Tennessee State Library or in the National Archives in Washington, D. C.

16. Letter to writer dated October 30, 1947.

17. *War of 1812*, Vol. 8, Photostats Nos. 7-c-1(2) and 7-c-2(2).

18. *Knoxville Sunday Journal*, August 17, 1930, News Section B, p. 1.

Chapter 3

1. I have discussed this matter in more detail in an article, "David Crockett and North Carolina," pp. 298-315. The tombstone and monument to Elizabeth in Texas states that the marriage took place in "Lawrence County, Tenn., 1815," though Lawrence County was not even created until October 21, 1817, and even so it is eighty miles from where the marriage took place. The marriage did not take place in 1815. We will not speculate here on the possible reason for this predating of the marriage.

2. J. A. Henderson, "Unmarked Historic Spots . . . ," *Tennessee Historical Magazine*, pp. 111-20.

3. *Tennessee Commission Books*, Tennessee State Archives, Book 3, p. 374.

4. J. A. Henderson, "Unmarked Historic Spots . . . ," *Tennessee Historical Magazine*, pp. 118 ff.

5. T. M. Owen, *History of Alabama and Dictionary of Alabama Biography*, I, 140, 155-57; II, 807, 814-15.

6. The Tennessee village of Jamestown, in Fentress County, near the Kentucky line in the Cumberland Mountains of east Tennessee. Twain's father, John M. Clemens, a lawyer residing there in 1827, drew up the plans for the courthouse which was built in 1828, was the first Circuit Court Clerk of the county, and was by far the largest landowner. A brother of Crockett's father, "deaf and dumb Jimmy Crockett," lived there at this time, as established by surviving court documents. It is possible that David's father likewise lived there for awhile and that David visited there.

7. *Journal of the House of Representatives of Tennessee*, First Session, Twelfth Assembly, 1817, pp. 308-12. Among the records of the Tennessee Historical Society survives one of the twelve original certificates issued these twelve justices.

8. The original handwritten proceedings of this first court of Laurance, now Lawrence, County still survived at the time of the writer's examination of them in August, 1947. The book had been removed from the court house and was in private hands. A word is necessary to describe this valuable documentary source since it may not be indefinitely preserved.

It was in quite a mutilated condition, the first eleven pages were missing, and pages twelve through sixteen were individually loose. The first dozen pages were not inscribed on the reverse sides, but succeeding pages were. The last numbered page was 292, for Thursday, October 10, 1820, but the volume continued for 229 more unnumbered pages, making a total of 521, through Saturday, April 6, 1822. Some later admirer had pasted on its front, "David Crockett J. P. Record 1818." The cover was leather-bound cardboard, very old and worn in appearance, about 7 x 13 inches, the back binding edge disintegrating at top and bottom. It was entitled *Lawrence County Court Minutes*, Volume I, 1818-23. For a photograph of this open volume, as well as of the beautiful site of Crockett's mill in Lawrence County, see *Nashville Tennessean Magazine* for November 3, 1946, pp. 7-8. David's authentic signature occurs at several places as one of the present and authenticating justices.

9. *Lawrence County Court Minutes, 1818-23*, I, 18-28.

10. *Tennessee State Commission Book*, No. 4, 1815-27, p. 96.

11. These depositions are not the original records of the commissioners' minutes but are true copies made nineteen months afterwards by the clerk of court, who was also one of the original commissioners signing the original records, in order that the party attempting to establish his property rights might have evidence of the testimony in the case to file with his land title in event of renewal of the dispute. The original records seem to have perished during the Civil War. Thus the original documents preserved in facsimile, or equivalent, do not contain the original signatures. These five documents are owned by the Tennessee Historical Society.

12. *Lawrence County Court Minutes*, I, 68, 72.

13. *Ibid.*, I, 95.
14. *Ibid.*, I, 151-55.
15. *Ibid.*, I, 193.
16. S. H. Stout, "David Crockett," *American Historical Magazine*, VII, 16-17.
17. *Lawrence County Court Minutes*, I, 299.
18. "This speech," say an authentic sounding marginal note in an old volume I once ran across, "was made at the present site of Centreville on the north side of the Public Sq." In view of the dispute between Centerville and Vernon concerning the county seat, and the fact that David says he went next to Vernon, the marginal note would seem to be accurate. Centerville was to become the county seat in 1822, during David's incumbency, and has so remained to date.

Chapter 4

1. Andrew Jackson and Isaac Shelby made a treaty with the Chickasaw Indians on October 19, 1818, acquiring for the United States all their lands east of the Mississippi River. Within the limits of Tennessee, this became the Western District. On November 7 of Crockett's first session an act to "Form and Establish New Counties West of the Tennessee River" was passed, and after that frontiersmen, eyes always focussed on available lands further west, came in ever-increasing numbers and new counties were formed. See *Acts of 1821*, Chap. XXXII, p. 39.
2. T. P. Abernethy, *From Frontier to Plantation in Tennessee....*
3. Published in Cincinnati in 1833. See Chapter IV, pp. 51 ff. This volume contained the origin of the famous coon-skin story about David. The story was later elaborated in a much better version by Richard Penn Smith in the *Texas Exploits*. David does not mention it in his own *Autobiography*.
4. J. Parton, *Life of Andrew Jackson*, 1860, I, 256-57.
5. An entry for the previous day reveals that David's round-trip travelling distance was 160 miles, that he had served sixty-two days, and that his salary was $273.60.
6. The reader should see a modern map as well as that of 1832. Some of the boundaries were slightly changed after 1832. Originally, for instance, the Obion-Weakley County line extended beyond the South Fork of the Obion River, instead of conforming to that river as at present. And inasmuch as David lived so close to the conjunction of the three counties, these boundary changes later cause some confusion as to just what county he was living in.
7. For all these, and other suits for indebtedness, see *Lawrence County Court Minutes, 1818-23*, I, 420, 421, 422, 471, 480, 500, 502-3, 504-5, 507-8.
8. *Journal of the House of Representatives*, Second Session, Fourteenth General Assembly, 1822, p. 129.
9. *National Banner and Nashville Whig*, August 14, 1822. These reports of Crockett's legislative speeches were made by Mr. John P. Erwin, lawyer and business man, who had taken over the publication of this paper.

Chapter 5

1. *Carroll County Court Minutes, 1821-26*, I, 20.
2. It is well to point out that David Crockett records existing in *Madison* County for August and October, 1822, and March, 1823, pertain to a different David Crockett. The Madison County Crockett bought a shotgun for $6.50 at the sale of the estate of Jesse Richmond in Madison County on August 24, 1822 (See *Madison County Wills and Inventories*, I, 17-18). Whereas the Crockett of this biography, the Crockett of

Carroll County, was *on that day* present in Murfreesborough, middle Tennessee, many miles away, attending the adjournment of the second session of the Fourteenth General Assembly.

3. *Carroll County Court Minutes, 1821-26,* I, 37, 61-62, 72.

4. *Ibid.,* I, 50, 75.

5. *Ibid.,* I, 87-88. Crockett pled not guilty and was so found.

6. *Ibid.,* I, 102, 244.

7. In his introduction to Scribner's edition of David's *Autobiography,* Hamlin Garland vouched for the authenticity of these expressions even as late as his own time.

8. From W. A. Nelson, "Reelfoot—An Earthquake Lake," *National Geographic,* XLV, 106-7. Sources for the story of the creation of Reelfoot, legendary and scientific, including eye-witness accounts, are, in the order of their importance: Nelson, "Reelfoot—an Earthquake Lake," pp. 94-114; "Earthquakes of 1811," pp. 235-37; H. S. Halbert and T. H. Ball, *The Creek War,* pp. 70-72. Two less scientific ones, both interesting, are those of the anonymous *Life* of Crockett of 1833, pp. 57-59; and Allen, *David Crockett, Scout, Small Boy, Pilgrim,* etc., Chapters XI and XII. Crockett himself gives incidental descriptive insights, but little about its causes. The Nelson article includes photographs, where trees may be seen growing on ridges out of the water, showing the effect of the earthquakes' "frozen waves."

9. This was the earliest west Tennessee newspaper, first issued in November, 1822, and supplanted on May 20, 1824, by the Jackson *Gazette.* Unfortunately, only two issues of the *Pioneer* survive, one for January 28, 1823, at the University of North Carolina, and the other for September 9, 1823, at the Library of Congress, too early and too late respectively for this Crockett announcement.

10. The best evidence I have found to authenticate this story comes from the reminiscences of a contemporary acquaintance of David's, Colonel Robert I. Chester. Colonel Chester implied his belief in the accuracy of the story when he remarked that Crockett "defeated Colonel Butler for Congress by ridiculing him for having carpets on his floors," though Chester's memory was wrong in attributing the defeat to a Congressional rather than to a legislative encounter. For his account, see H. S. Turner, "Andrew Jackson and David Crockett: Reminiscences of Colonel Chester," *Magazine of American History,* XXVII, 385-87.

11. E. I. Williams, *Historic Madison....,* footnote to pp. 50-52.

12. Marquis James, *Life of Jackson,* p. 61.

13. *National Banner and Nashville Whig,* Sept. 29, 1823.

14. *Ibid.,* Oct. 13, 1823.

15. *Ibid.,* Sept. 4, 1822; Sept. 27, 1824.

16. J. M. Keating, *History of the City of Memphis and Shelby County Tennessee,* I, 169.

17. *Knoxville Register,* Nov. 4, 1823.

18. The expense account of the House members reveals that David's mileage allowance was for 400 miles, that he served 76 days, and that his salary was $368.00.

19. *Gibson County Court Minutes, Book A, 1824-28,* pp. 36-37.

20. *Carroll County Court Minutes, 1821-26,* I, 201.

21. *Gibson County Wills and Bonds Book I, 1825-33,* p. 73, items 1, 4, 13.

22. *American Book Prices Current,* XL, for 1939.

23. *House Journal,* Second Session, Fifteenth General Assembly, 1824, p. 4 (bound with the volume of the *Senate Journal* for this year).

24. *National Banner and Nashville Whig,* Sept. 27, 1824.

25. *Ibid.,* Sept. 27, 1824.

26. His mileage allowance was again for 400 miles, his length of service 33 days, and his salary $196.00.

Chapter 6

1. Just one month after the legislature adjourned, the Gibson County Court fined David $25.00 for failing to answer the summons to appear as a Grand Petit Juror the previous month. On November 9 of the following year the fine was remitted in recognition of the fact that insufficient time had been allowed for him to arrive at the local court from the legislature two hundred miles away. In January, 1825, David was appointed on a Jury of Review. On September 24, David was issued a Military Land Grant for twenty acres of land in Lawrence County, for services in the War of 1812. It is likely that he sold this immediately, for there is no record of his having ever returned to Lawrence County, except for a visit. In October he was a bondsman on the constable's bond of Samuel Gordon in Gibson County. In the same month he was ordered to appear for jury duty and on November 8 was chosen a member of grand inquest and jury for the state for the current term. On the following day he helped as juryman to find John Gray guilty of gaming. *Gibson County Circuit Court Minute Book A, 1824-32*, pp. 9-10, 24, 25, 30-31; *Gibson County Court Minute Book A, 1824-28*, pp. 53, 113; *Gibson County Wills and Bonds Book 1, 1825-33*, p. 35; J. S. French and Z. Armstrong, *The Crockett Family and ....*, p. 580.

2. I have been unable to locate a single copy of this Circular Letter. Mr. E. J. Aston of Asheville, N. C., sent a copy to Governor Brown of Tennessee, with a letter of transmittal dated June 25, 1872, certifying to the existence of the circular. Another inclosure which accompanied the letter, a Crockett holograph, still survives; but the circular letter of 1824 is lost. The Tennessee Historical Society owns Mr. Aston's letter.

3. Of all the strange portions of the *Autobiography*, this is perhaps the most difficult to believe. Yet Dr. S. H. Stout states that it was related to him by a "reliable person in Gibson County" in 1843-44. The *Autobiography* had already been published and become widely popular by then, however, so that the story is in no way verifiable except as being consonant with the general temper of the times and of the man. And since David was alone, its reliability must in any event come back to David's own recounting. Inasmuch as David brought a witness, McDaniel, back to observe the scene and the evidence next day, and in view of the fact that David was still living among the same neighbors and was calling on their support again for his Congressional seat when he was writing the *Autobiography*, it seems highly improbable, to say the least, that he would have been foolish enough to invite the derision of his neighbors by telling a story of idle brag out of keeping with his courage and physical powers. At the very least it describes what David's neighbors well knew he truly *might* have done; and it may indeed be literal truth.

4. *Tennessee, A History, 1673-1932*, ed. Philip M. Hamer, I, 108.

5. S. H. Stout, "David Crockett," *American History Magazine*, VII, 12, ff.

6. H. S. Turner, "Andrew Jackson and David Crockett: Reminiscences of Colonel Chester," *Magazine of American History*, XXVII, 385-87.

7. J. O. Davis, *History of the City of Memphis*, pp. 140-50; J. M. Keating, *History of the City of Memphis and Shelby County, Tennessee*, I, 180.

8. J. D. Davis, *History of the City of Memphis*, p. 150.

9. *Gibson County Circuit Court Minute Book A, 1824-32*, p. 42.

10. *Gibson County Court Minute Book A, 1824-28*, p. 161. "David Crockett Jr" may here be employed in the sense of "younger" rather than of "son." He was possibly the son of Patterson Crockett, a name frequently occurring with David's in the west Tennessee records, since Patterson lived in David's neighborhood and was doubtless a relative. Patterson signed his name with a mark.

11. *Ibid.*, p. 161.

12. *Ibid.*, p. 197.

13. *Gibson County Circuit Court Minute Book A, 1824-32*, pp. 53-54. Slightly earlier than this David Crockett had sold a piece of property to Benton R. White in Giles County (*Giles County Minute Book, 1825-27*, I, 170). Mr. Curtis Bray of Jackson, Tennessee, allowed me to examine several old Crockett documents in his possession, among which was a "Return of Taxable property & free poles for the year 1826," made by Benjamin White, one of the first commissioners of Gibson and a justice of the peace there. For date of June 7 David was listed under both free poles and free males.

14. *Gibson County Court Minute Book A, 1824-28*, p. 201.

15. The original is owned by the Tennessee Historical Society, Nashville. The letter was addressed from Paris (Henry County), Tennessee, to Mr. C. G. Dunlap in Huntingdon (Carroll County) and was carried by a messenger whose name appears to be "Mr. Henry." Perhaps Dunlap was a schoolmate of John's.

The language of this letter should receive brief attention. "In the gunter" was equivalent to contemporary slang, "in the groove," or the earlier "in the high cotton," and meant *fine* or *excellent*. It was derived from the Gunter Measure, a highly reliable standard of the time. "A Gunter's measure" was a measure full and true. The *Dictionary of American English* does not list the expression as used above, but for a much later date (1843) does list the related "gunter's measure."

"Cut out" (for Orleans) is one of the most characteristic expressions of David's *Autobiography*, occurring in various combinations well over thirty times. Though we do not find it in David's own holographs, its use here establishes it as contemporary slang.

Another expression, "a going a head," seemingly a form of David's motto, is likewise frequently found in the *Autobiography*. It is the most frequently employed of all expressions, occurring in one variation or another at least forty-two times, though it is seldom found in David's own correspondence. The *DAE* lists "go ahead" as first occurring in 1839, but whenever it originated, it had surely been made popular by David as early as 1834.

The several meanings of "hook" as used here ("for Orleans in the hooks"; "I...am a whole hook"; his father, "the old hook") must be judged from context. The *DAE* does not list it in any of these meanings. I suspect it is related to a vulgar expression still current today.

16. E. I. Williams, *Historic Madison*...., pp. 37-38, 54. Dyer had fought under Jackson as a Lt. Colonel in the Natchez expedition, in the Creek War at New Orleans, and in the Seminole Campaign of 1818, had been one of the earliest settlers in Madison County, and at the time of the contest with Arnold, was one of the commissioners for the improvement of navigation in the Western District.

17. *Ibid.*, pp. 100-1.

18. Whoever this unnamed friend was, David says that his first action after arriving in Washington in 1827 was to repay the $250.00. He also says he paid it by check.

19. *Public Acts of the State of Tennessee*, 1823, Chapter 1, p. 5.

20. James D. Davis, *History of Memphis*, pp. 150-51. He seems to refer to this election.

21. While Crockett was pro-Jackson, this charge was made more than once by the anti-Jacksonites. When David deserted Jackson, followers of the latter pressed similar charges. According to Davis (p. 176), the Missouri *Republican* charged him with adultery and drunkenness, and the Jackson *Gazette* (August 15, 1829) replied editorially that "all his friends admit that he is somewhat eccentric, and that from a defect in his education, his stump speeches are not famous for polish or refinement, yet they are plain, forceful, and generally respectful."

22. Miss E. I. Williams, in what may be an unintentional transposition, gives it as

2,784 (*Historic Madison,* p. 71). And J. M. Keating says it was 3,400 (*History of Memphis and Shelby County,* I, 169-70).

23. Before he left, however, he decided for some reason to buy a bit of land in Weakley County contiguous or very close to the land upon which he had been living in Gibson. I find no account of his selling his land in Gibson, yet he seems to have moved onto this new purchase not many months later. He also seems to have continued to occupy land at the same time in Gibson; for in the *Congressional Directory* he listed his home address for all his terms in Congress as Gibson. (Trenton for 1827; Crockett Post Office, Tennessee, for 1831 and 1833. A Crockett holograph of May 26, 1834, tells us that Crockett, Tennessee, was in Gibson County. Wherever he lived in Gibson, Weakley, and Carroll Counties, it was hardly out of sight of his first location on Rutherford's Fork in what, at the time of his arrival, had been Carroll County.)

On October 1, 1827, Crockett went to the land office of west Tennessee and entered a purchase. (*West Tennessee Land Office Records,* Book 2 "A", p. 474, Tennessee State Archives, Nashville.)

24. J. A. Shackford, "David Crockett and North Carolina," *North Carolina Historical Review,* XXVIII, 298-315.

25. *Ibid.,* pp. 298-315. This article contains complete references to all source material in connection with the duel.

26. Though written in Pleasant Gardens, the letter was carried first to Jonesboro, Tennessee, and re-routed from there to prevent technical infringement on the North Carolina laws against duelling. The complete letter has been published only once, I believe, in an article by A. C. Avery in the Raleigh (N. C.) *News and Observer,* "North Carolina Review Section," for March 2, 1913, pp. 1-2, 11.

27. A copy of this letter was given me by Miss Mary M. Greenlee of Mooresville, N. C., who is a direct descendant of the brother of Elizabeth Patton's father, Robert. Miss Greenlee read the original letter in the possession of its addressee, the late Mr. W. C. Ervin, and with his permission made a copy which he authorized her to make public. Ervin was first cousin once-removed as well as step-nephew to the writer of this letter, Rebecca Carson Whitson.

Chapter 7

1. Washington City, December 27, 1827. Original owned by Mr. Curtis Bray, Jackson, Tennessee.
In all Crockett quotations I have followed his capitalization, spelling, paragraphing, punctuation (or lack of it), and other details except his hyphens and flourishes, exactly. Parts enclosed in brackets represent my reconstructions where the letter-creases have been worn or torn beyond legibility.

2. Letter for February 5 is owned by the Tennessee Historical Society.

3. The February 11 letter is owned by Mr. Carlos Dew, Trenton, Tennessee.

4. I have not discovered the owner of this March 11 letter—the photostat came to me from the University of Texas.

5. See footnote 3 above.

6. He so voted on April 22, 1828. See *Congressional Debates,* IV, 2471.

7. *Congressional Debates,* IV, 2086. Edward S. Ellis has confused the vote on Mrs. Brown with one on a fire in Georgetown (really in Alexandria), but he gives a possible explanation for David's reversal of his usual position on bills for relief of the needy. See his *Life of Colonel David Crockett,* Philadelphia: Porter and Coates edition, 1884, Chapter 14, pp. 137-56.

8. Chilton and Crockett were both elected to Congress for the first time in 1827. Both were Jackson supporters at this time, both served until 1831, both became Whigs

and were then defeated, and both were re-elected as Whigs for one more term, 1833-35, after which the Congressional career of both ended. Finally both migrated to Texas and died there, the one in the Alamo in 1836, the other presumably in bed at Montgomery, Texas, in August, 1854. For information about Chilton, see *Biographical Directory of the American Congress*, 1928, p. 807.

9. I take the essential facts and Tennessee's position on them from Polk's explanation. See *Congressional Debates*, IV, 2495 ff.

10. *Congressional Debates*, IV, 2518-19. Crockett's speaking ability was far superior to his ability to write, or else someone, editors of the *Debates* or others, was already improving his words. I think his speeches were not yet being written for him, but that they were spoken with a great deal less polish than the record shows. Such editing was usual and served the publisher's interests by helping to insure his continued selection as the printer of the House proceedings.

11. *Congressional Debates*, V, 161-66, 199-200; the Circular Letter is contained in the *Blair and Rives Papers* in the Library of Congress.

12. Courtesy Library of Congress, Division of Manuscripts. Polk stated on this copy that it was the substance of similar letters addressed "about the same date" to three other men whom he names.

13. *Congressional Debates*, VII, 383.

14. *Ibid.*, VI, 474, 480.

15. *Ibid.*, VII, 391.

16. *Ibid.*, VII, 418.

17. *Ibid.*, VI, 819.

18. *Ibid.*, VI, 869, 870, 873.

19. *Ibid.*, VI, 873.

Chapter 8

1. *Congressional Debates*, VI, 716, 692.

2. *Ibid.*, XI, Part 2, Appendix.

3. *Ibid.*, VI, 1147.

4. Keating, *History of Memphis*, I, 178.

5. *Congressional Debates*, VII, 788-89.

6. *Ibid.*, VI, 553.

7. *Ibid.*, VI, 583-84.

8. *Ibid.*, VI, 722.

9. *Ibid.*, VI, 634-35.

10. *Speeches on the Passage of the Bill for the Removal of the Indians, Delivered in Congress of the United States*, April and May, 1830, pp. 251-53. Perhaps it should be said that Mr. Everett of Massachusetts did make a speech in Congress on May 19 on that subject which, in a few interesting respects, resembles the "speech" which David did not make. *Congressional Debates*, VI, 1079 ff.

11. *Ibid.*, VII, 543.

12. *Ibid.*, VII, 680, 717-19.

13. Original owned by Tennessee Historical Society. It has been published in transcript in the *American Historical Magazine*, V (1900), 43-44.

14. He was later to be "the only Georgia politician of the first rank who was an avowed nullifier," though he was to be perhaps as bitter an opponent of the Second United States Bank as Jackson himself.

Chapter 9

1. *Gibson County Wills and Bonds Book I, 1825-33*, p. 97.
2. *Weakley County Court Minutes, 1827-35*, I, 43.
3. *Ibid.*, I, 60.
4. *Gibson County Court Minutes, Book A, 1824-28*, p. 386.
5. *Weakley County Court Minutes, 1827-35*, I, 89.
6. Charles and Mary Beard, *Rise of the American Civilization*, p. 541.
7. Original owned by New York Public Library.
8. It was this very Whig account which seems to have initiated that stereotype of the Crockett vernacular, employed to excess by some biographers: "if I didn't, I wish I may be shot"—though the newspaper story itself made the expression read, "I wish I may be d----d."
9. *National Banner and Nashville Whig*, XVI, 4.
10. The comment on Houston will be of interest to the historian as a sidelight into a knotty problem over which the debate still waxes vigorously.
11. Keating's confusion of dates is so masterful that it is impossible to work out his chronology, but I believe that this is the approximate date he assigns for this quandary of David's.
12. Keating, *History of Memphis*, I, p. 176 ff.
13. *Gibson County Circuit Court Minutes Book A, 1824-32*, p. 178.
14. *Weakley County Court Minutes, 1827-35*, I, 131, 149, 176, 183, 200, 233, 250, 268, 317, 323.
15. *Ibid.*, p. 130.
16. *Ibid.*, I, 184.
17. *Weakley County Will and Record Book, 1828-42*, p. 56.
18. The original is owned by the Historical Society of Pennsylvania.
19. Published on February 27, 1831, by Stephen C. Ustick in Washington. Copy available in the Library of Congress. So far as I know, this is the only published work of Chilton's, though I have discovered an unpublished holograph by him.
20. Copy available in the Library of Congress.
21. The account is a contribution by a "correspondent of the Nashville *Banner* ... from Paris, Tenn." printed in *Every Saturday*, XI (1871), 515. It cannot be accurate in all its details, and I believe it confuses matters concerning the elections of 1833 and 1835 with the election of 1831. In the first place it calls David's opponent James Fitzgerald instead of, properly, William. Further, another version of this story (footnote by editor James D. Porter to S. H. Stout's article "David Crocket," p. 7) says David made the mileage charge against Fitzgerald, rather than vice versa, which could only have been in 1833 after Fitzgerald had been to Congress; and David's letter of August 11, 1835, refers to these same charges as having been made against himself by Adam Huntsman and Andrew Jackson in the 1835 canvass. I believe the reported incident took place in 1831, but that the charge Fitzgerald brought dealt with David's excessive absences from roll-calls, as the *Autobiography* implies—rather than with his excessive charge for mileage.
22. *Niles Weekly Register*, ed. H. Niles, XLI, 150.
23. The *Congressional Debates* do not record it, but *Niles Register* does for December 31, 1831, XLI, 332.
24. It was dated August 22, 1831, and addressed to Doctor Jones, Madison County, Tennessee. The original is owned by Mr. Ed Knox Boyd of Bolivar, Tennessee. It has been published in transcript in E. I. Williams, *Historic Madison*, p. 422. Notations on the letter indicate that David took the lease (expiring on January 1, 1838) and that the land leased lay adjoining David's in Carroll County, being part of a 2,560 acre tract.

25. See M. Clarke, *Life and Adventures....*, chap. IX for two allusions quoted as remarks David made to the author on his visit and for an interesting description of David's family and "new" home.

26. R. C. Catterall, *The Second Bank of the United States*, p. 243.

27. R. C. McGrane, *Correspondence of Nicholas Biddle*, pp. 53-54. The correspondence is highly selective and suggests more than it reveals. Biddle knew and kept records on how representatives stood with reference to the bank charter, and obviously tried to influence their votes.

28. R. C. Catterall, *The Second Bank of the United States*, p. 256.

29. The original letter, dated January 7, 1832, is owned by the Historical Society of Pennsylvania.

30. *Weakley County Court Minutes, 1827-35*, I, 233, 250, 260.

31. Mr. W. J. White of Dresden, Register of Weakley, assured me by letter dated August 30, 1947, that this is exactly as the motto occurs on both.

32. For a transcript of the complete documents, see J. S. French and Z. Armstrong, *The Crockett Family and....*, pp. 378, 546-47, though they give the motto inaccurately. The court registration may be found in *Weakley County Court Minutes, 1827-35*, I, 264. The deed was recorded on April 14, 1832, the Bill of Sale on December 21, 1831. The land deed was certified for registration in both Weakley and Gibson Counties and we have another indication that David was living in two counties or that the land sold lay first in the one and then in the other. This left David with 200 adjoining acres to which two items in the *Record of Occupant Entries, 1827-33*, allude: Entry No. 482 for Yandrel Rece refers to "an entry for 200 acres in the name of David Crockett," and Entry No. 520 for Michael Israel includes the phrase "thence south 93 poles to a poplar David Crockets Crockets Corner" (pp. 108, 115, respectively). This may have been land David "entered" but had not bought—200 acres of that very public land which his bill in Congress intended to give to his neighbors—and to himself.

33. *Weakley County Court Minutes, 1827-35*, I, 279.

34. *Ibid.*, I, 308.

35. *Gibson County Wills and Bonds Book I, 1825-33*, pp. 222-24. The will was dated the 26 day of 1832. The month was omitted.

36. T. C. Richardson, "The Girl Davy Left Behind," *Farm and Ranch* (June 25, 1927), pp. 3, 4. According to the author, the teapot was owned in 1927 by a lineal Texas descendant, Mr. R. A. Parks.

Chapter 10

1. The first record I found relating Crockett and Huntsman was an indirect connection through David's brother-in-law, Hance McWhorter. In *Gibson County Circuit Court Minute Book A, 1824-32*, p. 297, under date of April 4, 1832, is recorded an acknowledgement of indebtedness by Huntsman to McWhorter for $125. Later it was Hance McWhorter who brought David into court over the executorship of the Patton estate, and in that suit *Huntsman was defending David*, just a couple of months before he defeated him for re-election to Congress!

2. They are quoted in their entirety, or nearly so, at pp. 115-26 of Clarke's *Life*, though neither there nor anywhere else that I know of, except in the quotation cited from the *Autobiography*, is the name of their author revealed. The complete title seems to have been "Book of Chronicles, West of Tennessee, and East of the Mississippi Rivers."

3. *Public Acts of the State of Tennessee*, Extra Session (1832), Chapter 4, p. 14. The other three counties left over from his old Ninth District went into the Eleventh District.

4. Photographically reproduced in *Dallas Morning News* (December 25, 1927),

Feature Section, p. 5. The *News* unfortunately no longer has the plates for the photograph.

5. Original, to A. M. Hughes, dated December 8, 1833, is owned by the Tennessee Historical Society.

6. *Congressional Debates*, X, Pt. 4, Appendix, 63, 59-79; 131-204 for the various papers of the controversy.

7. It is not carried in the *Congressional Debates* of Gales and Seaton, but in *The Congressional Globe*, published by Francis Preston Blair, a leading member of Jackson's "Kitchen Cabinet." Beginning with this Congress, the proceedings were printed by both for a few years, so that for David's final sessions we have a double source for his remarks, one by his new Eastern friends, one by Jackson's supporters. The discrepancies are sometimes not only revealing but amusing. For David's two motions, see *The Congressional Globe*, I, 37.

8. Original letter to William Rodgers is owned by the Tennessee Historical Society.

9. This original letter may be permanently lost. It was owned by Dr. Alexander Dienst, of Temple, Texas, but was not found among his effects by his son-in-law and administrator of his estate, Mr. J. W. Williams, of Austin. Mr. Williams did find, however, what for this study is just as good, a photograph of that letter which he kindly sent for my examination.

10. Perhaps the most widely "travelled" of all of Crockett's remains. It was discovered early in the present century by a second cousin of the writer, James W. Atkins, among papers of Mr. Atkins' father. It was published verbatim in the family paper, the *Gastonia (N.C.) Gazette*, and then sold to the firm of Walter R. Benjamin of New York. I have been unable to trace its present owner. It was republished from the *Gazette* in the *Confederate Veteran*, XI (1903), 162. The University of Texas Library has a typed copy, and photostatic copies of the *final page only* are owned by the New York Public Library and the Library of Congress. Portions of the first two pages have been directly quoted in various sales catalogues. *American Book Prices Current* shows that it sold at auction on December 3, 1923 (Vol. 30, 1924), and again in 1928 (Vol. 35, 1929), the last time for $210.00.

11. *Congressional Debates*, X, 2614; *Congressional Globe*, I, 153.

12. *Congressional Debates*, X, 2782; *Congressional Globe*, I, 197.

13. February 25 letter owned by the Historical Society of Pennsylvania; that for March 8, by the New-York Historical Society.

14. Original to Colonel Thomas Henderson owned by Mr. Tom McCorry of Jackson, Tennessee, great grandson of the addressee.

15. *Congressional Debates*, X, 2955; *Congressional Globe*, I, 230.

16. I traced the original to Miss Mary E. Benjamin, of the firm of Walter R. Benjamin, of New York City, but professional interests made her unable to allow me either a photostat or a transcript thereof. She did supply me with a tear sheet from an advertisement with the quoted portions and describing the letter as an autographed one of two quarto pages from Washington. The letter included an engraved Octavo portrait, likely that by Welch after Osgood.

17. *Congressional Debates*, X, 3549, 3573.

18. *Congressional Debates*, X, 3573; *Congressional Globe*, I, 298, 300. By this time the *Globe* had ceased to give David as much free space. For instance, on the first passage, the *Globe* omits the humorous remarks, recording only that "After some remarks by Mr. Crockett, Mr. Brown said...."; and the next passage is almost as briefly treated, the humor of "good nonsense" being smothered.

19. David refers to this matter in his first surviving letter, dated Dec. 17, 1827, and in his letters of Feb. 11, 1828, and Feb. 13, 1831.

20. *Congressional Globe*, I, 302.

21. D. Crockett, *An Account of Col. Crockett's Tour...*, 1835 edition, p. 157.

22. A heretofore unpublished letter owned by the Yale University Library.

23. *American Book Prices Current*, XXXIV (1928).

24. The last record of David from any source before he left on his political "towar" of the East is one described by the sales catalogue as a "sentimental manuscript" written on "Shakespeare's birthday." And though I have not located the original, the text establishes it clearly as Crockett's. The catalogue explanation is illuminating and I quote it in part:

> At the time, Crockett's great friend Samuel Houston was very attentive to Octavia Claudia Walton Le Vert, one of the acknowledged bells [*sic*] of Washington. He took Crockett to meet her and Mrs. Le Vert, in her Album.... Unfortunately we sold the poem Houston had composed and written on the opposite page....
> Mrs. Le Vert...was the most accomplished woman of her time, and considered the greatest living American Woman, second to none, not even the brilliant Dolly Madison....

Text of Crockett's Album Inscription:

> I take great pleasure in recording my name in Miss Octavia Walton's Album as a testimonial of my respects for her Success through life and I hope she may enjoy the happiness and pleasures of the world agreeable to her expectation as all Ladys of her sterling worth, merits. I am with much respects her obet. Servt.,
> David Crockett.

This was dated April 23, two days before David commenced his "towar." My information comes from a catalogue advertisement of April, 1936 (from the American Autograph Shop, Merion Station, Pennsylvania), owned by the New York Public Library. I was unable to elicit response from the autograph shop. I should be inclined to question the commas in the transcription, the periods, the *e* in "obet. Servt.," and possibly the correct spelling of *testimonial*. But there is sufficient evidence to establish it as Crockett's writing.

Chapter 11

1. V. L. Parrington, *Main Currents....*, II, 176. Italics added by author.

2. See Crockett holographs of May 11, 1834, and June 15, 1834, to that gentleman.

3. *American Book Prices Current* records the sale in 1913 of a "short autograph note signed" by David, written from Boston on May 4, 1834. This verifies the itinerary given in the *Tour* up to this point.

4. A holograph addressed to Mr. J. M. Sanderson of Philadelphia "making an appointment, and stating that he was much pleased with his Eastern tour," was written from New York on May 11. Either Crockett wrote it before leaving on that day, or else he spent one more day in Providence or New York than his account reveals. The May 9 arrival in Providence is the last date positively identified. *American Book Prices Current*, XXXVI (1930).

5. A bad error, since his stay in Boston was from May 3 to 9—a month earlier.

6. The dispatch must have been written about May 22 and printed late. Crockett returned on about May 14 and in fact spoke in Congress on May 17.

7. *Niles Weekly Register*, ed. H. Niles, XLVI, 252.

8. The original is owned by Mr. Joseph E. Wallis, of Los Angeles, California, great great grandson of the addressee. The University of Texas has a photostatic copy.

9. First published by S. G. Heiskell, *Andrew Jackson and Early Tennessee History*, III, 18, and republished from Heiskell's inexact transcript by E. E. Williams, *Historic Madison*, pp. 424-25. Both spell addressee's name Dobyns. The original is owned by

Mr. Josiah K. Lilly, Jr., of Indianapolis, Indiana. It is similar to a speech in the *Boston Tour*, pp. 150-58, delivered by David on July 14, 1834.

10. Original owned by Tennessee Historical Society which has published it in *American Historical Magazine*, Vol. 2, No. 2 (April, 1897), pp. 179-80. My own transcriptions, here and elsewhere unless otherwise indicated, have been made from photostats of the originals.

11. *Congressional Debates*, X, 4327; *Congressional Globe*, I, 413.

12. *Congressional Debates*, X, 4467; *Congressional Globe*, I, 445.

13. The *Globe* and the *Debates* differ amusingly on these resolutions. All the *Globe* recorded of these remarks of David's was: "Mr. Crockett moved a call of the house, which was ordered."

14. *Congressional Debates*, X, 4133; *Congressional Globe*, I, 392. The entry is from the *Congressional Globe*.

15. *Congressional Debates*, X, 4586-88. For the much-abbreviated account of the *Congressional Globe*, see I, 465. "Mr. Crockett made some desultory remarks... and was replied to by Mr. Dunlap.... Mr. Crockett briefly rejoined."

16. *Congressional Debates*, X, 4701-2; *Congressional Globe*, I, 469.

17. *Congressional Globe*, I, 477; *Niles Register*, XLVI, 321, for July 5, 1834.

18. The first letter has not survived in holograph. It was published by James D. Davis in 1873 in his *History of Memphis*, p. 155. It has evidently been improved by the newspaper editor from whose paper David took it (as in his reference to Cromwell, Caesar, Bonaparte; his spelling, punctuation, and so on), but there is sufficient internal evidence to identify it as stemming from an authentic Crockett letter.

19. The occasion of this gift of a gun to Crockett provides an opportunity to touch on the subject of Crockett's guns in general. There has been much discussion as to whether his earlier gun or guns were named "Betsy" or whether this one from the young Whigs was the real "Betsy"; which one he took with him to the Alamo, and so on. The 1833 *Life* stated that David called his gun "Betsey," so at least one earlier gun than the Whig gift of 1834 was so-named. The reader may recall David turned in a gun to Mr. Kennedy as partial payment for a "courting horse." Mrs. A. M. Felknor, aged resident of Dandridge (Jefferson County), Tennessee, gave me the following description of that early gun on my visit there in the summer of 1947: "The Kennedys soon sold it to Mr. James McCuistian who lived near, and at his death he bequeathed it to his son, Major Samuel S. McCuistian, who later moved from the Long Creek vicinity to Dandridge where he lived until his death. It has not been out of the McCuistian family since and is now owned by Mr. Samuel Gwin of Modesto, California."

About the other gun which the Whigs were to give him in Philadelphia (he owned enough guns during his lifetime to cause much confusion for those interested in such matters), I quote the following from a letter to me dated October 26, 1947, from Mrs. A. Sidney Holderness, great great granddaughter of David Crockett: "The rifle which I own... is the one presented to the Honorable Davy by the young men of Philadelphia in 1834 and was left by him at home when he went off to Texas and the Alamo. I understand that in his will he provided for it to be handed down in each generation from eldest son to eldest son and as I had no brothers, it came to me on my father's death and I am the only female to have ever owned it. It came from David Crockett to his eldest son, John Wesley Crockett; from him to his eldest son, Robert Hamilton Crockett; from him to his eldest son, John Wesley Crockett; and thence to me in 1920 at my father's death. My father had loaned the rifle to the Arkansas State History Commission for display purposes and as I was quite young when he died, the rifle was allowed to remain there.... I have a son who... will, of course, inherit it upon my death.... It is my recollection... that my mother said that Davy called this rifle 'Pretty Betsy' to distinguish it from 'Betsy.' It is an old flintlock rifle and is inscribed with gold 'Presented by the Young Men of Philadelphia to Hon. David Crockett of Tennessee.' Of course, some of the letters have fallen out by now—also on the barrel are the words 'Go ahead' in silver. . . . The barrel of the gun is shorter than it originally was as my Grandfather Crockett used it to hunt with and found the barrel a trifle too long for comfort and had it cut down some." In the files of the Tennessee Historical Society is a letter from this Robert Hamilton Crockett mentioning his having cut off the barrel of this gun.

Mrs. Holderness has also inherited David's watch, with the name of each owner, beginning with David, inscribed therein, and an 1825 edition of Ben Franklin's *Autobiography* inscribed with David's signature, in addition to the portraits described in Appendix IV.

20. Original owned by Historical Society of Pennsylvania. It includes a portrait of Crockett, the T. B. Welch engraving of the Osgood painting, with Crockett's authentic signature beneath.

21. Quoted by W. Frederick Worner, "David Crockett in Columbia," *Lancaster County Historical Society Papers*, XXVI, 176-77.

22. *Ibid.*, XXVII, 176.

23. A Crockett letter for August 20 from Weakley County was sold at public auction on January 21, 1921, but I have been unable to locate it. *American Book Prices Current*, XXVII, 1921.

24. *Gibson County Bonds and Will Book B, 1833-41*, pp. 36-37. I was unable to find John's will.

25. Mr. Curtis Bray of Jackson, Tennessee, owns David's handwritten plea and the writ of *supersedeas*.

26. Published photographically in *Dallas Morning News* (Dec. 25, 1927), p. 5.

27. The rest of the book is taken up with what went on after he arrived in Congress (about December 1), matters adequately treated by the *Congressional Debates* and the *Congressional Globe*, preferable sources.

28. The original of this previously unpublished letter is owned by the Historical Society of Pennsylvania. The stationery was embossed "Donaldson N York U. S. Gov." It was addressed to Biddle in Philadelphia and was postmarked Dec. 9 in Washington.

29. R. C. H. Catterall, *The Second Bank of the United States*, p. 254, note.

30. *Congressional Globe*, II, 20, for December 9, 1834.

31. *Congressional Debates*, XI, 781.

32. Original owned by the Rosenbach Company of New York City and Philadelphia.

33. I have a photostatic copy of only the second page, but the sales catalogue transcribed most of the first page in quotation marks, so that it is practically complete. It has been sold at auction four times. The New York Public Library has a photostatic copy of the second page and the sales catalogue transcription of the remainder.

34. To John P. Ash. The coversheet has been lost. The original is owned by the University of the South at Sewanee, Tennessee. It has been published in transcript with some inaccuracies by E. I. Williams, *Historic Madison. . . .*, pp. 425-27.

Chapter 12

1. The original is among the James K. Polk papers in the Library of Congress; photostats in the Tennessee State Library, Nashville. Published by E. I. Williams, "Letters of Adam Huntsman to James K. Polk," *Tennessee Historical Quarterly*, p. 339.

2. The original is owned by the Maryland Historical Society.

3. J. S. Bassett, *Correspondence. . . .*, IV (February 16, 1835), 199.

4. *Ibid.*, V (May 12, 1835), 345-46.

5. *Ibid.*, V (October 5, 1835), 371.

6. *Ibid.*, V (October 31, 1835), 374.

7. *Ibid.*, V (June 30, 1838[?]), 554. If Bassett is correct in his dating, David had by then been dead for more than two years. The date is probably too late, since the letter seems to have been written shortly after White's defeat for nomination and to contain a prophecy of future events which were bound to follow; and by 1838 Judge White's defeat was a matter of past history. A more likely date would be June 30, 1836.

8. *Niles Register*, XLVII, 452-53, for Feb. 28, 1835. Though the original has not survived, I believe it was based on an authentic letter, both because of its content and of such expressions as "office holders," "come out," "I do hope the people," "did believe," "I do believe," "I hope to see them stand firm." Most of the newspaper letters purporting to be Crockett's are spurious, but this one is so only to the extent, I believe, that one or more Whig editors through whose hands it passed paraphrased it in places to improve its language and spelling.

9. Mr. William D. McCain, Department of Archives and History of Mississippi, informed me on December 30, 1949, that he could locate no letters "to or from David Crockett or Thomas Hart Benton." These letters, however, were addressed to individuals and, if they survive, would be among the papers of those individuals. The publication and acknowledgement of the letters attest to their validity. See next two notes.

10. *National Banner and Nashville Whig*, XXIII, No. 1371, 2.

11. *Ibid.*, XXIII, 3.

12. Original owned by the New-York Historical Society.

13. *Biographical Directory of the American Congress, 1774-1927*, p. 116.

14. *Congressional Debates*, XI, 1391.

15. *Congressional Globe*, I, 48. The *Congressional Debates* also verify this statement.

16. It was sold at auction in 1912 and again on Dec. 23, 1923. It has not before been published or referred to in Crockett literature, but was so described by *American Book Prices Current* (a two-page autographed letter) XIX, 1913; XXX, 1924.

17. To Carey and Hart, dated Jan. 22, 1835. The original is owned by the Rosenbach Company of New York City and Philadelphia. The letter was described and partially quoted in *The History of America in Documents: Part Two*, pp. 113-14, and called to my attention by Mr. C. C. Davis of Baltimore.

18. Another unlocated letter to Carey and Hart for Feb. 6, referring "to the publication of one of his works," may refer to the *Van Buren. American Book Prices Current*, XXII, 1916.

19. C. G. Bowers, *The Party Battles of the Jackson Period*, p. 256, note.

20. Shepard may be right that the book was issued *after* instead of *before* the convention of May 20, for the Convention date had been moved up and may have caught the publishers unprepared, though the writing of the book was aimed primarily at influencing that convention. The catalogue of books bound in with the work was dated June, 1835. If this is the basis of Shepard's dating, then I suspect he is in error. The custom was to date the catalogue a month later than the date of printing to allow plenty of time for the printing, distribution, and sale of the book.

21. Edward M. Shepard, *Martin Van Buren*, p. 436. Italics added by author.

22. J. A. Shackford, "Authorship of David Crockett's 'Autobiography,'" *North Carolina Historical Review*, XXVIII, 265-68.

23. Stephen F. Miller, *The Bench and Bar of Georgia*, I, 185.

24. Lunia Paul Gresham, The Public Career of Hugh Lawson White (Ph. D. dissertation Vanderbilt University, 1943), p. 300.

25. *Congressional Debates*, XI, 953; *Congressional Globe*, II, 104.

26. *Congressional Debates*, XI, 1004; *Congressional Globe*, II, 135.

27. *Congressional Debates*, XI, 1051 ff; *Congressional Globe*, II, 157.

28. *Niles Register*, XLVII, 390, Feb. 7, 1835.

29. *Congressional Debates*, XI, 1191-92.

30. *Congressional Debates*, XI, 1193; *Congressional Globe*, II, 266.

31. *Congressional Debates*, XI, 1354; *Congressional Globe*, II, 241.
32. *Congressional Debates*, XI, 1422; *Congressional Globe*, II, 262.
33. *Congressional Globe*, II, 274. Not recorded in the *Congressional Debates*.
34. *Congressional Globe*, II, 331. Not recorded in the *Congressional Debates*.

Chapter 13

1. From the reminiscences of Dr. S. H. Stout. "It was written in good and forcible English, and was evidently of his own composition," says Stout naively; "I regret that it has been misplaced." In "David Crockett," *American Historical Magazine*, VII, 20.
2. S. Smith, *Life and Writings of Major Jack Downing of Downingville Away Down East in the State of Maine.*
3. M. A. Wyman, *Two American Pioneers.*
4. D. Crockett, *An Account of Col. Crockett's Tour...*, pp. 220-28.
5. *Downing Gazette*, I, No. 37, March 14, 1835.
6. *Ibid.*, I, No. 47, May 23, 1835.
7. *Ibid.*, I, No. 48, May 30, 1835.
8. *Ibid.*, I, No. 50, June 13, 1835.
9. *Ibid.*, II, No. 5, August 1, 1835.
10. J. M. Keating, *History of the City of Memphis and Shelby County*, I, 180.
11. C. M. Rourke cited "a [sales] catalogue of John Heise, Syracuse, N. Y." From a sales catalogue of Thomas F. Madigan of N. Y. she quotes two sentences from another supposed Crockett letter (*Davy Crockett*, pp. 150, 262) of August or September, but from the sentences quoted I believe it is spurious. *American Book Prices Current*, XVI, 1910 lists another from the Mouth of Sandy, Henry County, Tennessee, for June 26 of this summer; and another (VIII, 1902) which it lists for "1855" but must have meant "1835."
12. I have made little effort to duplicate Crockett spelling, grammar, or phraseology, but have rather tried to recover the part that I think was in content a section of his original letter.
13. The letter of one day earlier, August 10, appears to survive only in the columns of the *National Intelligencer*, Sept. 2, 1835. It is so nearly like that of the next day, surviving in holograph, that we can accept it as completely authentic except for a few small changes. The editors in publishing it admitted that they had "ventured indeed to soften his language in one or two passages, where it was rather too *energetic.*"
14. The original is owned by the Maryland Historical Society.
15. The entire records of this case, here abstracted, may be found in the *Gibson County Chancery Court Minutes, Book A, 1834-47*, pp. 1-6.
16. There is a strange inconsistency in this name. It occurs as "Trosper" in David's letter of January 27, 1829, the suit of complainants, Robert Patton's original will, and elsewhere. Yet it appears as "Hooper" in the defendant's reply, in their additional reply, and in the *copy* of the Patton will appended to their second reply.
17. The solicitors for David in this first reply were Huntsman and Miller—the former, to defeat David for Congress ten months later. Miller had earlier withdrawn from a Congressional race with David.
18. The original is owned by Mrs. Percy B. McCord, of Portland, Maine. Constance Rourke quoted three short sentences in her *Davy Crockett*, p. 262. Because of David's salutation, she says the letter was written to David's brother. If she saw the original, she could have given it only a hurried and careless glance.

Chapter 14

1. Dr. Stout, ten years younger than Davis, but a resident of the area, thought this "an exaggeration," as are many of the sayings attributed to Crockett ("David Crocket," p. 11); though it sounds to us rather characteristic of David's humor. Davis records it in *History of Memphis*, p. 143.

2. J. D. Davis, *History of the City of Memphis*, p. 140.

3. *Niles Weekly Register*, XLIX, 225.

4. *Ibid.*, XLIX, 281, December 26, 1835.

5. Republished in *Niles Register*, L, 432-33, for August 27, 1836, from the Jackson, Tennessee, *Truth Teller*.

6. A surviving holograph of David's friend Sam Carson, of North Carolina, states on Sept. 8, 1835, that "We start '*Lock Stock & Barrels*' on the 22nd inst." for the same country, where he was to become the first Secretary of the State of Texas. Original letter owned by the Tennessee Historical Society, Nashville.

7. Henry Stout was frequently a guest for protracted visits in Mrs. Clark's home when Judge Pat B. Clark was dwelling there, and Judge Clark had heard him tell many stories of the olden times.

8. The story is told by Claude V. Hall, who states that he got it from Judge Pat B. Clark. Judge Clark spent most of his early manhood in the home of his grandmother, Mrs. Isabella H. Clark, who went to David's aid in this story, and he had heard his grandmother tell it many times. C. V. Hall, "Early Days in Red River County [Texas]," *Bulletin of East Texas State Teachers College*, XIV, 49-79.

9. Original was owned in 1946 by Mr. J. D. Pate, of Martin, Tennessee.

10. *Niles Weekly Register*, LIV, 258.

11. Letter to Writer from Major General Edward F. Whitsell, the Adjutant General, dated November 19, 1947.

12. Letter dated November 26, 1947, from General William H. Martin.

13. C. M. Rourke, *Davy Crockett*, p. 174.

14. For an account of its activities, see Zoe Allison, "Notes on the Journal of the Proceedings of the General Council of the Republic of Texas...," *Bulletin of the East Texas State Teachers College*, XIV, 84-88.

15. *The Writings of Sam Houston*, ed. Amelia W. Williams and Eugene C. Barker, VI, 6-8.

16. "Jackson wanted Texas, and Houston went there to get it for him," says Marquis James, in *The Raven*, p. 344.

17. The original is in the Controller's Military Service Records, Texas State Library.

Chapter 15

1. *Writings of Sam Houston*, ed. Amelia W. Williams and Eugene C. Barker, VII, pp. 306-33, for his Senate speech; VI, 8, note, for correct date of his departure, according to editors.

2. Original owned by Mr. Thomas W. Streeter. Photostat furnished author by the New York Public Library, where the Streeter Collection is deposited.

3. H. S. Turner, "Andrew Jackson and David Crockett; Reminiscences of Colonel Chester," *Magazine of American History*, XXVII, 385-87.

4. E. S. Ellis, in his *The Life of Colonel David Crockett*, went so far afield in fiction as to state at p. 232 that David came to Texas bearing a letter from Andrew Jackson which introduced him as a "God-chosen patriot"! But perhaps the reader will recall the Jackson letter of Chapter Twenty-one, written the day before David left for

Texas, referring to the "miserable caucus" of "Crockett and Co" and reflecting a somewhat different sentiment from that invented for this occasion by Ellis.

5. *Writings of Sam Houston*, ed. Amelia W. Williams and Eugene C. Barker, VI, 8.

6. Complete letter published in *Niles Weekly Register*, L, 122-23.

7. *Writings of Sam Houston*, ed. Amelia W. Williams and Eugene C. Barker, I, 363-65; *Niles Weekly Register*, L, p. 121.

8. *Writings of Sam Houston*, ed. Amelia W. Williams and Eugene C. Barker, I, 373-74.

9. *Ibid.*, I, 363-64, footnote 3.

10. *Ibid.*, IV, 547, note.

11. H. P. N. Gammel, *Laws of Texas*, X, 326-27.

12. He is mistaken. Sam Houston had reported it in his letter to Fannin of March 11, partially quoted earlier. Mrs. Dickerson denied the story, saying her only child was the young daughter whom she brought away with her. For Houston's report of it, see his *Writings*, Vol. 1, pp. 362-65, and p. 364, note 5.

13. W. Corner, *San Antonio De Bexar....*, pp. 117-19.

14. He reports her as saying it was 100 years and 3 months. Here he or the interpreter evidently erred, for she must rather have said 103 years and a few months in this 1888 interview. For in April, 1891, the Texas Legislature gave her age as 107, and in another interview with Corner she said in 1890 that she was 105 years old; and this explanation would make all three dates fairly well agree.

15. M. Elfer, *Madame Candelaria, Unsung Heroine of the Alamo....*, 23 pages.

16. The *San Antonio Daily Express*, Feb. 11, 1899; and the *San Antonio Light*, Feb. 19, 1899, which was reprinting it from the *St. Louis Republican!*

17. M. Elfer, *Madame Candelaria, Unsung Heroine of the Alamo....*, pp. 14-15.

18. *Writings of Sam Houston*, ed. Amelia W. Williams and Eugene C. Barker, I, 364, note 5.

19. J. M. Morphis, *History of Texas*, pp. 176-77.

20. *Niles Weekly Register*, L, 121-22, for April 16, 1836.

21. J. S. French and Z. Armstrong, *The Crockett Family and....*, pp. 346-56, 376.

22. *Gibson County Wills and Bonds Book II, 1833-41*, p. 112.

23. Original owned by the Tennessee Historical Society.

24. S. H. Stout, "David Crockett," *American Historical Magazine*, VII, 3-21.

25. *Niles Weekly Register*, LIX, 407, for February 27, 1841.

26. *Ibid.*, LVIII, 128.

27. *Ibid.*, LVIII, 224.

Chapter 16

1. W. Blair, "Six Davy Crocketts," *Southwest Review*, XXV (July, 1940), 443-62.

2. J. Leach, "Crockett's Almanacs and the Typical Texan," *Southwest Review*, Summer, 1950. Italics added by author.

3. R. M. Dorson, in *Davy Crockett: American Comic Legend*, has published a volume of these almanac stories to which the reader may refer. Professor Howard Mumford Jones in a preface to Dorson's book assures us that they have truly epic proportions, comparing them to the Maginogion. Dorson followed Jones' suggestion and made the comparison elaborate: "Davy Crockett and the Heroic Age," in the *Southern Folklore Quarterly*, VI (June, 1942), 95-102.

4. V. L. Parrington, *Main Currents in American Thought*, II, 179.

Appendix 1

1. Letter to writer from Vincent L. Eaton, Assistant Chief, Rare Books Division, Library of Congress, dated December 19, 1947.

2. W. I. Paulding, *Literary Life of James K. Paulding*, p. 218. Italics added by author.

3. N. F. Adkins, "James K. Paulding's *Lion of the West*," *American Literature*, III, 254.

4. *Ibid.*, III, 251.

5. *Ibid.*, III, 251.

6. W. I. Paulding, *Literary Life.* . . . , pp. 218-19.

7. N. F. Adkins, "James K. Paulding's . . . ," *American Literature*, III, 250. Italics added by author.

8. *Ibid.*, III, 253.

9. Amos L. Herold, *James Kirke Paulding, Versatile American*, p. 99.

10. *New York Traveller, Spirit of the Times and Family Journal* for Dec. 21, 1833. This was called to my attention by Mr. Joseph Leach.

11. N. F. Adkins, "James K. Paulding's . . . ," *American Literature*, III, 255-56.

12. W. I. Paulding, *Literary Life.* . . . , p. 219. Italics added.

13. N. F. Adkins, "James K. Paulding's . . . ," *American Literature*, III, pp. 255-56.

14. French's dates, 1807-1885, together with certain other information about him were supplied me from the notes of Mr. Clayton Torrence, Secretary of the Virginia Historical Society. Mr. Curtis Carroll Davis, authority on William Alexander Caruthers, also supplied information on French.

15. *Diary of Christopher Baldwin in Transactions and Collections of the American Antiquarian Society*, VII (1911), 239-40. Italics added by author.

16. J. S. Derby, *Fifty Years Among Authors, Books, and Publishers*, p. 551.

17. *Ibid.*, pp. 552-53.

18. E. A. Poe, *The Complete Works.* . . . , IX, 116.

19. Complete title, M. Clarke, *Sketches and Eccentricities of Colonel David Crockett, of West Tennessee*. Harper deposited it for copyright on November 14, 1833, according to the previously cited letter from Eaton, Library of Congress, dated December 19, 1947. (Footnote 1, above.)

20. E. A. Poe, *The Complete Works.* . . . , XV, 219.

21. V. L. Parrington, *Main Currents in American Thought*, II, 45.

Appendix 2

1. The present owner of this letter I do not know. The Library of Congress has a negative photostat.

2. *American Book Prices Current*, XIII (1907), shows that it was sold at public auction in 1906 and describes it as a two-page letter writen from Washington City on January 28, the day the book was completed. It has never been published, nor ever before referred to in Crockett literature.

3. Original owned by the Maine Historical Society, a part of the J. S. H. Fogg Collection. It was erroneously sold as an autographed Crockett letter in 1916 (*American Book Prices Current*, XXIII 1917), and I have informed the Maine Historical Society of my discovery of its true writer. The italics in the letter are those of Chilton. This letter was first published by the present writer in "The Author of David Crockett's Autobiography," pp. 297-98.

4. The original is owned by the Boston Public Library.

5. Miss Constance Rourke explained away David's letter assigning half the copyright to Chilton, and concluded that the *Autobiography* was truly all David's own. Professor John Donald Wade maintained in an article that a native Georgian son, Judge Augustin Smith Clayton, wrote the *Autobiography* and used for proof selections about Georgia taken from two entirely different Crockett books (*The Boston Tour* and the *Texas Exploits*) which some publisher had included in the same covers with the *Autobiography*. By this procedure he concluded that whoever wrote the

Autobiography certainly thought frequently in terms of Georgia—whereas in point of fact the real *Autobiography* itself never so much as mentions or alludes to Georgia or any Georgian once in the entire work. For Rourke's treatment see *Davy Crockett* (New York: Harcourt Brace & Co., 1934). For Wade's article, see "The Authorship of David Crockett's 'Autobiography,'" *Georgia Historical Quarterly*, VI (Sept., 1922), 265-68.

6. E. Mims and B. R. Payne, *Southern Prose and Poetry*, p. 98.

7. Charles and Mary Beard, *The Rise of the American Civilization*, I, 540.

8. V. L. Parrington, *Main Currents in American Thought*, III, 390-91; for the second, *Ibid.*, II, 172-73.

9. R. Blankenship, *American Literature*, p. 225.

Appendix 3

1. J. S. Derby, *Fifty Years Among....*, pp. 552-53.

2. C. M. Rourke, "Davy Crockett: Forgotten Facts and Legends," *Southwest Review*, XIX, 159; also in the concluding chapter to her *Davy Crockett*, called "Behind This Book."

3. *Burton's Gentleman's Magazine and American Monthly Review*, V (Sept., 1839), 121.

4. E. A. Poe, *The Complete Works of....*, XV, 255-56.

5. *Ibid.*, XV, 200.

6. However, this single letter Miss Rourke managed to multiply into two letters. In her book she gave it correctly as being from St. Augustine—she corrects David's spelling of the word—on January 9 (*Davy Crockett*, pp. 174-76); but in her article she published about half of *the same letter* and this time addressed it from Nacogdoches and dated it January 5 ("Forgotten Facts and Legends," p. 149)! She attributed the ownership of this letter to David's granddaughter, Mrs. T. M. (T. H.) Hiner, who in fact writes me that she has never owned or known the owner of the original.

7. Letter to author dated October 26, 1947.

8. *Ibid.* (November 23, 1947).

9. *Ibid.* (November 30, 1947).

10. Dr. Dienst had one holograph mentioning the name of Crockett's helper, the letter David wrote his son on January 10, 1834. Unfortunately in that one David had omitted a letter from Chilton's *CHLTON*, and Dr. Dienst could not be sure, on that single bit of evidence, that David had not meant the *Clayton* for whom Wade contended.

11. Letter dated March 6, 1923. It appears in transcript in Margaret Haynes Gates' Master's Thesis, University of Illinois, pp. 152-55. The transcript had what I am sure was a typographical error, which I have here corrected ("There is not one *work*" instead of *word*).

Bibliography

(NOTE: a complete annotated bibliography—also collated for all of Crockett's works, including books, letters, circulars; and for biographies about him—may be found as Appendix II, pp. 563-715, of the writer's doctoral dissertation submitted to Vanderbilt University in the spring of 1948: The Autobiography of David Crockett; an Annotated Edition, with Portraits, Maps, and Appendices. It is divided into ten parts: Crockett's Works; Book-Length Biographies (40 pp. or over); Other Books Partially or Wholly Relating to Crockett; Periodical Literature; Reminiscences; Genealogy; State and County Records and Documents; Legislative and Congressional Records; Newspapers; and Miscellaneous Material—Maps, Mythological Material, Letters to the Writer, and Background Material. All Crockett literature of any possible interest up to May of 1948 is included there, with an evaluation of each item.

Of the County Court Records listed herein, the writer was able to examine only those of Jefferson and Lawrence Counties in the original, the remainder having been obtained from transcripts on deposit at the State Library, Nashville, Tennessee. A number of individual items from the other counties, however, were doubly verified by means of personal correspondence with the County Registers concerned. There are, of course, many county records of David and his family which would have been too tedious to list in this volume. This is by no means a complete bibliography of David Crockett.)

1

UNPUBLISHED MATERIAL

County Records:

Carroll County, Tennessee: *County Court Minutes, 1821-26,* I.

Gibson County, Tennessee: *Chancery Court Minutes, Book A, 1834-47; Circuit Court Minutes, Book A, 1824-32; County Court Minutes, Book A, 1824-28; Marriages, 1824-60; Wills and Bond Books I, 1825-33,* and *II, 1833-41.*

Giles County, Tennessee: *General Index to Deeds, Vol. A, 1810-59; Minute Book, I, 1825-27.*

Greene County, Tennessee: *Minutes of Court of Pleas and Quarter Sessions, 1783-96.*

Hawkins County, Tennessee: *Circuit Court Minutes, 1810-21; Deed Book Number One, 1788-1800.*

Jefferson County, Tennessee: *County Court Minute Book No. 5, 1810-11; Deed Record Book C-D, 1792-99; Deed Record Book Q, 1797-1802; Marriage License and Bond Book, 1792-1840; Will Books No. 1, 1792-1810, and 2.*

Lawrence County, Tennessee: *County Court Minutes, I, 1818-23.*

Lincoln County, North Carolina: *County Court Minutes.*

Lincoln County, Tennessee: *Minute Docket Book No. 1, 1811-12; Minutes of Court of Pleas and Quarter Sessions, 1810; Minutes of Court of Pleas and Quarter Sessions, 1814-17.*

Madison County, Tennessee: *Wills and Inventories, I, 1822-35.*

Sullivan County, Tennessee: *Deed Book, I, 1775-90; Deed Book, II, 1784-96; Deed Book, III, 1795-1802.*

Washington County, Tennessee: *Minutes of Court of Pleas and Quarter Sessions, 1778-98,* I.

Washington County, Virginia: *First Minute Book; First Will Book.*

Weakley County, Tennessee: *County Court Minutes, 1827-35, I; Will and Record Book, 1828-42; Records of Occupant Entry, 1827-33.*

In the Tennessee Land Office:

North Carolina Land Grants, Books 1, 2, and 6. Tennessee Land Office, Nashville.

North Carolina Land Grants for Revolutionary Services, Books F#6 and G#7, Tennessee Land Office, Nashville.

In the Tennessee State Archives:

Surveyor's Entry Book C, Surveyor's District II. Tennessee State Archives.

Tennessee State Commission Books, Nos. 3 and 4. Tennessee State Archives, Nashville.

West Tennessee Land Office Records, Book 2 A, Tennessee State Archives.

Miscellaneous:

Crockett's Commission as Justice of the Peace and five "true copies" of depositions taken before David and others as commissioners of Lawrenceburg, Tennessee (Tennessee Historical Society).

Marriage Bond, Polly Findley. Dandridge, Jefferson County, Court House.

Muster and Payroll Records, War of 1812, II, III, VII, VIII. War Records Division, National Archives, Washington, D. C.

2

GOVERNMENT PUBLICATIONS AND RELATED MATERIAL

Biographical Directory of the American Congress, 1774-1927. Washington, D. C.: U. S. Government Printing Office, 1928.

Colonial Records of North Carolina. Edited by William L. Saunders. Raleigh: P. M. Hale, 1886-1890. 10 vols.

The Congressional Globe. Debates and Proceedings of the Twenty-Third Congress. Edited by Blair and Rives. Washington, D. C.: Globe, 1834-35.

Journal of the House of Representatives: State of Tennessee: First Session, Twelfth Assembly, 1817; First and Second Sessions, Fourteenth General As-

sembly, 1821, 1822; First and Second Sessions, Fifteenth General Assembly, 1823-24.
Laws of Texas, 1822-97. Edited by H. P. N. Gammel. Austin: Gammel Book Co., 1898.
Niles Weekly Register. Edited by H. Niles. VIII, XLI, XLV, XLVI, XLVII, XLIX, L, LIV, LV, LVIII, LIX. Baltimore.
Public Acts of the State of Tennessee. 1821, 1822, 1823.
Register of Debates in Congress. III, IV, V, VI, VII, VIII, X, XI. Washington: Gales and Seaton.

3

CROCKETT'S WORKS AND BIOGRAPHIES

Allen, Charles Fletcher. *David Crockett, Scout, Small Boy, etc.* Philadelphia: J. P. Lippincott Co., 1911.
Clarke, Mathew St. Clair. (anonymous) *Life and Adventures of Colonel David Crockett of West Tennessee.* Cincinnati: For the Proprietor, 1833. Republished the same year as *Sketches and Eccentricities of Colonel David Crockett of West Tennessee.* New York: J. & J. Harper, 1833.
Crockett, David. *An Account of Colonel Crockett's Tour to the North and Down East, etc.* Philadelphia: E. L. Carey and A. Hart, 1835.
——. *Address of Mr. Crockett, to the Voters of the Ninth Congressional District of the State of Tennessee.* Washington: Gales and Seaton, 1829.
——. Circular Letter to Constituents, 1824; late 1834, early 1835.
——. *Col. Crockett's Exploits and Adventures in Texas.* Philadelphia: T. K. and P. G. Collins, 1836.
——. *David Crockett's Circular. To the Citizens and Voters of the Ninth Congressional District of the State of Tennessee.* Washington: February 24, 1831.
——. *The Life of Martin Van Buren, Hair-apparent to the "Government," and the Appointed Successor of General Jackson.* Philadelphia: Robert Wright, 1835.
——. *A Narrative of the Life of David Crockett, of the State of Tennessee* (The *Autobiography*). Philadelphia: E. L. Carey and A. Hart, 1834.
——. "Reply-to-Benton Letters," *National Banner and Nashville Whig,* January 26, 1835, p. 3.
——. "A Sketch of the REMARKS OF THE HON. DAVID CROCKETT, Representative from Tennessee, On the Bill for the Removal of the Indians ... May 19, 1830," *Speeches on the Passage of the Bill for the Removal of the Indians, Delivered in the Congress of the United States, April and May, 1830.* Boston: Perkins and Marvin, 1830.
——. *Speech of Mr. Crockett, of Tennessee, on a Bill Proposing to Construct a National Road from Buffalo to New Orleans.* Washington: Duff Green, 1830.
Dorson, Richard M. *Davy Crockett: American Comic Legend.* New York: Spiral Press, 1939.
Ellis, Edward S. *The Life of Colonel David Crockett.* Philadelphia: Porter and Coates, 1884.

French, Mrs. J. Stewart and Zella Armstrong. *The Crockett Family and Connecting Lines*. Bristol, Tenn.: King Printing Co., 1928.
Gates, Margaret Haynes. Fact and Fiction in the Early Biographies of David Crockett. Unpublished master's thesis, University of Illinois, 1929.
Mayer, Edwin Justice. *Sunrise in my Pocket: or the Last Days of Davy Crockett*. New York: Julian Messner, Inc., 1941.
Rourke, Constance M. *Davy Crockett*. New York: Harcourt, Brace and Co., 1934.
Shapiro, Irwin. *Yankee Thunder: The Legendary Life of Davy Crockett*. New York: Julian Messner, Inc., 1944.

4

NEWSPAPERS

Cincinnati *Gazette* (July 14, 1834).
Columbia, Pa. *Spy* (July 12, 1834).
Dallas *Morning News* (December 25, 1927).
Downing Gazette (February 28, March 14, May 23, May 30, June 13, August 1, 1835).
Jackson *Gazette* (July 2, August 6, October 30, November 13, 1824; August 15, 1829).
Jackson *Pioneer* (January 28, 1823; September 9, 1823).
Jackson *Southern Statesman* (March 12, 1831).
Knoxville *Register* (November 4, 1823).
Knoxville *Sunday Journal* (August 17, 1930).
Memphis *Commercial Appeal* (November 23, 1941).
Morning Courier and New York Enquirer (December 15, 1830; November 21, 1831).
National Banner and Nashville Whig (August 14, September 4, 1822; September 29, October 6, October 13, 1823; September 27, 1824; November 25, 1828; January 9, January 23, 1829; January 21, January 26, February 23, 1835).
National Intelligencer (September 2, 1835).
New York *Evening Post* (August 27, 1831).
New York *Mirror* (December 18, 1830).
New York *Traveller, Spirit of the Times and Family Journal* (December 21, 1833).
Poulson's American Daily Advertiser (July 7, 1834).
Raleigh, N. C. *News and Observer* (March 2, 1913).
San Antonio *Daily Express* (February 11, 1899).
San Antonio *Light* (February 19, 1899).

5

ARTICLES IN PERIODICALS

Adkins, N. F. "James K. Paulding's *Lion of the West*," *American Literature*, III (Nov., 1931), 249-58.
Allison, Zoe. "Notes on the Journal of the Proceedings of the General Council of the Republic of Texas," *Bulletin of the East Texas State Teachers College*, XIV (June, 1931), 84-8.

American Historical Magazine, II (April, 1897), 178-80; and V (Jan., 1900), 41-7.

Bishop, H. O. "Davy Crockett—Bear Hunter," *National Republic,* XVII (Aug., 1929), 31-7.

———. "Col. Crockett Goes Visiting," *National Republic,* XVII (Oct., 1929), 24-5, 39.

———. "Col. Crockett in New York," *National Republic,* XVII (Nov., 1929), 28-9, 39.

Blair, Walter. "Six Davy Crocketts," *Southwest Review,* XXV (July, 1940), 443-62.

Bray, Curtis. "David Crockett Autographs," *Hobbies,* XLVIII (July, 1943), 17.

Chittick, V. L. O., "Review of *Davy Crockett* and the *Adventures of Davy Crockett," American Literature,* VI (Nov., 1934), 368-70.

Crowell, Chester T. "Davy Crockett," *American Mercury,* IV (Jan., 1925), 109-15.

Davis, Curtis Carroll. "Virginia's Unknown Novelist: James Strange French, a Southern Colonel of Parts," *Virginia Magazine of History and Biography,* LX (Oct., 1952), 551-81.

Dorson, Richard M. "Davy Crockett and the Heroic Age," *Southern Folklore Quarterly,* VI (June, 1942), 95-102.

Franklin, P. L. "Col. Crockett Gives Advice," *National Republic,* XVII (Jan., 1930), 31, 44.

———. "Col. Crockett Visits Boston," *National Republic,* XVII (Dec., 1929), 30-31, 45.

Hall, Claud V. "Early Days in Red River County [Texas]," *Bulletin of the East Texas State Teachers College,* XIV (June, 1931), 49-79.

Henderson, Mrs. Jessie Arn. "Unmarked Historic Spots of Franklin County," *Tennessee Historical Magazine,* Series II, III (Jan., 1935), 111-20.

Leach, Joseph. "Crockett's Almanacs and the Typical Texan," *Southwest Review,* Summer, 1950.

Nelson, Wilbur A. "Reelfoot—An Earthquake Lake," *National Geographic,* XLV (Jan., 1924), 94-114.

Reynolds, Louise Wilson. "The Pioneer Crockett Family in Tennessee," *DAR Magazine,* LV (April, 1921), 186-91.

Richardson, T. C. "The Girl Davy Left Behind," *Farm and Ranch* (June 25, 1927), 3, 11.

Rourke, Constance M. "Davy Crockett: Forgotten Facts and Legends," *Southwest Review,* XIX (Jan., 1934), 149-61.

Shackford, James Atkins. "The Author of David Crockett's Autobiography," *Boston Public Library Quarterly,* III (October, 1951), 294-304.

———. "David Crockett and North Carolina," *North Carolina Historical Review,* XXVIII (July, 1951), 298-315.

Simms, William Gilmore. "Michael Bonham: or the Fall of Bexar," *Southern Literary Messenger,* XVIII (1852).

Stout, Dr. S. H. "David Crockett," *American Historical Magazine,* VII (Jan., 1902), 3-21.

Turner, H. S. "Andrew Jackson and David Crockett: Reminiscences of Colonel Chester," *Magazine of American History,* XXVII (May, 1892), 385-87.

Wade, John Donald. "The Authorship of David Crockett's 'Autobiography,'" *Georgia Historical Quarterly*, VI (Sept., 1922), 265-68.

Williams, Emma Inman. "Letters of Adam Huntsman to James K. Polk," *Tennessee Historical Quarterly*, VI (Dec., 1947), 337-69.

Worner, William Frederick. "David Crockett in Columbia," *Lancaster County History Society Papers*, XXVII (Dec., 1923), 176-7.

Wright, Marcus J. "Colonel David Crockett of Tennessee," *Magazine of American History*, X (Dec., 1883), 484-9.

6

GENERAL WORKS

Abernethy, Thomas Perkins. *From Frontier to Plantation in Tennessee: A Study in Frontier Democracy*. Chapel Hill, N. C.: The University of North Carolina Press, 1932.

American Book Prices Current. Vols. I-LVIII, 1895 to 1952. Edited by Edward Lazare. R. R. Bowker Co.

Bassett, John Spencer. *Correspondence of Andrew Jackson*. Washington, D. C.: Carnegie Institution of Washington, 1931. 7 vols.

———. *Life of Andrew Jackson*. New York: The Macmillan Co., 1931.

Beard, Charles A. and Mary R. *The Rise of the American Civilization*. New York: The Macmillan Co., 1941.

Beazley, Julia. *Texas and Southwestern Lore*. Number 6, publications of the Texas Folklore Society, 1927.

Blankenship, Russell. *American Literature*. New York: Henry Holt, 1931.

Boone and Crockett Club, Brief History of, With Officers, Constitution, and List of Members for the Year 1910. Edited by George Bird Grinnell. New York: Forest and Stream Publishing Co.

Botkin, B. A. *A Treasury of American Folklore*. New York: Crown Publishers, 1944.

Bowers, Claude G. *The Party Battles of the Jackson Period*. New York: Houghton Mifflin Co., 1922.

Caruthers, William Alexander. *The Kentuckian in New York, or, The Adventures of Three Southerns*. New York: Harper & Brothers, 1834. 2 vols.

———. *The Knights of the Horseshoe*. New York: A. L. Burt.

Catterall, Ralph C. H. *The Second Bank of the United States*. Chicago: University of Chicago Press, 1930.

Chilton, Thomas. *The Circular Address of Thomas Chilton, of Kentucky, to His Constituents*. Washington City: Stephen C. Ustick, 1831.

Chittick, V. L. O. *Ring-tailed Roarers: Tall Tales of the American Frontier, 1830-1860*. Caldwell, Idaho: Caxton Press, Ltd., 1941.

Clayton, Augustin Smith. *"The Mysterious Picture," by Wrangham Fitzramble, Esq*. New York: Collins & Hannay, 1825.

Coke, E. T. *A Subaltern's Furlough*. New York: 1833, vol. 1.

Colyar, A. S. *Life and Times of Andrew Jackson*. Nashville: Marshall Bruce, 1904. 2 vols.

Corner, William. *San Antonio De Bexar*. San Antonio: Bainbridge and Corner, Christmas, 1890.

Davis, Curtis Carroll. *Chronicler of the Cavaliers. A Life of William A. Caruthers.* Richmond: The Dietz Press, Inc., 1955.

Davis, James D. *History of the City of Memphis.* Memphis: Hite, Crumpton, and Kelley, 1873.

De Morgan, Augustus. *The Book of Almanacs.* London: Taylor, Walton, and Maberly, 1851.

Derby, J. S. *Fifty Years Among Authors, Books, and Publishers.* New York: G. W. Carleton, 1884.

Dictionary of American English, A. Edited by W. A. Craigie and J. R. Hulbert. Chicago: University of Chicago Press, 1938. 4 vols.

Elfer, Maurice. *Madame Candelaria, Unsung Heroine of the Alamo,* etc. Houston: The Rein Co., 1933.

French, James Strange. *Elkswatawa, or, The Prophet of the West.* New York: Harper & Brothers, 1836. 2 vols.

Gresham, Lunia Paul. The Public Career of Hugh Lawson White. Unpublished Ph. D. dissertation, Vanderbilt University, Nashville, 1943.

Halbert, H. S., and T. H. Ball. *The Creek War.* Chicago: Donohue and Hennebury, 1895.

Heiskell, S. G. *Andrew Jackson and Early Tennessee History.* Nashville: 1920. 3 vols.

Herold, Amos L. *James Kirke Paulding, Versatile American.* New York: Columbia University Press, 1926.

Houston, Sam. *The Writings of Sam Houston 1813-1863.* Edited by Amelia W. Williams and Eugene C. Barker. Austin: University of Texas Press, 1938-43. 8 vols.

James, Marquis. *The Raven.* Indianapolis, Ind.: Bobs-Merrill Co., 1929.

————. *Andrew Jackson: Portrait of a President.* New York: Bobbs-Merrill Co., 1937.

Keating, J. M. *History of the City of Memphis and Shelby County, Tennessee.* New York: D. Mason and Co., 1888. 3 vols.

Lomax, John A. and Alan. *American Ballads and Folk Songs.* New York: The Macmillan Co., 1934.

McGrane, R. C. *Correspondence of Nicholas Biddle.* Boston: Houghton Mifflin Co., 1919.

Meine, Franklin J. *Tall Tales of the Southwest: An Anthology of Southern and Southwestern Humor, 1830-60.* New York: Alfred A. Knopf, 1933.

————, and Walter Blair. *Mike Fink: King of Mississippi Keel-Boatmen.* New York: Henry Holt and Co., 1933.

Miller, Stephen F. *The Bench and Bar of Georgia.* Philadelphia: J. B. Lippincott Co., 1858.

Mims, Edwin, and Bruce R. Payne. *Southern Prose and Poetry.* New York: Charles Scribner's Sons, 1910.

Morphis, J. M. *History of Texas.* New York: U. S. Publishing Co., 1874.

Owen, Thomas M. *History of Alabama and Dictionary of Alabama Biography.* Chicago: S. J. Clarke Publishing Co., 1921. 4 vols.

Parrington, Vernon Louis. *Main Currents in American Thought.* New York: Harcourt, Brace and Co., 1927.

Parton, James. *Life of Andrew Jackson.* New York: Mason Bros., 1860.

Paulding, William I. *Literary Life of James K. Paulding.* N. Y.: Charles Scribner's Sons, 1867.
Poe, Edgar Allan. *The Compete Works of Edgar Allan Poe.* New York: Univ. Society, 1902. 17 vols.
Randolph, Vance. *Ozark Mountain Folks.* N. Y.: Vanguard Press, 1932.
Reid, John, and John Henry Eaton. *Life of Andrew Jackson.* Philadelphia: M. Carey and Son, 1817.
Sandburg, Carl. *The American Song Bag.* New York: Harcourt, Brace and Co., 1927.
Schlesinger, Arthur M., Jr. *The Age of Jackson.* Boston: Little, Brown and Co., 1945.
Shepard, Edward M. *Martin Van Buren.* New York: Houghton, Mifflin Co., 1899.
Smith, Richard Penn. *The Sentinels and Other Plays.* Edited by R. H. Ware and H. W. Schoenberger. Princeton: Princeton University Press, 1941.
Smith, Seba. *The Life and Writings of Major Jack Downing, etc.* Boston: Lilly, Wait, Colman, and Holden, 1833.
———. *My Thirty Years Out of the Senate.* N. Y.: Oaksmith and Co., 1859.
Tennessee, A History, 1673-1932. Edited by Philip M. Hamer. New York: American Historical Society, Inc., 1933.
Williams, Emma Inman. *Historic Madison, The Story of Jackson, and Madison County, Tennessee, from Prehistoric Moundbuilders to 1917.* Jackson, Tenn.: Madison County Historical Society, 1946.
Wyman, Mary Alice. *Two American Pioneers.* New York: Columbia University Press, 1927.

Index

Index